Lines in the Sand

A Carpenter and Philly Novel

(Sixth in a Series)

Ken Behar

Lines in the Sand
(Sixth in a Series)

978-0-9961462-8-9 (paperback)
978-0-9961462-9-6 (eBook)

Library of Congress Control Number: 2020918644

Published by: Ken Behar
Lexington, Massachusetts

Cover design and cover photograph © by Angela Valenti.

To Linda and to the Holmes Hall Cliffies she brought into my life

Chris
Debbie
Emily
Lisa
Meredith
Paula
Sandy
Sherrie
Stephanie

To George Gilliam

In Memory Of

Jim Kolb
Paul Arkema

Also by the author:

Ghosts Can Only Go Straight
(Turn of the Century Tales)

Not Too Shabby
(Barrister Tales from Ed's Breakfast Emporium)

HOOPS

Carpenter and Philly Novels:
Turn The Page
No Right Answers
Coin Flips
Full Circles
All
Lines in the Sand

Contents

January

From Meredith's Playlist

"Take a Walk on the Wild Side"

Lou Reed

1

"Stop dreaming; here it is!" Detective Evelyn Rodriguez turned right into the drive of Sanborn Assisted Living Center and followed the arrows to *Visitor Parking* at the rear of the building. She eased the unmarked motor pool car into a free space and opened her door. "We don't know what this is about, right?"

Detective Paul Sullivan, Evelyn's partner and superior officer, startled. "Right," he answered as he opened his door, hoping the frigid, January morning air would focus his attention on police work. He couldn't tell Evelyn why he was preoccupied. It wasn't every morning that your wife leapt out of bed, sprinted to the bathroom, threw up, and returned to bed with the bombshell announcement that she was ninety-nine percent sure she was pregnant.

"It's got to suck living in a place like this," Evelyn said as they approached the main entrance. Paul silently agreed. He was still getting used to his new partner. Evelyn was tall and thin and walked with a swagger. She was such a no-nonsense type that Paul wondered whether they would ever freely joke with each other. But she knew her stuff and seemed to have memorized most of the department manuals.

The Center was a large, three-story brick building. An inverted V-shaped canopy supported by four white columns crowned the main entrance. Inside, residents, for the most part elderly, were sitting along the side walls of the broad entryway, just sitting, not reading, not conversing, a few staring straight-ahead with vacant looks. Several glanced their way as they approached the reception desk.

"Mr. Masterson to the main lobby," the receptionist paged after Evelyn announced their arrival.

A ruddy-faced, smiling man who looked to be in his early forties approached them.

"Good afternoon," said Evelyn, nodding to the man. "I'm Detective Rodriguez and this is my partner, Detective Sullivan. We understand that you placed a call to the Cambridgeport station of the Cambridge Police Department saying that there were photographs the police should view. Have we got that right?"

"Grant Masterson," the man responded. "I'm the executive director here. Yes, that's why I called. Thanks for coming. I'm sure you're busy so why don't we get to it? Follow me please."

Masterson led the way out of the entryway, turned left and proceeded at a brisk pace. "This wing has smaller units and is mostly for people living alone," he said over his shoulder. “A couple would find these units cramped.” He paused before a door numbered 133 and used a key to open the door revealing an all-purpose room that served as a living room and dining area. The few mismatched furnishings looked used. In a corner, two darkly stained wooden chairs were positioned on the short sides of a small rectangular table. A microwave was at one end of the table and a small refrigerator under the table. Next to Masterson was a recliner facing a TV mounted on a rolling stand.

“A guy lives here, right?” Evelyn said.

“Lived here,” Masterson clarified. “Dennis France passed away two days ago. We were packing up his things when we found some photographs that are very disturbing. I gave instructions that nothing was to be touched until the police gave the okay. This way, please.”

Masterson opened the door to a small bedroom and stood aside. A narrow bed and dresser were the only furnishings. The door to a small closet stood open and Paul estimated roughly a dozen hangers were in use.

“They’re over here,” Masterson said, pointing to the bed. “Housekeeping found a box under the bed and opened it. When they saw the photographs, I was called.”

“Why weren’t this guy’s relatives going through his things?” Evelyn asked.

“Mr. France doesn’t have any relatives, as far as we know.”

Photographs and papers were strewn on the bed. Evelyn slipped on gloves before picking up a photograph by a corner. “Shit,” she muttered.

Paul donned gloves and took the photograph from Evelyn. A nude boy who couldn’t have been more than ten years old was tied to a straight-backed wooden chair, slash marks on his arms, legs, and torso, possibly the work of a knife. The boy’s eyes were closed. He looked dead but Paul wasn’t sure; the head was out of focus, blurry. It was a black and white shot, but Paul visualized bloody red lines laddering the boy’s upper body and extremities.

“Shit!” Evelyn repeated as she moved on to the next photo.

“Who was this France guy?” Paul asked.

“We don’t know much about him,” Masterson replied. “A copy of his file is ready for you at the front desk. When he took up residence, he was seventy years old. That was roughly a year and a half ago. I remember meeting with him when he signed the admission papers. A week later, he paid for two years in advance, which was very unusual. The money was wired to us from a bank in Georgia. I have no idea where to send the money for the six months he’s never going to use.”

“Did he have any friends here?” Evelyn asked.

"I don't think so, but I can't be sure. He declined our meal plan. As far as I know, he never used our dining room."

"How did he get around?' Evelyn continued.

"He didn't have a car. I believe he called for a taxi on occasion. There's also a bus stop near our facility."

"Do you require identification when you admit someone?" Paul asked.

"We do. We usually see a driver's license, but France produced a passport which we copied. That's in the package waiting for you at the front desk."

"Did he have a Social Security number?" Paul followed up.

"He put one down on the admission form. I don't believe we ever checked it out."

"Fingerprints," Evelyn said, more to herself than to Masterson.

Paul turned to Masterson. "We're going to take the photographs with us, if you don't mind. I'll try to get a forensics team here this afternoon, so leave things as they are until they're through."

Masterson nodded. "We'd like to clean out the room so it can be shown as soon as possible. When do you think that will be?"

"Two days is my best guess," Evelyn said as she placed the photographs into a cellophane bag.

"I guess we'll have to live with that," Masterson said, with a rueful smile. "From one perspective, we lost a model tenant. France kept to himself, never bothered anybody. He was never any trouble. Until now."

When they were first teamed up, Evelyn had announced that she preferred to drive. She said driving helped her think. Paul decided this was one accommodation he would make throughout their partnership. It was a small thing that he didn't feel strongly about.

"There were thirteen photographs," Evelyn said. "We could have a serial killer here."

Paul remained bothered by the blurry look of the one photograph he had examined. "Do you think the photographs were staged with live children?"

"That doesn't make any sense," Evelyn said, glancing briefly at him before turning her attention to the road. "Sorry," she added. "I shouldn't have been so quick to dismiss what you said."

"But you still think what I said doesn't make sense, right?"

Evelyn smiled. "Right."

"What if we get no leads on this guy?" Paul said. France had gone out of his way to live in shadows.

"We'll find that out soon enough," Evelyn said. "You think this guy's smoke?"

"Something like that," Paul said. "The guy kept a profile lower than low."

After work, Paul made the drive from Cambridge to his house in Brighton along roads bordered by mounds of recently plowed blackened slush. He parked in the driveway beside the house, sprinted up the steps and in the front door, quickly closing it behind him to keep out the raw, January cold. In the living room, Daisy thudded giddily about, pulling a wooden duck that quacked as it rolled. She wasn't aware Paul had entered, and he prolonged the moment before he announced himself to watch her. He hadn't adopted Daisy. Yet. He and Philly planned to make that happen. Philly had told Philip's parents that their granddaughter was going to have a new legal dad. But the timing still didn't feel right.

Of the five adults who shared the Brighton house, the only other one home seemed to be Isabella, who was holding her seven-month-old infant daughter, Rosalind, and walking with a distracted expression while managing to avoid a collision with Daisy. Philly was absent, as was Raul, Isabella's fiancé. Sarah Ferguson, the fifth owner of the house, and live-in babysitter extraordinaire, was also among the missing. Paul thought this scene was as far removed from gruesome crime photographs as any scene he could think up. He wriggled out of his overcoat and, as he turned to open the entry hall closet, Daisy's high-pitched screech announced that his cover was blown.

"Hey, pumpkin," Paul said, reaching down to pick her up with one hand while he finished wedging his coat onto a hanger with the other. "How's my big girl?"

Daisy's wet kiss landed on his nose and she squealed with delight. She had chunky, squeezable toddler legs and long, fine, black flyaway hair that was such a mismatch from Philly's tight, black curls and her father's thick blond hair that Paul sometimes wondered what recessive genes had been at work. Daisy wriggled to be let down and Paul glided effortlessly into the next role he was to play, a role he had played with Jennie, his daughter from his first marriage. "I'm going to catch you," he said as Daisy sped away from him, nearly running into Isabella.

Paul offered a smile to Isabella and a cheek squeeze to Rosalind before heading after Daisy in earnest. "I'm getting closer. I've almost got you."

Daisy darted behind the living room couch. Paul saw her hair above the couch back but played along. "Where did Daisy go? I don't see her anywhere."

Daisy's giggle produced a grin from Isabella.

"Where could she be?"

Rosalind now demanded to be let down and Isabella obliged. Soon Rosalind was in motion, slowly crawling after a fashion toward the couch.

"I think Rosalind knows where Daisy's hiding."

Rosalind disappeared behind the couch and now two giggles sounded.

"Oh no!" Paul exclaimed. "I can't find Rosalind!"

Paul heard footsteps on the stairs and soon Philly came into view. She stepped over the bottom stair guardrail with her game face on, a sign that she wasn't about to get involved in hide and seek. She gave Paul a curt wave and headed for the kitchen. Probably, Paul thought, some legal case she was working on wasn't going well. Or maybe she was just eager to get a meal on the table.

"Do you think they're hiding behind the couch?" Paul asked Isabella.

"I don't know. Should we take a look?"

Daisy's giggle drowned out Rosalind's softer laugh.

Paul and Isabella rounded the couch from opposite ends. "There they are," they said in unison.

Paul soon had each girl under an arm and plopped down on the couch with them.

"I'll help Philly with dinner," Isabella said.

"So how are my two favorite little girls?" Paul asked. He eased them off the couch and lay down on the floor. Soon the girls were climbing all over him. Their antics almost succeeded in providing a distraction from the assisted living center photographs. Evelyn had already uncovered two facts: Dennis France's passport was a forgery and his Social Security number a fake.

2

Philly marveled that she and Isabella were keeping their vow to go spinning outside in the mornings regardless of the weather. At six thirty, the sky was dark and the outside thermometer registered thirteen degrees. Philly had swept an area of the backyard blacktop clear of a light snowfall and, after upending a red-clay planting pot on the spot, placed her boom box on the flat surface of the pot's bottom. Pink's "U and UR Hand" was at medium volume.

Isabella wriggled out of her parka and tossed it on the snow and Philly soon followed suit. They were wearing stocking caps, lined mittens, sweatpants, and heavy sweatshirts with hoods. Five minutes into their workout, Philly felt sweat dampening the area between her breasts. She loved generating heat while seeing her breath materialize in the cold.

"Let's make this a hill," Isabella suggested as she turned her resistance knob to the right.

Philly matched Isabella and moving the pedals became harder. As often happened when her body was engaged, her mind drifted to work. In a few days, one of her new law partners, Simon Jeffries, would be taking a deposition in a suit brought by one of their clients, Martina Glass. Glass had been injured while attending a minor league hockey game when a large twenty-something guy, Fred Dunn, fell over a guard rail and landed on her. Dunn had claimed that he had been pushed by a person unknown. Philly's private investigators had found witnesses to the incident, an elderly couple, who were prepared to testify that Dunn had fallen while reaching for a bag of peanuts tossed to him by a friend.

"Purple Rain" began playing and Philly turned her resistance higher still, slowing her pace. Prince's classic was a perfect hill-climbing song—slow with a defined beat. Isabella's legs were also straining, and she and Philly exchanged a brief smile.

Then there was an upcoming, early-February trial in which Simon and her other new partner, Rachel Boyle, would carry the load. Their client, Fay Richardson, had aborted a fetus she had been carrying. The father, Al Townsend, a former boyfriend, had labeled Richardson as a killer on a billboard message he had designed. The billboard didn't mention Richardson by name. It depicted Townsend holding a baby he would never get to see because the mother had killed his baby without telling him. Last year Richardson had obtained an injunction ordering that the billboard be taken down.

Philly needed to carve out time to discuss the cases with Carpenter, their experienced, over-sixty partner. When was that going to happen?

Isabella had reduced the tension on her bike and was now sprinting, her legs a blur. Philly couldn't match Isabella's pace. Not for the first time, Philly wished she had Isabella's willowy body and strikingly long, powerful legs.

Light had been seeping forth by degrees but now, in a rush, the sun lit up the backyard. Philly wondered if she would now be puking her guts out if she'd put something in her stomach before exercising. Early on during her pregnancy with Daisy, she couldn't keep anything down in the mornings except dry toast coated with a thin layer of jam. She fought the impulse to tell Isabella she was pregnant; this early in her pregnancy it was prudent to let the pregnancy progress further before informing others.

3

An Owner of a Family Business

Standing in his rapidly emptying living room amidst the few pieces of furniture that were headed for the condo he and Maxine French were moving to, Carpenter studied the boxes that contained the contents of his life: cartons stuffed with financial records, correspondence, clothes, several tools he would be hard-pressed to figure out how to use, foodstuffs, photograph albums. Had his belongings really distilled to fit in fifteen good-sized moving boxes? There was traveling light but one box for every four-plus years he had lived bordered on the ridiculous. True, Maxine's belongings would make up for his meager possessions, especially when it came to furniture.

Moving day was less than a week away. Although he disliked change, Carpenter was looking forward to the start of the next phase of his life with Maxine.

He considered another surprising development as he desultorily paced about his living room. Yesterday, he and Philly had talked on the phone about the lack of billable-hour work on the horizon for 2012. Ordinarily, this would have troubled him. Yet for some reason, he was not actively fretting about their new firm's lack of cases. His primary focus was moving out of his present condo and settling in with Maxine at their new place. When the hell had he become one of those guys who had his priorities squared away?

Carpenter sat on one of the boxes, wishing Maxine was around. She was packing at her condo on the South Shore and had turned down his offer to help, pointing out, correctly, that he'd only be in the way. Still, he was lonely.

What the hell did a sixty-five-year-old guy do on a Sunday night? 'Of course,' he thought. 'Sports bar!'

Carpenter was only half paying attention to the Bruins game playing on the TV mounted at a downward sloping angle above the center of the bar. He had never gotten into hockey. But last year he *had* gotten caught up in the playoffs that ended with the Bruins winning the Stanley Cup. The Bruins' attitude had won him over. The team had never quit. Their resiliency had been remarkable.

"You must be a fan, the way you're grinning," came from his right, and Carpenter turned on his bar stool to find a new arrival, a forty-something guy in a gray business suit, tie loosened, pointing up at the TV screen.

"Not really," Carpenter replied. "I was just remembering how much fun the last Stanley Cup finals were."

His seat-mate was drinking what looked like a double of something which was halfway drained. The man hadn't ordered food. "Help yourself to some bread," Carpenter offered, pushing his bread plate closer to the man.

The man shook his head and signaled the bartender for another. "I'm not doing anything to dampen the buzz I'm trying to get."

His drinking neighbor had long, wavy blond hair, blue eyes, and a strong chin. "What's got you down?" Carpenter asked.

"You don't want to know."

The man drank silently and Carpenter returned to his cobb salad with garlic bread on the side. He sipped at his beer, a dark ale he had never heard of that was on tap.

"I got fired," the man next to him said. "Shit-canned, so I'm going to get shit-faced."

"Fired," Carpenter said, his interest picking up.

"More like forced out," the man clarified.

Carpenter pulled his wallet out from a back pocket of his jeans and searched out one of his business cards. "Carpenter," he said, handing the card over.

The man studied the card. "Figures I would park my ass next to a lawyer."

"It's your lucky day."

The man offered a weak smile. "Clyde Atkins," he said.

"What's this about being forced out?" Carpenter asked.

"I'm in this family business," Atkins said. "Or maybe I should say I *was* in this family business. We deal with lawn mowers, snowblowers, leaf-blowers. We sell them and repair them."

"What's this about being forced out?"

Atkins stuck a forefinger in his new drink and stirred the liquid. Carpenter wondered whether he was already three sheets to the wind.

"It's a lot of little things," Atkins said morosely.

'Life is about little things,' Carpenter mused silently. The little things added up and then you had a big thing bearing down on you. His cancer was a case in point. "What do you mean by little things?"

Atkins scowled, his look darkening. "I don't know you," he said, his words somewhat slurred.

"Well, I sure as hell don't know you," Carpenter respond. "And since you're not a client, any advice I give you will be free, which is the worst kind."

Atkins smiled ruefully. "My father started the business. He's retired now. He turned the business over to me, my brother, and my sister. That was probably his first mistake. We each have a one-third ownership interest."

"Why was it a mistake?"

"We basically can't stand each other."

Siblings running a business often proved to be a recipe for disaster, which Carpenter attributed to childhood grievances playing out in the business context. In his limited experience, businesses run by siblings had a poorer prognosis than businesses run by a husband-wife team.

"What about those little things?" Carpenter asked again.

Atkins absentmindedly took a slice of Carpenter's bread and began chewing around the edges at the crust.

"I'll tell you what the latest thing was," Atkins said. "I wanted to stop selling a snowblower model that's gotten lots of consumer complaints. My brother and sister wouldn't hear of it. They insisted we sell off our remaining stock."

"Would there have been a loss on the remaining stock?" Carpenter asked.

"Yeah, but so what? You need to understand something. This business has been pretty good to us. It's been profitable—sometimes highly profitable. It made my father a wealthy man, and I can tell you his three kids have done all right for themselves. I'm reasonably well-off. It hasn't hurt that I've done really well in the market. But even with that aside, I'd be sitting pretty."

"What are the other little things?" Carpenter probed.

"Times are tough for a lot of people. I didn't want to bill people for repeat repairs, especially if we screwed up the initial repair. Things like that. I was always outvoted."

"Why do you think that was?"

"I *know* why that was," Atkins said with some heat. "My brother and sister have families. I'm a bachelor. Money is more important to them than it is to me."

"Are you saying this business with the line of crappy snowblowers was the final straw for your brother and sister?"

Atkins was silent for a long moment. "I never thought of it that way," he finally said, "but that could be right."

"So how were you forced out?"

"Each of us has an employment contract with the company. My brother and sister voted to terminate my contract. I still have my ownership interest in the company. They could buy me out if they wanted to. But it would cost them. By terminating my contract, they can pay themselves more and cut off my income from the business."

"What do *you* want, given the situation?" Carpenter asked.

The question momentarily silenced Atkins. "I guess I want to be rid of my brother and sister. It might be okay with me to be bought out. I'd have to think about it. Maybe it's time for me to try something new. Or maybe I should be the one buying them out. I could probably afford to do that if I borrowed some money, but there's no way in hell they'd go for that."

"Where does your father stand on all of this?"

Atkins emitted a contemptuous snort. "He'd back my brother and sister. For him, it was all about the money. Plus, he gets paid a small percent of profits for about ten more years. He's going to want that percent of profits to be as high as possible. He'd never agree to take a hit by eating a loss on a lousy product."

Carpenter digested what he'd been told as Atkins finished up his remaining bread. "Sounds like you need a lawyer," he said.

"I thought I was talking to one," Atkins replied.

4

The computer in the conference room faced one of the long sides of the conference room table where Carpenter sat between Simon and Rachel. When Simon hooked Philly up to the call by Skype, Daisy appeared. "Guess who's filling in for me?" Philly's voice sounded.

"Hey, cutie!" Rachel cooed. "What are you up to?"

Carpenter grinned. Philly's daughter always cheered him up. She was smiling and pointing in their direction. Even Simon responded with a faint smile.

"What have we got?' Philly asked as Daisy remained visible.

"Did I tell you the one about the lawyer who walked into a bar?" Carpenter said, as he directed a wave in Daisy's direction.

"This better be good," Philly said. "I could use a laugh."

"It turns out the lawyer ended up with a client," Carpenter continued, and he went on to outline Clyde Atkins' situation. "I sent Atkins an engagement letter this morning," he concluded, "and I just got it back signed."

"Nothing like a billable-hour case to start off a new year," Philly said above Daisy's babbling.

"I'm not clear what we're supposed to do for the guy," Simon said.

"First, we're going to look at the company's corporate documents and the siblings' employment contracts," Carpenter explained. "It may turn out that Atkins is screwed if his employment contract can be terminated by a two-to-one vote."

"Do the siblings actually do any work for the company?" Rachel asked.

"Clyde Atkins oversees sales and service," Carpenter said. "His brother Malcolm handles the books. The sister, Mary Ellen Pines, deals with personnel. According to Clyde, they all show up and put in a full day."

"Do the brother and sister plan to replace Clyde?" Rachel continued.

"He's not sure," Carpenter said. "If he had to guess, he thinks his sister is going to take over his job and bring in someone new to deal with personnel."

"Can one of the siblings force the other two to buy him out?"

After Rachel's question, Philly replaced her daughter on the computer screen. She looked good, Carpenter thought. She seemed to have put behind her the stress of two major trials that had concluded last year. "Clyde didn't think that he could force his siblings to buy him out, and he doubted they would agree to do it willingly. We need to make our own assessment as to whether a sibling can force a buyout."

"Does he want to bring a lawsuit?" Simon asked.

"That depends," Carpenter said. "It depends on whether there's anything to sue over. He'd like to be able to prevent his siblings from pocketing his salary if there's legal support for him to do so."

"He's going to be in a stronger position if he's not replaced and his brother and sister put his salary in their pockets," Rachel observed.

Carpenter had had the same thought. "I agree," he said.

"Anything else new?" Philly asked.

Simon broke the silence that followed her question. "I wish there was a way to market those two million-dollar verdicts at the end of last year."

"I have a wild thought about that," Philly said. "I'll get back to you guys."

Carpenter wondered what Philly had in mind as she led the discussion to next steps for the few cases that had carried over from last year. In the decades he'd been practicing law, he had never marketed himself. Now that their group had formed a four-way partnership, he foresaw that marketing decisions would proceed whether he was on board or not. 'It could be worse,' he thought.

5

A Fired Lawyer

Paul viewed the case of the assisted living center photographs—if it was a case—as two mysteries: the identity of the deceased resident and the photographs. They had come up empty on both fronts and now Evelyn was plainly looking to him for direction. They had positioned their desks in the large work area of the Cambridgeport Police Station so that they faced each other. At times like this the arrangement was less than optimal. There was nowhere to hide from Evelyn's direct gaze. "No Dennis France matches up with the dead guy, right?" Paul asked, more to say something than to move their investigation along.

"Right," Evelyn confirmed. "There are a number of Dennis Frances, but age and other factors confirm there's no match. Also, there's no match with the fingerprints on some of the photographs."

"What about the photographs?" Paul responded.

"I've searched every missing person data bank I could think of," Evelyn said. "I've looked at available photographs and didn't come up with anything."

"What do you make of the initials on the backs of the photographs?" Paul asked.

"LFLS," Evelyn said. "Beats the hell out of me."

Paul had spent time studying the initials. The handwriting was shaky, wavy, and it made him think that someone was using the opposite hand he or she wrote with. "What about the Georgia bank check that paid for two years of France's stay at the assisted living center?"

"I talked with a vice-president of the bank," Evelyn responded. "He's supposed to call me back tomorrow. Says he has to run it by legal. Legal might hide behind confidentiality."

Paul didn't disagree. "Right now, it's all we've got."

Rachel usually tried to save money by bringing her lunch to work, but last night she never got around to making a sandwich. It was her boyfriend, Josh's fault. He had wanted to fool around and they had started early and then early morphed into late.

Standing in line at a deli, Rachel was relieved to be out of the office. She had spent the morning wading through copies of corporate documents and contracts that Clyde Atkins had delivered to the office. Atkins and his brother and sister were the family corporation's sole stockholders and directors. Stockholder and director decisions were to be decided by majority vote, which meant that two siblings could gang up on the third. The three siblings rotated the corporation's officer positions. Currently Clyde served as president, his brother Malcolm was the treasurer, and their sister Mary Ellen, was the corporation's secretary.

Each sibling's employment contract could be terminated without cause either by the corporation or by the sibling giving sixty days' advance notice of termination. The contract could also be terminated immediately by either party for cause. The letter terminating Atkins' employment contract, signed by his brother as treasurer of the corporation, stated that the termination was effective immediately because Atkins was not acting in the best interests of the corporation. That stated reason was vague and lacked specifics. Corporate minutes contained no record of any board of directors meeting at which a vote was taken to terminate Atkins' contract.

Rachel had outlined possible grounds for Atkins to legally challenge the termination of his contract. No corporate vote authorized the termination action. The termination letter cited no specific cause for termination so, at a minimum, Atkins was entitled to his contract for another sixty days because termination without cause required sixty days' notice.

Rachel thought that obtaining sixty more days of paid employment following a proper board of directors' vote might be the best Atkins could achieve.

In her e-mail memo to Carpenter, Philly, and Simon with her preliminary thoughts, Rachel also noted that Atkins' director and stockholder positions were protected by the corporation's bylaws. There could be no change in the existing directors or stockholders unless all directors and stockholders agreed.

Rachel paid for her club sandwich and tried to find a seat. The tables on the periphery of the seating area were filled. A large rectangular table with stools on each long side ran down the center of the room. Rachel hustled forward and pounced when she saw an elderly man surrender his stool at the long table.

"Rachel? Rachel Boyle?"

Rachel was startled to see Meredith Sweeney, in a seat across and to her left, offering a somewhat forced grin accompanied by a tentative wave. So much for privacy during this lunch break. Her law school classmate hadn't changed much since graduation. She was tall and thin with short dark hair, full lips, and prominent cheekbones. Each of them had graduated from Spencer Law School *summa cum laude,* but the directions of their legal careers had nothing in common. Despite her stellar academic record, Rachel had been unable to find a job after graduation. Meredith, in contrast, had promptly landed an associate position at one of the big downtown law firms. Rachel had attributed the differences in their career paths to Meredith having achieved honors in moot court competitions. Law firms must have figured that she had potential courtroom skills in addition to academic smarts. In contrast, Rachel had stayed away from moot court and other elective programs that involved the possibility of litigation or an oral presentation. She had avoided participation in classroom discussions and only spoke in class when directly called upon by a professor. The law firms she had applied to probably thought—rightly—that there was nothing to distinguish her from scores of other job applicants who had displayed only academic proficiency in law school.

"How have you been?" Meredith asked above the noise of orders being shouted and plates and silverware making contact.

"Good," Rachel said, silently thankful that her personal and professional lives were where she wanted them to be.

"What are you doing?"

"I'm a partner in a boutique litigation practice," Rachel said, trying not to gloat or to break into an idiotic grin when she said the word partner.

"You? Litigation?"

"Don't sound so surprised," Rachel replied, although she knew that Meredith's reaction would be shared by any other classmates who remembered her from law school. "What about you?"

Meredith frowned and fell silent. When the person seated directly across from Rachel got up to leave, Meredith slid over to take the vacated stool. "I didn't want to shout out my tale of woe so anyone could hear."

"Tale of woe?"

Meredith nodded. "I'm no longer working at Pinkerton, Ashley & Rosewood. In fact, I'm probably going to end up suing them."

Rachel considered following her instincts and remaining silent. But she thought of Carpenter, Philly, and Simon, reminded herself that she was now a partner in a law firm that needed clients to survive, and put her natural inclinations on the back burner. "What happened?"

Meredith glanced at her food and then briefly scanned the deli. "How about a coffee after you finish your sandwich?"

"Works for me," Rachel said, and she started in on her club while Meredith moved salad around on her plate.

No one was within earshot at the corner table they chose in a nearby Dunkin' Donuts. Observing her classmate, Rachel noticed dark patches under Meredith's eyes and a tenseness in the way she held herself. In law school, they had been acquaintances at best. Rachel had been envious of Meredith, awed by her boldness in pursuing varied extracurricular activities, her assertiveness, and her palpable confidence.

"I don't know why I'm talking to you," Meredith said, ignoring her coffee. "I haven't told anyone what's happened."

"You wouldn't have suggested coffee if you didn't want to talk about it," Rachel said.

"We don't really know each other. It's not as if we've ever been friends."

"Maybe that's a good thing. I'll treat what you tell me in confidence. Maybe I can help."

As Meredith weighed her offer, Rachel thought it would be beyond ironic if Meredith Sweeney was the first client she brought to her new firm.

"All right," Meredith said. "This stays between us. I was fired from Pinkerton, Ashley & Rosewood two weeks after I complained to one of the managing partners that I was being sexually harassed."

Rachel was taken aback by Meredith's revelation, but she borrowed a page from Carpenter's book and did her best to maintain a neutral expression.

"In what way were you sexually harassed?"

"A junior partner in the litigation department pressured me to date and on one occasion kissed me."

"I assume you told the guy you wanted no part of him."

"Her. The junior partner is a woman."

"Are you gay?" Rachel asked, knowing her neutral expression had left the building.

Meredith sighed and sagged in her chair. "I'm bisexual."

"Did you mention that to your harasser?"

"No. But I made it clear to the woman that I wasn't interested getting involved with anyone at work."

"What did the managing partner do when you complained?"

"She said she'd look into it and that she'd discuss it with the two other members of the firm's management committee."

"Did that happen?"

"I don't know," Meredith replied with some heat. "I can tell you what I do know. I was asked to meet with the three members of the management committee. They told me that my complaint had been thoroughly investigated and that there was no credible, independent evidence to back it up. Then I was told that my performance in the litigation department was not up to snuff and that I was terminated immediately with three-months of severance."

"Had your job performance been criticized before?"

Meredith hesitated a beat. "Yes. At my previous full review, my second-year review, I was told that my performance in arguing motions was mediocre at best, and that my drafting of pleadings and discovery responses needed more work."

Meredith's litigation duties were those of the stereotypical associate toiling in the litigation department of a large law firm. She probably hadn't been directly involved in any actual trials, but instead had been relegated to litigation grunt work dealing with motions and discovery requests. Rachel imagined Meredith's shocked expression if she were to reveal that at the end of last year, she had delivered the opening argument in a jury trial, had handled all the direct testimony presented to the jury on behalf of her client, and had substantially contributed to the client's obtaining a seven-figure jury verdict. It was possible that Carpenter and Philly's generosity in distributing collected contingency fees meant that she had made more money last year than Meredith.

"Did that previous full review come before or after the harassment started?"

"The review occurred before."

'That will be the firm's defense,' Rachel thought. "Did you think the criticism was justified?"

"Frankly, the negative review came as a surprise. I won most of the motions I either drafted or argued. I thought my success rate was decent. From time to time a partner in charge of a case would ask me to rewrite something. But I don't recall having to do any major rewrites."

"Was your harasser the source of the criticism of your work?"

"I don't know."

Rachel didn't see a smoking gun that would make a sexual harassment suit a winner. "Why are you thinking of suing your firm?"

"The woman who came on to me is probably going to be made a full partner. She's brought in a major client to the firm. There's a family relationship behind her bringing in the client. The client throws a lot of business the firm's way, and I don't think my complaint against the junior partner was ever taken seriously."

"Did your harasser have any reason to assume you were gay?" Rachel asked.

"You'd have to ask her."

"Did you tell her she was wasting her time because you weren't gay?"

"I only told her that she was wasting her time because I wanted to stay away from any involvement with anyone at the firm."

"Are you saying you weren't attracted to her?"

"No. I didn't want a personal relationship with anyone I worked with. But if you must know, I *was* attracted to her."

Meredith was looking at her expectantly and Rachel felt that she owed her classmate a response. "I'm pleased you trusted me with your story. If it's solely your word against the word of the junior partner, you may have a tough time prevailing given the negative evaluation you received before the harassment started. We both know that the firm will use that negative evaluation to claim it had a business reason to let you go."

Meredith nodded. Rachel hadn't told her classmate anything Meredith hadn't already concluded.

"Do you have any problem with me discussing your situation with my partners? I won't mention any names."

"No," Meredith replied after a brief hesitation.

"How do I get in touch with you?"

Meredith produced a business card and jotted personal contact information on the reverse side. "This is so embarrassing," she said. "I can't believe I got fired. I've got one more month of severance, so I've got to find another job. I'm not going to get a recommendation from the firm, that's for sure."

Rachel handed over one of her newly minted business cards. "Let me know if you think of anything else that might be helpful."

Meredith studied Rachel's card. "Is the Jeffries in your firm Simon Jeffries?"

Rachel nodded.

"No shit. Back in law school I figured Simon for litigation. The guy never shut his mouth." Meredith became lost in thought. "I always wondered whether Simon was gay," she said with an inquiring look.

"You'd have to ask him," Rachel replied.

"Whatever. If you don't want to tell me, just say so."

Rachel tried to think of a painless way to end this meeting.

"Would it help if the junior partner had made advances to someone else?" Meredith asked.

"Of course," Rachel said. "Do you have evidence of that?"

"I'm working on it."

6

Whenever in the course of police business Evelyn had been told that a matter had to be run by legal, the end result was a lawyer telling someone to clam up. So she was pleasantly surprised when Alfred Maitland, a vice-president of Atlanta Savings Bank and Trust Company, asked how he could help her.

"I've faxed you a copy of the wire transfer received by an assisted living facility in Cambridge, Massachusetts. The wire was from a branch of your bank. I need to know anything you can tell me about the wire, including who sent it."

Evelyn heard papers rustling. "I want to confirm that this is part of a criminal investigation," Maitland said.

"We believe it is," Evelyn said, stretching the truth since the photographs found in Dennis France's room were no guaranty that any crime had been committed.

"A man named Daryl Finch had a savings account with us for about a year. The day the wire was sent he closed the account. The money left in the account after the wire was paid over to him by bank check."

"How much was left over?" Evelyn asked as she took notes.

"One hundred and two thousand, three hundred and forty-nine dollars and thirteen cents."

"What do you have for an address for this guy Finch?"

"A post-office box in one of the poorer sections of the city," Maitland said before reading off the box number. "I can give you his Social Security number," Maitland added, and Evelyn took it down.

"Anything else?"

"The assistant manager who handled the closing of the account remembers Mr. Finch. She described him as medium height, thin, thinning sandy hair, and freckles or age spots on his forehead. If you have a picture you want to send down here, I can have the assistant manager take a look at it."

There had been no photographs of France in his condo unit. "Let me see what I can come up with," Evelyn replied. "You've been extremely helpful. I'm grateful."

After Evelyn hung up the phone, she ran the Social Security number she had been given for Daryl Finch. This time there was a match. She saw no need to make inquiries about the post-office box number Maitland had provided; she was reasonably confident that France and Finch would turn out to be the same man. But there was one way to make sure: she needed a photograph of France's face. France's body had been moved to the morgue. She dug out the number and placed the call.

Trial preparation in the billboard abortion case was proving to be a tortuous grind taking more time than Simon had anticipated. He looked up from the desk chair in Philly's office and noticed that Rachel's expression suggested she had her own aggravations. Rachel had turned in her chair at the workstation that had been added to Philly's office and nursed a dejected air. "What's got you down?" he asked.

"It's about someone from our law school class I ran into the other day."

"Who was it?"

"I said I wouldn't mention her name?"

"So it's a woman. How about a hint?"

"I shouldn't be playing this game."

"Just one hint."

"Confidence bordering on arrogance," Rachel blurted out.

Some clues were giveaways. Simon hadn't thought of Meredith Sweeney in years. He didn't want to think of her now. "How is Meredith?"

"I gave it away, didn't I?" Rachel said, sounding crestfallen.

Simon nodded. "So, how is she?"

"Actually, she's in trouble."

"Who's in trouble?" Carpenter asked appearing in the doorway. He was carrying a gym bag, and Simon figured he had just returned from one of those spinning classes he had begun going to at the end of last year. It was difficult to imagine Carpenter exercising on a bike. But a spinning Carpenter was proving to be a mellower Carpenter, so Simon was content to have his senior partner pedal his brains out.

"It's this woman we went to law school with," Rachel said.

As Rachel recounted Meredith Sweeney's problem, Simon tried to focus. Memories of his last one-on-one encounter with Meredith had surfaced and he needed to submerge them if he was going to retain anything of what Rachel was saying.

"She said she had no problem with me discussing this with you without mentioning names," Rachel concluded, "but Simon guessed who I was talking about."

"That firm she was with has a reputation," Carpenter said. "They're mainly litigators and the word is, they are not very nice. I've never had a case with them, but a few of my Barrister friends have run into them."

Carpenter had explained that he had Sunday breakfasts with a group of attorneys his own age whom he referred to as the Barristers. Simon wanted to get a look at this breakfast crew, if only to see for himself whether Carpenter clones were on the loose.

"What do you think of her suing her firm?" Rachel asked.

Carpenter left his gym bag by the door and moved to the visitor's chair across from Simon's desk seat. "I'll tell you this," he said. "Pinkerton, Ashley & Rosewood will never settle a case like that. If your friend sues, she's in for a trial."

"Why wouldn't they settle?" Rachel asked.

"Word would get out somehow even if the settlement agreement contained a confidentiality provision." Carpenter scowled. "Besides, from what I've heard about those guys, they can never admit when they're wrong."

"If the firm was sued and could walk away from the suit for small dollars," Simon said, "I think they'd jump at the chance."

"If word got out that there was a settlement and what was settled," Carpenter countered, "would any woman apply for a position with that firm?"

"In today's economy, yes," Simon said with an assurance he didn't feel.

Carpenter shrugged. "Who knows? Even if your classmate's story is true, the firm can say she was a lousy lawyer and that they pointed that fact out to her before she was allegedly harassed. I think she's got a tough road ahead."

"What if she comes up with evidence that someone else was harassed?" Rachel probed.

"Then I would seriously consider taking her case," Carpenter said.

"I wouldn't want to personally get involved in representing her," Simon said.

"Since when did you start having second thoughts about taking on a case that would get you into court?" Carpenter asked.

Simon had deliberately brought the issue into the open, so there was no turning back. "In this case, it would be beyond awkward. At the end of our last year of law school, she came on to me."

Rachel's draw dropped, and Simon couldn't hold back a smile.

"What do you mean she came on to you?" Rachel asked.

"She asked me to have dinner with her and was pretty clear that the evening would end at her place with the two of us in bed."

"I don't believe this!" Rachel exclaimed. "When Meredith looked at my business card she asked if you were the Jeffries mentioned. When I said yes, she asked me whether you were gay."

"What did you tell her?"

"I told her to ask you."

'Well played," Simon said. He remembered Meredith Sweeney's explicit invitation. He also remembered how close he had come to accepting it. Had he done so, the evening probably would have ended in disaster. It was not curiosity that had him thinking of accepting Meredith's offer. Rather, it was Meredith. She was beautiful and he had found her cockiness exciting. He had figured that if he were ever to experiment with switching teams, Meredith Sweeney would be the one to lure him to the dark side. Somehow, he had told her no; thinking back on the event—which he had done frequently afterwards—there were times when he replayed the scene with the word "yes" leaving his lips.

"I'm not sure Meredith would want us to represent her," Rachel said, "but I did say I would get back to her. I'll tell her my partners concurred with my analysis and we're not prepared to represent her without something more."

Simon watched Carpenter tense in the visitor's chair, his jaw muscles working, which meant he was assessing the pros and cons of Meredith's case. "Tell her we'll consider representing her," Carpenter said, "if she can come up with something else to support her harassment claim. She might want to look at each woman who left the firm in the last three years. And I'm not talking just lawyers. I'm talking paralegals and secretaries as well."

"I still don't see how I can get involved if we take the case," Simon said.

"You need to expand your vision," Carpenter replied. "But don't dwell on it. We're far from taking this woman on as a client."

'Carpenter doesn't know Meredith,' Simon thought. If Meredith told Rachel that she was working on getting more evidence, Simon was willing to bet she'd succeed.

7

A Hockey Fan

As the stenographer set up her equipment for the deposition, Philly assessed the young man who had fallen on Martina Glass during a Salem Stampede hockey game last year. Fred Dunn was huge, a beefy guy with a noticeable gut and thick appendages. If you were going to imagine a cartoon hockey fan, this would be your guy. He had to be over six foot two and weigh in at close to two hundred and forty pounds. Recalling Glass' slight build, Philly considered it a miracle that their client hadn't been killed. The man's lawyer, William Ward, was a physical match for Dunn with a gut so substantial that Philly doubted he could successfully button his suit jacket to cover the bulge. But where Dunn was taciturn, Ward was outgoing. His greeting had been loud and friendly, his handshake firm.

The other lawyer in attendance was Wayne Martin, representing the hockey team, the Salem Stampede. He was young, dark-complexioned, and rugged-looking. Philly pegged him for a former hockey player. Last year, Martin had unsuccessfully moved to have Martina Glass' lawsuit against the Salem Stampede dismissed.

The stenographer, Jeanne Smith was closer to eighty than seventy. She was Carpenter's stenographer of choice, and her pendulous jowls shook as she signaled that she was ready.

Simon, Ward, and Martin quickly established the deposition ground rules, and Simon began with background questions. Dunn worked for a moving company. After high school, he had completed one year of junior college. He had played hockey in high school as a defenseman. He and some of his friends from work attended Stampede games from time to time.

"Do you remember attending a Salem Stampede game during which you fell from where you were sitting and landed on a woman below you?" Simon asked.

"Yeah."

"What period in the game did that occur?"

"I'd guess the beginning of the third period."

"Who attended the game with you?"

"Frank Madden and Jerry Lynch."

"Who are they?"

"Friends of mine from work."

"What caused you to fall on the woman you landed on?"

For a moment Dunn seemed confused by the question. "Somebody pushed me," he finally said with a sullenness that Philly regarded less as actual belligerence but more as manufactured toughness to mask a lie.

"Who pushed you?"

"I don't know. I didn't see who it was."

"Did your friends Frank and Jerry see who pushed you?"

"I don't think so. You'll have to ask them."

"Rest assured, Mr. Dunn, I will ask them," Simon said in a tone that could cut glass and that caused Dunn to drop his eyes. "When you were pushed, where were your friends, Frank and Jerry?"

"I think Frank had gone to get something to eat. Jerry was sitting next to me."

"Have you ever discussed with Jerry who pushed you?"

"I guess so." Dunn again didn't meet Simon's gaze. Philly glanced at Ward, who was unperturbed by the questions directed at his client.

"Did you and Jerry discuss who pushed you to prepare for this deposition?"

"I might have. I don't remember."

"Did Jerry ever tell you what he observed of your falling?"

"We talked about it. I think he said he didn't know how it happened."

"Did he see you pushed?"

"I don't think so, but you'd have to ask him."

"When you were pushed, were you sitting or standing?"

"Standing."

"Why were you standing?"

"I don't really remember. There must have been something exciting on the ice."

"Were you standing in front of your seat?"

"Yeah."

"Was it the kind of seat that left more room to stand when the seat was pulled up?"

Dunn frowned in concentration. "Yeah."

"Was your seat pulled up when you were standing before you fell?"

"I don't remember," Dunn said in a barely audible tone.

"Where exactly was your seat?"

"I think it was the third level up from the ice."

"Was it an aisle seat?"

Dunn shook his head. "It was like four or five seats in from one of the aisles."

"Was your seat at center ice?"

"No. It was off to the side of center ice."

"Was there a lot of leg room?"

Martin stopped taking notes, looked up, and stared at Dunn.

"Not really. It was sort of cramped."

"Was there a railing near your seat?"

"Yeah, in front of the seat."

"How high was the railing?"

Dunn shrugged. "I don't think it came up to my waist when I was standing. It was a low railing."

"Before you were pushed, did you drink any alcoholic beverages at the game?"

Dunn glanced briefly at Ward. "Yeah."

"What did you drink?"

"Beer."

"How many beers did you have before you got pushed?"

"Probably a couple."

"Could it have been more than two?"

"Maybe. I don't think so, but I suppose that's possible."

"How many beers do you usually have when you attend a Stampede game?"

Dunn again looked toward Ward. "Three, maybe."

"Did you eat any peanuts before you were bumped?"

"I don't remember."

"At any time before you were bumped, did either of your friends—Frank or Jerry—toss you a bag of peanuts?"

Dunn glared at Simon for a long moment. "I don't remember that," he finally replied.

"Did you ever discuss your fall with your friend Frank?"

"Yeah."

"Did he tell you what he saw of your fall?"

"I don't think he saw anything. Like I said, he was getting food."

"You said you were pushed. How were you pushed?"

Simon was jumping from topic to topic, then circling back to the alleged push. Philly recognized the approach as a way to keep Dunn off balance, making it difficult for him to recall whether he'd previously said something inconsistent with what he was about to utter.

"I don't really remember."

"Were you pushed from behind?"

"I think so."

"You think so," Simon repeated not bothering to conceal incredulity. "You weren't pushed at all, were you?"

"No, that's not true," Dunn said without much conviction in Philly's estimation.

"Do you recall any signs at the arena warning fans not to lean over railings?"

"I don't remember seeing anything like that."

"Were there any posted warnings telling fans not to stand during play?"

"I don't think so. I never saw anything like that. Fans like to stand and cheer."

"What did you do after you fell on the woman below you?"

"I got off her."

"Did you call for help?"

"No, I think somebody else did."

"What was the condition of the woman you landed on?"

"She wasn't moving. I heard her moan a few times."

"What happened next?"

Dunn slouched in his chair. "I'm not totally sure. I was shaken up. Eventually help came and they took the woman away."

"Was she still moaning?"

"I'm not sure. I was in the aisle so people could get to her."

"Did you drink alcohol before the hockey game?"

"I'm pretty sure I did. I think we stopped off at a bar before the game."

"How many drinks did you have before the game?"

"I don't remember."

Simon's questions wound down in the next twenty minutes. When he consulted her, Philly agreed that he had asked what needed to be asked. Ward quickly announced that he had no questions for his client. "I have a few questions," Martin said.

"You said you were pushed, is that correct?" Martin began.

"Yeah."

"Did anybody working for the Salem Stampede push you?"

"I don't know who pushed me."

"Did you see anyone during the game wearing a Salem Stampede uniform or wearing an article of clothing with the name or logo of the team?"

"There may have been someone in the lobby area where you go into the arena."

"What about where you were sitting?"

"I don't think so. But I can't be sure."

"Who was sitting behind you at the game?"

"I don't know."

"Did you ever turn around in your seat?"

"I don't remember. I might have."

"Was the push you say you got a hard push?"

"Objection for the record," Ward said.

"It was hard enough to send me over the rail," Dunn said.

"Where exactly were you pushed? What part of your body?"

"My lower back, I think."

"You think?"

"That's what I said."

"Did you read the back of your ticket stub?"

"I don't remember."

Martin had Jeannie Smith mark a ticket stub that had been stamped void as a deposition exhibit.

"Read the back of the stub out loud," Martin instructed.

"'Hockey is a contact sport and any fan purchasing a ticket does so at his/her own risk. The Salem Stampede is not responsible for any injury that a fan may incur. An individual purchasing this ticket is responsible for acting in a manner that does not result in injury or discomfort to any other individual. A fan not complying with these instructions may be directed to leave the premises.'"

"Do you agree that you are responsible for the injury to Martina Glass?" Martin asked.

"Objection," Ward said sharply.

"No," Dunn answered. "Like I said, I was pushed."

"Did the railing you described provide a barrier between where you were seated and the seating level below you?"

"Objection!" Ward nearly shouted.

"Not really," Dunn said. "It didn't stop me from falling."

"Nothing further," Martin said.

"Then the deposition is concluded," Simon declared.

"Now there's a guy who acted like he had something to hide," Jeannie Smith remarked as she packed up her stenographer gear.

Smith's observations had often been pretty sound, so Philly asked, "Do you think a jury would find him believable?"

"With a jury, who knows?" Smith replied. "I can tell you I didn't trust him worth a damn. He wouldn't meet your eyes at times," she said to Simon.

"Good to hear," Simon said. "Too bad the guy's a working stiff and doesn't have money."

"What was all that about a bag of peanuts?" Smith inquired.

"That," said Philly, "is what is known as a mixed bag."

With the Dunn deposition behind him, Simon waited until Rachel left the office they shared so he could have some time alone to think. He and Frank Stevens had spent a lot of time together over the holidays, and had phoned a lot when Frank went back to college. But ever since Meredith Sweeney loomed as a potential client for the firm, Simon had not returned Frank's calls and had responded to e-mails perfunctorily. Simon knew that wasn't fair to Frank. He picked up his cell phone.

"What's going on?" Frank demanded after brief hellos.

Simon hesitated. He could follow his natural instincts and conceal what was bothering him, use work as an excuse. Or he could break tradition and level with Frank. He liked Frank, maybe even loved him. Their nine-year age difference no longer troubled him. And the fact that Frank was a jock and loved sports was something he could live with. 'What the hell,' Simon thought, 'time to break the mold.' "It's a goddamn girl," he blurted out.

"What the hell are you talking about?"

For a moment Simon was tongue-tied. "Were you ever attracted to a woman?" Simon found his voice.

"I assume we're talking sexually, and the answer is no. I thought we had similar senior prom stories."

"There was a moment at the end of my last year of law school when I was very close to accepting an offer to have sex with a woman classmate."

"Close only counts in horseshoes," Frank responded.

Simon didn't appreciate the joke. "I'm trying to be serious here," he said sharply.

There was silence at the end of the line and Simon couldn't picture the expression on Frank's face.

"Sorry," Frank said. "You surprised me. Sorry. Who is this woman?"

"In some ways, she was a female me," Simon began. "She loved to argue. She was smart as hell, maybe as smart as Rachel. We were on opposite sides in the finals of a major moot court competition. There was nothing that fazed her. She was cocky, arrogant even, and unafraid of anybody or anything."

There was a brief pause.

"Who won?" Frank asked.

"What are you talking about?"

"Who won the moot court competition?"

"She won best speaker. My team won the overall."

After another pause, Frank asked, "So why did you turn down her offer?"

Simon remembered what he had told Rachel and Carpenter. He hadn't been completely honest with his partners. "I just chickened out. It was very tempting." It was the truth, though not what he had told Rachel and Carpenter.

"What brought this on? You've been out of law school a while."

"She may become a client of the firm. I told Carpenter and Rachel that I couldn't be involved in the case if that happened."

"You still have feelings for her," Frank said, and Simon noted that it wasn't a question.

This time the silence was longer, and much more tense. Maybe Frank was reassessing their relationship.

"The important thing," Frank said, at last, "is that you said no. You knew who you were then, and you know who you are today. You did the right thing. In my opinion, we are both clear on our sexual orientation."

Simon let out the breath he'd been holding. Leveling with Frank had been the right move. He had needed to hear Frank say what he'd just said. It sometimes struck him that the nine-year age difference between them was misleading when it came to maturity, since at times Frank had a better read on big picture issues than he did.

"Also, don't be so quick to stay away from her case. If the case comes in, listen to what she has to say before you make up your mind."

'Another bit of sound advice,' Simon thought. The question was whether he would take it.

8

Dennis France and Daryl Finch were one and the same. The assistant bank manager mentioned by Alfred Maitland had viewed an unflattering photographic head shot of a dead Dennis France and positively confirmed that the photograph was of Daryl Finch, the man who had closed out his Atlanta account. "She'll swear to that under oath," Maitland had assured Evelyn, who had just now passed on this news to Paul.

"This information isn't exactly unexpected," Paul said. "Go over what you have on Daryl Finch."

"No criminal record. He'd lived and worked in Medford. His wife died seven years ago. He started receiving Social Security benefits when he turned sixty-six. That's when he left Medford. The benefits were first direct deposited into an account in Miami and then were changed to the bank in Atlanta. While Finch lived at the Cambridge assisted living center, his Social Security checks were sent to a Cambridge post-office box. He had a family: two sons and a daughter."

"For some reason, Finch left Massachusetts and then came back," Paul said more to himself than to Evelyn. "I think we start with the sons and daughter."

Evelyn jotted a few notes on her notepad. "We could also publish the photographs of children we found in his room."

"That option is lower down on my list," Paul said. The photographs continued to bother him.

"Why not throw everything out there?" Evelyn asked. "There could be kids in danger. I don't see a reason not to move forward on several fronts."

Paul stuck to his instincts. "There's something off about the photos. They look staged to me. And if Finch was responsible for the photos, he's not going to be responsible for any future photos."

"What reason would someone have for staging those photographs? They look real to me. But let's say they were staged. If we put them in the public domain and someone confirms the staging, we'd have made some progress."

"You're making logical points," Paul acknowledged, "but I'm going to take this incrementally. I'm not ready to go public with the kids' pictures."

"What if there are kids who have gone missing?" Evelyn pressed. "Those photographs are sick."

"You're thinking Finch was a predator of some kind, right?"

"Looks that way to me. It looks like he had a need to keep mementos of his handiwork."

"But there's another way to look at this," Paul said. "Finch was really going out of his way to stay invisible. It makes me think he didn't want to be found because there was someone out there gunning for him."

"That doesn't explain the photographs."

"No, it doesn't," Paul admitted. "But the fact that Finch had the photographs doesn't mean he took them. Maybe someone sent them to him."

"I still peg him for a predator."

"Maybe you're right. But I want to stick with what I outlined before. See if you can find out whether anyone's contacted Social Security trying to locate Finch or his address."

"Okay," Evelyn said without enthusiasm, and Paul knew that she was disappointed. And maybe Evelyn was right. What if kids would be put in harm's way by his incremental, cautious approach?

Paul stood up and stretched. "I need coffee," he announced and made his getaway, not for the first time in their relationship perturbed by Evelyn's concentrated stare.

Rachel took a call from Meredith Sweeney curious where her classmate's situation stood. She had previously called Meredith to deliver her firm's collective judgment on the merits of her case against Pinkerton, Ashley & Rosewood. Meredith hadn't reacted when informed they were not interested in representing her without more.

"I'm making no progress," Meredith said. "What I need is a private detective to dig up some dirt on the junior partner who came on to me."

"Can you afford a private detective?" Rachel asked, thinking of the two former Cambridge cops, now PIs, who had been instrumental in digging up witnesses for the jury trial she won last year.

"I'm willing to throw some money away, but I don't have a lot of spare cash. I'm going to need something to live on while I search for a job. I haven't exactly been diligent in lining up something else."

Rachel checked her contacts and passed on the information for Barney Freedman and Herb McCauley. "These guys really delivered for us last year."

"Thanks." Meredith paused. "Is Simon around?" she finally asked. "I'd like to say hello."

"I'll have to put you on hold while I check," Rachel lied. She was sitting behind Philly's desk and looked across the room to the workstation where Simon was typing. "Meredith Sweeney wants to say hello. Are you in?"

Rachel had rarely seen Simon discomfited but, when he turned to face her, he was red in the face and flustered. "I'm not in," he said lamely.

"But you are in. What's going on?"

"You know damn well what's going on. I told you and Carpenter about my last run in with her. I don't want to talk to her."

"You're acting like a baby."

"Frankly, I don't give a damn."

"I'll leave the room, give you some privacy."

"Tell her I'm not here."

"She could use a few friends right now." Rachel had opted for sympathy and saw immediately that she had struck the right chord. Simon's defensive wall exhibited cracks.

"We weren't exactly close, and *I* took the time to talk to her," Rachel added. "Come on. This isn't like you."

Rachel was right: he *was* acting like a baby. "All right. I'll take you up on the privacy."

Simon waited until Rachel left the room before moving behind Philly's desk and staring at the blinking green light announcing that a call was on hold. He picked up the phone. "Hi, it's Simon."

"How are you?"

"Rachel and I are good."

"I know Rachel's good. I've seen her. She's transformed. It's amazing actually. But as for you, the person I asked about, since I'm not eyeballing you, I guess I'll just have to take your word that you're good."

Meredith's jocular little barb reminded Simon of what had attracted him to her: her directness, her refusal to take any crap. And speaking of eyeballing, *he* wanted to eyeball *her*. Did she still have that haughty carriage, those dark eyes that held your gaze like they would never let go? Rachel had said Meredith was feeling down. Was that even possible? Would Meredith deign to let vulnerability or disappointment show?

"Then that's what you'll have to do." Simon said.

"What do you think of my chances if I sue my former firm?"

"Did Rachel tell you what she thought?"

"Yeah."

"She was also speaking for me and one of my other partners."

Meredith fell silent. If Rachel was right that Meredith needed support, he certainly wasn't providing any. His tone had been business-like to a fault.

"You know," Meredith said, "I sometimes think about that pass I made at you at the end of our senior year. Do you ever think about that?"

Simon was not about to admit that he had periodically obsessed over the event after it occurred. However, there was a truthful response he could make that might keep the discussion open. "When Rachel said she ran into you, I thought about it."

"I've always wondered why you turned me down. It looked like you were about to take me up on my offer."

"At the time, it seemed more prudent to say no."

"There was something about you that made me take the initiative. Maybe I totally misread the situation."

Simon remained silent. Let Meredith wonder whether her intuition was correct.

"Are you gay?" Meredith asked. "I asked Rachel and she said to ask you."

Simon saw no reason to lie. "Yes."

"Well, maybe that explains why you said no."

"Not completely," Simon conceded. "I was tempted to say yes."

"Well, if you had said yes, it would have been interesting."

"That's one way to describe it."

"If I come up with more information and your firm takes my case, will you be working on the case?"

"I'll probably decline. I'd just as soon stay clear of it."

"That's too bad," Meredith said. "If I come up with more evidence and hire your firm, I'd want you front and center."

'That's not going to happen,' Simon thought. "I'll think about it," is what he said.

9

Carpenter couldn't find anything to complain about when it came to the three-bedroom condo he and Maxine had moved into. The decision to opt for an extra bedroom had been the right one. They had turned it into an all-purpose room that now housed a refurbished spinning bike, a flat-screen TV facing a newly purchased couch, his work desk, a three-drawer file cabinet housing his work-related papers and just enough room for Maxine to unroll her yoga mat. Both Carpenter and Maxine regarded the third bedroom as his room. Maxine recognized that he needed a space with clutter and none of the fancy furniture she had brought over from her condo. So she had claimed the second bedroom for her desk.

Maxine was handy. Since they'd moved in, she'd been sanding, painting, putting up shelves. He'd offered to help but was relieved when she directed him to stay out of her way. He was a klutz when it came to repair work.

His fear of having Maxine around 24/7 had proved baseless. On weekdays, they went to work. On weekends, they did things together but also spent considerable time alone. Maxine knew that he liked to obsess about work in solitude. Living together was turning out okay. But that didn't mean he had run out of subjects to fret about.

He wasn't sleeping well. It was tempting to attribute his wakefulness to the new surroundings. But other factors were in play. The firm's inventory of active cases was depressingly small, similar to last year. Then there was the result of his last blood test which had showed a small increase in his white cell count, an increase that his oncologist dismissed as of no moment because he was well within a stable range. Still, any increase, however modest, dismayed him for it meant that his hope that his white cell count might decrease over time was fantasy. Of course he knew that Fred, as he had named his chronic lymphocytic leukemia, wasn't a fantasy. But a guy could hope, even a curmudgeon like him. And lastly there was the fact that their new surroundings had made Maxine absolutely randy, and he'd been unable to match her desire. True, they had christened the new couch in the third bedroom. But he knew that the drop in his sex drive was a disappointment to Maxine, and he also knew she would never let on that it was.

Last night he had abruptly opened his eyes a little after four in the morning and had known immediately that he wouldn't be able to fall back to sleep. He had eased out of bed, gently closed the bedroom door, and paced about their new home in the dark. He had thought about his concerns—work, health, sex—and wondered whether his worries in these areas would increase over time and be joined by other concerns he couldn't yet imagine. During his fifties, no issue had managed to weigh him down. He'd bitch about work or the lack of it, but he had never felt that he didn't control his destiny. His cancer diagnosis—chronic lymphocytic leukemia, or CLL—had changed that mindset for good. CLL took its own sweet time—or not—and did its own thing. You could work with it, manage it some, but you were never really in control.

Maxine had found him at six this morning on his spinning bike, pedaling at a leisurely pace, not really getting any kind of workout but finding comfort in his legs being in motion. She had given him a kiss and unfurled her yoga mat. Silently she had gone through stretches and poses that he could never replicate. When her workout was over, she'd given him another kiss and left the room, closing the door behind her, reminding him that one of the things he loved about her was that she knew when to keep her mouth shut.

Now, standing before the mirror in their bedroom, Carpenter adjusted his tie knot. It wasn't that he was dressed up with no place to go. It was that he had a place to go with nothing much to do.

Barney Freedman was pleased with his first impression of Meredith Sweeney. She was prudent in carefully checking them out. If she hired them, she'd be entrusting them with helping her deal with a major, traumatic event in her life. They were in a Dunkin' Donuts off Davis Square in Somerville having breakfast, Herb telling Sweeney it was their treat. She took a bite of her bacon and egg sandwich and studied them. If staring was impolite, Sweeney had never been so advised.

"You guys are big," Sweeney said. "I always pictured detectives as thin, wiry guys."

"You've watched too many movies," Herb McCauley said. "Big has its benefits. When we were on the force, a suspect never liked having me and Barney tower over him." He took out his notepad. "Why don't you tell us what happened. Then we'll tell you if we think we can help you."

"This is confidential, right?"

"Right," Herb said.

Sweeney breathed in deeply and let the air out slowly. She was one of those women, Barney thought, who didn't have any particular feature that caught your attention but presented a total package that made you take notice. Maybe it was her height. Maybe the measuring look in her dark eyes. Maybe it was her deliberateness as she assessed whether to level with two guys she didn't know from Adam.

"Right after law school, I landed a job with one of the largest and most prestigious Boston law firms: Pinkerton, Ashley & Rosewood. I was assigned to the litigation department. When I was interviewing, I made it clear that litigation was what I wanted to do."

Barney had been cross-examined by enough criminal defense attorneys to know that litigators' abilities ranged from formidable to clueless. He suspected that Sweeney would land on the competent end of the spectrum.

"Gwen Cantor was a junior partner in the litigation department. Beginning my second year with the firm, I worked on a number of cases with her. When I was assigned to work with Cantor, I thought I did well. We got along and there were occasions when she took the time to teach me and discuss strategy. Out of all the litigation partners, I considered her to be the closest thing to a mentor I was likely to have."

"What's the difference between a junior and senior partner?" Herb asked.

"The way I understand it is a senior partner gets to share in the firm's profits while a junior partner is treated more like an employee. At the end of a year, a junior partner can look forward to a significant bonus but that's nothing like having a share of the profits. A junior partner also gets the title of 'partner' that she can point to when dealing with clients.

"After finishing my second year, I was given a major review. The review was largely negative, which took me by surprise. I'd been going along thinking that I was doing a decent job and out of the blue my oral argument skills, writing ability, time management—you name it—were called into question as needing improvement. It was pretty harsh and unexpected. I was disappointed. Some of the criticisms of my work were brought up for the first time. I had no clue I'd been screwing up in anybody's eyes."

"Who did this review?" Herb asked.

"Eleanor Hightower, a senior partner."

"Had you worked with her before?" Barney asked.

"Once."

"What happened next?" Herb prompted.

"I think the negative review had an effect on me that wasn't intended. If the idea was to make me work harder, I did. I put in more hours. But the criticism made me more tentative. I began to doubt my judgment. I didn't think this at the time, but now I realize that I wasn't all that happy.

"In the fall last year, I asked to meet with Gwen Cantor. She saw me after hours in her office. I told her about the negative review and how unexpected it was. I told her the review bothered me and was negatively affecting my work. I asked her for her reaction and advice.

"She was sitting behind her desk and I was in one of the two visitor chairs opposite her. She came around to my side of the desk, held out her hand. When I took her hand, she pulled me up to a standing position and kissed me square on the lips. She said, 'I've been wanting to do that for a long time.'"

Herb was writing. Barney was struck by the lack of emotion on Sweeney's part as she relayed her superior's advance.

"I pushed Gwen away and asked her what the hell she was doing. She said, 'I thought you'd be pleased. I'm pretty adept at reading people and I sensed you feel the same way as I do.' I was so stunned I couldn't say anything."

"Did you feel the same way as she felt?" Herb asked.

Sweeney colored slightly but met Herb's gaze. "Gwen is attractive and I'm bisexual so yes, on some level I *was* drawn to her. But there was no way in hell I was going to get involved with anyone where I worked."

"Did you tell Ms. Cantor that?" Herb followed up.

"Yes."

"Is that it?"

Sweeney shook her head. "Gwen said something like she wasn't about to give up and take no for an answer. She asked me if I was free for dinner that night and I walked out of her office."

"Did she keep after you?" Herb asked.

"Yeah. She did. She kept asking me to have dinner with her. There came a time when I was alone with her in her office and she tried to kiss me again. I told her I was going to report her if she wouldn't promise to leave me alone and she more or less smirked at me and told me that if I reported her, I'd probably end up getting fired."

Barney envisioned where this tale would end up. "What happened when you reported her?" he asked.

"Nothing," Sweeney said with some bitterness. "I reported her to Eleanor Hightower, the partner who gave me the poor review. This was only after Cantor had gotten me alone and again came on to me. Hightower is one of the three senior partners who are on the firm's management committee. She told me that my allegations were serious and they would be fully investigated."

"Were they?" Barney asked.

"Hightower told me they were and that there was no credible, independent evidence to substantiate my claims. Then she told me that I was fired immediately with three months of severance."

Herb finished writing and looked up. "What are you looking for us to do for you?'

Sweeney pushed her plate to the side. "I couldn't have been the first person Gwen came on to. I want you to find someone else she harassed."

"We can do that," Herb said.

10

Carpenter now couldn't complain he had nothing to do. Clyde Atkins wanted to bring suit immediately against his brother Malcolm and his sister Mary Ellen for forcing him out of the company they all owned. Usually when a client said, "Sue the bastards, I don't care what it costs," those words were music to his ears. When Atkins let loose with this directive, it struck a faint, discordant note. Carpenter wondered whether he had mellowed too much. Why was he more concerned with the obstacles to Atkins prevailing in litigation than with a billable-hour, paying client?

Philly had agreed that Rachel was the right person to work with him on Atkins' case, and she now sat in his office's visitor chair poised to take notes.

"I'm thinking that you take first shot at a court complaint," Carpenter said. "We're going to try to get a preliminary injunction and you know what we need to establish because we sought a preliminary injunction in the abortion billboard case."

Rachel nodded. "I assume we should ask to have Atkins paid his salary for sixty days."

"Right. But what's more important that we should ask for?"

Rachel chewed at her lower lip. She was so transparent that Carpenter could tell she was disappointed in not thinking immediately of an answer to his question.

"In Atkins' place," Rachel said after a long pause, "I wouldn't want his brother and sister to take money out of the business that would have gone to him."

"Exactly," Carpenter said. "I think we should ask that the money that would have been paid Atkins after he was properly terminated be placed in escrow and not pocketed by his sister and brother."

Rachel wrote for a time. When she looked up, she was still chewing on her lower lip. "Can we do anything with getting the brother and sister to buy Atkins out?"

"I thought of that," Carpenter replied, "and didn't come up with much."

"I wish I knew more about corporations," Rachel mused.

"By the time you're finished with this complaint, you'll have gotten your wish. I'll do the affidavit for Atkins. I want you to allege that by terminating Atkins' employment agreement, his brother and sister breached the good faith obligation they had to Atkins as a minority stockholder."

"Okay," Rachel said standing. "This is fun."

Not the word he would have used but Carpenter nodded.

Barney didn't have the patience for computer grunt work, but Herb did. Herb found he worked best if he holed up in the new Cambridge Public Library. This got him out of the house, out from under his wife's surveillance, and gave him a chance to check out the students from the nearby high school. If nothing else, the students provided a fashion display that revealed just how far the country had landed in the crapper.

Herb had printed out the attorney list on Pinkerton, Ashley & Rosewood's website. The firm currently had 120 lawyers comprising 50 partners and 70 associates. Then there was a small army of paralegals. What he really wanted to know was who had left the law firm in the last five years.

Herb called the Board of Bar Overseers and asked his question. The woman who fielded his call tried to be helpful. "Lawyers are required to update their contact information," she explained. "We then update our public records so a member of the public will have updated information on a lawyer he or she wishes to contact. The old contact information is no longer a public record visible on our website. However, the old contact information could probably be found in an individual lawyer's paper file."

The last thing Herb was going to do was sift through a boat load of individual attorney files in the hope of flagging a lawyer who had left Pinkerton.

"I just remembered," the woman said. "We saved the current information for lawyers and paralegals on separate data discs at the end of 2009 and 2010. I can't remember if we did that at the end of 2011, but I'm pretty sure we did."

"Where are you going with this?" Herb asked.

"We could do a search of the firm you're interested in. You would have to do some work to figure out who dropped out from one year to the next."

That sounded more manageable than searching individual attorney files. "The firm is Pinkerton, Ashley, & Rosewood," Herb said.

"I'm familiar with them," the woman replied. "Check back with me in two days. Make sure you ask for Jocelyn Weaver."

"Why are you going beyond the call of duty here?" Herb couldn't resist asking.

"What makes you think I'm going beyond the call of duty?" Weaver replied. "I'm just a humble public servant trying to respond to a citizen inquiry."

"Then keep up the good work."

Herb ended the call and immediately dialed a personal cell phone number on his contact list.

"Fisher."

"I need a favor, Hank."

"You always need a favor, so what else is new? How about leading up to it? You could ask me about my family, how I'm doing. Small talk. You remember small talk?

"How are you and your family doing?"

"Don't ask. I thought when your kids were teenagers that was as bad as it was going to get. I was wrong. When your grandchildren are teenagers it's worse."

"Can Barney and I help?"

"Let me sleep on that. What do you need this time?"

"I need to know who filed unemployment compensation claims against a law firm in the last five years."

"What's in it for me?"

"The usual tickets you like."

"Who are we talking about?"
"Pinkerton, Ashley & Rosewood."
"Call me in two days."
"Consider it done."

February

From Meredith's Playlist

"The Best of You"

Foo Fighters

11

An Alleged Killer

Entering the Worcester County Superior Court courtroom, Philly remembered the jury trial she had litigated while pregnant with Daisy. Back then she had subsisted on black tea and toast and jam, her fare this morning. Fay Richardson's trial promised not to be as taxing as that jury trial: Simon and Rachel were trying the case in a bench trial with no jury present. Philly had advised Richardson of her right to a jury trial and her client decided to trust her luck with the judge who had ordered her ex-boyfriend Al Townsend's billboard message to be taken down.

But the first order of business for Judge Terence Murray was to deal with the defendants' motion that he disqualify himself from hearing the case. Late last year, Simon had found news stories that Murray's daughter had been stalked by an ex-boyfriend who wanted her to have an abortion. Patrick Lassiter, the defendants' lawyer, cited this incident in requesting the judge to recuse himself. If the judge allowed the motion so that a new judge took his place, Philly wondered whether Fay Richardson would be kicking herself for giving up her right to a jury trial. For that matter, why hadn't the defendants claimed a jury trial to take the ultimate decision out of Murray's hands?

Judge Murray took his seat on the bench promptly at nine. He had gray hair and an unsmiling mien, and he ran his courtroom with authority. When the court clerk announced the case, Murray took a moment to study the attorneys arrayed before him. "The first order of business is the defendants' motion that I recuse myself from this case. The plaintiff opposes the motion. Tell me, Mr. Lassiter, is there anything you wish to add that is not in your motion?"

Lassiter rose. He was a tall, trim man. This morning he was wearing a charcoal-gray pinstriped suit and a patterned maroon tie. Philly thought of only one additional point Lassiter could make and she wondered whether he had the balls to make it. It turned out that he did.

"Your Honor came down unduly hard on the defendants at the end of the hearing on the preliminary injunction heard late last year. Respectfully,

Your Honor's strong words seemed uncalled for. The defendants believe that the inference can be drawn that the subject of abortion triggers an untoward emotional response in Your Honor and therefore they request that you recuse yourself."

Lassiter sat down promptly. "Does the plaintiff care to respond to Mr. Lassiter's comment?"

Simon rose. "The judicial response last year was proper given the harm to the plaintiff that was occurring daily. It's hard to imagine any issue that doesn't trigger an emotional response at some level. The question is whether Your Honor may fairly consider the evidence and judge the case, and nothing the defendants have put forward suggests that you can't."

"I agree," Murray declared before Simon was seated. "I'm prepared to decide this case based on the evidence. The defendants' motion is denied."

Philly would not have wanted to be in Lassiter's position. Lassiter had basically accused the judge of being prejudiced against the defendants and now had to live with a judge who had rejected his prejudice charge.

"Is the plaintiff ready to call her first witness?" Murray asked Simon.

"Yes, Your Honor. The plaintiff calls Selena Boyd as her first witness."

Selena Boyd was the first of a trio of witnesses who had seen the billboard message authored by Al Townsend and immediately knew that the killer allegation had been directed at their friend, Fay Richardson. Boyd was short, of compact build, and seemed unperturbed by being in a courtroom. Philly had suggested to Simon that he lead off with the woman he thought would be the strongest witness.

Boyd had known Fay Richardson since high school and considered her a close personal friend. She and a boyfriend had once double-dated with Fay and Al, and she had visited their apartment when they had lived together.

"At some time did you alert Ms. Richardson about a billboard you saw?"

"I did."

"How did that come about?"

"I was driving south into Mercer when I saw this billboard coming up on my right. I recognized Al's picture immediately and I slowed down to get a better look. Al was holding a baby and there was a message in large print that you couldn't miss. It said something like, 'My baby will never be several months old because its mother killed it.' I may not have it exactly but that was the gist of what I read."

"What did you do next?"

"I drove on until I could make a U-turn. I headed north and when I passed the billboard, I made another U-turn, and this time I stopped and pulled over in front of the billboard and got out of my car."

Simon paused. Judge Murray was writing. When the judge looked up, Simon directed his attention back to Boyd. "What did you do?"

"I wrote down the message on the billboard. I had a notepad and a pen with me and I remember it took me a while to write it all down because my hand was shaking."

"Why was your hand was shaking?"

"Because I was furious." Boyd paused and looked behind the counsel table where Lassiter was sitting. "That gutless bastard over there," she said, pointing at Al Townsend, "had no business calling my friend a killer. He's one sick person, a control freak who has no sense of decency whatsoever. Fay is well rid of him."

"Objection, and move to strike the witness' answer," Lassiter said in a raised voice.

"Overruled," Judge Murray declared.

"You pointed while you gave your last answer. Please clarify who you were pointing at."

"Him," Boyd said, her voice an angry snarl. "Al Townsend. I don't see any other gutless bastard in the room."

"Please just answer the question posed to you," Judge Murray directed. "It's not appropriate for you to make speeches."

"Sorry, Your Honor," Boyd said, sounding anything but.

"No further questions."

Lassiter rose. "Are you married, Ms. Boyd?"

"No."

"Have you ever been pregnant or had children?"

"No."

"Did Ms. Richardson talk to you about having an abortion before she went ahead and had one?"

"Yes."

"When did that discussion occur?"

"Maybe a week before she had the procedure."

"What was said during that conversation?"

Lassiter hadn't taken Boyd's deposition, so Philly wondered why he had asked her an open-ended question, the answer to which might hurt his case. Maybe Lassiter believed that with Judge Murray deciding the case he had nothing to lose by taking risks, which again raised the question why Lassiter hadn't insisted on a jury trial.

"I remember Fay was crying. I offered to go over to her place, but she said that wasn't necessary. She told me what she had decided and said that it had been a wretched decision. What tipped the scales for her was that she was fearful of Al. She believed that he was capable of harming her. She needed to make sure that he was totally out of her life and she didn't want a baby with someone who terrified her." Boyd paused. "I told her that I thought she was making the right decision. At first I had thought Al was an okay guy, but as soon as they moved in together, he seemed to change and I told her so. He was always checking up on her. He plainly didn't like it when Fay and I and other friends got together. And he had this thing about Fay's weight. Fay's weight is fine, but he was always warning her not to eat anything fattening. Like he should talk! He's one of those plump guys who doesn't have a muscle inside of him."

"Did you ask Ms. Richardson if she had shared her abortion decision with Mr. Townsend?"

"No. It was apparent from our talk that she hadn't, and I didn't blame her one bit. Like I said, he's a sicko. Why tell him anything?"

"When you talked with Ms. Richardson after seeing the billboard, did it sound to you as if she was wrestling with an important decision?"

"Yes."

"Do you agree that Mr. Townsend was affected by her decision?"

Boyd frowned. Philly nudged Simon.

"Objection," Simon said, moving to his feet.

Judge Murray had the stenographer read back the question. "Do you understand the question?" Murray asked Boyd.

"I'm not sure. If he's asking whether Fay's decision might have an effect on Al, I would answer yes, indirectly. But if he's asking whether Fay's decision concerned Al, I'd say no because this was totally a decision that Fay got to make herself as I understand a woman's right to choose in Massachusetts."

Philly was impressed with Boyd. The woman was smart and wasn't going to be pushed around.

"Is it your belief then, Ms. Boyd, that a woman may proceed with an abortion without even notifying the father?"

"Absolutely. Especially if the father is a sicko."

"Nothing further."

Simon's next two witnesses recounted run-ins with the billboard. Neither witness exhibited Boyd's assertiveness and confidence, but each held her own under Lassiter's questioning. Lassiter's cross-examination of the second witness, Janice Waverly, produced an exchange that Philly thought, on balance, would help Richardson's case.

"Isn't it true, Ms. Waverly, that only you and a few friends who are close to Ms. Richardson were even aware of the billboard?"

"No, that's not true," Waverly replied, mustering more combativeness than she had so far displayed.

"Didn't you just testify that you've only discussed the billboard with maybe three or four other people?" Lassiter asked.

"Yeah, but I was talking about one-on-one discussions. I was around when people were talking about this, and for a while it seemed like this was all anybody was talking about."

"What did you mean by your last comment?" Judge Murray intervened.

"A lot of us stayed in Mercer after graduating from high school," Waverly explained. "I work in town and a lot of us get together for lunch at various places. The women I went to high school with are behind Fay one hundred percent. With the guys, it's a different story. A lot of the guys I went to school with think it's okay for Al to do what he did with the billboard. You can talk all you want about a woman's right to choose, but there are a lot of guys out there who don't get it."

After a short recess, Simon called Professor Shannon Kane to the witness stand. It had been Rachel's idea to use Kane as an expert witness. She had argued for a scorched earth approach: an attack that left no point likely to be raised by Al Townsend unchallenged during Richardson's direct case. Kane taught criminal law at Spencer New England School of Law and Rachel and Simon had taken her class. The professor had been only too glad to help and had agreed to charge a flat fee of $1,000 for all the time she spent on the case—whether in court or during out of court preparation.

Simon quickly established Kane's credentials. The professor had achieved tenure three years ago and taught introductory criminal law and two advanced criminal law seminars. While practicing law, she had been both a prosecutor and a defense attorney. She was tall and broad-shouldered and had an imposing presence as she sat in the witness chair.

"Have you read the billboard message that is a focus in this case?" Simon asked.

"Yes. I've read the message and viewed a photograph of the billboard."

"Is there any basis in criminal law for labeling the mother of a fetus aborted in the first trimester of pregnancy a killer?"

"Objection!" Lassiter shouted.

"What's the basis of your objection?" Judge Murray asked.

"The question asks for a legal opinion, which is the role of this court, not a witness."

"Objection overruled. The word 'kill' appeared on the billboard. We've heard testimony that the billboard was directed at the plaintiff. I'm of the view that this witness is qualified to answer the question. You may answer, professor."

Kane squared her impressive shoulders. "The short answer to your question is no. By way of explanation, the word 'kill' suggests that there has been the commission of a homicide of some kind by the mother of an aborted fetus. I've read various pleadings in this case and understand that the abortion occurred well within the first trimester of pregnancy. Such an event is not a homicide; it is not murder, manslaughter, or any other category of criminal conduct. The right of a woman to abort a fetus in the first trimester of pregnancy is protected by both the federal and the Massachusetts constitutions. This has been established for years. The word 'kill' is therefore a false allegation."

Simon leaned over to confer with Rachel and Philly joined their huddle.

"I'm inclined to leave her testimony where it is," Simon said.

Rachel nodded her agreement and Philly followed suit.

"No further questions," Simon declared.

Lassiter stood. "When did the life of the aborted fetus begin?"

Philly nudged Simon, who said, "Objection."

Judge Murray sighed. "Are you able to answer the question?" he asked Kane.

"I don't believe the question may be answered since in Massachusetts a fetus is not a life," Kane replied.

"When were the living cells comprising the aborted fetus first formed?" Lassiter followed up immediately.

"Sometime prior to the time the fetus was aborted. I couldn't tell you when."

"Those living cells belonged to both the mother and father, correct?"

Philly delivered another nudge, and Simon duly rose and objected.

"Where are you going with this, Mr. Lassiter?" Judge Murray asked. "We seem to have strayed a bit from the billboard that gave rise to this case."

"The questions go to Mr. Townsend's state of mind at a minimum," Lassiter responded. "The questions also bear on the appropriateness of the word 'kill' that appeared on the billboard."

"Your latter comment loses me, Mr. Lassiter. I believe it is common knowledge that cells of a developing fetus come from the mother and father. What does that have to do with this case?"

"I've already explained Mr. Townsend's position," Lassiter said. "The question goes to his intent, to his state of mind, and to the appropriateness of a word that appeared on the billboard."

"Objection sustained," Murray ruled. "Ask another question."

"Please note my objection," Lassiter said evenly. "With my cross-examination limited, I have no further questions of this witness."

"Next witness," the judge requested.

Rachel rose and switched seats with Simon so that she was now between Simon and Philly. "I call the plaintiff, Fay Richardson," she announced.

Richardson moved toward the witness chair slowly, her head lowered. Philly was worried by her distant look. Richardson was plain-looking, in her early thirties, and likely had been consumed by worry during the weeks leading up to this trial.

Rachel started off with basic background questions that produced brief responses from Richardson. Their client kept her eyes lowered, rarely looked at Rachel, and only once cast a sideways glance in Judge Murray's direction. Philly was about to nudge Rachel for a brief colloquy, but Rachel had picked up on Richardson's lack of affect.

"Ms. Richardson?" Rachel raised her voice.

Richardson looked up startled.

"I can barely hear you. Please try to keep your voice up, okay?"

Richardson nodded.

"I'm sorry. I didn't hear you."

Richardson offered up a weak smile. "Okay."

"I don't really have a clear picture of what you do in publishing," Rachel continued. "Would you please give the judge some examples of what your job entails?"

Richardson again nodded, and when she looked in Judge Murray's direction, Philly believed that Rachel had gotten through to her.

"As I said, I work for a small publishing company. Because the company is small, we all tend to be jacks-of-all-trades. We specialize in non-fiction books but recently we've branched out into previously unpublished authors who have written novels. I handle manuscript edits, typeface, layout, and jacket design.

I've been playing the editor role for two novelists. I've helped out with marketing from time to time, but mostly the marketing is done by others."

Philly hadn't thought Richardson capable of such a long speech, and she started to relax. Rachel had been a calming influence on witnesses before, and it seemed to be working again.

"When did you first meet Al Townsend?" Rachel shifted gears.

"We met at a party. I think one or two of our friends had in mind introducing us if we both showed up. Anyway, we met and seemed to hit it off and we began dating afterwards."

"Please describe the course of your dating."

"We went out for several months. Movies, dinner. I remember we went to a play. We seemed to have similar interests and got along. At some time, we became intimate."

"At some time did you move in together?"

Richardson nodded. "He proposed that, and I agreed."

"Was that the first time you had lived together with a boyfriend?"

"Yes."

"How was your relationship once you moved in together?"

Richardson leveled a long look at Townsend. "He changed once we moved in together. It was as if he thought that my moving in with him meant he owned me in some way. I had a group of friends I was close with and he seemed to resent us getting together. He'd try to talk me out of seeing them and became angry when I kept up with them. He would buy clothes for me without consulting me and would insist I wear them even though most of what he bought didn't suit me. I couldn't get him to stop doing that. And he was constantly on me about what I ate. He kept on saying, 'You don't want to get fat.' It went so far that he would try to get me to change my mind when I ordered something I liked at a restaurant. It was embarrassing. All these little things left me feeling smothered."

Philly turned in her seat. Townsend was regarding Richardson with a distant look that she couldn't read.

"What did you do about this change in Mr. Townsend's behavior?"

"I confronted him. I said I thought we should live apart for a while. I told him he was suffocating me, and I needed some time to breathe."

"What was his reaction?"

"He got angry. He got red in the face and said, 'You can't do this to me. I won't let you.' It was scary really. He never said he would try to change or that he would try to be more understanding of my needs. He kept on saying, 'You can't do this to me,' as if it was all about him and I didn't count. That was when I realized I had to get away from him."

"To your knowledge, was this the first time Mr. Townsend had lived together with a woman?"

"I don't know. I asked him about past relationships, and he would always say that he didn't want to talk about them. I had been honest with him when he asked me about prior boyfriends, but he wouldn't say anything to me about his previous involvements."

"At some point did you leave the place where you were living together?"

"Yes."

"How did that come about?"

"I pretended to go off to work one morning. When I was sure he had also left for work, I came back with some friends and moved my things out. I stayed with Selena Boyd for a week until I could find a place of my own."

"What was Mr. Townsend's reaction when he discovered you had moved out?"

"He called me on my cell phone and said I was a 'fucking bitch.' He was furious. I told him to never call me again, but he would call my cell phone at all hours of the day and night. Finally, I had to get a new cell phone number."

"Did he ever physically confront you after you moved out?"

"Once. He came to where I worked and demanded to see me. I refused to come out and see him. I told the receptionist to call the police if he wouldn't leave. Fortunately, he left."

"At some point did you find out you were pregnant?"

"Yes," Richardson answered with a rueful look. "About two weeks after I moved out."

"Did you inform Mr. Townsend that you were pregnant?"

"No."

"Why not?"

"I didn't want him to know. I didn't want him in my life. He scared me. I had totally misjudged him."

"What did you decide to do about the pregnancy?"

"I talked to my closest friends, like Selena, and decided to get an abortion. Which I did."

"After the abortion, did Mr. Townsend re-enter your life?"

"You could say that."

"How did that come about?"

"Selena told me about this billboard that I needed to see. So I took the long way coming back from work and saw this billboard with Al holding this infant that said the mother killed his baby. I nearly drove off the road, I was so upset."

Rachel paused. Judge Murray was writing but Lassiter was not.

"What did you do next?" Rachel resumed.

"For a time, I was paralyzed. I didn't know what to do. My friends were urging me to sue Al. I had a meeting with a client who saw I was upset, and I told this client my story. The client gave me Ms. Sullivan's name and said that Ms. Sullivan had helped her with a legal problem some years ago. So I called her, and your firm took my case, for which I'm eternally grateful."

Rachel sat down and held up her notepad to block Judge Murray's view. "I think I should leave it here," Rachel said.

Philly took her time considering Rachel's request. "Ask her how she felt while the billboard was up. Otherwise, I think we're good."

"While the billboard was up," Rachel said, rising, "what was your reaction?"

"It was humiliating and horrible," Richardson replied with feeling. "I had done nothing wrong. And that bastard was publicly calling me a murderer. I want him to pay for what he put me through. He had no right to do what he did."

"No further questions," Rachel announced.

"Did Mr. Townsend ever physically abuse you?" Lassiter asked to begin his cross-examination.

"Not physically, just verbally."

"Did you ever raise your voice to him?"

"I'm sure I did when we were arguing."

"When you raised your voice to him, was that verbal abuse on your part?"

"Not in my opinion."

"When Mr. Townsend raised his voice to you, was that always verbal abuse on his part?"

Richardson shook her head. "Not always, but when he became angry and insistent he scared me, and I felt I was being abused. His face was like a barometer. When he was shouting and red in the face, I found him abusive."

"Did you ever criticize Mr. Townsend's choice of clothing?"

Richardson stared at Lassiter unblinking. For a brief moment, a smile played across her face. "He had this sports jacket I didn't like. It didn't go with anything. It was brown with a faint yellow stripe and he would wear it with anything. It was ugly and I told him so."

"Did he change the sports jacket when you objected to it?"

Richardson frowned in concentration. "I think he did once. The other times he would say something like it was his favorite jacket and no one would notice."

"Did you in fact have the fetus you told us about destroyed?"

"Objection!" Rachel said, springing to her feet.

Judge Murray regarded Lassiter. "The witness has testified that she had an abortion. That terminated her pregnancy. I find your use of the word 'destroyed' argumentative, and so I'm going to sustain the objection."

"Did you give any thought to Mr. Townsend's feelings when you proceeded to have an abortion without telling him?" Lassiter followed up smoothly with another question.

"No."

"Would you agree, Ms. Richardson, that anger is a legitimate reaction on the part of a father who learns that a fetus he fathered was aborted without his knowledge?"

"Objection!" Rachel said forcefully.

Judge Murray had the question read back. "Are you able to answer the question?" the judge inquired of Richardson.

"I guess I can understand anger as a reaction, but I'm not going to say it was legitimate."

"Why not?" the judge inquired.

"Because it was my decision to make and any emotional response by anyone else doesn't make my decision illegitimate in any way."

Philly silently applauded Richardson. Their client was exhibiting the same resoluteness as Selena Boyd.

"Is it your view, Ms. Richardson, that Mr. Townsend has no right to criticize your decision to abort the fetus without telling him?" Lassiter resumed.

"I don't believe he has a right to publicly criticize me for anything," Richardson replied, and Philly was pleased to see that Rachel had prepared their client well for Lassiter's questions.

"Do I understand from your answer that you have no issue with Mr. Townsend privately criticizing your decision?"

"No. You haven't told me the form of this private criticism."

"Would you object to his calling you to talk about the matter?"

"Yes, I'd object to his calling me. As I said, he frightens me."

"So what form of private criticism of your decision by Mr. Townsend would you be okay with?"

Richardson met Lassiter's stare. "None that I can think of at the moment."

"Let's see if I understand your position," Lassiter said sarcastically. "You made a decision to abort the fetus that Mr. Townsend fathered, you refused to take his calls, and your position is that Mr. Townsend is powerless, both publicly and privately, to object to your conduct. Do I have it right?"

Richardson smiled. "Yes, you do," she said with conviction.

When Lassiter's cross-examination concluded, Philly, Rachel, and Simon huddled.

"I wouldn't ask any questions on redirect," Simon urged.

Philly met Rachel's questioning look. "I'm thinking," she said. "Do you think Richardson came off as unreasonable by saying Townsend had no right to criticize her actions?"

Simon shrugged. "Maybe. But so what? She said she was scared of him. I think that came across."

Rachel nodded in agreement. "The abortion decision was hers alone to make."

"Any redirect examination?" Judge Murray prompted.

Rachel rose. "Nothing on redirect," she announced.

Judge Murray consulted his watch. "Does the plaintiff have any other witness?"

"No," Rachel responded. "The plaintiff rests."

"Then we'll break for lunch," the judge said. "Mr. Lassiter, be prepared to start your case when we return. With luck, perhaps we can finish this trial today."

'Not a chance,' Philly thought. Especially if the other defendant, the owner of the billboard, took the stand.

Lassiter's direct examination of Al Townsend had concluded without any surprises, in Philly's opinion. Townsend had been in love with Richardson; he wouldn't have suggested they move in together if that were not the case. Yes, there were stressful moments in the relationship once they started living together, but on balance, Townsend believed they had gotten on well. Richardson's leaving had caught him totally by surprise. He was angry that she hadn't tried to work things out and had left surreptitiously. There were times when he commented on Richardson's attire and food choices, but he never insisted that she do anything she didn't want to do. Townsend believed Richardson had killed his offspring. There was no other word to describe what she had done. He had decided on the billboard posting as the best method to protest Richardson's action.

Simon rose and regarded Townsend for a long moment. "When you moved in with Ms. Richardson, was that the first time you had cohabitated with a woman?" Simon began.

Townsend reddened. "No," he said barely audible.

"On how many prior occasions had you lived with a woman?"

"Once."

"What was the woman's name?"

"Objection," Lassiter intervened.

"Overruled," Judge Murray ordered.

"Cecelia Whatley."

"How long did that cohabitation last?"

"About three months. She was subletting a room in an apartment I'd rented."

"Who broke things off?"

"She did."

"Did she give a reason for breaking things off with you?"

Townsend fidgeted in his seat. If anything, Philly thought he had colored further.

"She said things weren't working out."

"Did she provide you with any specifics as to things not working out?"

"She said she felt tied down and that she realized she didn't want to be tied down at that point in her life."

"How long was it between the end of your relationship with Ms. Whatley and the beginning of your cohabitation with Ms. Richardson?"

Townsend paused briefly. "About a year, give or take."

"Where did you and Ms. Whatley reside when you were living together?"

"In Southborough."

"Do you remember the street address?"

Townsend rattled off the street address and, in response to a follow up question, said he believed that Whatley still lived in Southborough. Philly wrote down Whatley's available contact information and immediately texted the details to Barney Freedman.

"Have you ever been married?" Simon resumed his questioning.

"No."

"Did you and Ms. Richardson ever discuss children before you moved in together?"

Philly glanced behind her and saw Richardson shaking her head.

"Not that I recall."

"Did you ever call Ms. Richardson a bitch?"

Townsend reddened further, something Philly hadn't thought possible. "On one occasion."

"Are you paying your legal fees in this case?"

"Objection!" Lassiter said angrily.

"Overruled."

Townsend slumped in his seat. "There's an organization called Massachusetts Citizens to Preserve Life that's paying my fees."

"Is it correct that Rita Stout, the woman who manages the company that put up your billboard, is a vice-president of that organization?"

"I believe that's the case," Townsend said grudgingly.

"Have you ever filed a criminal complaint against Ms. Richardson?"

"No."

Simon let Townsend's answer hang in the courtroom. "Isn't it true that in response to Mr. Lassiter's questions you testified that Ms. Richardson killed your fetus?"

"That's what I said."

"Isn't it true that you never filed a criminal complaint against Ms. Richardson in connection with the fetus because you knew that she had not committed any crime?"

"In my eyes she did."

"But in the eyes of the law, you knew that she had not committed a crime, correct?"

Townsend glared at Simon, but Philly knew that in a staring contest, it would take a stronger man than Townsend to best Simon.

"I guess so," Townsend said, lowering his eyes.

"Can you point to any instance in your relationship with Ms. Richardson in which you changed your behavior to accommodate her?"

"Objection," Lassiter said. "The question is vague."

Judge Murray had the stenographer read back the question. "Do you understand the question?" the judge directed at Townsend.

"I think so."

"Then let's have your answer."

The silence lengthened as Townsend contemplated an answer. "I can't think of anything at the moment," he finally said.

"Were there times when you objected to Ms. Richardson spending time with her friends?"

"Yes."

"Why didn't you want her to spend time with her friends?"

"I preferred that she spend time with me."

"Did you have any friends that you spent time with during the time you were living with Ms. Richardson?"

"I'm sure I did."

"Did Ms. Richardson object to your spending time with your friends when you chose to do so?"

"No, but I would clear it with her first."

"Give me the name of one friend you spent time with while you were living with Ms. Richardson."

Townsend pondered the question. "Sam Goodyear."

"Where does Mr. Goodyear live?"

Philly texted Goodyear's name and the town he lived in to Barney Freedman immediately after Townsend provided the information. Townsend had been unable to recall a street address.

"Are you still friends with Mr. Goodyear?"

"I still consider him my friend, but we haven't seen each other in a while."

"Are you currently involved in a romantic relationship?"

"Not currently."

"When you had the billboard put up did you consider Ms. Richardson's feelings should she learn about it?"

"Not really. She didn't give a damn about my feelings."

"Was one purpose in your putting up the billboard to humiliate Ms. Richardson?"

"I didn't think of it that way. I wanted to protest what she did so my voice would be heard."

"But you knew that suggesting Ms. Richardson was a killer was a harmful allegation, didn't you?"

"I didn't think of it that way. Like I said, I wanted to protest what she had done."

"Just so I have this correctly, is it your testimony that you gave no thought to whether the billboard you had put up was harmful to Ms. Richardson?"

"I didn't think about harm to her. My focus was on making my voice heard."

"So you wanted your voice to be heard regardless of whether your voice harmed Ms. Richardson, is that correct?"

"You're twisting my words around. I've told you what my motivation was."

"Yes, you did," Simon said mincingly. "You wanted your voice to be heard regardless of who it harmed, correct?"

"I didn't consider harm, if that's what you mean."

"I think you've exhausted this line of questions, Mr. Jeffries," Judge Murray interjected.

"Thank you, Your Honor," Simon said. "Was it your view that you had a right to veto Ms. Richardson's decision to have an abortion?"

"I don't think I could have vetoed her decision, but I should have been informed about what was going on."

"Are you saying that if you were informed about what was going on and Ms. Richardson stuck by her abortion decision, you would have no complaint against her?"

"I still would have objected to her decision to have the abortion."

"But so long as you were informed about what was going on, is it correct that you wouldn't have put up the billboard?"

Townsend frowned. "I don't know," he finally said.

After Simon concluded his cross-examination and Lassiter declined to pose redirect questions, Judge Murray glanced at his watch. "We'll adjourn for today," he declared. We'll begin promptly at nine tomorrow with the defendant's next witness."

Fay Richardson and Selena Boyd joined the firm legal team outside the courtroom. Philly took charge to shield Simon and Rachel. She remembered how Carpenter had fielded questions from a client at the end of one of her jury trials last year and how grateful she was for his dealing with her client while she was both dead on her feet and still caught up in an adrenalin rush from the trial.

"I would say the case is going as well as can be expected," Philly responded to Boyd's, 'How do you think it's going?' question. "We should conclude testimony tomorrow."

"Townsend really is creepy," Boyd observed. "There's something off about the guy."

"Now you tell me," Richardson said, making a halfhearted attempt at humor.

"I can't tell if he's some kind of crazed psycho or fucked up in other weird ways," Boyd said.

Philly agreed with Boyd's assessment. There *was* something off about Townsend. She doubted he would be an anti-abortion crusader if he had to pay his own legal fees.

"Can you come tomorrow?" Richardson asked Boyd, a hint of pleading in her voice.

"Wouldn't miss it for anything," Boyd responded, and this time Richardson smiled in earnest.

12

Rita Stout was a buxom, bleached blonde who Philly judged to be in her early forties. There were nicotine stains on her right hand and Philly expected her to have a raspy smoker's voice, but instead Stout's voice was annoyingly high-pitched. In response to Lassiter's questions, Stout testified that Townsend had called Massachusetts Citizens to Preserve Life and had inquired about making a public protest over what had befallen him. The intake worker who fielded Townsend's call remembered that Stout owned a billboard company and provided Townsend with Stout's number.

"Who came up with the idea for Mr. Townsend to protest through the use of a billboard?" Lassiter asked.

"I'd say we both did," Stout answered. "He was clear that he wanted to publicly protest what had happened to him, and we both focused on using a billboard to make the protest."

"Did your company charge Mr. Townsend for the billboard?"

"No. I totally supported his cause and offered to provide the billboard at no charge."

"Is Massachusetts Citizens to Preserve Life paying for Mr. Townsend's legal fees and your legal fees?"

"Yes. The organization is totally behind Mr. Townsend. We believe that getting his message out is an important public service. We want Mr. Townsend's voice to be heard."

"Who wrote the words that appeared on the billboard?" Lassiter inquired.

"Mr. Townsend did the first draft. I offered some comments and I think he incorporated some of my suggestions."

"How would you describe the mission of Massachusetts Citizens to Preserve Life?"

"We are against abortion for any reason. We do not believe that the Bible endorses what happened to Mr. Townsend."

"Are you aware that in Massachusetts, the courts have established a right to obtain an abortion?"

"We're aware of all that, but it doesn't make it right. We believe the First Amendment permits us to protest court decisions that violate basic Christian values."

"No further questions," Lassiter said.

"Did anyone other than you and Mr. Townsend come up with the words and picture that appeared on the billboard?" Simon fired off his first question.

"No."

"Which of you came up with the word 'kill?'"

"I believe that word was in the first draft Mr. Townsend came up with. I was totally behind using that word."

"You said that you were aware that the courts in Massachusetts have established a woman's right to obtain an abortion, correct?"

"Yeah, I'm aware of what the courts have done."

"How does the word 'kill' square with the fact that a woman has an absolute right to obtain an abortion during the first trimester of pregnancy?"

"Just because a bunch of judges have lost their moral center doesn't mean a citizen can't call a killing what it is," Stout retorted, her voice coming close to chalk squeaking on a blackboard.

"So you don't care what the law provides as to a woman's right to obtain an abortion, is that correct?"

"Yes, that is correct. Just because something is the law doesn't make it right and doesn't mean a citizen can't protest the law."

"The billboard you approved of claimed that Ms. Richardson, the plaintiff in this case, killed a fetus, correct?"

"Her name wasn't mentioned."

"The billboard referenced the mother of a fetus, correct?"

"Yes."

"That mother would be Ms. Richardson, wouldn't it?"

"I suppose so, indirectly."

"Could the billboard be referring to any person other than Ms. Richardson?"

"I suppose not."

"As a legal matter, Ms. Richardson didn't kill anyone, correct?"

"Not under the joke that passes for the law."

"So the law that guarantees a woman's right to an abortion is a joke to you? Is that what you're saying?"

"The law is more like an abomination."

"Is it an abomination for a woman who is raped to abort the fetus that resulted from the rape?"

"It is in my opinion."

Simon regarded Stout for a long moment before huddling with Rachel and Philly. "I don't see the point in further sparring with her," he whispered. "Either the judge is going to consider Stout an asshole or he isn't."

Philly also didn't see an upside in eliciting further polarizing statements from Stout. "I agree," she said, and Rachel also nodded.

"Nothing further," Simon said.

"The defendant rests," Lassiter declared.

"Any rebuttal?" Judge Murray directed at Simon.

"Yes, Your Honor. Rebuttal will be brief. The plaintiff calls Cecelia Whatley."

As a court officer opened the door to the rear of the courtroom, Philly glanced at Townsend. The defendant was no longer blushing. He was ashen.

Barney Freedman held the door for a tall, dark-haired woman dressed in a black power suit who moved with a purposeful stride to the front of the courtroom. The woman stopped when she drew abreast of where Townsend was sitting, gave him a hard stare that he avoided, and then proceeded to the witness chair. Philly suspected that her "I do" after the oath had been administered could be heard in neighboring courtrooms.

"Do you know the defendant in this case, a Mr. Al Townsend?" Simon began.

"Yes, I know him. He's sitting right over there." Whatley pointed in Townsend's direction in what Philly regarded as an accusatory fashion.

"May the record reflect that the witness has identified Mr. Townsend?" Simon requested.

"It may," Judge Murray said.

"How do you know Mr. Townsend?"

"We lived together for about three months maybe a year or so ago."

"How did you come to live together?"

"I had lost a job, couldn't afford the apartment I was living in, and someone told me about a guy who was looking for a roommate. The guy turned out to be Al and I checked his place out. I'd have my own room and I'd be saving a lot on rent, so I said yes."

"Did the two of you get along?"

"For a time we did."

"What was the nature of your relationship while you were getting along?"

Whatley sighed. "We slept together a few times, if that's what you want to know. The first time I had gone out drinking with a bunch of friends, came back to the apartment horny, and made a pass at Al. That was probably a mistake. After that, I probably should have left it as a one-time thing, but there were two other times when we hooked up."

"Did the intimate relationship continue during the time you shared an apartment?"

"No, not during at least the last month I was there. Al asked me out a bunch of times, but I always said no. It was clear to me that he made more out of our hooking up a few times than I had. I remember one time when I told him I didn't want to go out and he became angry. He demanded to know why I wouldn't go out with him after the nights we spent together. I told him I just wasn't interested. He pleaded with me to give him a chance. He said something like, 'If you give me a chance, I know you'll feel about me the way I feel about you.'"

"What happened next?" Simon asked.

"I got another job and began to look for my own place. I finally found a place, but I was going to have to wait three weeks before a tenant moved out. I told Al I was going to leave at the end of the month and he went nuts. He began yelling at me. He said, 'You can't do this to me.' He said he cared about me. Then he said he wouldn't let me leave."

"What did you do?"

Whatley glanced briefly at Townsend. "I didn't do anything for a time. When I needed to move, I had my brothers come over. I've got an older and a younger brother. Let's just say they're big guys."

"What happened?"

"My older brother walked up to Al and said, 'Are you the guy who said you weren't going to let my sister leave here?' Al mumbled something and my brother just hauled off and hit him in the stomach. He crumpled up and dropped to the floor holding his gut. My younger brother helped me pack and bring things down to his car. When I was moved out and ready to go, my older brother jerked Al to his feet and told him that if he ever came near me or contacted me, he would beat the shit out of him. Al nodded that he understood but my brother again busted him in the gut for good measure."

Simon let Whatley's last statement hang in the air. "Did Mr. Townsend ever get in touch with you after that incident?"

"No."

"No further questions."

Lassiter rose to his feet slowly. In Lassiter's position, Philly wouldn't have cross-examined Whatley, but she suspected that Lassiter would feel compelled to ask at least a few questions.

"Did Mr. Townsend ever strike you or hurt you in any way?" Lassiter asked.

"No."

"And yet you felt the need to have one of your brothers beat Mr. Townsend up, is that correct?"

Whatley appraised Lassiter for a long moment. "Let me put it this way," she said. "Al threatened that he wouldn't let me leave. You'll have to ask him whether he meant it or not. I took what he said seriously because people are capable of anything. Maybe Al's got a screw loose. Who the hell knows? Besides, I didn't like being threatened. So I told my brother to do whatever was necessary to get Al out of my life forever."

"This man you say you felt threatened by is the same man you initiated sex with, correct?"

"Yeah, but what's your point? I was horny and Al was around. It was no big deal."

"Did you ever think it was a big deal to Mr. Townsend?"

"I thought he'd be happy to get his rocks off. That first time he had to know I was pretty drunk. If he was looking for a religious experience or true love, he could have told me no."

Lassiter glanced at his notepad. "No further questions," he said as he took his seat.

"Any other rebuttal witness?" Judge Murray inquired.

"The plaintiff calls Sam Goodyear," Simon announced.

Barney Freedman exited the rear of the courtroom and returned with a short, red-headed young man who paused briefly after entering the courtroom and then followed Barney's directive to move to the front of the chamber. Townsend looked like he wanted to be elsewhere.

"Do you know Al Townsend?" Simon inquired after Goodyear had been sworn in.

"Yeah, I know him in passing. He's seated over there behind the lawyer's table."

"What do you mean, you know him in passing?"

"We have a friend in common who threw a couple of parties and we were introduced."

"Do you consider Mr. Townsend to be a friend of yours?"

"Not really. More like a casual acquaintance. I don't think I ever spent time with him alone. The few times we ran into each other were at parties. We talked some. I remember he was interested in some of the computer games I like. But that was about it."

"No further questions," Simon declared.

"A moment, Your Honor," Lassiter requested, as he huddled with Townsend.

Philly took the time to assess the impact of the rebuttal witnesses. Whatley had helped Richardson's case by pointing to Townsend's threat against her. Goodyear had debunked Townsend's testimony that the two men were friends. Philly thought that Simon had done a good job trying to portray Townsend as a creepy loner who might be capable of violence.

"No questions on cross-examination," Lassiter said.

"That concludes the plaintiff's rebuttal case," Simon said.

Judge Murray leaned over to confer with his court clerk. When he resumed his seat, he addressed counsel. "I'm going to give each of you three weeks to make any further submissions you wish me to consider. I'm particularly interested in any new arguments the parties wish to make on the first amendment issues that are presented by this case. Once I receive your submissions, I'll do my best to issue a decision promptly. In the meantime, I'm reminding the parties that the preliminary injunction remains in effect. Court is adjourned."

Lassiter led Townsend and Stout from the courtroom once the judge had departed. Philly, Simon, and Rachel took their time packing up their papers. Soon they were joined at their counsel table by Richardson and Boyd. Barney Freedman had brought the rebuttal witnesses to the barrier separating attorney seating from public seating.

Philly motioned to Richardson. "You might want to thank the rebuttal witnesses for appearing. They helped your case."

Richardson nodded and headed for Barney's group.

"Al Townsend is one sick puppy," Selena Boyd declared.

"But even a sick puppy has first amendment rights," Simon pointed out.

"If this judge rules for Townsend, the law is totally fucked up," Boyd retorted. "Townsend's nuts. End of story."

Richardson came near. “I’m taking everyone out to lunch,” she said. “I hope you’ll join me.”

Philly declined but urged Simon and Rachel to take Richardson up on her offer.

“I have one question,” Richardson said. “I’ve sued Al and Stout for damages. I think you called it emotional distress. Do you think there’s a chance of winning damages?”

Philly fielded the question. “Yes, you have a chance. Your complaint alleges that the defendants intentionally caused you emotional distress. They knew what the law was, but they chose to disregard the law and label you a killer. You may get lucky and be awarded damages.”

Richardson nodded without expression and then led Simon and Rachel to join the others.

When Philly finally moved to the rear of the courtroom, she found Barney waiting for her. “Nice job on the rebuttal witnesses,” she said.

Barney held the door for her. “It was a piece of cake. They were happy to help, especially Whatley. What’d you think of her?”

“Your basic piece of work,” Philly replied. “Essentially fun-loving and fearless—a dangerous combination.”

“Yeah, she’s a pistol,” Barney agreed.

“How come you’re passing on lunch?” Philly asked.

“I don’t do well in social situations.”

“I can identify with that.”

13

“Go over again what you found out about Daryl Finch’s kids,” Paul requested.

“The oldest son, Wilson, lives in Medford. I don’t have any leads on the daughter, Heather. She’s the middle child. The younger son, Edwin, lives in Cambridge.”

“Did you get anything else from Social Security?”

Evelyn flipped through her notepad. “Fifteen months ago, Social Security received a call from someone who said he was Finch’s son. The caller wanted to know if Social Security had a current address for his father. According to the caller, the family had lost track of his father and hadn't heard from him in a while."

"Did Social Security release the address?"

"Yes, the Cambridge post-office box."

"Do we know which son called?"

"No."

Paul opted for a simple division of labor. "You pay a visit to the son who lives in Cambridge. I'll deal with the older son living in Medford."

Evelyn snapped her notepad closed. "Sounds like a plan. Maybe the sons kept an eye on the post-office box and followed the father back to the assisted living facility when he checked the box."

"That's what I was thinking."

Philly hadn't seen Muriel Parker in years. But when she and Daisy arrived in Parker's office, the advertising executive hadn't changed for the most part. She was short and trim and athletic-looking. This morning she was wearing a yellow silk blouse and black slacks. She had kept her brown hair short framing her round face. There was still the intensity in her brown eyes. Missing were the vertical worry lines between her eyes that had been pronounced while Philly had represented her in litigation.

"Who is this beautiful girl?" Parker gushed.

"Say hello to Daisy. I'm giving her babysitter a respite."

"Hi, cutie."

Daisy smiled at Parker. Her bouts of "stranger anxiety" had been brief and now seemed behind her.

Inside Parker's office, Philly took off her own parka and then Daisy's. Then Philly emptied onto the office rug a small canvas bag filled with brightly colored blocks and small fuzzy animals. Daisy grinned broadly, put a bunny's ear in her mouth, and started pushing the blocks around. "I brought along some toys to keep her busy while we talk," Philly said.

"It's great to see you," Parker said. "You got me the money to start this business. You also helped my partners and they're sorry they won't get to see you this morning. They've got appointments outside the office."

Parker and her partners had been bilked by an advertising agency that had misappropriated work they had done and submitted to the agency while applying for jobs. All of the cases had settled in favor of the job applicants.

Philly got right to the point. "First, I want to thank you again for sending Fay Richardson our way. The case seems to be going well, but of course it's not over till it's over. Second, and more to the point, I want to hire you to do a website for our firm. Four of us have formed a firm. You probably remember Carpenter. He's sixty-five years old and has never advertised or had a website. I'm next in seniority. Then there are two younger lawyers who will be full partners in two years. I've had each lawyer do a write up of himself or herself. Getting Carpenter to come up with a statement was like pulling teeth."

"I remember Carpenter."

"We specialize in litigation. At the end of last year, I got two jury verdicts of over a million dollars. There must be a way we can market that."

"We've never done anything for a law firm," Parker admitted, "but it's something I always wanted to try. This is great. This is going to force me to come up with an image and marketing strategy for a law firm. And because it's you, you're going to get a special, discounted rate."

Philly felt a tug on her sleeve, and Daisy handed over a bright blue wooden cube. Philly held it up for Parker to see.

Parker nodded solemnly. "Nice," she said. "Clean design. Lots of color. Very impressive, young lady."

Daisy smiled and searched out another block.

"I'm guessing she's eighteen months old," Parker said.

"Nineteen months."

"Talk about blue eyes!"

It never failed, Philly thought. People meeting Daisy always noticed Philip's blue eyes.

"I take it things are well?" Philly asked.

"Very well. We've hired two associates. We've decided to stay small. I can see hiring one more associate but that's going to be it."

"I hope you're right that small is good," Philly said. "That's our plan."

"I'm right. The three of us who are partners get along. We each remember when we had nothing. We're dedicated to not screwing this up."

"Words to live by," Philly said as she accepted another block from her daughter.

14

Herb thought it was a minor miracle that he was now face-to-face with Stephanie Manley in a Dunkin' Donuts in the Boston Financial District. He had used the information provided by the helpful woman at the Board of Bar Overseers to identify twenty women who had left Pinkerton, Ashley & Rosewood in the last three years. Seven women had flat-out refused to talk to him once he explained the purpose of his call. Manley, a paralegal, was his eighth contact.

'Honesty is the best policy' was a dictum Herb tried to live by, but sometimes the bald truth tended to send a potential witness running for the hills. He had been zero-for-seven when he'd called Manley but had decided to stick with the direct approach. When he'd explained that he was a private investigator hired by a former attorney at Pinkerton, Ashley & Rosewood who believed she had a harassment claim against the firm, Manley had clammed up, her frosty silence somehow making its way over the phone line, and Herb thought that he was about to go zero-for-eight.

"Hear me out," Herb had said before launching into a general description of how his client had been subject to sexual harassment by a junior partner in the litigation department of the firm. When his account produced no reaction from Manley, Herb had then explained that he was contacting individuals who had left the firm to try to discover whether harassment had been responsible for their leaving. Manley said nothing for such a long time that Herb expected to shortly hear a dial tone signaling that she had hung up. "I'd prefer not to get involved in anything having to do with that firm," Manley finally said, and Herb knew he was talking to someone who could possibly help Sweeney's case. He had then done what he thought he did best—he had wheedled and cajoled and appealed to the greater good and justice for all and when Manley grudgingly said she'd think about it and get back to him, he had figured he at least had a foot in the door. Then, out of the blue, she had called him back and had agreed to hear him out.

Manley had missed her calling. She should have gone in for modeling. She was tall and lithe with flowing black hair and she had that finely chiseled bone structure that Herb associated with cover girls. If he wasn't careful, he could get lost in her light blue eyes. He had brought coffee to an out-of-the-way table and decided to continue on the honesty-is-the-best-policy course.

"Thanks for agreeing to meet with me. I want to be clear about the ground rules up front. You don't have to say a word to me. But if you do tell me something, you need to be clear that I may mention what you say to my client."

"Who is your client?"

Herb had been given authority to release Sweeney's name, but he preferred not to on the theory that the less he had to reveal, the better. "I'd rather not say," Herb replied.

Manley took a sip of coffee and rose. "Then I think we're done here."

"Please sit down," Herb said evenly, for the first time wondering if he was being played.

Manley sat and Herb contemplated his next move.

"If I reveal my client's name, will you give me your word you won't share that information?"

"No," Manley said, and it was the way she said it that Herb was no longer concerned about getting lost in the woman's eyes.

Herb took his time, wanting Manley to think he was going through a gut-wrenching decision process. "Okay," he said. "I'm going to tell you my client's name and I'm also going to ask that you keep it to yourself. I understand you're not making any promises, but that's my request to you."

Manley continued to remain silent. She was probably a hell of a poker player, Herb thought. He had no read on what she was thinking.

"The woman who hired me is Meredith Sweeney." Manley showed no surprise at the name and Herb wondered whether she was expecting it. "Do you know her?"

Manley nodded. "I know her by sight."

"Ms. Sweeney registered a sexual harassment claim that the firm rejected for lack of evidence."

"Who was the claim against?"

Herb had been thinking how he would handle this inevitable question. 'In for a penny, in for a pound,' he thought. "Gwen Cantor."

Manley didn't respond but Herb again believed that his answer hadn't come as a surprise. "You've made no promises to me but I'm going to ask you to keep that information to yourself as well."

Manley sipped at her coffee. Herb decided to take the offensive. "Do you have any reaction to what I've told you?" he asked.

"I'll think about what you've said."

"Are you in a position to help Ms. Sweeney?"

"I just told you that I'd think about what you've said."

Herb reflected on another thing he did well; he knew when to shut his mouth. "Here's my card," he said sliding his business card across the table. "It took a lot of guts for you to meet with me. I appreciate it and I'm sure Ms. Sweeney will as well."

"Stop trying to butter me up," Manley said.

"No, I won't stop. I admire courage when I see it. You might want to learn how to take a compliment."

Manley didn't respond. Her eyes remained cold, but Herb thought he saw a smile briefly play across her lips.

Carpenter couldn't tell whether Rachel was disappointed or relieved when he told her that he would be arguing Clyde Atkins' motion for a preliminary injunction. The truth was he hadn't been before a judge in a while and he wanted to get back into court. Philly, Simon, and Rachel had handled all of the court work in recent months and his lack of court time made him feel that he wasn't pulling his weight.

"Do you think we have a chance on getting the injunction?" Rachel asked.

"I think it's less than a tossup," Carpenter said. "A lot depends on the judge. It's hard to tell how this will play out until we see affidavits from Atkins' brother and sister. We don't know what they're going to say about why they terminated Atkins' employment contract."

Rachel nodded glumly. She was sitting in his visitor's chair, deep in thought. She'd done an excellent job drafting a court complaint and her edits to his legal memorandum had improved that document.

"What's bugging you?" Carpenter asked.

"It's the fact that the sister and brother could legally gang up on Atkins and vote to terminate his employment contract. That's the elephant in the room. We may be able to dance around that issue for a time, but eventually, if the matter is voted on at a properly scheduled meeting of the board of directors, I think Atkins is screwed. It bugs me that all our efforts might end up buying him some time—sixty days—but not helping him in the long run."

"I don't disagree with what you said. But cases like this can be funny. You start poking around, taking depositions, and suddenly facts start turning up that can be useful to you. Also, if we win some opening skirmishes, that might bring the brother and sister to the negotiating table."

"I don't like feeling we have the weaker side of the case in the long run," Rachel said.

"Nobody likes being on the weaker side. But it doesn't take much to turn the weaker side into the stronger side."

Rachel nodded but Carpenter could tell that she wasn't convinced.

Evelyn had parked the unmarked police car across the street from Edwin Finch's two-story house in East Cambridge and had been waiting a half hour. She didn't like confronting someone before dinner but had decided to make an exception in Edwin Finch's case. She was uncomfortable talking to him at his workplace. Daryl Finch's younger son worked as an electrical engineer in a company located on Route 128. His driver's license photograph revealed an unsmiling man with thick black hair, a strong chin, and dark, hard eyes.

Evelyn shivered. The day had had started out cold, warmed to over fifty, and now, as darkness settled in, returned to cold. Out of pure cussedness, she'd resisted the urge to start her car and get the heater running. She'd rather suffer in silence then give in to the elements, and there were times when she wondered whether this trait revealed something flawed about her.

A sedan coming from the opposite direction her car was facing slowed and made the turn into the driveway of Finch's house. The license plate was visible under a street light. "It's about fucking time," she muttered as she got out of her car.

Finch paused beneath a light by the walkway to the front door. He resembled his driver's license photograph. He was of medium height, medium build, and was gripping a leather satchel that bulged from its contents. "Mr. Finch!" Evelyn called out as Finch began heading for his front door.

Finch stopped and watched her approach. Evelyn tried to banish the frustration of waiting in a cold car and offered a smile. "Hi, Mr. Finch. I'm Evelyn Rodriguez with the Cambridge Police Department. I'm sorry to catch you when you're just getting home, but I need a few minutes of your time. This has to do with your father."

Finch's expression darkened and he tensed. Evelyn opted for directness. "We believe that your father recently passed away. He was living in an assisted living facility in Cambridge under a false name, but we believe we have correctly identified him." Evelyn paused but it became clear that Finch was going to wait her out. "When's the last time you saw your father?"

Finch's expression remained cold. "Do I have to talk to you?"

"No, you don't. Is there any reason why you wouldn't help me out and provide me with some basic information?"

Finch didn't reply immediately. "Here's the only thing I'm going to say to you. I haven't seen my father in years. When I was growing up, he was a vicious bastard. If he's dead, good riddance to him."

Finch started to head toward his front door.

"Can you tell me how I can reach your sister?" Evelyn called out.

Finch stopped, turned, and faced her. "I'm repeating myself but apparently you didn't get it the first time. I've said all I'm going to say to you."

Finch moved to his front door, worked his key, opened the door, and went inside the house. "That went well," Evelyn directed at the closed front door.

15

Herb thought about playing hunches. There were times when your gut told you that you were on the right track and when that happened, it made it easier to forge ahead even though half the time your gut was giving you a bum steer. Then there were times—like now—when your gut was silent, and you were just winging it with no clue whether you were doing the right thing or headed for disaster. Winging it was more stressful than relying on false hope from your gut. Somehow, without that subtle gut suggestion lulling you into believing that you knew what you were doing, winging it inevitably proved more nerve-racking.

Herb saw his hunch—Gregory Madison—leave his State Street office building and head in the direction of the waterfront. Without enthusiasm, he followed Madison, still not sure how to approach the man. Madison had been a partner at Pinkerton, Ashley & Rosewood for ten years. When he separated from the firm, he had applied for unemployment compensation and the firm had not opposed his application. Correlating the information provided by Jocelyn Weaver at the Board of Bar Overseers with the information obtained from his friend, Hank Fisher, Herb had concluded that Gregory Madison was the only partner who had recently separated from Pinkerton, Ashley & Rosewood and claimed unemployment compensation. There had to be a story there since a partner in a business was considered an employer and employers weren't entitled to workers' compensation. But now, trailing Madison, Herb began doubting that a story existed.

Madison entered a deli and Herb followed. It was another fifty-degree afternoon and it made Herb think that the global warming argument had something going for it. True, last year, New Englanders froze their collective asses off and were buried up to their eyeballs in snow. But this winter was scary mild.

Herb watched Madison order and move to a table for two in the back of the eatery. Herb thought, 'What the hell,' and took the seat across from Madison.

"Do you mind if I join you, Mr. Madison?"

Madison looked up and regarded him intently. Herb pegged him for one of those guys in his fifties who aged gracefully. The touch of gray in his dark hair added distinction instead of making you think of old age. Madison was clean-shaven with a long, angular face and lively gray eyes. In the unseasonably mild weather, he wore no overcoat, but had wrapped a maroon scarf around his neck that matched the color of his tie.

"Do I know you?"

"No, you don't. My name is Herb McCauley. I'm a private investigator. I'm looking into a matter for a client and I'm interested in learning whether you can help her."

Madison's expression didn't change. Herb had found that typically, once the words "private investigator" left his lips, the person he was talking to retreated mentally and physically making it clear that the conversation had just ended. But Madison had yet to give off those vibes.

"My client claims that she was sexually harassed at Pinkerton, Ashley & Rosewood." Herb paused. No reaction by Madison to the mention of his former law firm. "Her claim was rejected by the firm's management committee purportedly after the claim was investigated."

"When did this harassment take place?" Madison asked.

"Recently."

"Then I don't see how I can help you. I haven't been with the firm recently."

"I know that. You separated from the firm a while back and claimed unemployment compensation."

"How did you learn that?"

"I'm not going to answer that question. As far as I can tell, you're the only partner who left the firm and claimed unemployment compensation afterwards. I thought that was peculiar. I'm interested in knowing whether there's a story behind your leaving the firm that might be of help to my client."

Herb met Madison's probing gaze. The lawyer seemed at ease, though cautious.

"I don't see any reason why I should talk to you," Madison said.

"To be honest," Herb came back, "neither do I. I'm playing a hunch talking to you. Your situation has me curious because it's unique. But you're right, you don't have to talk to me."

Madison had ordered a club sandwich and he took his time making inroads on his lunch. Watching Madison eat, Herb felt his stomach growl; he was hungry. Madison must have heard the noise because he pushed a side of fries in his direction. "Help yourself," Madison said, and Herb thought, 'Why not,' and used his fingers.

"Do you have a card?" Madison asked after finishing half of his sandwich.

Herb fished out a business card and handed it over. Madison studied the card and placed it in a shirt pocket.

"The firm basically let me go," Madison said. "My son was in an automobile accident and I spent time with him. My billable hours dropped and, to be frank, my heart wasn't in practicing law. It's possible my judgment wasn't the best at that time."

This information wasn't helpful to Meredith Sweeney. "Did you leave on good terms?" Herb asked.

"Not really. The relationship was strained. Watching my son battle for his life made me wonder what I was doing with *my* life. Suddenly, the pressures of life in a large law firm seemed… I don't know… unacceptable. It's hard to explain."

"Are you back practicing law?"

"I am. I'm of counsel to a small litigation practice. I work when I want and on what I want. I'm paid a fair percentage of the cash I generate. My life has slowed down and become more manageable. I've got no complaints."

"Did you ever work with Gwen Cantor?"

Madison showed no reaction to the mention of Meredith Sweeney's harasser, and now Herb was convinced that his hunch was dead in the water.

"I knew her. We never worked together. She had brought in a big client through a family connection."

Herb had run out of questions and had nothing to show for it.

"I'm not helping you, am I?" Madison said.

"No, you're not. But I appreciate your talking to me."

"Don't mention it."

"My client's case is bugging me. She was an associate at the firm. She strikes me as a young woman who's got her head screwed on right. But proving sexual harassment is a bear."

"I don't doubt that."

"Plus, your former firm can always say my client was a lousy lawyer. She wasn't expecting it, but she got a lousy review after her second year."

"Oh, yes, I remember. The second-year review."

"What about it?"

"Every associate got a lousy second-year review in whole or in part. Every single one. It was pretty much firm policy. The idea was to lay a paper trail in case the associate had to be let go down the road. The idea was also to try to get the lawyer to work harder. It was a clever, sadistic approach, but I can tell you it worked."

"Would you be willing to testify about that?"

"No," Madison said.

"Shit!" Herb muttered.

"I suppose I could be subpoenaed," Madison said, offering up his first smile. "Also, if the matter ended in litigation, I suppose you could subpoena all the second-year associate reviews that occurred during the year your client was reviewed."

"I'll keep that in mind," Herb said. "You helped me after all. My hunch just paid off."

"Glad to be of assistance," Madison said, another smile in place.

Herb felt he was missing something and was relieved when he remembered what it was. "I'm sorry. I forgot to ask you the most important thing. How's your son?"

"Thank you for asking. No one at Pinkerton, Ashley & Rosewood ever asked during most of his recovery. And the answer is, he's nearly fully recovered."

"Good for him and you."

"Yes," Madison agreed. "Good for us."

Wilson Finch worked for an insurance agency in downtown Medford. Paul hadn't wanted to embarrass or bother the guy at work, but he was pressed for time and needed to put this interview behind him. He had given Finch a heads-up call at work, which had been greeted with stony silence. After pressing, Paul had gotten Finch to agree to meet with him at two o'clock.

"I'll let Mr. Finch know you're here," a receptionist said.

Five minutes later a large, burly guy with dark hair wearing a black leather jacket marched into the reception area and nodded toward the front door to the office. Paul recognized Finch from his driver's license photo. "Let's walk," Finch said before turning to the door.

It was a mild afternoon again. The pale blue sky overhead, the bright sunlight, the few wispy clouds scudding west before a light breeze all made it feel like a spring day. Paul was wearing a light windbreaker and he unzipped his jacket.

"One of your officers paid a visit to my brother," Finch said. "It wasn't appreciated. In fact, your visit isn't appreciated. After this, neither of us is going to say a word to any of you."

Paul realized that he was at a disadvantage; Evelyn hadn't yet briefed him on her visit with Finch's younger brother. "We believe that your father passed away," Paul said.

"That's what the other cop said to Edwin. He told her that he didn't give a shit. Just so we're clear, I don't give a shit."

"Would one of you be willing to identify him?"

"I'm not going to and I doubt if Edwin will."

"What's behind all the hostility to your old man?"

Finch stopped walking and faced Paul. "My brother told your partner that our father was a vicious bastard, and I can second that emotion. He used to beat the shit out of me and Edwin and he laid into our mother when he tied one on. He was a rat bastard so if he's dead, I don't give a shit."

"What about your sister? Did he abuse her too?"

"No," Finch said, scowling.

"Why not?"

"You'll have to ask him. Oh, my mistake. You can't ask him if he really is dead."

"We haven't been able to locate your sister. Can you tell me where we can find her?"

"I'm not going to answer that question. Your partner asked Edwin the same question and got the same answer."

Paul debated bringing up the subject of the photographs. He wondered whether Evelyn had raised that subject with Finch's brother. Finch had resumed walking and Paul picked up his pace to catch up.

"Did your father ever hit kids outside your family?"

Finch slowed briefly—it was barely noticeable—before shaking his head. "I couldn't tell you one way or the other."

'Couldn't or wouldn't,' Paul thought. He could understand sons hating an abusive father. But even if the elder Finch was the prick his sons said he was,

Paul couldn't understand why the sons weren't curious enough to confirm their father was dead.

"Why don't you want to verify that your father's dead? We know you or your brother learned where he was living."

"Because I don't give a shit whether he is or not. My brother and I have moved on. I don't want to know anything about my father. He's been out of my life for years and I want it to stay that way."

Paul stopped walking and it was a long moment before Finch stopped and turned around. "Does this mean we're done?" he called out.

"Since you're not going to help me, I guess we are done."

"And I'm done talking. I don't want to hear from you or any other cop about my father."

"Don't worry. You won't hear from me again. But you may hear from a grand jury and, if you do, I might just sit in."

Paul turned around and headed back to his car. As exit lines went, he thought his last comment to Finch was pretty good. He couldn't pinpoint why he had mentioned a grand jury. The likelihood of a grand jury being convened was between slim and none, and slim had left the building. Still, it had sounded good.

16

Carpenter was looking forward to this court hearing. He was feeling good—physically and mentally—and his competitive juices were flowing. Clyde Atkins was experiencing serious jitters, so Carpenter had assigned Rachel the task of calming their client down. Judge Timothy Manningham had four cases scheduled for motion hearings this morning and Atkins' case was last on the list. The order of cases would give Carpenter and Rachel time to review the defendants' pleadings, once the other side arrived.

The rear door to the courtroom opened and Carpenter turned to view the new arrivals. He was certain he was looking at Atkins' brother and sister, Malcom and Mary Ellen, and their counsel. He recognized their attorney, Benjamin Learner, a seasoned business litigator who practiced with one of the large Boston firms. Learner had to be in his mid-fifties, a tall, lean man with wavy graying hair. He was accompanied by a woman who must have spent a fair amount of time in front of a mirror before coming to court: not a hair out of place in the cascade of blond hair sweeping up from where it touched her shoulders, bright red lipstick, heavy eyeliner. The man accompanying her was wearing a dark gray suit; he was of medium height and build and seemed to be viewing the courtroom with a mix of awe and nervousness. 'Was it possible,' Carpenter mused, 'that Learner had shown up unaccompanied by the requisite associates? Wasn't that against the rules of large firm litigation departments?'

Carpenter approached the trio. "You're here on the Atkins case, I would guess," he said to Learner. Learner nodded and made introductions. Carpenter gestured for Rachel to join him and he introduced her to the opposition.

"Let us get settled," Learner said. "My associates are on their way. I've got some pleadings to give you."

Carpenter and Rachel had retreated to the rear of the courtroom and sat on either side of Clyde Atkins. Learner had submitted a legal memorandum opposing Atkins' request for a preliminary injunction. Also, Mary Ellen Pines had submitted an affidavit. Carpenter started with the affidavit and gave Rachel the legal memorandum. By the time each of them had reviewed both documents, the first case of the morning had been called. Carpenter motioned for them to leave the courtroom so they could talk.

"She's full of shit!" Atkins erupted when they regrouped in the corridor outside the courtroom.

Carpenter considered Pines' affidavit. She had portrayed her brother as a man out of touch with business realities who was therefore a detriment to the family business. Atkins had wanted the business to take a loss by refusing to sell a product that he had regarded as inferior but that had never been subject to a recall. When a product required more than one repair, Atkins favored charging lower fees for a subsequent repair even if the initial repair had been done correctly and charging no fee when a preceding repair had been done incorrectly. The business' costs were continuously rising, and Atkins' uniform response was to reduce revenue. Mary Ellen Pines and her brother had become convinced that Atkins no longer had the family business' best interests in mind, but instead was committed to a course of action that would ensure that the business failed.

"Is anything she said false?" Carpenter asked.

Atkins sputtered for a moment. "She's putting a ridiculous spin on things."

Carpenter didn't respond to Atkins' outrage.

"The sister says nothing about the lack of a board of directors meeting at which Mr. Atkins' contract termination was discussed," Rachel pointed out.

Carpenter nodded. "And she said nothing about not giving sixty days' advance notice."

"The defendants will argue that there was cause to terminate the contract," Rachel said.

"But the cause was never spelled out in the contract termination letter," Carpenter replied.

"Are you going to let her get away with this?" Atkins asked.

"I'm going to do my best to put her in her place," Carpenter said. "But whether I succeed is not within my control. It depends upon what the judge is going to do."

"Shit!" Atkins exclaimed.

"Do you have the article on the snowblowers?" Rachel asked Carpenter.

"I do."

"Remember that a lot of what Mary Ellen is pointing to occurred months before the contract was terminated," Rachel said.

Carpenter smiled. He had thought of that. Rachel was on her game.

"I have to say," Judge Manningham said when the Atkins case was called, "that the injunctive relief the plaintiff is seeking is novel to say the least. You want the plaintiff to be paid his full compensation for at least sixty days from the time of a valid notice of termination. You also request that the compensation he would have received thereafter be escrowed until the case is decided. Since the plaintiff could recover damages from the defendants, why shouldn't I deny the injunction request because damages are available to the plaintiff and it's a basic rule of law that an injunction should not issue if a plaintiff has a damage remedy?"

Carpenter rose and studied the judge. Manningham was a recent appointee to the superior court bench. It was rare for a young judge to be assigned to the Business Litigation Section of Suffolk Superior Court. But Manningham apparently was up to the task. His first question cut to the heart of the matter. Carpenter suspected that in private practice, Manningham had been a bulldog litigator. He looked like a tough customer with his rugged build, craggy face, and a mop of sandy colored hair brushed in a halfhearted way.

"I would like to respond to your question in stages," Carpenter began. "The request for sixty days' compensation has to do with a fact put forward by the plaintiff, which is not disputed by the defendants' pleadings. The plaintiffs' brother and sister terminated his contract without a meeting of the board of directors taking place. The siblings met in secret and terminated the plaintiff's contract. As a director of the corporation, the plaintiff was entitled to have the termination of his employment contract considered at a directors' meeting because it is the directors who are responsible for corporate decisions. In addition, since the notice of contract termination didn't specify any particular cause for contract termination, the termination letter was based on no cause and the plaintiff was entitled to sixty-days' salary following a valid board of directors vote before any termination without cause could take effect."

"What would have been the point of a directors' meeting?" the judge asked. "The directors were aligned two to one against the plaintiff."

"On this issue, the board of directors was required to meet to discharge its fiduciary obligations to the corporation, and the plaintiff was entitled to speak at the meeting. Moreover, as the president of the corporation, the plaintiff never gave approval to the contract termination decision and was not even informed of that decision. Under the corporation's bylaws, the president was the officer who had to implement any contract termination decision."

"Even his own contract termination?" the judge asked.

"Especially his own contract termination," Carpenter said.

"According to the defendants," the judge continued, "the termination letter states that the plaintiff was not acting in the best interests of the corporation. Therefore, the letter states a cause for termination and the sixty-day provision has no applicability."

"I respectfully disagree," Carpenter said. "The letter is generally worded and lacks specifics. The letter does not identify what, if anything, the plaintiff did that was contrary to the best interests of the corporation."

Manningham stared at Carpenter. "Well, we certainly now know what the defendants claim the plaintiff did."

"The defendants are sixty days late and thousands of dollars short when it comes to being specific," Carpenter responded. "Besides, most of what the defendants point to in an affidavit occurred months ago. If what the plaintiff did months ago didn't justify his contract being terminated back then, it makes no sense that his previously accepted conduct can now be characterized as somehow detrimental to the corporation."

"You still haven't answered my question about the plaintiff having a right to obtain damages. Where he has that right, injunctive relief is not proper."

"Nothing the defendants have submitted to this court indicates that any money will be available to pay the plaintiff if he prevails at trial. The defendants are simply going to pocket the money that would have gone to the plaintiff, so the money will be gone. In the event the defendants hire someone to replace the plaintiff, the money will also be gone in payments to that person."

"I think that's a reach," the judge replied.

"Again, I would respectfully disagree. The defendants' scheme is transparent. Two owners are effectively freezing a third owner out of the business so that they can line their pockets. Two owners are deliberately ganging up on and breaching their fiduciary duty to a minority stockholder."

Manningham took a deep breath and let the air out slowly. "Before I direct questions at Mr. Learner, I'm curious as to the plaintiff's response to the defendants' claims about his business judgment."

"To help satisfy Your Honor's curiosity, may I pass a document to you for your consideration?"

"You may."

Carpenter delivered a copy of the document to Learner before handing a copy to the court clerk.

"Before you," Carpenter said, "is a Consumer Reports article rating snowblowers. The lowest-rated model is model number AZ9500 named the Snow Blaster. The ratings list appears on the last page of the article."

Judge Manningham studied the document handed to him by his clerk. The judicial inquiry took some time and Carpenter realized that the judge was going to read the entire article.

"I suppose you're going to tell me that the Snow Blaster was the snowblower model the plaintiff wished to stop selling."

"Your supposition is correct," Carpenter said, enjoying the moment. "The Snow Blaster ranked worst in the categories of breaking down and frequency of repairs. It appears that on two occasions, the Snow Blaster blew up. Fortunately, no one was injured. Yes, Your Honor. The plaintiff urged his siblings to discontinue selling this explosive device to the public."

"I think I've heard enough from the plaintiff for the moment," the judge said. "Your turn, Mr. Learner. Let me first ask you whether the plaintiff's various requests, in particular to lower repair charges and to provide free repairs where a machine broke down frequently, were ever implemented."

Learner rose, glancing briefly at the associates seated beside him. "No, Your Honor. Those suggestions of the plaintiff were never implemented."

"Is that because the individual defendants outvoted the plaintiff?"

"I don't know whether there was a formal board of directors meeting. However, it is safe to say that the defendants on the board refused to go along with the plaintiff's proposals."

"Would it also be correct that the defendant directors were against the plaintiff's proposal to scrap the business' stock of Snow Blasters?"

"That is correct," Learner said.

"I'm having difficulty seeing how the plaintiff acted contrary to the interests of the corporation. Every proposal he made was voted down. Why was his employment contract terminated when suggestions he made as a director were never adopted?"

Learner hesitated a beat. "As Ms. Pines' affidavit makes clear, the plaintiff's employment contract was an at-will employment contract. Thus, there didn't have to be a reason for its termination. Her affidavit also makes clear that there was justification for terminating the employment contract because the plaintiff's proposals were consistently detrimental to the financial success of the business."

"Mr. Atkins' affidavit states that he oversaw sales and service," the judge pointed out. "Was Mr. Atkins at all deficient in doing his job related to sales and service?"

"In the view of the defendant directors, yes. He wanted to take a loss on the line of snowblowers that has been mentioned and he proposed losing money on repairs."

"But since the plaintiff's proposals were never implemented, the company was never harmed by them. Is there anything else that the plaintiff did that in the defendants' view harmed the company?"

"Nothing beyond what is set forth in the affidavit of Ms. Pines."

"Is it true that the money that would no longer be paid to the plaintiff would increase the business' profit?" the judge asked.

"That might occur. It depends on what the business decided to do in terms of replacing the plaintiff."

"The plaintiff claims that the defendant directors will simply increase their compensation by the amount the business is no longer paying the plaintiff. What is to stop the defendants from doing that?"

"The defendants might elect to do that," Learner replied. "But to date they have not elected to do that. To my knowledge, the employment contract salaries of the defendants have not changed since the plaintiff's employment contract was terminated."

The judge held up the Consumer Reports article. "Why would your clients want to continue to sell a product that was not only rated lousy, but also presented a danger of blowing up?"

"Respectfully, Your Honor, a business does not have to conform its conduct to ratings provided by an outside source that is not a government authority. A few disgruntled consumers might skew a product's rating."

"It's hard to skew the fact that two of the Snow Blasters exploded."

"No government agency ordered a recall," Learner retorted.

Judge Manningham took his time reviewing the papers in front of him. "Does counsel have anything new to add?" he said when he looked up. "I place stress on the word new."

"No, Your Honor," Carpenter said promptly.

Learner consulted his notes. "No, Your Honor," he echoed.

"This is a difficult and complicated case," the judge said. "I conclude that the plaintiff has the better of it on the manner in which the plaintiff's employment contract was terminated. There was no board of directors' vote on this issue and had there been a meeting of the board, the plaintiff, as a director, would have been given his say. Also, and equally important, the termination letter does not identify any specifics that would amount to termination for cause. In fact, the plaintiff has never acted contrary to the best interests of the business because the defendants have consistently vetoed any suggestion by the plaintiff that they didn't like. In my view, the plaintiff's employment contract couldn't be terminated without him being provided with sixty days' advance notice following a directors' vote. That didn't happen. Therefore, I am going to order that the plaintiff be paid through sixty days following the date of a duly conducted corporate vote to terminate his contract."

Carpenter glanced to his left. Rachel was smiling. 'And she should be,' he thought. She'd been the one to frame the argument the judge had just adopted.

"The plaintiff's other request for injunctive relief is more complicated," the judge continued. "The plaintiff wishes to have the money he would have been paid after sixty days escrowed. I'm going to allow that request for further injunctive relief for a period of six months. I'm setting this case down for trial in four months. The individual defendants have no intention at the moment of increasing their salaries, so the defendants are not harmed if the money that would have been paid to the plaintiff is segregated. Secondly, given the fact that the decision to terminate the plaintiff's contract was made without a director vote and cited no specific cause for termination, I conclude that the plaintiff has made a sufficient showing that he is being forced out of the business improperly. Specifically, I determine that his claim that his rights as a minority stockholder are being abridged by the majority stockholders has merit at this point in the case. Majority stockholders hold a duty to deal fairly with a minority stockholder and the actions of the defendants suggest unfair, unilateral dealing with respect to the termination of the plaintiff's employment contract."

Manningham paused and asked his court clerk to produce his electronic calendar. "Discovery is to be concluded within the next sixty days. I'm going to have a pretrial conference in ninety days. As I previously said, trial will be in one hundred twenty days. The clerk will send you by facsimile a copy of my order. We're adjourned."

Atkins was shaking his hand with such force that Carpenter considered the possibility of injury. "Easy," he cautioned their client. "This is a nice preliminary battle victory, but you're a long way from winning the war."

Atkins released his grip. "Not a bad job for a guy I happened to meet in a bar," Atkins gushed. "My sister and brother are going to be spitting nails. Serves the bastards right."

"We have a lot of work to do," Rachel said. "You will likely be deposed, and we need to consider taking the depositions of your brother and sister. We will need to request documents from the defendants and we're going to need your help in deciding what documents we should ask for."

"Can't I gloat a little bit longer?" Atkins griped.

"The party's over," Rachel said. "You can count on our being papered to death by your siblings' lawyer."

Carpenter watched Atkins return to earth. "Should we consider whether this case can be settled in some way?" he asked.

Atkins shook his head. "That would be a waste of time," he said, "and you've made the point that we're going to be pressed for time. I don't see my brother and sister settling. They're going to be pissed off, especially my sister. I think you need to keep the pressure on them. You need to make them understand that I'm serious."

Carpenter considered the upcoming months. He was not put off by an expedited discovery schedule. He now had a firm behind him although, admittedly, Rachel and Simon were not as impressive an army of lawyers as Learner's firm could muster. "Okay," he said. "We'll try to launch the first discovery missile. I think we can get your siblings' attention."

17

"We need to locate the sister," Paul said. He and Evelyn had just finished comparing notes on their respective interviews with Daryl Finch's sons. Evelyn had shared his puzzlement over the brothers' refusal to provide information about their sister.

"I'll start with the high school," Evelyn said. "Maybe the sister showed up for a class reunion."

"Something's screwy," Paul responded. "We've got two brothers who won't tell us the time of day, an allegedly abusive father, a sister who could be anywhere, and photographs that hint at foul play."

"Did you just say foul play?"

Paul laughed. "In this case, I think the words fit the bill."

"Foul play," Evelyn muttered. "Not to be confused with fair play."

Paul studied his partner. Evelyn was smiling. She had just joked around with him. Maybe now was the time to worry.

Carpenter and Simon sat beside Rachel waiting for Philly's face to appear on the conference room computer through Skype. Carpenter realized that Philly's daughter was inching closer to two years old. Maybe the time was coming soon when Philly would feel comfortable leaving her kid with a babysitter and spend full days in the office.

"Sorry I'm late," Philly said as Daisy's face showed on the computer screen.

"Hi, cutie," Rachel said as she bent over and positioned herself so Daisy could see her.

Daisy, looking serious, pointed at Rachel. Carpenter considered that with Philly in the office more often, he would see less of Daisy. There was always a trade-off, he reflected.

"Great job on the Atkins case," Philly said. "Not much new business as far as I can tell." She displaced her daughter and came into view. "There are two matters I want to discuss. The first is our firm website."

"Don't think I had forgotten about that," Rachel said. When she looked his way, Carpenter rolled his eyes, but it was more to put up a show of token resistance than anything else. Rachel had insisted on a firm website as a condition of joining the firm, and he'd agreed.

"When we ring off, I'm going to forward each of you some rough outlines done by the advertising firm I told you about. Let me know what you think."

"What's the other thing you wanted to discuss?' Carpenter asked.

"I'm pregnant," Philly announced.

"Jesus!" Carpenter exclaimed, and immediately wished he could take the word back. Philly had probably seen his surprise and disappointment.

"Congratulations," Rachel said. "What great news!"

"Congratulations," Simon echoed. "When are you due?"

"September."

Carpenter considered how the year would play out. Philly would be limited by her pregnancy beginning sometime in July and would not be back in full swing until the beginning of next year. And when she was back in full swing, what the hell would full swing be? She'd have *two* kids to deal with.

"You certainly know how to top anything we have to discuss," Rachel said.

"That's what I'm here for," Philly replied.

Stephanie Manley had refused to talk on the phone and had requested another face-to-face meeting. She had chosen a soup-and-salad luncheonette near Cambridge City Hall, and Herb picked up the tab. They were seated at a corner table and were not likely to be disturbed. The luncheonette did a brisk take-out business and the tables were largely empty.

Herb started to speak, but Manley cut him off with a raised hand. "Let me get something in my stomach first," she said. "I'm famished."

Manley worked on her soup. Herb was also hungry, but he wouldn't be able to eat until he heard whether Manley could and would help Meredith Sweeney. He thought she would. If she was going to stay out of the case, she would have delivered that news with a phone call.

Manley finished half her soup before looking up. "I left Pinkerton, Ashley & Rosewood because Gwen Cantor had made a series of passes at me," Manley finally said.

"Are you willing to testify to that?" Herb asked.

"I'd prefer not to. But if I was served with a subpoena I would have to obviously."

"Are you willing to provide a written statement as to your testimony?"

"No," Manley said with a vigorous shake of her head. "I'm only going to go through this once and that once is in court when the case is tried."

"Will you meet with Meredith Sweeney's attorneys?"

"No."

Herb wasn't as familiar with civil cases as he was with criminal cases, but he was reasonably certain that Sweeney's attorneys would have to provide a summary of what each of her witnesses would testify to. At a minimum, Manley would have to be identified as a witness and once that occurred, the other side could opt to depose her. "I appreciate your willingness to testify if you are subpoenaed into court," he said. "I'll leave it up to Ms. Sweeney's lawyers, but I don't think they will use you without a written statement." 'I wouldn't use you without a written statement,' was the thought he kept to himself. "And by the way, you may not get to do this just once in court. Ms. Sweeney's lawyers would probably have to identify you as a witness. Once that happens, there's a chance the law firm could take your deposition."

Manley frowned in concentration and Herb questioned her puzzlement. As a paralegal, she probably knew a hell of a lot more about witnesses and depositions than he did.

"I've told you my terms," Manley said evenly. "I'll take the risk of Pinkerton deposing me. You need to understand that this is painful for me. It dredges up a lot of unhappiness. I'm going to minimize my involvement to as little as possible."

Herb knew that there were times when he was too trusting. Barney trusted nobody and was always giving him shit about accepting people at face value. Yet when it came to Manley, Herb was in Barney's camp—he didn't trust her.

"Thanks for lunch," Manley said. "I've got to get going."

"You're welcome. Thanks for meeting with me. Why don't you run along? I'm still working on my soup. I'll pass along what you've said to Ms. Sweeney's lawyers and get back to you."

Manley made a hasty exit and Herb pondered his next move. He'd sound out Barney on what he had found out and get his partner's read on Manley. Then he'd report to Sweeney. Was Manley trying to set him up? What if she was telling him that she'd been harassed but would deny that harassment had occurred on the witness stand? Such a U-turn might bury Sweeney's case.

Herb finished his soup and started in on his oyster crackers. 'Let the lawyers figure it out,' he thought. Sometimes it helped to be a lowly private investigator. You didn't get paid the big bucks, but the upside was that you didn't have to make the hard calls.

18

There were only six people present, but maybe it was the two investigators who made the conference room feel cramped. Barney Freedman and Herb McCauley were huge guys.

This was Carpenter's first look at Meredith Sweeney. There was a presence about her that reminded him of Simon. She was recently fired, out of work, probably wondering how she was going to support herself and yet, despite these miseries she looked composed, resolute, and prepared to do battle. It was difficult to imagine Sweeney coming on to Simon and even more difficult to picture Simon's response.

"Thanks for meeting with us on short notice," Meredith said. "You know Mr. Freedman and Mr. McCauley. Rachel gave me their names and I've hired them. I want you to hear directly from them what they've found out."

Herb cleared his throat. "I'm going to start out with the easy one. A litigation partner was let go a while back by the Pinkerton firm. He ended up filing for unemployment compensation and the firm didn't contest the filing. I thought it was unusual and I decided to chat the guy up. The guy's name is Gregory Madison. I approached him and we had a long talk. The bad news is that he is of no help on the sexual harassment claim. The good news is that he let drop the fact that the Pinkerton firm gives every associate a lousy two-year review in whole or in part."

Every time he heard a story like this Carpenter counted his blessings that over the years, he had never gotten involved with a law firm, especially a big law firm. True, there were numerous notable exceptions, but the internal bureaucracy and shameful shenanigans at big firms that from time to time had come to his attention made him wonder why any sane lawyer would join a leviathan of a firm. Carpenter noted the reactions of his colleagues: Simon took in Herb's information without expression while Rachel's jaw dropped.

"Madison won't give a statement. He said that he would prefer not to be subpoenaed. He suggested that you might want to subpoena all the two-year reviews that took place around the time Ms. Sweeney was reviewed. Maybe that would make his testimony unnecessary."

"Why would they do such a thing to their associates?" Rachel wondered aloud.

"Because they're bastards," Meredith said. "That lousy review was devastating to me."

"Because they wanted to have a review with something lousy on the record to justify firing an associate down the road," McCauley explained. "Also, they thought a lousy review would cause an associate to work harder."

"Maybe I was lucky I didn't get a job at a big firm," Rachel said. "Our firm is small, but I can't imagine us treating an associate that way."

"I also made contact with a woman named Stephanie Manley," Herb resumed. "She claimed that she left Pinkerton because Gwen Cantor made several passes at her."

"Why is this the more difficult situation?" Simon asked. "This is the kind of evidence Meredith needs for her case."

Herb and Barney exchanged a glance. "She won't provide a written statement," Herb said. "She won't meet with any of you. She claims she only wants to go through things once in court."

"If we list her as a witness, Pinkerton could take her deposition," Rachel said.

"I explained that," Herb replied. "She said if that happened, she'd have to live with it. I'm not a lawyer, but something seems off to me."

Carpenter agreed with the private investigators. The woman claimed that she was willing to help Sweeney but wouldn't confirm anything she would say on Sweeney's behalf. At the moment, it was her word against Herb's as to whether she had stated she'd been harassed.

"Herb and I smell a rat," Barney spoke for the first time. "Manley may be a set-up. If she doesn't provide a written statement, there's nothing to stop her from getting on the stand and saying she was never harassed."

Carpenter reasoned that if Manley was a plant of some kind, the Pinkerton firm wouldn't take her deposition. Rather, the firm would wait for Manley to give Gwen Cantor a clean bill of health from the witness stand.

"Did you exhaust all other leads on someone Cantor may have sexually harassed?" Carpenter asked Herb.

"No. After finding Manley, I stopped searching. Ms. Sweeney doesn't exactly have an unlimited budget and I thought one witness would do the trick. Before reaching Manley, I contacted seven women and each refused to speak with me. What it comes down to is that Barney and I aren't sure she's for real."

Carpenter regarded Herb's discovery of Pinkerton's two-year review policy as huge. If Sweeney's negative two-year evaluation was bogus, the firm would have difficulty claiming that her work was poor.

"I thought I'd add," Herb said, "that Stephanie Manley is drop-dead gorgeous. She should have been a model."

Carpenter put Herb's observation to the side. He was inclined to trust the private investigators' instinct that there was something off about Manley. If Manley was some kind of a plant, then Pinkerton knew that Meredith Sweeney was contemplating a lawsuit.

"You need to continue following leads on another witness who was sexually harassed," Carpenter said. "I don't see any way around that."

"That's going to have to wait," Meredith said. "I need to find a job before taking on any more financial obligations."

Carpenter noted Rachel's downcast expression. Rachel would probably opt for taking Sweeney's case on the spot and having their firm foot the investigators' costs.

"How much is it going to cost to finish your investigation of other witnesses?" Rachel asked.

Herb shrugged. "A thou give or take. That's just a guess."

Carpenter wouldn't have asked Rachel's question, but accepted his new world in which his new partners were going to do things their own way. "Why don't we talk internally and get back to you?" Carpenter said to Meredith. "The new information on the two-year review is extremely helpful to you. Nice job coming up with that," he directed to Herb.

"Do you think I have a case?" Meredith asked.

"You had a case before today," Carpenter said. "The question for us is whether it's a good or bad case. Your case is better today than it was yesterday. That's all any of us are going to say about your chances. We'll discuss things and get back to you."

Meredith took the hint. "Thanks for your time," she said, rising.

They reassembled in the conference room with mugs of fresh coffee, and Carpenter decided that he wasn't going to start the discussion on Meredith Sweeney. Rachel appeared eager to begin, but it was Simon who led off.

"Don't take this the wrong way," Simon said to Rachel, "but you can't appear so obvious about wanting to take Meredith's case. We need to discuss things among ourselves before we take on a case like this. Philly would need to be involved."

Rachel reddened. "Okay, maybe I was obvious. But so what? She got screwed. She was right: the partners in her former firm were bastards. I want to help her."

"We need to be cautious," Simon responded. "Meredith can't afford to pay our hourly fees. The Pinkerton firm is going to treat this case as a major crusade. If we take them on, every inch of ground is going to be contested."

Carpenter realized that Simon shared his approach to taking on a new matter, and that Rachel's attitude to a potential new case was similar to Philly's. Was a gender-based thing at work here?

"Remember what Philly said when she took on Fay Richardson's case?" Rachel asked. "She said that Richardson needed immediate help and our job was to help people. Meredith's situation is similar. I'll remind you that Richardson also couldn't pay our hourly fees."

"Well, maybe we shouldn't have taken on Richardson's case," Simon replied. "We're never going to be paid for the hours I put in getting the case ready for trial."

"How can you say we shouldn't have taken her case?" Rachel exclaimed. "We would have ended up feeling horrible if we'd abandoned her. And we'll feel equally horrible if we leave Meredith high and dry. And besides, in Richardson's case we may get lucky. We have a damage claim for intentional infliction of emotional distress."

Carpenter's young partners had run out of gas and were staring at him as if they expected him to draw on his years of experience and come up with a solution to their irreconcilable differences.

"It would help to have another witness who will say Cantor came on to her," Carpenter said. "Before we sign on to represent your law school friend, we have to think through whether we will be paid and whether Sweeney will win." Carpenter paused for effect. He had his young partners' attention and soldiered on. "We would have to represent Sweeney on a contingency basis. There would be no cash flow coming in. If we win, because her sexual harassment claim is basically a discrimination case, we'd recover our reasonable attorney fees. As you know, none of us are put off by contingency cases. They made our year last year. So the real question is whether Sweeney can win."

Rachel and Simon had settled down. Carpenter felt like a father dealing with quarreling children but knew that comparison wasn't fair to his partners.

"I meant what I said when I told McCauley he had made a real breakthrough by coming up with Pinkerton's policy of giving all associates negative two-year reviews. I was trying to think through whether that would be enough to take on Sweeney's case. McCauley's information helps on the issue of whether Pinkerton had a non-discriminatory reason for letting Sweeney go. The firm is going to be hard-pressed to claim that Sweeney did lousy work. But it still leaves open the question of whether Cantor came on to Sweeney. We know that Cantor will deny that charge and so the case becomes a 'she said—she said' battle."

"But won't Pinkerton's policy of giving all associates negative reviews cast doubt on anything the firm claims at trial?" Rachel asked.

"Maybe," Carpenter acknowledged. "But Cantor is only a junior partner. She had nothing to do with that policy. The firm's policy may hurt the *firm's* credibility, but it doesn't hurt Cantor's. That's why another witness would help."

Rachel looked deflated by his assessment, but Carpenter saw no reason to sugarcoat his analysis. "Here's another thing to consider," he added. "If we take her case, I'm inclined to charge her a modest non-refundable retainer. I'm thinking of six thousand dollars."

"Divisible by four," Simon said.

"That may turn Sweeney off completely," Carpenter continued. "If she can't afford a thousand dollars for the investigators to finish their job, she'll probably end up saying no to a retainer."

"Shit!" Rachel muttered, and Carpenter saw that Simon was as taken aback as he was by her swearing.

"What if we can't find another witness?" Simon asked.

"At the moment, I wouldn't be in favor of taking on the case," Carpenter answered.

"Listening to the private investigators," Simon said, "I began to wonder whether if Manley was lying—if she and Cantor are in a relationship."

"Where are you going with this?" Carpenter asked.

"What if those investigators came up with photographs of Manley and Cantor together?"

"I see where you're headed," Carpenter said. "But we have no reason to believe such a relationship exists."

"Maybe that's why Manley left the firm," Rachel said. "Maybe Cantor and she are involved, and they decided they didn't want anyone in the firm to know about their relationship. But if they were involved, why would Cantor come on to Meredith?"

"Does the word threesome ring a bell?" Simon asked.

"Oh my God!" Rachel exclaimed.

Carpenter tried to maintain a neutral expression in response to Rachel's shocked reaction. "Enough," he said. "I want both of you to go through everything we just talked about with Philly. Tell Philly to call me after she's thought about what you tell her."

Dr. Specter favored him with a wry smile that Carpenter decided not to read anything into. It was pointless to speculate on what would pop out of his oncologist's mouth. His young, blond, blue-eyed physician was constantly surprising him, shocking him on occasion. Specter had poked and prodded him, listened to his heart and lungs and, now that he was dressed, prepared to deliver her exit interview.

"Go figure," Specter said. "You're stable. And since you say you're feeling okay, you are okay."

Carpenter thought of the expression "as good as it gets." He would never be excellent or even good. He would always be saddled with a fucking incurable disease and with having to settle for stable if he was lucky.

"What's the matter?" Specter asked. "You just had a good checkup. I suppose now you're going to try to find something to complain about."

"Stable," Carpenter said. "What I have to hope for is stable."

"Don't knock stable. There are a lot of people out there who would give a lot for stable. Are you still exercising regularly?"

Carpenter nodded. He had made it a point to hook up with Camellia Kim, his personal trainer, at least once a month. The sessions with Kim probably weren't necessary; he had memorized her prescribed exercise routines and could perform them on his own. It was probably superstition that made him continue paying Kim's hourly session fee and continue to drink down the herb mixture her grandmother had made up for him. Since working with Kim, he had felt more and more like his old self and he was not about to change a routine that seemed to be working.

"You look fit," Specter said. "Keep at it. How's your sleeping?"

"I drop off as soon as my head hits the pillow. But there are times when I wake up around four in the morning and I can't fall back to sleep."

"On those days, do you get tired later on?"

"Sometimes."

"If you get tired, take a short nap. Naps are wonderful. I take naps whenever I get a chance."

Carpenter emitted a noncommittal grunt. Naps were a hit-or-miss proposition. He didn't like the idea of dropping off in the office and wasn't sure that he could.

"Is that it?" Specter said. "Don't tell me you've run out of things to bitch and moan about."

"There is one other thing," Carpenter forced himself to say. "I'm not up for sex as much as I used to be."

"I take it the way you phrased your concern describes the problem."

Carpenter felt himself reddening. "It partly does," he admitted, embarrassed.

Specter sat down at the small desk in the examining room and began to write on a notepad. She ripped off the page she had been writing on and handed it to Carpenter. "Here's a prescription for Viagra," she said. "See how that works for you."

"Jesus!" Carpenter exclaimed.

"You just complained about not being up for sex. There's something you can do about that. What's the problem?"

At least Specter hadn't uttered the words erectile dysfunction. If he saw one more fucking TV commercial on that subject, he couldn't be held responsible for his actions. "Is it okay to take Viagra with my CLL?"

"There's no medical reason you can't that I'm aware of."

Carpenter thought of having to call a doctor when an erection lasted more than four hours. Four hours! He should be so lucky.

"Get out of here," Specter said. "You're good to go."

"I'm stable," Carpenter corrected her. "I'm stable to go."

"In your case, there's no difference."

19

Evelyn sat at a small table in the administration area of Medford High School paging through the 1995 high school yearbook. Heather Finch's photograph showed a girl with black eyeglasses and long, springy, dark hair who would likely pass as a nerd today. She had the look of a shy, retiring, loner. On her first pass through the yearbook, Evelyn hadn't been able to locate a picture of Heather in any school activity. Then she went through the yearbook a second time, more slowly, carefully reading the captions under each of the photographs. She almost missed the reference to Heather. Seven girls were decked out in aprons and chef's hats. Cooking Club? Evelyn couldn't remember a cooking club at her high school. The girls were standing in a line behind a long table on which were arrayed mixing bowls, pots, pans, long-handled spoons and forks, a set of knives. They were not a cheery bunch. Only one member of the club sported a smile, a short, thin blond girl.

Evelyn caught the eye of the helpful secretary who had set her up with the yearbook. "I've marked two pages I would like copied before I leave. Is there any teacher around who taught back in 1995?"

"There are several," the secretary said. "What are you looking for?"

Evelyn pointed to the Cooking Club picture. "Someone familiar with the Cooking Club back then."

"You're in luck," the secretary said. "Mrs. Avery is still with us. She teaches science. Back in 1995 she was the faculty advisor to the Cooking Club. I'll make your copies."

"We no longer have a cooking club," Constance Avery said with a note of regret. "I got roped into being the club's faculty advisor. I was new to the school, lacked clout, and didn't have the guts to say no to the principal. But as it turned out, I enjoyed the experience."

Avery was seated behind her classroom desk and Evelyn had drawn up a chair to sit across from her. Evelyn had warmed to Avery as soon as they had made introductions. The science teacher had a twinkle in her blue eyes, exhibited warmth and good humor, and wanted to be helpful. Evelyn was hard-pressed to guess her age.

"Do you remember Heather Finch?" Evelyn asked, handing over the yearbook photo of the Cooking Club.

"I certainly do," Avery said, smiling. "I remember all these girls," and she proceeded to name them, going left to right, clearly not looking at the printed information below the photograph. "It's odd about memory," Avery continued. "I can't remember what I had for breakfast three days ago and I have those moments when I go into a room and can't remember what led me to do so. But when it comes to the youngsters I taught, I remember names and faces very well."

"I'm trying to locate Heather Finch," Evelyn explained. "She's not in any kind of trouble as far as I know. But she might have information that could be helpful in an investigation we're conducting."

"I don't think I can help," Avery replied. "I haven't seen her in years. I can tell you that when it came to cooking, Heather Finch excelled. From what I remember, she wasn't much of a student. But she only had to read a recipe once and she could repeat it back to you verbatim. I remember that she often wanted to experiment. We'd be making something, and she'd ask if she could substitute this for that or add more of this and less of that—that kind of thing. Cooking Club was the one place where she shined. I never had her in a class, but teachers talk and I learned that she was shy and retiring and never volunteered in class."

So far Evelyn hadn't heard anything useful. "Her brothers won't tell me where she is. Do you have any idea why they won't tell me her whereabouts?"

"Sorry, I have no idea."

"Well, thanks for talking to me."

"Things are coming back to me," Avery said, as Evelyn rose. The teacher was staring at the Cooking Club photograph, which Evelyn had forgotten to reclaim. "Do you see that girl standing next to Heather?" she asked pointing. "That's Jacqueline Templeton."

Evelyn leaned over and saw that Avery had identified the only girl who was smiling in the photograph. "Heather and Jacqueline were inseparable. I always wondered if there was something going on between them. In those days, if there was, it probably wasn't something they would have advertised. But I remember thinking there might be something between them at the time. God! I can't believe I remembered that. Jacqueline's mother still lives in Medford. She's a member of my church. Her husband died a couple of years ago. If the two girls kept in touch or are together, I'm sure Jacqueline's mother would know where to find them."

'Now we're getting somewhere,' Evelyn thought, as she wrote down Jacqueline Templeton's name and the name of her mother.

"What the fuck are we doing here?" Barney bitched. "We're freezing our asses off and the chance of us finding out anything is less than zero."

It was after nine o'clock at night and they had been parked for over three hours outside the Esplanade Condominium complex where Gwen Cantor lived. Herb had figured Barney would have snapped an hour ago; he was amazed his partner had lasted as long as he had. "Stop complaining," Herb said. "You've got nothing better to do and, besides, you like hanging out with me. Our deal is that we leave at midnight if she doesn't show."

Barney grunted and shifted in the passenger seat. Herb guessed that Barney would keep his frustration bottled up for about fifteen minutes before going off again. He checked his watch so he could time it. "Do you want me to turn the heater on?" he asked.

Barney shook his head. So far they had taken the chill out of the truck's cab only three times. For this stakeout, Herb had borrowed his son's pickup truck because the cab was roomy and they could stretch their legs.

"Are we going to charge for this?" Barney asked.

"I already told you no," Herb replied. "Sweeney said to stop work for the time being."

"Fucking great!" Barney exclaimed.

When frustrated, Barney liked to focus on as many negatives as he could call to mind. Herb remembered stakeouts back in their Cambridge PD days that lasted for days and Barney's list of things to bitch about was never-ending.

"Remind me why we're doing this?" Barney asked.

"Because we like Sweeney and we want to help her and because we've got nothing better to do."

"And if we see this Manley broad go inside, what's our plan again?"

Herb knew that Barney remembered his plan. In all the years they worked together, Barney rarely wrote down anything but remembered everything.

"I told you. I scouted this place out. In the morning, I'm going to park my ass off to the right of the front door by that tree over there, and I'm going to wait for Manley to leave. She's supposed to be at work by nine. I'm going to take her photograph when she leaves, and I should be able to get the condominium name in the picture."

"Manley knows you by sight. If she sees you, you can forget about photographs."

"I'll risk it," Herb said.

"If you get a photograph, Manley will say the photograph was doctored. It'll be your word against hers."

"I was hoping it would be *our* word against hers."

"Don't push your luck," Barney said with a dismissive snort.

Herb was confident that if they saw Manley entering the building, Barney would stick around with him until she left.

Herb changed the subject. "Philly and this guy Carpenter are throwing business our way. What's your read on them?"

Barney shrugged. “Philly’s okay. I don’t have a feel for Carpenter yet.”

“Are you saying Philly’s okay because she’s married to Paul?”

“That’s part of it,” Barney admitted.

“You got any ideas how we’re going to dig up dirt on that brother and sister?” Herb asked.

“I’m thinking about it.”

Herb had been thinking about it as well. Carpenter wanted them to get a read on the personal financial situation of Mary Ellen Pines and Malcolm Atkins. He also wanted them to find out whatever they could about the family business, Atkins Equipment, Supplies and Services, Inc. “I could start on the company...” Herb began before Barney cut him off.

“That looks like the woman you described,” Barney said pointing.

Herb reached for his night vision glasses and zeroed in on the figure walking purposefully toward the entrance to the condominiums. “Bingo!” he exclaimed.

“Christ! That means we’re here all fucking night. I’m getting too old for this.”

“We’re both too old for this,” Herb replied. “But we’re going to do this and you know it, so time to put a sock in it.”

Herb glanced at his watch. Twenty minutes since his last time check. Barney had held out for five minutes longer than he had predicted. There were going to be a lot more time checks before the night was through.

20

Barney leaned against the tree Herb had planned to hide behind and wondered whether, when the moment came to spring into action, he would have any circulation in his fingers to work the camera. Last night and this morning had proved to be exceptions to the relatively mild winter. He checked his watch. Eight in the morning. Manley had better get a move on.

It had taken some convincing, but Herb had finally agreed that Barney should be the one to photograph Manley since Manley had never seen him.

Barney took off his mittens and blew on his hands, wriggled his fingers. Then he sited with the camera, using the zoom lens on the entrance door. And just like that, the Manley broad emerged, walking toward him on the path Herb had figured to be her route, obviously heading for the parking garage. Barney began to snap photographs—'the more the merrier,' he thought. Manley was wearing a tall fur hat but her face was visible. She walked purposefully, seemingly oblivious to her surroundings. Barney figured he had at least two good head shots with the entryway in the background. He debated whether to leave well enough alone and decided not to. He imagined Herb quietly going ballistic at the sight of him following Manley.

The parking facility had four levels, two below ground, one at ground level, and one above ground level. Manley took the stairs to the top level and Barney offered up a silent thank you. In the lower levels he would have had to use a flash and Manley couldn't have failed to notice.

Manley fumbled with her keys beside a white Toyota Camry and Barney memorized the license plate as he approached. The timing was working to perfection. As he drew abreast of the car, Manley opened the front door and started to get inside. Barney slowed, sited the camera, and squeezed off two photos in the direction of the license plate before picking up his pace and hoping to look like someone heading for his car. He darted behind a SUV parked five spaces beyond where Manley's Camry had been parked. He heard Manley's car start and, peeking from behind the SUV, saw the Camry begin to back out. Manley turned her car and began driving away from him. Barney thought, 'What the hell, one more for the road.' He moved from behind the SUV and clicked three more photographs with his zoom lens, capturing the license plate. Then he aimed the camera higher and took his time with two final photographs. He caught the top of Manley's car and a sign above it: *Esplanade Condominium Parking—Exit to the Right.*

Manley's car slowed and Barney hustled to get back behind the SUV. He counted off two minutes before venturing a look. Manley's car was still there. She was staring out the driver side window in his direction and he scrunched down out of sight. If she got out of the car and walked his way, he was toast. There was no explanation for his behavior.

A horn sounded. Barney hazarded another quick glance. Another car was trying to get around Manley's car and he saw her backing the Camry up at an angle and then moving forward, making room for the other driver to get around her. The Camry's brake lights flashed and then the car again moved forward and turned right, following the exit arrow. The other driver pulled into the space Manley had vacated.

Barney wouldn't have put it past Manley to have pulled over outside the parking garage to wait for him to emerge. He could stay put until nine when she was supposed to be at work. But he'd had it with waiting. The driver of the car that had pulled into Manley's space slammed his door and began walking toward the exit. Barney moved quickly to try to catch up. "Hey!" he called out.

The man turned and waited. He was a heavyset guy wearing a long black winter coat and a red and white woolen cap.

"I'm checking out the condos here," Barney said. "Is the parking facility big enough for owners and guests?"

"I've never had any trouble getting a space, and none of my guests has complained," the man said before turning and heading for the exit.

Barney tailed along. He had stuffed the camera into a side pocket of his ski parka. "What's your candid opinion of this place?"

"To be frank, it's been great for me. I work downtown and most days I can walk to work. But I've been away on business and just came in on a red-eye. You'll like it here. They've got an indoor pool, a workout facility, the works."

Outside Manley had in fact pulled over and was eyeing them as they headed toward her.

"Is there a market nearby?" Barney asked as they drew abreast of Manley. She was glaring at him, but Barney focused on his companion.

"Yeah, it's within walking distance. It's pricey but has pretty much everything you need."

"What's housekeeping like?" Barney asked as they moved past Manley.

"Reasonably efficient."

"Thanks," Barney said. "I didn't mean to bend your ear."

"No problem."

Barney walked past where Herb had parked, ignoring the pickup truck. He felt Manley's gaze boring into his back. Herb knew how to improvise so Barney hoped that he'd put two and two together. Herb had to have seen Manley get out of her car when she exited the parking garage.

Barney kept walking. Herb would slouch down, stay put, and wait for a call. This wasn't the first time their cover had been blown.

Florence Templeton had made tea for Evelyn—she had no coffee in the house—and the detective sipped at it for the sake of politeness while wishing it was a jolt of high-test coffee. Jacqueline Templeton's mother was a wispy thing—thin, short, thinning white hair. Templeton was wearing faded jeans and a red flannel shirt and work shoes. After Evelyn had rung the bell to Templeton's small cape house and been invited inside, Templeton had said she'd been about to work on her backyard garden to get it ready for the spring. With the unseasonably warm weather, Templeton predicted an early spring. Now they were sitting in her kitchen at a small round wood table and Evelyn was debating how to approach her host when Templeton solved her problem.

"You said you were here on police business," Templeton said.

"The Cambridge Police Department is trying to find someone who we believe was a friend of your daughter in high school."

"That was a long time ago," Templeton said.

"I was over at the high school looking at the yearbook for your daughter's senior year. There was a picture of the Cooking Club. Standing next to your daughter in the picture was the girl we're trying to locate—Heather Finch. Does that name ring a bell?"

"Yes, it does. She was a close friend of my daughter in high school. I remember her."

"When was the last time you saw Heather Finch?"

"Probably sometime just after the high school graduation."

"May I ask where your daughter is living?"

"Omaha, Nebraska. She's been there for years."

"Have you ever visited her there?"

"No, but Jackie comes back here about once a year."

"Do you know whether your daughter has kept up with the Finch girl?"

"You'd have to ask Jackie. I don't know."

Evelyn wrote down contact information for Jacqueline Templeton and studied her host. It seemed rude to bolt immediately after receiving the only useful information she was likely to obtain. "Does your daughter still like to cook?" she asked to make small talk.

"I don't think she's ever liked to cook," Templeton said. "To this day, I don't understand why she joined the Cooking Club. Whenever I'd ask her to help with a meal, she'd tell me she hated to cook."

Templeton's gaze wandered and Evelyn suspected that she was thinking back to her daughter's youth.

"I never really understood my daughter," Templeton said in a soft voice. "I suppose that's an awful thing to say, but it's true. When she comes to visit, we get on okay. But there's a closeness that's missing. It's sad, really."

Evelyn set down her teacup, already thinking about the coffee she would stop for en route back to the station. She didn't have much sympathy for mothers who didn't understand their daughters. She'd come up with a solution to her own mother's ever-present look of disappointment over her career choice: keep visits and calls to a minimum.

21

"The Dog Days Are Over" sounded from her boom box, and Philly adjusted the volume. Morning temperatures had started to inch upwards. This morning she and Isabella had started their spinning routine without pulling up the hoods on their sweatshirts. The sky was already beginning to lighten, and Philly guessed the sun would emerge in minutes. Rosalind was asleep in a stroller beside their bikes, covered with a heavy wool blanket.

"How did Sarah take the news of your pregnancy?" Isabella asked as "Kids" next sounded from the boom box

"I think she's worried about whether she can handle it," Philly replied.

"I don't blame her. She's finally settled into a routine with Daisy and Rosalind and you and Paul had to go ruin it."

"I'm thinking of getting her some help," Philly said. With misgivings, she was considering using a teenager in the late afternoons. Even if she could find one, was a teenager the solution? Sarah would be around to supervise because she lived in the house, but even so, Philly was hesitant to entrust Daisy and a new baby to a teen.

"What's going to happen with your law office?" Isabella asked.

"What's with all the questions? This is my time to forget about the nagging details of my life." Philly checked the time on her heart rate monitor watch. "In twenty-five minutes, I've got to eat breakfast and then throw up."

Isabella laughed. "It's my job to ask you questions. I need information to help you come up with solutions. Your problems are mine and Raul's and Rosalind's."

"I really don't know what to do about work," Philly admitted. Carpenter had probably looked forward to her spending more time in the office, but her immediate work future was likely a continuation of working from home and Skype conferences. He had never complained about this arrangement, yet Philly sometimes felt she was letting him down.

"Last year you worked from home and you told me you had a very good year. Why not simply continue?"

"Because sometimes working from home makes me feel like I'm not pulling my own weight. It's complicated."

"You pulled your own weight last year. You had two big trial victories at the end of the year."

Philly refrained from delivering Carpenter's standard message that this was a new year and past-year accomplishments no longer counted for anything.

The back door opened, and Daisy emerged in her new, red winter snow suit. Paul closed the door behind them and turned her loose, then left for the station. Philly was grateful for the appearance of her daughter. Daisy's presence would put a stop to Isabella's questions.

Daisy was wearing little red boots and began wobbling about the backyard. The swish of her snow pants could be heard above "Born This Way."

"I'm thinking of continuing to work half-days," Isabella said. "I've discussed that option with my boss. That should be a help if he goes along with that plan."

Philly didn't want to feel dependent on Isabella. "It'll only be a help until Rosalind has a little brother or sister."

"Don't even think about that."

Daisy shuffled up to Philly's bike and held up her hand. Philly dutifully admired the desiccated pinecone in her daughter's red mitten.

"We'll work it out," Isabella said. "We always do."

Philly picked up her pace, hoping that Isabella was right.

"I love it," Rachel gushed.

Rachel and Simon had moved close together; Philly could easily see them on Skype. Carpenter's visage eluded the Skype eye and Philly pictured him with a sour look.

"When will the final website design be done?" Simon asked.

"As a favor to me, Muriel Parker said it would be done within two weeks of our giving the go-ahead."

"Awesome!" Rachel exclaimed. Philly wondered when the elephant in the room would be heard from. She didn't have long to wait.

"Don't you think they've gone overboard with the million-dollar verdicts?" Carpenter said.

"That's the best part," Rachel said, and Philly hoped she could sit out this debate and let Rachel and perhaps Simon carry her water.

"But the caption," Carpenter insisted. "'Stunning Litigation Successes.' Isn't that overkill?"

"Didn't you say last year that back-to-back million-dollar verdicts were extraordinary?" Simon asked, exhibiting his prodigious memory.

"What if I did? It *was* extraordinary but that doesn't mean we have to become shills about it."

"But we should," Rachel said. "This is our chance to tout our accomplishments. I like the way the agency wrote up this part. We pulled off something major and the agency came up with a way to toot our horn that I thought was reasonably restrained."

Philly heard a grumble from Carpenter but still couldn't see his face.

"I like it as well," Simon said. "We want to stand out from the crowd. This is a way to do it."

Philly heard an unintelligible noise she suspected came from Carpenter. "What about the rest of it?" she asked.

"It's totally user-friendly," Simon said. "I have a minor edit on how they wrote about the work we do, but outside of that I say we go for it."

"Agreed," Rachel said.

When Carpenter remained silent, Philly spoke up. "I'm with Rachel and Simon. I think they did a good job."

Carpenter's continued silence struck Philly as ominous. She wanted to see his face and debated asking for the Skype camera to be rotated so that she could.

"I suppose it doesn't matter what I say since I'm outvoted," Carpenter finally said.

"Of course it matters what you say," Rachel responded immediately. "Don't be like that. Maybe what you have to say will change our minds."

"I doubt that. I guess I'm still ambivalent about a website. This is a big step for me. But I agreed to go along with a website so I'm going to make it unanimous."

"Yes!" Rachel cheered. "This is going to be great."

"How's the pregnancy going?" Simon asked.

"Great," Philly said, thankful for the subject change even though she would have preferred a different subject. "I know it's going great because I can't keep anything down in the morning except tea, toast, and jam. It was the same way with Daisy."

"Another Daisy would be wonderful," Rachel said, and Philly prayed that would be the case.

22

Carpenter closed the door to his office so he could talk alone with Philly on Skype. "We need to sort out this Meredith Sweeney mess," he said.

"Shouldn't we be hashing this out with Simon and Rachel?" Philly asked.

"Yeah, we should," Carpenter responded, Philly's question raising anew for him the problems of a firm operating as a democracy. "But for the moment, you and I are the senior partners and I need to get your read on the situation. Then we'll talk to Simon and Rachel."

Carpenter filled Philly in on Meredith's latest call to Rachel. Barney and Herb's report finding a link between Gwen Carson and Stephanie Manley was a new complication that he was having trouble wrapping his mind around.

"I guess this *is* a mess," Philly said when Carpenter finished his account. "I assume Rachel is even more eager to take on the case."

"You've got that right. She's champing at the bit. We have to assume that Manley won't provide testimony that would help Meredith. That leaves us with no witness who will say she was harassed by Carson. We have going for us the firm's policy of giving every associate a shitty two-year review, which is big. I think we can prove that Sweeney performed her job well. But is it enough?"

Philly didn't answer right away. She was staring at him, concentrating. Then she ducked out of view and resurfaced holding her daughter. Carpenter waved at the toddler reflexively and she smiled in return. He grinned back.

"We'd be suing the firm and Cantor," Philly said. "The firm would have to explain its policy on negative two-year reviews. Cantor would have to explain what Manley was doing at her condo."

Carpenter had considered the latter point. "Cantor might say that Manley wanted to meet with her after being approached by McCauley. She might come up with a story that McCauley was trying to get her to say she was harassed by Cantor. Manley would probably deny that she ever told McCauley that Cantor had come on to her."

"Is that why Manley spent the night at Cantor's place?" Philly asked.

"Good point," Carpenter conceded.

Daisy began squirming and Philly set her down. "I'm leaning toward taking the case," Philly said. "We can allege that Sweeney was fired because she made a complaint of sexual harassment. It will be interesting to learn how Sweeney's harassment complaint *was* investigated."

Carpenter had always enjoyed back and forth with Philly on a problem. The exchange usually helped his thinking. "What the fuck," he said. "Let's go for it."

"What about Simon?" Philly asked.

"If he's ambivalent about getting involved, I say we let Rachel do most of the work."

"Okay," Philly said. "Go over this with Simon and Rachel. At least one of them will be pleased."

March

From Meredith's Playlist

"Wake up Call"

Maroon 5

23

An afternoon spent at the Cambridge Public Library reaffirmed Herb's belief that people had a right to bitch and moan about their lack of privacy. From searches of public records, he now knew the names and home addresses of the officers and directors of Atkins Equipment, Supplies and Services, Inc. who, in this case, were one and the same. He also knew the security interests the company had granted to several equipment suppliers, the assessed valuations of the houses owned by Malcolm Atkins and Mary Ellen Pines, and the amount of the mortgages on those houses. He knew that Mary Ellen Pines and her husband had taken out a substantial home equity loan. He could infer from the downturn in the real estate market that the siblings had little real equity in their homes; he suspected that the outstanding mortgages and home equity loan in the case of the sister pretty much represented the values of the properties. The siblings might be people who owned expensive houses but lived paycheck to paycheck.

Cornerstone Commercial Bank had a lien on the company's accounts receivable. Herb figured that the bank had given the company a working capital loan that was secured by the company's revenue stream. Maybe it would turn out that Atkins Equipment, Supplies and Services, Inc. was leveraged up to its eyeballs. That was probably what Carpenter and Philly were hoping.

Herb felt his cell phone vibrate and he took the call, whispering "hello" so as not to disturb anybody. He still thought of libraries as solemn institutions, which, back when he was a kid, they were. These days he probably could have shouted into his cell phone; the high school kids spread out at the tables surrounding him were talking up a loud storm.

"Hi, it's Meredith Sweeney."

"Hold on a minute. I need to go outside so I can talk freely."

Herb got up from his computer table and gathered his notes. Outside, he found an unoccupied bench and again said hello.

"I just wanted to thank you," Meredith said. "You and Mr. Freedman went beyond the call of duty."

"Don't mention it."

"I'm damn well going to mention it. I'm very grateful."

"Glad we could help."

"Rachel's firm is going to take my case. I thought you and Mr. Freedman would want to know."

"That's great news."

"Yeah, it is. They want a retainer and that presents a problem but you're right, it is good news."

"You'll let us know how it comes out?"

"I have a feeling you're not done with me," Meredith said. "By the way, I picked up a freelance brief writing job that should buy me about six weeks."

"Good for you."

"Anyway, when I get back on my feet, somehow I'm going to make it up to you guys."

"That's not necessary. I mean that."

"Yeah, it is necessary. I won't forget what you've done for me."

When Meredith rang off, Herb stayed seated, taking in the scenery. The warm winter had caused trees in the spacious area abutting the library entrance to start to bud. For the most part, people entering and leaving the library had abandoned winter wear and had donned light jackets. The weird weather probably had plant-life and humans equally fooled. Herb wouldn't be surprised if the beginning of spring brought a whopping snowstorm that screwed up the biological clocks of every living thing in New England.

Herb stood up and stretched. He'd have to break it to Barney that they needed to put in some more free time. If Gwen Carson had come on to another woman besides Meredith Sweeney, he needed to contact the remaining women who had left the firm. Also, it would be helpful to get a photograph of Manley and Carson together. Even if it killed him, Herb knew that he wasn't going to stop until he found one more thing to help Meredith. Then again, maybe Barney would kill him, put him out of his misery.

Driving home, Herb felt his cell phone vibrate and he pulled off the road to take the call. "Carpenter," announced the voice on the other end after he said hello.

"What can I do for you?" Herb asked.

"You're supposed to get back to Manley, right?"

"Right." Herb had been wondering if and when he would contact her and what message he would deliver if directed to make the call.

"We've had a brainstorming session and we want you to call her back in a week."

"Why the delay?"

"To let a little time go by after your partner's run in with Manley at the parking garage."

"Makes sense," Herb said, although he didn't think the timing of the call would make a difference. Manley would be suspicious of anyone and everyone from here on out.

"When you talk to her, thank her for getting back to you. Then tell her that Sweeney's lawyers aren't willing to list a witness who isn't prepared to give a signed statement as to her testimony."

"That should be the end of that," Herb said. Manley had been adamant about not giving a statement.

"Maybe, maybe not," Carpenter said.

"What if Manley brings up that she thinks someone's following her?"

"Play dumb," Carpenter answered. "Ask her why she thinks that?"

"What if she asks me if I'm following her?"

"Tell her she's nuts."

"So you want me to lie?"

"Yeah, I do."

Herb didn't like lying. He'd have to think of a response to Manley that didn't involve a lie. "I'll play it by ear," he said.

"I don't like the sound of that," Carpenter said.

"When are you filing suit?"

"In the next few days."

"Let me know if there's anything else we can do."

24

Simon had just finished reviewing the defendants' post-hearing legal memorandum filed in the billboard case. His bottom-line assessment was that Patrick Lassiter had not offered any new argument on behalf of Al Townsend and Rita Stout.

He stared at the home page on his office computer and his thoughts turned to Meredith Sweeney. Mercifully, Rachel was drafting the complaint that would be filed with the Massachusetts Commission Against Discrimination on Meredith's behalf. That meant he could briefly further delay the moment when he'd have to decide whether to involve himself in the case.

Simon knew the source of his ambivalence. If he had taken up Meredith's offer years ago and slept with her, it would have been a one-and-done event. Had they hooked up, he would have no hesitation in participating in her lawsuit against the Pinkerton firm. But he had unfinished business with Meredith because not taking her up on her offer still rankled in a way he didn't fully understand. If he slept with her tomorrow, would he be willing to get involved in her case the day after? Simon was surprised to find that the answer was yes. So what was that all about?

Evelyn consulted notes as she briefed Paul on her discussion with Jacqueline Templeton. "So when I told her that she didn't have to speak with me, she said that she'd rather not. But you know me. I kept pressing."

Paul *was* beginning to know his partner. Her doggedness and thoroughness were slowly winning him over.

"I asked her if she could help me locate Heather Finch and she said, and I quote, 'Sorry, I'm not able to help you.'"

"She didn't say she couldn't help you," Paul observed.

"Right. For all we know, the Finch woman was standing next to her during my call."

"Did you tell her why we wanted to talk to Finch?"

"I thought about that but decided against it. I told her that if Finch got in touch with her, Finch might be interested in learning that her father had died. I explained that there was a question we wanted to ask Finch in connection with her father's death."

Paul thought that Evelyn had revealed just the right amount of information. It would have been a mistake to mention the photographs.

"I was hoping Templeton would ask me what my question was, but she didn't. I asked her when she last saw Finch. Templeton again said that she wasn't able to help me."

Paul digested Evelyn's information. There was only one logical next step in their investigation.

"So which one of us is going to Omaha?" Evelyn asked, reading his mind.

Frank was holding him, and Simon wondered whether his heart would ever stop thudding. He should have been spent but his mind was racing and nervous energy continued to make him feel revved up. He had driven to Wesleyan to talk with Frank face-to-face and now he wondered whether he had the nerve to raise the subject he needed to discuss.

"This is a pleasant surprise," Frank said in a soft, low voice. "It's not like you to hit the road after dark and it's even more unlike you not to call first. But I'll take it. Is everything okay?"

Frank had given him a lead-in. "There's something I need to ask you," Simon said, having no clue how he would get the words out.

"So ask."

"It's about that girl—that woman—I was telling you about."

"The one who made a pass at you at the end of law school?"

"That's the one."

"So ask," Frank repeated.

"I want to ask her if her offer is still open," Simon admitted. He felt Frank's grip tighten and wondered whether his obsession with Meredith—if that's what it was—would cause him to lose the most important person in his life.

"And what if her offer is still open?"

"I want to take her up on it."

Frank's grip loosened and he didn't say anything for a long moment. "I thought we had a monogamous relationship," he finally said.

"We do. This has nothing to do with monogamy."

"Then what does it have to do with?"

"I can't really explain it. It's not curiosity, exactly. It's more that I've always regretted not taking her up on her offer when she made it."

Frank was holding him from behind and Simon was grateful that they weren't looking at each other. Not that he would be able to see Frank's face in the darkness. It was totally dark in Frank's bedroom. His roommate had crashed in another dorm room to give them some privacy.

"This makes no sense to me. At the risk of being insensitive and unsupportive, I think you're being ridiculous."

"I probably am. It's just something I need to do."

"What if I say no?"

"Then I won't ask her, and I won't work on her case, which we've decided to take on."

"But if she says yes you will work on her case?"

"Correct."

"What if she says no?"

"Problem solved, and I'll work on her case."

"This is insane!"

Simon didn't disagree. His heart was still going a mile a minute and he began to second-guess his impulsive nighttime drive. He tried deep breaths to steady himself and after a time he felt weariness begin to take over. He closed his eyes.

"Use a fucking condom, asshole!" Frank said, and Simon jolted awake.

25

"Well, that was… different," Meredith said.

They were lying in Meredith's narrow bed and Simon began to catalogue other adjectives Meredith might have used: "pathetic," "horrifying," and "humiliating" topped the list that quickly came to mind. "Can we agree never to speak of this again?" he asked.

"You can't be serious; we simply have to tell Rachel," Meredith replied, and Simon was so mortified that he couldn't speak.

"God! I don't know what I was thinking," Simon said when mortification slightly released its hold.

"I'm teasing you," Meredith said. "Agreed. This stays between us."

"Shit," Simon muttered. "I have to tell my partner. That has to be the one exception."

"Your partner?"

"I'm in a relationship."

"And he knows about this?"

"Yes."

"And he's okay with this?"

"Not really."

Meredith fell silent and Simon hoped she would stay that way.

"You're a lucky guy," Meredith finally said, and there was a rueful tone to her words. "Your partner must like you a lot."

"I like him a lot. This is probably going to screw things up between us."

"Appropriate choice of words. Do yourself a favor and forget about this."

Simon found forgetting all but impossible. Obliterating this experience from his memory would have required use of that flashing device in the *Men in Black* movies that was used by the alien monitors to permanently erase an earthling's memory.

"I'm serious," Meredith said. "We need to move on."

Simon replayed the various moments when he could have backed out. He had gone to Meredith's apartment unannounced and when she opened the door, he had asked her, without so much as a hello, whether her offer at the end of law school was still on the table. When she said yes, he could have said he was just curious and turned around and left. But, no, he had entered her apartment. She led him directly to her bedroom, told him to sit on her bed, and slowly stripped naked. At that moment, having experienced no reaction, he could have owned up to his mistake and left. But, no, he had proceeded to lie back on the bed while Meredith undressed him. When Meredith had settled beside him and gave him a soft peck on the cheek, he could have taken his continued lack of reaction for the sign it was and admitted his error. But, no, he had let the farce continue to play out and had only himself to blame.

"When my case goes to trial," Meredith said, "I want you to be the lead counsel."

"My partners might have other ideas. I know Rachel wants to be involved in the trial."

"I want you front and center. I'm the client. I should have the final say. I've had to borrow money from my folks to pay your retainer. I've got a lot riding on this."

"It's not that easy when you're in a firm."

"Then make it easy," Meredith said with some heat. "I trust you. I don't have the same confidence in Rachel."

"Last year Rachel made the opening argument in a jury trial, presented the plaintiff's direct case by herself, and helped land a million-dollar verdict."

"No shit! I'm envious. But I still want *you*."

"I'll definitely be involved. I promise you that. I'll do what I can on taking the lead." Simon had no idea how Carpenter and Philly envisioned the handling of Meredith's case. He was about to find out. "I think I better go."

"No," Meredith said. "I want you to spend the night. This is the last time we're going to be able to really talk. I want to know why you're here."

"It's a long, unintelligible story."

"That's why you have to stay. I want to hear everything."

Meredith eased out of bed and began rummaging in her dresser. Simon found her unselfconsciousness unnerving. "Here," she said, tossing him a sweatshirt and a pair of running shorts. "Time to cover up," she added, as she went to her closet and returned in a robe.

They lay facing each other and it struck Simon that Meredith looked sad. "Is there a guy in your life?" he asked.

"There is neither a guy nor a gal in my life at the moment. I haven't ruled either out."

Simon wondered whether Meredith had had any romantic expectations once he showed up at her door.

"This is not all your fault," Meredith said. "You had told me you were gay, and I should have told you no when you asked if my law school offer was still open."

"Don't go there," Simon said. "I should have walked out the door after your striptease didn't produce a rise in my interest."

Meredith laughed and for the first time in her presence, Simon felt himself relax. "We're a pair," he said.

"I'm hoping we come out of this friends," Meredith said. "And if you need help with the man in your life, let me know."

"It's a deal," Simon said, realizing that he did in fact want to talk. The hell with Carpenter preaching it was a mistake to become friends with a client. "Now, as to why I'm here, I was always…" He paused. "I was going to say I was always attracted to you but interested in you might be a better way to put it."

"What do you mean?"

"You were a force to be reckoned with in law school. As far as I could tell, you were the only student besides me who took on the professors in class. I noticed you. I was aware of you. You have no idea how close I came to saying yes when you came on to me."

"Should I be flattered?"

"You can be anything you want."

Meredith's expression turned serious. "Sometimes I think I'm a freak," she said. "Have you ever felt that way?"

"No," Simon replied, surprised he didn't really have to think about his answer. "Growing up I was often unhappy and frustrated. But I knew who I was and what I wanted, and I was okay with who I was. Why would you say something like that about yourself?"

Meredith sighed. "Because it's true. Because I'm a mess. Look at me. At the end of law school, I was attracted to you but had no clue you were gay. I was attracted to Cantor and probably would have taken up with her if she wasn't one of my bosses. And then tonight, I joined you in something I knew deep down was stupid. What the hell's the matter with me?"

"I don't know," Simon admitted. "I don't understand the way you're wired. But I do know that you're not a freak. If I had your smarts or Rachel's smarts, I'd be truly dangerous. You've got it all."

"A lot you know," Meredith said with a put-upon air that Simon knew was feigned. "But keep talking. I like what I'm hearing."

26

Daisy held up a dried-out oak leaf that had escaped last fall's raking.

Philly smiled, tried to show interest, but her mind was elsewhere. So far this morning she hadn't been a helpful spinning companion to Isabella, her mind flitting from topic to topic, at the moment settling on Sarah Ferguson after a stint of worrying about work.

"Very pretty, pumpkin. Can you find another one?"

Daisy clomped off and began to look intently about the backyard.

"I bet she starts talking this month," Isabella observed.

Philly nodded, only half paying attention to her daughter and Isabella.

"Are you all right?"

"Yeah," Philly said with a sigh that belied her assertion. "I talked to Sarah about getting her some help with the kids and she said she'd nose around. I guess I was secretly hoping she would say she didn't need help. Now she's got me really worried."

"Sarah's being practical. She's thinking ahead. It really is too much to ask of her to take care of three little ones. I don't think I could do it."

They were working on a simulated hill climb and Philly had noted that at the start of the ersatz hill, Isabella had ramped up the resistance on her bike. Philly was just too tired to add tension.

"Sarah knows the neighborhood," Isabella added. "If anyone can find someone to help it's her."

Isabella was talking sense, but Philly was in one of those moods where she preferred to nurse crabbiness.

Daisy moved close to her bike and held up a blackened mass that might once have been a leaf but was now unrecognizable.

"Thank you, pumpkin," Philly said as she got off her bike, scooped Daisy up, and held her daughter as she remounted the bike. She got her legs working and breathed in the scent of Daisy's flyaway hair. The morning was cool but pleasant. Philly was wearing a long-sleeved running shirt and her biking shorts. For the first time, Daisy was not in winter wear. Global warming had to be real if this morning was an accurate barometer of things to come.

"No fair," Isabella said. "You've got someone to help you."

Philly forced a smile. At the moment, her pregnancy appeared daunting. If she were to put on weight at the rate she had with Daisy, morning spins would shortly be a thing of the past. Dealing with work would be that much harder once she started to waddle around. Even with an extra set of hands—assuming a set could be found—she foresaw being overwhelmed by life in the near term.

"Cheer up!" Isabella said.

Philly forced another smile, but the smile turned real when Daisy started to babble. She wondered what was going on in her daughter's head. The nonsense words Daisy uttered never failed to raise her spirits. But then she thought of another complication she needed to deal with. Daisy needed to start interacting with kids her own age. Where the hell was she supposed to find them? For some reason she and Paul didn't want to resort to daycare.

"You're no fun," Isabella chided.

"Sorry," Philly said. "I've got a lot on my mind."

"Let me help. That's the whole idea of our communal living. We can help each other."

Philly believed she had come to terms with accepting help. Now she considered that she wasn't as far along on that path as she thought.

The gathering at the evening AA session in the basement of Saint Sebastian Church was well-attended. Philly counted more than thirty people. Her sponsor, Melanie, waved her over and she joined Melanie in the front row. Recently, Melanie had been more understanding about her sporadic attendance and tonight Philly was relieved to see that her sponsor was not regarding her with disappointment. Charlie, the group leader, was resplendent in one of his trademark Hawaiian shirts, this one bearing an orange and yellow pattern that would stand out anywhere but appeared particularly gaudy in the drab basement surroundings. Charlie clapped his hands and the room fell silent.

Charlie quickly determined that there were no new attendees. He asked whether anyone wanted to share and Philly promptly raised her hand surprising Melanie.

"I have some news," Philly began. "I'm pregnant. I'm due in September."

There was a smattering of applause and Melanie reached over to give her hand a squeeze.

"This morning I was exercising with one of the women I share a house with, and I started to feel overwhelmed. When my daughter was born, I didn't see how I was going to juggle motherhood and job, and I still don't have a clear idea of how I've been able to do that. But this morning I was visualizing a life with two little ones to take care of and I didn't see how I was going to make it work."

"Did any of this cause you to want to drink?" Charlie asked.

"No," Philly responded. "But it made me want to come here tonight and share, so I think subconsciously I may have been thinking of booze."

"You have a husband now," Melanie pointed out. "And by the way," she added, "the guy is a hunk." When the laughter subsided, Melanie grew serious. "I'm just saying that you're going to have help right at the start, which is something you didn't have before."

Melanie had made a valid point. Yet there was always a *but*. "You're right, but Paul works during the day and he can't work from home."

"I've seen how he is with your daughter," Melanie said. "He's wonderful and you know he's going to help with your second child."

Philly nodded. "I still felt overwhelmed this morning."

Charlie had been pacing behind the table he had placed in the front of the room. "We've talked about coping techniques when you're feeling overwhelmed," he reminded the group.

Philly sensed that her feeling this morning had touched on something deep and ultimately troubling and that standard coping techniques wouldn't do the trick. She didn't totally dismiss the idea that thinking positive thoughts, reaching out to Melanie, or trying relaxation techniques would be helpful. It was simply that her anxiety this morning was qualitatively different. "I've felt overwhelmed before," she said. "This morning was bad in a different way that I can't really explain."

"You came here to share with us," Charlie said. "That tells me you're not going to let yourself be overwhelmed without seeking help to fight back. That's a good thing. Second, you've recognized that this feeling you had this morning might be a prelude to a drinking issue. That's also important. It shows self-awareness and not wanting to drift back to a pattern that was destructive for you."

Charlie paused and Philly hoped that he'd continue. She had come to the meeting to hear someone suggest something she could do.

"If I remember correctly, you live in a house with a lot of people around," Charlie said. "I'd recommend mentioning your fears to your hunk and housemates."

Philly couldn't hold back a smile and Melanie was grinning broadly.

"If you and the hunk think it's a good idea," Charlie resumed, "I would bring up this feeling you had at a house meeting. You may find help is right there under your own roof."

What Charlie had just said was pretty much what Isabella had told her. Philly couldn't remember whether they had ever had a house meeting.

"Try these suggestions," Charlie urged. "And report back to us. Maybe you'll have a lesson for us."

Philly nodded reflexively.

"We must not forget your most important news," Charlie said. "Congratulations."

"Hip hip hooray," Melanie whispered, but Philly wasn't in the mood to cheer.

27

Paul spread the photographs found in Daryl Finch's bedroom on his desk. He idly moved them around, studying each new configuration. He began to make notes on what was common about the pictures: only boys were in the photographs; the head shots were blurry so it was difficult to make a facial identification; the markings on the bodies were similar; the chair displayed in about half the photographs looked to be the same. These common features didn't produce a breakthrough revelation, but Paul believed the exercise was useful.

Yesterday he'd talked to his captain about springing for the expense of a trip to Omaha; his superior officer viewed the Finch case as low priority—they may not be dealing with a crime. Evelyn would have to wait and delay wouldn't sit well with her. On one point he and his captain were agreed: publication of the photographs was premature.

Paul stacked the photographs and returned them to the case folder. His thoughts turned to Philly. Last night she was subdued, seemed troubled, and when he had asked how she was doing she had replied fine. He figured that her morning ritual was taking a toll: spinning, breakfast, throwing up. Now that Daisy was constantly on the move, Philly couldn't always carve out blocks of time to devote to her work. They hadn't had any alone time since their marriage and by alone time he meant time when Daisy wasn't present. That had to change—it wasn't good for any of them.

Rachel studied the financial information for Malcolm Atkins and Mary Ellen Pines produced in discovery. Last year—2011—each of the siblings was paid a base salary of $250,000. At the end of 2011, each sibling received a $15,000 bonus. Their company picked up their health insurance, disability insurance, and life insurance.

Malcolm Atkins' expenditures for 2011, including taxes, totaled $209,000 which meant that he was living within his salary. Malcolm's wife didn't work.

Mary Ellen Pines' expenses for 2011 including taxes topped $300,000. Her husband was a high school teacher who was paid a salary of $70,000. The Pines were pretty much spending whatever income they brought in. Medical expenses for Mary Ellen's family totaled nearly $50,000 last year. Uninsured medical expenses were eating up a major portion of the Pines' disposable income. Rachel placed a call to their client to ask about the situation.

"That has to be Timothy," Clyde Atkins explained. "He's their eight-year-old son. He's got autism and he's in a special school and has one-on-one sessions with a host of therapists. It's a sad situation. Medication helps somewhat, but the kid's got problems."

"Do they have other kids?"

"Two. The other two are fine. Timothy is not fine."

"Thanks," Rachel said after promising to send Atkins copies of his siblings' financial information.

Carpenter peered into her office. "Everything under control?" he asked.

"Pretty much," Rachel said, and she filled him in on the financial information she just reviewed.

"The sister won't be able to afford costly litigation," Carpenter said, "if the costs require a reduced salary draw. The sister is the weak link for the defendants."

"What are you getting at?" Rachel asked.

"Big firms paper you to death in litigation," Carpenter replied. "We're going to become a big firm. We're going to paper the defendants and take their depositions and generally drive them bat shit. Learner will do the same to us. When the company gets its first significant legal bill from Learner's firm, the brother and sister are going to have a coronary."

"But why would we stoop to doing what a big firm does?" Rachel persisted, concerned that she was missing something obvious.

"To bring the sister and brother to the negotiating table. Remember, our client may want the opportunity to be bought out by his siblings or to buy them out. Putting financial pressure on the siblings is a way to make that happen."

"So we're going to take advantage of the sister because she has a kid with serious disabilities?"

"That's exactly what we're going to do," Carpenter said without any apparent misgivings.

Rachel wanted to show appropriate aggressiveness, but she didn't like taking advantage of Mary Ellen Pines' misfortune.

"Do you think Learner would try to use leverage if our client had a kid with medical problems?" Carpenter asked, and Rachel realized that her own reservations had been evident.

"I guess so," Rachel said.

"Of course he would. Learner's a shark. He'd stick it to Clyde Atkins in any way he could."

'This sucks,' Rachel thought. "It's great to be in a big firm," is what she said.

"Great sex is supposed to cheer you up," Josh said, as his right hand stroked her side, briefly cupping her hip whenever it landed there.

Rachel didn't say anything. She continued to nurse her discomfort over Carpenter's strategy to take advantage of Mary Ellen Pines' sick child.

"Are you going to fill me in on what's bugging you?"

"What makes you think something's bugging me?" Rachel snapped.

Josh started laughing in earnest and Rachel willed herself not to join in. Which was no small task. Josh's enjoyment was contagious. He was happy with his life, and why not? Teaching tennis and golf didn't involve gut wrenching decisions on whether to take advantage of someone's misfortune.

Josh settled down. "You forget I'm a poker player," he said. "Admittedly I'm out of practice since the government has shut down online poker. And true, online poker doesn't involve face-to-face contact. But you have no poker face. You're plainly upset and that's not like you."

Rachel had to constantly remind herself not to underestimate Josh. With his long dirty blond hair, a tan that never totally faded even in winter, and a tall, finely muscled body, he often came across as a laid-back, slacker jock. But he was competitive and perceptive. "All right," she said, and related to Josh her discussion with Carpenter.

As Josh took his time considering her account, Rachel realized that she had never seen him in a hurry. He approached anything that came his way in a calm, deliberative manner. His hand continued to stroke her side and Rachel felt herself getting aroused again. Maybe arousal had to do with unburdening herself to Josh.

"I think Carpenter is right," Josh said. "I'm not saying what he wants to do is nice. But you guys have a client to represent and Carpenter wants to be aggressive to help your client get what he wants. It's not like he's suggesting anything illegal."

"Some help you are!"

"We've talked about this," Josh said. "Your natural instinct is to be nice. It's one of many things I love about you. But there are times when what you have to do is not nice. There are times when you have to be aggressive and combative."

Rachel wondered whether Clyde Atkins would agree that his nephew's illness should be used to his advantage.

"Let's say I'm playing tennis," Josh said, "and my opponent slips and, when he gets up, he's favoring his left leg. I play to win and I'd do whatever I could to take advantage of my opponent's injury. I'd try to run him around, try to get him to aggravate the injury. And I have to tell you, I can't think of a guy I've played against who wouldn't do the same to me. If I was hurt and my opponent didn't try to take advantage of my injury, I would lose respect for him."

Rachel reflected that she didn't have a killer instinct and wondered whether you could be a lawyer without one.

"Being a lawyer must be great," Josh said.

"Why is that?"

"You get paid to be a prick."

'Great,' Rachel thought. She snuggled closer to Josh. She hadn't much liked what he'd said, but she did feel less grumpy having heard it.

"Feeling better?"

"Besides my being nice, what else do you love about me?" Rachel asked. It never got tired hearing Josh praise her good points.

"I love it that you're beautiful and smart and that you put up with me. I love it that I trust you completely and I can say anything to you."

Rachel thought about Philly's pregnancy announcement. Josh had damn well better be the father of her kids.

28

In this morning's mail was a motion by Pinkerton, Ashley & Rosewood to dismiss the complaint filed by Meredith Sweeney with the Massachusetts Commission Against Discrimination. That was no surprise. What did surprise Carpenter was that the law firm had taken less than half the permitted time to file its motion. Carpenter believed that his suspicion had been confirmed: Stephanie Manley was a plant who had informed Pinkerton that Meredith was going to sue. The law firm must have begun preparing its response before the suit was filed.

Carpenter studied Meredith across the conference room table. She'd been working in the nearby library in the courthouse where the commonwealth's appellate courts conducted their business when Rachel's e-mail informed her of the law firm's action. She had arranged to come over to pick up her copy of the pleadings. Carpenter was impressed. Meredith was reviewing a document that substantially affected her life but, observing her, you might have concluded that she was reading a weather report.

Carpenter had gone through the Pinkerton firm's papers twice as had Simon and Rachel. Big firms had a way about them. Any legal memorandum they submitted was crammed with citations and was written in a style that showed barely concealed contempt for the position of the opposing party. An affidavit from Gwen Cantor denied Meredith's sexual harassment allegations. Another affidavit from a managing partner of the firm—Eleanor Hightower—detailed the thorough investigation of Meredith's harassment charge and the lack of any evidence to substantiate her claim. She pointed to Meredith's negative two-year evaluation as the primary reason for terminating Meredith's employment.

Meredith finished her reading and looked up as Simon and Rachel entered the room. "There's nothing unexpected here," Meredith said, and this assessment coincided with Carpenter's own. "How are we going to get into evidence the firm's policy about giving all associates a negative two-year review?"

"We've requested copies of all two-year associate reviews for the six months before and after your review," Carpenter said. "We'll argue that the firm's motion to dismiss should not be acted upon until we have that information."

"The firm talks about that in its legal memorandum," Rachel said. "Its position is that reviews of other associates are irrelevant and also confidential."

"The firm can redact names for all I care," Carpenter said.

"But what do we say is the basis for thinking that the two-year reviews will all be negative?" Meredith asked.

"As a last resort," Carpenter replied, "we can submit an affidavit from McCauley saying he interviewed a partner who will not consent to be named and was informed by that partner of the firm's policy."

"That's going to open up discovery as to who that partner is," Rachel said. "The guy's name is going to come out and McCauley may not want to compromise the guy."

"Maybe McCauley should take another run at him," Simon suggested. "Maybe the guy would agree to McCauley filing an affidavit along the lines you mentioned."

Meredith stood. "I've got to run," she said. "You guys need to figure this out."

'Easier said than done,' Carpenter thought, as Meredith made her exit.

Herb didn't want to have this discussion on the phone. He had followed Gregory Madison to the same deli where they had their initial meeting. He waited for Madison to order lunch and take a seat and then approached his table.

"Sorry to bother you, Mr. Madison, but I'd like a minute of your time."

The attorney looked up and it took him a moment to place Herb. "Have a seat."

"Thanks. I see that you remember me."

"Mr. McCauley. I was wondering whether I might hear from you again. Or maybe it was *when* I might hear from you again."

Herb sat down. He owed it to Madison to be as direct as he was at their first meeting. Madison didn't seem bothered that his lunch was being interrupted. The lawyer was calm, focused.

"Your former firm has moved to dismiss my client's sexual harassment claim. The firm is relying on her two-year evaluation to say she wasn't doing a good job. I told you that I wouldn't use your name. What I would like to do is file an affidavit that doesn't mention you but does say that I spoke with a former partner who wishes to remain anonymous but informed me that all associates received negative two-year evaluations. I would like your permission to do this."

Madison sighed. "If you file such an affidavit, it is likely that my name would surface. If you've talked to the lawyers representing… Ms. Sweeney, isn't it?... they probably told you as much. I probably shouldn't have told you about the firm's two-year negative evaluation policy. I believe there's something in the partnership agreement I signed that required me to keep the firm's policies confidential. I thought about that after we met."

Madison was raising the point that the Pinkerton firm might sue him. Herb felt for the guy. There was nothing Madison could do if Herb broke his word and named Madison as the source of his information. "Shit!" Herb said.

"My sentiments exactly," Madison said.

"Are you saying that you don't want me to file the affidavit that I just mentioned?" Herb asked.

"It would make my life easier if you didn't file the affidavit. There's probably nothing I can do to stop you from filing whatever you want. You told me you wouldn't use my name but if you did, I don't suppose there's a hell of a lot I could do about it."

"Is that a no?" Herb asked.

Madison took a bite of his sandwich and became lost in thought. Herb wondered whether he could live with himself if he broke his word to Madison.

"You don't need my permission to file the affidavit you want to file," Madison said. "Nevertheless, you have it."

"Wow!" Herb exclaimed.

"Wow indeed."

Herb marveled at the guts people displayed at unexpected moments. Here was Madison giving permission to do something that could come back to haunt him. It was guys like Madison who belied Barney's belief that nobody acted against self-interest. "Why are you doing this?"

Madison shrugged. "The senior partners at Pinkerton never treated me very well at the end. They showed no genuine concern for my son's recovery after his accident. Therefore, I don't feel any strong duty of loyalty to them. If they come after me, so be it. I've talked this over with my wife and she's okay with this. Pinkerton's two-year evaluation policy was dishonest. I'll take my chances if they learn about me and sue me. Maybe you'll be able to recommend a good lawyer if they take me to court."

"The ones representing Sweeney appear to be on their game."

"They're going to need to be. Pinkerton will fight Sweeney's suit to the death."

"I could mention in the affidavit that you're concerned about retaliation," Herb said.

"Please don't do that. That would be a mistake on many levels."

Herb nodded. Madison was right. "Ms. Sweeney and her counsel will be grateful to you. Thank you."

"Don't mention it," Madison said. "I want you to do two things for me. First, I want you to send me a copy of your affidavit. I don't need to review it before it's filed." Madison took out a business card and began writing on the back. "Send the copy to my home address. Second, if you file an affidavit, I want a call from you telling me the time and place of the hearing on the motion to dismiss Sweeney's case."

The last request surprised Herb. "Are you thinking about attending the hearing?"

"Thinking is the operative word. That's all I'm doing. Thinking about it." Madison paused. "I wrote my cell phone number on the card I just gave you. I'm probably not going to attend the motion hearing. But if, during the hearing, Sweeney's lawyer wishes to talk to me, my cell phone will be on."

29

Simon and Rachel sat side by side in the conference room going over a report Barney Freedman sent to them on Guiding Light Construction Contractors, LLC, the company that Gwen Carson brought in as a client to Pinkerton, Ashley & Rosewood through a family connection. Carson's uncle was an officer of the company and no doubt a part-owner. The building contractor had several major construction projects underway in suburbs to the north and west of Boston. Simon considered the legal work a major building contractor threw off: the negotiation and drafting of construction contracts, subcontractor contracts, sorting through complaints by a construction project's owner of shoddy work, and arbitration proceedings to resolve disputes that couldn't be settled informally. He puzzled over why having brought in such a substantial client, Gwen Carson hadn't been made a senior partner. Perhaps she was a lousy lawyer.

"How does any of this help us?" Rachel asked.

"How does any of what help us?" Carpenter said as he entered the conference room and took a seat.

"We were looking over Barney's report on the client Gwen Carson brought to the Pinkerton firm," Simon replied. "We can't think of anything it would accomplish."

"I'll take a look at it," Carpenter said in an offhand way. "I think it was worth a gamble. You never know what will turn up. Maybe we can claim that the firm sided with Cantor to make sure the client she brought in wouldn't bolt the firm. But you're probably right; there may be no way to use the information."

"I've drafted an affidavit for McCauley to sign," Rachel said. "I think it's great that McCauley was able to get this lawyer Madison to agree to the affidavit."

"I agree," Carpenter said.

"Do we have to file the affidavit with our papers opposing Pinkerton's motion to dismiss?" Simon asked.

"That was the whole purpose of having McCauley contact Madison," Carpenter said. "If we don't file the affidavit, the hearing officer will never see it."

"Can we file the affidavit at the hearing on the motion to dismiss?" Simon persisted.

"Where the hell are you going with this?" Carpenter demanded. "A hearing officer may not let you file the affidavit at the hearing because Pinkerton wouldn't have seen the affidavit before the hearing."

"The Pinkerton firm didn't bring in an outside law firm to defend this suit," Simon replied. "Pinkerton is defending itself. I think we can do some damage to them at the hearing."

"I'm not following you," Carpenter said, and Simon saw that Rachel looked equally puzzled.

Simon laid out what he was thinking and was relieved to see what passed for a smile appear briefly on Carpenter's face.

"You're saying keep the affidavit in reserve, take our chances that the hearing officer might not let it into evidence, and see if your idea will work," Carpenter summarized.

Simon nodded. "I guess that's what I'm saying."

"What do you think?" Carpenter turned to Rachel.

"I like Simon's approach," Rachel said. "No matter what happens before the administrative agency, we're going to move this case to court because we want a jury trial. So I don't think it ultimately matters what happens before the administrative agency. Plus, maybe we can keep Madison's name out of it, which he would appreciate."

Carpenter went into one of his trances. His gaze wandered and his jaw muscles began grinding. "Okay," he finally said. "But make sure that Sweeney's affidavit contains an allegation that she believes the two-year evaluation was a fraud that was perpetrated on her. You can base her statement on the fact that her work had never been criticized before the evaluation."

"You're probably wondering why I called us all together," Philly began, striving for a light tone as she took in the confusion on the faces of three of her housemates. Paul was the only one who had been briefed on what she intended to say. They were seated in the living room following dinner and the washing up. Sarah had joined Raul and Isabella on the couch and she and Paul occupied the easy chairs. Daisy and Rosalind were down for the night.

"A little while back I had this overwhelming feeling of panic. I was thinking ahead to child number two being born and it occurred to me that I had no idea how I was going to deal with *two* little ones, what should be a full-time job, and all the minutia of everyday life. Even with Sarah's help, I didn't see how I was going to keep it all together. I brought this up at an AA meeting and the group leader reminded me that I wasn't alone, that I had you guys. He wanted me to share this feeling with you and report back on how that went."

Raul's expression was unreadable. Isabella immediately relaxed, which probably meant she had anticipated something graver than what she had just heard. Sarah looked concerned.

"I just want to clarify one thing. I don't want Sarah to think that I want her to do more. If it were possible, I'd like her to do less. I feel guilty that sometimes I forget that Sarah has a life that doesn't center around Daisy and Rosalind. Paul and I are still reluctant to send Daisy to daycare."

Sarah offered a weak smile, but Philly couldn't tell whether she was reassured.

"I would like to say something," Raul announced, as he put an arm around Isabella. Raul looked good, Philly thought. He had remained thin and wiry with soulful eyes.

"I feel that I have not pulled my weight in our communal project. I leave the house early every morning because world markets never sleep. I return home late because world markets never sleep. I like to cook but my schedule has prevented me from making my share of our dinners. This is something that I have discussed with my business partner, Connie."

Philly hadn't thought about Carpenter's former significant other in some time. She and Raul ran a boutique international investment firm. Last year Carpenter had defended Connie's husband against a sexual harassment complaint.

"We are going to hire an employee," Raul continued. "This should free up my time. We have made clear to the candidates that the job requires long hours. I hope to be free of my early morning departures and many late-night returns. I will be around to do more."

"Raul and I have decided that I will continue to work only part-time," Isabella added. "I may have to fill in from time to time, but I'll be available most afternoons."

"I'm going to need some help," Sarah said, and Philly saw how difficult it was for her to make the request.

"Any luck finding some backup?" Paul asked Sarah.

"I'm looking," Sarah replied. "The problem is that the neighborhood has changed. I've lived here forever but a lot of the people I knew have moved. Not to mention passed away."

"Are you still happy with our arrangement?" Paul followed up.

"Yes," Sarah said, and Philly was relieved that Sarah sounded like she meant it. "But there are times when it does get wearing."

"Do you still have friends your own age who live around here?" Paul asked next, and Philly realized that since they had moved into this house, Sarah had never had visitors.

"The people I was close to are no longer around," Sarah said. "The ones who are left are more like casual acquaintances."

"Do you use the senior center?" Paul asked.

"Not really."

Philly realized that their oldest housemate was basically alone. The people in this room were her available family.

"Philly and I have been trying to figure out how to find little kids for Daisy to play with," Paul said. "It makes me think you might want to try the senior center to see if you like it."

"Are you saying I need to play with people my own age?" Sarah said with a forced smile.

"I guess I am," Paul said. "I think you might enjoy getting out of the house on some of your free time. I hope you give it a try."

"Just the name 'senior center' makes me feel old," Sarah groused.

"You're not old," Paul said with some force. "And speaking of getting out of the house, Philly and I want to take a long weekend. Without Daisy."

Philly smiled when silence followed Paul's pronouncement.

"We'll take Rosalind when you guys want a getaway alone," Paul told Raul and Isabella. "What do you say to a weekend swap?"

"I say that is a wonderful idea," Raul replied.

"So how do you feel now?" Isabella asked Philly. "What will you report back to your AA group?"

"I'm glad we talked," Philly said, meaning it. "I'm going to tell the group leader he had a good idea. The key to all this is getting backup for Sarah. If we can pull that off, I think we'll be okay."

"Let me see what I can do," Sarah said, and Philly was pleased with her upbeat tone.

30

Paul sat down at his desk across from Evelyn's just as she finished making on-line reservations to Omaha. Their captain had unexpectedly given them the okay, told them to get on it before he changed his mind, and Evelyn had taken him at his word. Paul had decided that Evelyn was the one to make the trip and she was pleased that he had.

"We need to talk through how you're going to proceed once you get to Omaha," Paul said. "We get one shot at this, so we need to make it count."

Evelyn had made arrangements to stay two nights. Essentially, she had forty-eight hours to complete her investigation. "I'm going to rent a car. Jacqueline Templeton lives in a suburb north of the city. I figured I'd check out the house. I've got tech guys working over the yearbook pages to come up with aged images of Templeton and Heather Finch. I'm hoping that I get to see two women who look like the women in the aged photographs."

"What if you only see the Templeton woman?"

"Then I confront her. I don't have all that much time."

Paul drummed his fingers on his desktop. 'God, the guy was good-looking,' Evelyn thought. She was grateful that he'd never made a pass at her or directed an off-color joke her way. She'd put up with enough of that crap before being assigned to work with him, but she couldn't totally suppress the part of her that made her wish he would. She had seen a picture of his wife and the woman was not what she'd expected: short and compact with tight black curls and a complexion so pale it made you wonder if sunlight had ever touched her features.

"Say you confront Templeton. What are you going to say?"

Evelyn hadn't fully organized her thoughts on the subject. "I'll introduce myself and remind her that we talked on the phone and she pretty much blew me off. I'll ask to talk to her and if she says no, I was planning to tell her that it was important we speak, that children's lives might be at risk if our department didn't get some answers to some questions we thought Heather Finch could help us with."

"I like that approach. You've kept it vague and haven't really told her anything. Laying a guilt trip on her if she doesn't talk is a nice touch. But what if she still won't talk to you?"

"I'm not above begging. I'll plead with her. If she still says no, I'll have to leave. I was thinking about asking the locals for help."

"I'll talk to the captain," Paul said. "I doubt we know anyone in the Omaha PD, but maybe we can reach out to them anyway. Lay it on thick. Maybe suggest that a grand jury may be convened in Cambridge and once that happens, the grand jury will be looking for ways to obtain statements from witnesses wherever they are."

A Cambridge grand jury couldn't compel an out-of-state witness to come to Cambridge, so Evelyn was surprised that Paul was willing to suggest that could happen.

"Yeah, I know. That's stretching things," Paul admitted as if reading her mind. "But I keep thinking about those pictures and those boys and it bugs the hell out of me."

"I want to be clear about something," Evelyn said. "From what the captain said, I can't mention what's in the photographs or show them to Templeton."

"That's correct."

"What if Finch is living with Templeton and I get to confront her?"

"I think you know what to do," Paul said.

"If Finch is there, at least one question will be answered."

"What's that?" Paul asked.

"Why Templeton joined a cooking club when she had no interest in cooking."

"I can't believe you're not going with an affidavit from McCauley! McCauley busted his ass to get that lawyer to agree to his filing an affidavit."

Simon took a deep breath. Meredith had read the documents that they planned to file opposing the Pinkerton firm's motion to dismiss her case, and she had called *him* even though Rachel had drafted most of the submission and had forwarded the papers to her. He was seated behind Philly's desk and was relieved that Rachel was not using the other workstation in the office.

"There's a method to our madness," he replied evenly. "We think this approach could work to your advantage in a big way." After he explained the strategy, Meredith fell silent.

"I don't want to risk a hearing officer ruling that there's no probable cause for my sexual harassment claim," Meredith finally said. "I don't want those bastards to have any moment of satisfaction that they bested me in anything."

"You have a point. But even if a hearing officer finds no probable cause for discrimination, you can still bring your case to court. But if the hearing officer does stick it to your former firm, you will have scored a major victory, both real and psychological, that will have Pinkerton on the run or at least having to consider that it could lose. I think it's worth the risk going with our approach."

"I don't like it," Meredith muttered.

Meredith, Simon realized, might be the proverbial difficult client. She would likely immerse herself in every strategy decision and insist on reviewing and approving every document filed on her behalf. True, she had paid them a retainer and had every right to be involved in *her* case. But micromanaging to a fault might hurt her chances of winning.

"It's ultimately your call," Simon said. "I've told you what we collectively think. Why don't you think about it and get back to Rachel or me?"

"You're probably convinced I'm going to be one of those difficult clients who won't let you do your job."

"There's no 'probably,'" Simon said, striving for both candidness and humor.

"Very funny. Okay, go with what you want to do. I don't like it, but I'll go along. When do you think there will be a hearing?"

"After we file our papers, I think a hearing will be scheduled promptly."

"I can hardly wait."

31

Paul chose a B&B on the outskirts of Falmouth that had ten rooms to rent for his Cape weekend getaway with Philly. When they checked in, the owner told them that only two of the other rooms had been rented so they pretty much had the place to themselves. Philly rolled her eyes when they were shown their room. Knickknacks occupied every flat surface and there were frilly curtains and a frilly fringe on the soft, queen-sized bed. Paul kept a straight face and assured the owner that the room was just fine.

They had left Brighton early in the morning and now it was approaching noon. They were walking slowly and holding hands, meandering along the waterline of Chapoquoit Beach, a beach that Carpenter had put in a plug for. The sun was bright and Paul figured it was wearing sunglasses that contributed to his upbeat feeling that he'd stepped out of his life for some earned R&R. No one was in the water. There was a slight chill in the air and a breeze met them head on, but the March day felt like a day in late spring. They passed a couple seated in folding chairs well back from the water. In another hundred feet, they would pass another couple seated close to the rock wall that served as a buffer for the parking area. Otherwise the beach was deserted.

"This is nice," Philly said.

Paul gave her hand a squeeze. She was wearing one of the heavy sweatshirts she had used for spinning in the winter topped by a windbreaker. Her Boston Red Sox cap barely contained her curls and her running shoes left crisscross indentations on the hard sand. Her recent admission that she was feeling overwhelmed had brought him up short. It struck Paul that he typically observed Philly in two modes: one where she was doing battle on a case or determinedly dealing with her home life, and the other, which belied the first, when she appeared fragile. He'd first met her shortly after she had arrived at the hospital where Daisy's father had been taken after being struck by a drunk driver. That was as fragile as she was ever going to be. At least, he hoped so. Then there was her courage as she dealt with her pregnancy and drinking problem, and her tenacity in dealing with a law practice and orchestrating the move to their present house. It had been such a long stretch of Philly dealing with whatever life threw at her that he had forgotten the time when she was on the verge of breaking down. Maybe her drinking should have been a tip off that any brave façade she presented thinly masked vulnerability that could surface in a flash.

"Do you think Daisy has given us a thought?" Philly asked.

Paul laughed. They had kissed Daisy before leaving and had said bye-bye, but Daisy was crawling around the living room with Rosalind and had paid them no mind. "She took our leaving well," he said.

They reached a low rock wall and turned around. The wind was to their backs and the sun's glare disappeared.

"How did you know I needed this?" Philly said.

"You? I wasn't thinking about you. *I* needed this."

"Very funny. I'm sorry I got so panicky these past days. I don't know what came over me."

"Has the panicky feeling gone away?"

Philly shrugged. "It feels that way. Right at this moment, it's hard to feel panicky."

Paul thought about what he wanted to say next. "It's okay to feel overwhelmed; everyone does at some time or another. If you ever get that feeling again, the only thing I ask is that you tell me and not keep it to yourself." He had stopped himself from saying *when* you get that feeling again.

"You don't seem to panic over anything," Philly said.

"A lot you know. I'm as nervous as you about life with another little one. There are times when I feel overwhelmed by the cases I'm working on, particularly when I'm not making headway."

"You seem to be coping pretty well."

"Some of it is putting up a brave front. But remember, I've been shot at. When I think about that, everything else becomes less scary."

"Do you think if I was shot at my perspective would change?"

Philly was plainly joking but Paul sensed a nugget of seriousness in her question. "I wouldn't recommend getting shot at under any circumstances," he said. "In your case, if you think about all you've been through and conquered, I think you'll find your perspective changing without the need for gunfire."

Philly gave him a playful bump, and he held her closer.

"Feed me," Philly said.

"I can do that."

"We're on the freaking Cape. Fish."

"Fish it is."

"I know you told me," Frank said, "but now I want details."

Simon had been dreading this discussion. Previously, also by phone, he'd told Frank that he'd taken the girl he mentioned up on her offer but hadn't elaborated. Now the only saving grace was they were again on the phone. If he had to meet Frank's steady, probing look in a face-to-face meeting, he'd crack in seconds. "There are no details worth discussing," he said halfheartedly.

"Don't give me that. Did you actually screw her?"

Simon felt himself redden even though Frank wasn't present. This was beyond embarrassing. "I'm not sure."

"What do you mean, you're not sure?"

"For a while I couldn't get it up and then there was a lot going on on her part. I closed my eyes, but I couldn't focus on anything. I must have got hard at some point. I really don't want to talk about this."

"Did you come?"

"Yeah."

"You're just not sure where?"

"Something like that. As I said, my eyes were closed, and part of me was trying not to think about what was happening."

Simon was grateful that Frank wasn't laughing.

"Are you involved in this woman's case?"

Simon realized that he had never mentioned Meredith by name to Frank. "Big time. I think she's looking to me to lead her charge."

"That's got to be awkward."

"Not really," Simon said, somewhat surprised that he could answer honestly. "That part is going to be okay." Whatever the hell had happened with Meredith had broken down any real and imaginary barriers he had been wrestling with when it came to her representation.

"Lawyers!" Frank said disgustedly.

"She made me a promise and I want you to make the same one."

"What was it?"

"We are to never speak of this again."

Frank paused and Simon didn't think it was for effect.

"Fine," Frank said. "Are you doing okay?"

"I am now."

32

Evelyn parked her rental car on a quiet residential street and studied Jacqueline Templeton's house across the street, a small ranch with white aluminum siding and not much of a front lawn. She felt conspicuous. The street had the feel of closely-knit neighbors keeping an eye on each other's property. The longer she sat without leaving her car, the more likely she would attract unwelcome attention. She decided to give it no more than thirty minutes before approaching the house. Although she had confirmed her arrival with the Omaha PD, she hadn't wanted local law enforcement on the scene. Yet.

Evelyn trained her binoculars on each window she could observe from her car. It was seven-thirty in the morning on a Saturday and there was no movement inside the house. A newspaper lay on the walk leading up to the front door, so she assumed that someone was around, perhaps sleeping in.

It was a cloudy, gray day. As her thirty-minute countdown continued, Evelyn felt her eyes growing heavy.

When the front door opened, it took Evelyn a moment to focus. The woman who retrieved the paper stood up, stared at her car, and turned back to the house. Even without binoculars, Evelyn knew that she was looking at Jacqueline Templeton. The aged photograph of the woman had accurately tracked her maturation.

There was no reason for further delay. Evelyn started her car, drove forward, and did a U-turn that landed her in front of Templeton's house. She wished she had her service revolver.

She knocked three times on the front door and waited. When the door opened, she was confronted with a cold look from a diminutive woman with blond hair and bright blue eyes.

"Ms. Templeton? My name is Evelyn Rodriguez. We spoke on the phone a while back. I explained to you that I was trying to get in touch with Heather Finch."

Templeton's expression didn't change. Evelyn half expected the woman to close the door.

"I remember the call. I told you then that I wasn't able to help you and nothing's changed."

"May I come in?"

"I don't see why. I don't have to talk to you and I'm not inclined to do so."

Evelyn had had it with persons of interest in this case refusing to give her the time of day. "Suit yourself," she said. "I've flown here from Cambridge, Massachusetts because it's important that I talk to Ms. Finch. The Cambridge Police Department has reason to believe that there's a predator out there preying on little kids. Somehow, Heather Finch's father is involved. Since her father's dead, I need to talk to her to try to prevent another child being put in danger."

Templeton's surprised look told Evelyn that the woman hadn't been expecting the purpose of her visit. True, she'd laid it on thick. She may have varied the approach that Paul had signed off on, but she thought that she was still pretty much on-script.

"Maybe you better come in."

Evelyn followed Templeton to a depressingly small living room. A threadbare couch was backed against one wall and two drab easy chairs faced it. There were no pictures on the walls. The room looked barely lived in. Templeton sat down on the couch and Evelyn took the easy chair closest to her. There were no sounds coming from the rest of the house so perhaps Templeton lived alone.

"I didn't follow what you said about Heather's father," Templeton said.

Evelyn noted the use of the first name. "I'll get to that," she said. "First, I want to confirm that I'm talking to Jacqueline Templeton."

"That's me."

"Do you know where Heather Finch is?"

"I'm not going to talk to you about Heather or anyone else until you answer my question. What's her father got to do with anything?"

Evelyn considered turning up the aggression. She wanted to control this conversation.

"While you're thinking about my question, how about some identification?"

Evelyn offered her badge and Templeton took it, left the room, and returned with a piece of notepaper and a pencil. She resumed her seat and began to copy information from the badge.

When Templeton handed the badge back, Evelyn decided against waging a battle of wills. "Ms. Finch's father died alone. He'd been living in an assisted living facility. He hadn't provided the facility with any next of kin information. In fact, he was using a false name. The facility staff packed up his things and discovered some disturbing information that involved children and called our department. Does that answer your question?"

Templeton was staring at her open-mouthed and Evelyn knew that she had taken control of the situation.

"Do you have a cell phone?" Templeton asked. "I'm going to need to get back to you."

Evelyn rattled off her mobile number and Templeton wrote it down.

"I don't have much time," Evelyn decided to press. "I need you to tell me whether you can help me get in touch with Heather Finch. Either you can or you can't. Why can't you just tell me?"

Templeton shook her head and Evelyn had to acknowledge that the woman looked torn.

"I just can't. You need to go. I'm not going to say another thing."

"Well I am. I don't know what game you're playing but it had damn well better stop. You probably don't know what obstruction of justice is, but I do, and I can tell you that's what I think you're up to. You're making a big mistake by not cooperating with me."

"You need to go," Templeton repeated. "And if you keep trying to threaten me, you can go to hell."

Templeton's anger was genuine. Evelyn had probably misjudged the woman and had never been in control of this conversation.

"When will you get back to me?"

"I'm hoping it will be early evening. Where are you staying?"

Evelyn provided the name of her motel and Templeton turned her notepaper over to record the information.

"I know my way out," Evelyn said, getting to her feet. "And for the record—you should feel threatened. If you don't do the right thing here, threats will be the least of your worries."

"Fuck you," Templeton snapped as Evelyn moved to the front door.

Paul looked up through the trees and caught a glimpse of pale blue sky. "I feel guilty," he said to Philly. "I've packed Evelyn off to Omaha and I probably should have been the one to make that trip." They had rented bikes in Dennis and were now bicycling along the Cape Cod Rail Trail toward Provincetown. Philly had finally gotten him on a bike.

"Better her than you," Philly said. "This is glorious."

"How far are we going to go?" he asked. Philly was pedaling effortlessly. With all the spinning time she'd put in, she could probably make it to Provincetown without breathing hard. He didn't think he'd be so lucky. He felt like he was using muscles for the first time.

Philly shrugged. "We'll go until you wimp out or I get hungry, whichever comes first."

Paul reflected that Philly was doing a better job than he was of putting work out of mind. It was as if she had downshifted to a lower gear. Last night's lovemaking had been different: languid, unhurried, no urgency. That hadn't happened in a while.

"Having fun?" Philly asked.

"Yes, definitely."

"Does this mean I'm going to get you to go biking with me?"

"Let's not get totally carried away."

Paul thought of Evelyn rattling around an unfamiliar city. If she didn't make a breakthrough in the case, they were nowhere. The case would be moved to a burner so far back it would never be seen again. Then again, was it really a case?

"That was fun saying good night to Daisy last night," Philly said.

"I loved the lullaby," Paul said, grinning at the thought of Philly's out of tune rendition of "Rock-A-Bye Baby."

"I wonder what she made of our voices?"

"She was babbling," Paul replied, remembering Daisy's nonstop, unintelligible chattering even during the lullaby.

They emerged from the trees and the sun was directly overhead. In unison they donned sunglasses.

"You know, if you're worried you could call Evelyn on her cell," Philly said.

Paul shook his head. Philly had picked up on him thinking about work. "No. She's a big girl. She can handle herself."

Nothing felt right to Evelyn about this meeting. The strip mall was nearly deserted. The sun had gone down but there was still light. Most of the stores had closed. A proprietor was locking up. Evelyn had considered letting her Omaha PD contact know what was up, but Templeton had threatened to back out of the meeting if she didn't show up alone, and her OPD contact would have insisted on backup surveillance.

She drove slowly toward the far end of the parking lot where Templeton had instructed her to wait. She suspected that Templeton wouldn't show up until dark. Again she wished that she had her service revolver with her.

Evelyn got out of her car and stretched. She considered the possibility that Templeton would arrive with protection—men. Paul would be irate; he would never have permitted either one of them to go it alone in this situation.

Evelyn tried to relax as darkness took over. She leaned against the driver's side door and began to breathe deeply, letting the air in through her nose, out through her mouth.

The minutes passed slowly. When the last car left the strip mall parking lot, dark had settled. Evelyn's eyes adjusted to the night. She heard a car before she saw it; when she turned, a car was approaching from the direction she had taken. The car cut its lights and came to a stop twenty feet from her own car. Templeton got out of the car on the driver's side. Evelyn thought she saw someone sitting in the passenger seat.

Templeton approached. "You can talk to Heather for thirty minutes, no more, no less. Are we clear?"

Evelyn nodded and Templeton waved toward her car. The passenger-side door opened. The woman who came into view was taller and larger than Templeton. The black eyeglasses and long, springy dark hair hadn't changed much since Finch's high school yearbook photograph. In her age-advanced photograph, Finch had been depicted with worry lines on her forehead and a pinched expression. This woman didn't look like she had a care in the world.

"I understand you want to speak with me," Finch said.

"I do," Evelyn said, noting that the two women were maintaining a distance of several yards.

"Then get to it," Templeton said.

"Why all the cloak and dagger stuff?" Evelyn asked.

"You're wasting time," Templeton replied.

"When's the last time you saw your father?"

"Probably fifteen years ago."

"Were you aware he died before I mentioned that fact to Ms. Templeton?"

Finch shook her head.

"Would you be willing to go back to Cambridge to make your own identification of your father?"

"No."

"May I ask why?"

Finch took a deep breath and sighed as she exhaled. "It probably has to do with the fact that he was a shit."

"When's the last time you saw your brothers?"

Finch's scowl was barely visible. Templeton moved closer to her.

"That would also be about fifteen years ago."

"Have your brothers or father been in touch with you in those fifteen years?"

"No."

"Your brothers know you're here in Omaha, right?"

"Unfortunately," Finch said with some heat. "That shouldn't have happened, but it did."

A picture began to emerge for Evelyn. "But I'm guessing your brothers don't know where exactly you're living."

"Right," Finch said.

"And it needs to stay that way," Templeton added.

Perhaps Finch was using an alias. That might explain why a search for Heather Finch in Omaha had turned up nothing. "Do you have any idea why your father would have evidence of young boys who look like they'd been abused?"

Finch shook her head. "Not really. Jackie told me what you had said about disturbing information. Maybe he just liked torturing young boys. He used to beat the shit out of my brothers, and I think the sick fuck enjoyed it."

"Your brothers say he never laid a hand on you. Why do you think that was?"

"I couldn't tell you. He just didn't."

Evelyn was running out of questions. She consulted her notepad. She felt that she was missing something that was in plain view.

"Do the letters LFLS mean anything to you?"

Finch flashed a brief smile. "Like father, like son. My brothers came up with that."

Evelyn jotted down Finch's answer. "Why did they come up with that?"

"Because they figured that they would end up as abusers."

"Did they?"

"You could say that."

"Who did they abuse?'

"Who the hell do you think?"

Templeton put her arm around Finch's waist. Evelyn felt her heart racing and she again resorted to deep breaths to calm down. "Did you ever do anything about that?"

"I left."

Evelyn tried to make connections. "You two are living in the house I was at this morning, right?"

"Ask another question," Templeton said.

"Did you keep track of where your father was over the last fifteen years?"

"No."

Evelyn closed her notepad. If there was a case, the case was back in Massachusetts. "Thank you for your time."

"I want to say something to you," Templeton said. "Heather doesn't need to hear this."

Evelyn followed Templeton back to Templeton's car, where Templeton turned and faced her.

"If Heather's brothers ever find out where she's living here, I promise you I will hunt you down and fucking kill you. Are we clear?"

Evelyn was debating her answer until Templeton eased her shirt above the belt on her jeans, revealing a revolver. Then instinct kicked in. Evelyn delivered a kick that caught Templeton in the chest and sent her crashing into her car. Evelyn was on her in a flash.

"If you ever again show me a weapon, I will ram it up your fucking ass. Are we clear?"

"Get off her!" came the cry from behind her, and before Evelyn could turn, her head exploded in pain.

33

A little before noon, they had just crossed the Bourne Bridge when Paul's cell phone sounded. Part of what had made the last few days blissful was not being called.

"We got a call from an Officer Benson in Omaha that Evelyn's in the hospital," the Sunday dispatcher said. "He left his phone number."

"Shit!" Paul exclaimed. "Hold on a minute." He pulled to a stop in the breakdown lane and noted Philly's look of concern. "Is she all right?"

"She's got a concussion, but she's okay. They're holding her for observation."

Paul took down the number of the Omaha officer and ended the call. He filled Philly in as he phoned.

"Benson."

"This is Paul Sullivan from the Cambridge, Massachusetts police department. I'm Evelyn Rodriguez's partner."

"My condolences. Your partner's a handful."

"Is she all right?"

"Yeah. She got clocked last night. She was lying near her rental car in the parking lot of a strip mall. A couple of teenagers discovered her. My guess is the teens were going to park to fool around."

"What do the doctors say?"

"She's got a concussion. We knew she was in the area. She checked in after arriving in Omaha."

"I need the number of the hospital where she's staying."

"She won't tell us a goddamn thing about what happened," Benson complained after providing hospital contact information.

"Maybe that'll change after I talk with her."

"I don't think so. That is one stubborn woman."

Paul wandered outside to have some privacy while Philly dealt with their take-out order. His cell phone reception wasn't great, but he finally got connected to Evelyn's hospital room.

"Hello?"

Evelyn sounded groggy. He could barely hear her. "It's Paul. How are you doing?"

"I've been better."

"What the hell happened?"

Evelyn didn't reply immediately. "Do you have some time to kill?" she finally asked. "It's a long story."

Philly emerged from the roadside eatery, gave him a wave, and headed for their car.

"You're going to need to keep your voice up," Paul said as he walked slowly to join Philly.

Paul sat down on the driver's seat but kept his feet planted on the gravel in the parking lot so his back was to Philly. Evelyn couldn't be that bad off, he figured. She had started from the beginning and was giving him a detailed report.

"Jesus!" Paul said when Evelyn finally finished. "What the hell were you thinking?" He immediately regretted his comment. There was no need to kick his partner while she was down. "Sorry," he said.

"No, you're right. I had that coming. I kind of got carried away."

Paul assessed Evelyn's information. She had come up with answers to a lot of their questions. And she was right—whatever case existed was in Massachusetts.

"Has this guy Benson been in to see you?"

"Yeah. He's not too happy with me. The guy is gorgeous by the way."

"Does he know Templeton's name?"

"No. When I checked in, I left it vague that I was running down a lead in a case we were working."

Paul understood Evelyn's current unwillingness to cooperate with the locals. She was trying her best to keep Templeton and Finch off the locals' radar. "I'd forget the two women. The daughter, Heather, seems to have suffered enough."

"That's the way I'm looking at it. By the way, they're letting me go at two. They don't want me flying out tomorrow. I've switched reservations and I got a seat on the first flight out the day after tomorrow."

"I'm glad you're okay," Paul said.

"Thanks."

"Do you think Benson will take another run at you?"

"He damn well better. He's picking me up at two to take me to my motel. He's taking me to dinner tonight."

"Good grief!"

"What can I say?"

"Say no."

"Not a chance. You should see this guy."

Paul ended the call and swung his legs into the car.

"No way," Philly said. "I'm driving and you're eating and filling me in."

34

"I need to stay another day," Evelyn said.

Paul glared at Evelyn's vacant desk chair. He'd been counting on her showing up for work tomorrow. "Are you okay?" he asked.

"I'm fine. It's just that something's come up."

Paul thought he heard giggling in the background. Christ! Evelyn was fooling around with that cop Benson.

"Jesus, Evelyn!"

"I'd like to take tomorrow as a personal day."

There was no mistaking the giggling this time. Paul debated giving Evelyn a hard time. She hadn't lied to him, hadn't made up a story that she was having headaches and had been told not to fly. Since they had started working together, she had never asked him for anything. "Okay," he said.

"Thanks. I really appreciate it."

"Don't mention it. I'll see you in two days."

"I'll be there."

Paul set down his phone. The weekend with Philly had been just what he needed. If Evelyn needed a few more romps in the hay, who was he to stand in her way?

35

The Massachusetts Commission Against Discrimination had moved quickly to hold a hearing on the motion of Pinkerton, Ashley & Rosewood and Gwen Cantor to dismiss Meredith Sweeney's sexual harassment complaint. Meredith had insisted that Simon argue against the motion and Carpenter saw no reason to oppose her choice. Whatever had happened years back between the two seemed to have sorted itself out.

The MCAD hearing room was small. Carpenter sat in a chair behind the counsel table occupied by Simon and Rachel. If necessary, he could slip them a note by leaning forward.

At the other counsel table, three lawyers from the Pinkerton firm had removed more files from their litigation briefcases than Carpenter believed the briefcases could hold. Predictably, the senior member of the Pinkerton team was a woman. Putting a woman forward as lead counsel sent the message that a female associate claiming sexual harassment was off base because a woman certainly wouldn't condone a valid charge. Juliana Patton exuded confidence. She was tall, had a touch of gray in her short, dark hair, and had a determined, resolute bearing. Rounding out the Pinkerton team was a man Carpenter judged to be a junior partner and a woman he pegged for an associate.

Until today, it had never appeared to Carpenter that Meredith's emotions were getting the best of her. Seated next to him now, she fidgeted and couldn't keep her hands still. It would only increase her agitation if he told her not to worry. Besides she had reason to worry. Any time your fate was to be determined by a judge or a hearing officer, you stood a real chance of getting shafted.

The Commission hearing officer moved to the desk in the front of the room and took his seat. "Good morning," he said. "My name is Francis McPhee and I'm the hearing officer assigned to this case. I've read all the papers. I'm inclined to simply begin the hearing and I would like to start with the respondents who are the moving parties."

McPhee was a young guy—short, stocky, with brown curly hair. He was wearing khaki pants, a blue shirt, a red tie, and a dark blue sports jacket. Carpenter would have preferred a female hearing officer but those were the breaks.

Patton introduced her colleagues and paused as she consulted a single page of notes. "My law firm is dismayed at the complaint filed in this case. The firm treated the complainant's harassment complaint seriously. Her allegations were fully investigated, and the investigation turned up no independent source of evidence that supported any of the allegations. The complainant never produced any evidence of any kind to corroborate her claims. As you know from reading the papers, Ms. Cantor has categorically denied the harassment allegations, and she makes the telling point that since joining the firm, no one has raised any such allegations against her. So, before you are allegations that have not been substantiated in any respect whatsoever."

Carpenter noticed that Meredith was no longer acting as if beset by nerves. She was sitting erect, taking notes, and glancing periodically at the hearing officer.

"Before the complainant claims she was harassed, she was given an overall evaluation following her second year as an associate. That evaluation is part of the record before you. The evaluation of the complainant was negative. Her research, writing, and litigation skills were all found wanting. It was this evaluation that led to the termination of the complainant's employment. Thus, there was an independent, non-discriminatory basis for the complainant's termination from employment."

"How long was Ms. Sweeney employed at your law firm after that negative evaluation?" McPhee asked, and because the question was a good one, Carpenter entertained the hope that they had drawn a hearing officer who was on his game.

"Approximately six months."

"After her performance was found to be so wanting, to use your word, why was Ms. Sweeney kept on for an additional six months?"

"The firm no doubt tried to be fair to the complainant," Patton responded. "The complainant was given a chance to display improved skills."

"What do you have to say to Ms. Sweeney's affidavit statement that she was never told before the two-year evaluation that she was not performing well?"

"The evaluation process is a time when there is an in-depth review of performance. That process may result in a finding of poor performance even though there had been no prior negative comments."

"Ms. Sweeney claims that the two-year evaluation was a farce and shouldn't be considered. She claims that once your firm produces copies of other associates' two-year evaluations, the farce will be exposed. What do you say to that?"

Patton had to have seen this question coming and she displayed no unease. "The complainant's labeling something a farce doesn't make it so. This is another unsubstantiated assertion that has no merit. How the firm evaluated other associates has no bearing on the complainant's case. In addition, associate evaluations that do not concern the complainant are entitled to confidentiality."

McPhee wrote in his notebook and turned to Simon. "What do you have to say about Ms. Patton's last points?"

Simon rose smartly, glanced briefly in Patton's direction, and faced the hearing officer. "First, confidentiality is a red herring. The respondent may redact associate names and Ms. Sweeney has agreed to that as her written submission shows. Second, there's an easy way to resolve this matter. The respondent's website discloses that Ms. Patton is a firm partner. Why not ask her if it is her firm's policy to give negative two-year evaluations to all associates? After all, she just self-servingly informed us that her firm tried to be fair to Ms. Sweeney by giving her a chance to improve performance. I submit that it will turn out that the respondent has never been fair to any associate."

"Is there a firm policy in place along the lines Mr. Jeffries has mentioned?"

Carpenter gave Patton credit. She couldn't have imagined this hearing would move in the direction it had, yet she remained unperturbed.

"As a partner in my firm, I have signed an agreement not to disclose firm policies to anyone, and I'm certainly not going to break my promise here because an attorney believes a certain policy is in effect."

Simon had remained standing. "May I offer a suggestion?" he said. "We have an associate of the respondent present here today. That would be Ms. Claire Smith, according to the names on the respondent's pleadings. Simply ask Ms. Smith whether her second-year evaluation was negative. If the answer is yes, you might want to inquire whether the negative evaluation came as a surprise to her."

Simon sat down abruptly.

"Objection," Patton interjected. "It is nothing less than outrageous that an attorney of record be subjected to questions relating to how she was evaluated by her law firm. That's not within this Commission's jurisdiction."

McPhee's expression gave no clue to what he was thinking. Carpenter noted that Simon was enjoying himself. Meredith was nervous but that was to be expected.

"You make some appropriate points, Ms. Patton," McPhee said. "But if your firm does in fact have a policy to give negative two-year evaluations to all associates, such a policy would undercut the reason you have given for Ms. Sweeney's termination. I want written confirmation from a partner in your firm as to whether or not such a policy exists. I'm not going to rule on your motion to dismiss Ms. Sweeney's complaint until I receive that confirmation."

"This is highly irregular," Patton said.

"I disagree with you," McPhee said. "Ms. Smith, did you receive a two-year evaluation?"

The fair-skinned associate turned red. Carpenter had no sympathy for the young woman.

"Yes," Smith said.

"Do you mind sharing with us whether the evaluation was positive or negative?"

"Yes, she does mind," Patton said angrily. "Ms. Smith is a counsel in this case. She is not a witness. I am not going to permit her to answer your question."

Smith looked relieved in Carpenter's estimation. But the extent of her coloring suggested that Smith had, in fact, received a negative evaluation.

"Very well," McPhee said. "Provide me with written confirmation of your firm's policy or the policy's non-existence within the next two days. We'll schedule the resumption of this hearing a week from today. But I will tell you now that if the respondent's written confirmation confirms a policy of negative two-year evaluations for all associates, I'm inclined to deny the respondent's motion to dismiss without a further hearing. Make sure Ms. Sweeney's counsel receives a copy of the letter you send me. We're adjourned."

McPhee left the hearing room. Meredith stood, moved toward Simon's chair, gave him a hug, and followed up by hugging Rachel. "Thanks, guys."

Carpenter put a finger over his lips and gestured toward the Pinkerton legal team who were stuffing file folders back in their litigation briefcases. When the law firm team left the hearing room, Meredith was the first to speak.

"Do you think they'll provide the letter?"

"If they don't, their motion to dismiss will be denied," Carpenter said. "Also, if they won't provide a letter, we can file a motion to have the fact established that the firm had in place a negative two-year evaluation policy."

"That hearing officer had some balls," Meredith said.

"Let's hope he retains them for a while," Simon said. "We may want to keep this case before the Commission for a longer time than we originally intended."

Carpenter preferred getting into court as soon as possible. But Simon had a point. If the Pinkerton firm submitted a letter acknowledging a negative two-year evaluation policy for all associates, the firm would have lost credibility before the hearing officer. The hearing officer might conclude that Patton had deliberately misled him. If that were the case, it might make sense to let the hearing officer beat up on the Pinkerton firm a while longer. In Pinkerton's position, Carpenter would turn over defense of Meredith's case to an outside law firm. Hopefully the Pinkerton firm would prove too pigheaded to take that commonsense step.

36

For a woman who had been concussed, Evelyn looked remarkably cheerful and fit. She claimed there was a sizable bump on the back of her head, but Paul couldn't discern any swelling.

"Were you able to withhold Templeton's name from officer Benson?" Paul asked.

"That was probably the only thing I withheld," Evelyn replied, grinning.

"Jesus!"

"Come on! You knew what I was up to. And here's the unexpected part. I really liked the guy. True, he kept going on that I was stubborn as a mule and a piece of work who wouldn't last two days in Omaha. But besides that, he was a flat-out nice guy. He had a sense of humor, and for a big guy there was a gentleness about him that I liked. I'm going to miss him."

"I know I'm repeating myself, but I'll say it again—Jesus! Now, enough about you. We've got to deal with the brothers."

"You really know how to kill a good mood," Evelyn said without any heat. She took a deep breath. "All right. I've actually been thinking about that. Do we have any leverage over them because they abused their sister?"

"Not if the sister is going to remain silent."

"But they don't know she's going to remain silent," Evelyn countered.

"If we play that card, what are the chances one or both of them will head out to Omaha to try to find Heather and silence her?"

From her expression, Paul knew that Evelyn hadn't considered that possibility. "I think she'd be easy to find," Paul continued. "If I was looking for her, I'd start by looking at restaurants. You mentioned that cooking was something Heather loved and was good at. My guess is that she ended up as a chef."

Evelyn looked crestfallen. "You know, I never got a chance to ask Heather what she did for work. The bottom line is I don't want to put her at risk even though she flattened me."

"Then we have a problem," Paul said. "If we confront the brothers with the abuse claim, they'll figure Heather talked."

Evelyn muttered, "Shit," stood up, and began pacing. Paul watched her in silence. Motion seemed to help Evelyn think in the same way driving helped her to order her thoughts.

"You know how kids who have been abused end up being abusers themselves?" Evelyn said. "Heather made that point," she went on, not waiting for Paul to answer her question. "Why don't we confront them with the photographs and tell them we think they're responsible for abusing the kids in the pictures? We tell them we're bringing this to the district attorney's office with a request that he convene a grand jury investigation. Then we ask them whether they have anything to say that might cause us to reconsider what we plan to do."

Evelyn abruptly took a seat, and Paul considered her reasoning. It was a stretch to believe that the brothers would simply break their silence after being confronted. Most likely they would clam up—maybe even lawyer up—and refuse to say anything if hauled before a grand jury. Assuming a district attorney would actually convene a grand jury based on the scant information they possessed. Still, what Evelyn had come up with was likely their best bet if Heather was a card that wouldn't be played.

"That's pretty clever," Paul said. "I want to think about it a little more even though I don't think I'm going to come up with anything better."

"If we do this," Evelyn said, "I'd like to confront the brothers together. It would give us a chance to read anything going on between them."

"I'll think about that also." It occurred to Paul that he rarely approved any proposal that Evelyn came up with straightaway. She was probably annoyed with his consistently deliberate approach.

"It's good to be back," Evelyn said. "I just wish Horace was around."

"Horace?"

"That's Officer Benson to you."

Simon opened the letter, not recognizing the name of the law firm on the envelope. The letter was addressed to the hearing officer in Meredith's case and was short and to the point. The firm of Case, Maxwell & Shine was taking over the representation of the Pinkerton firm and Gwen Cantor. The Pinkerton firm would not be advising the hearing officer as to any firm policy having to do with associate evaluations because firm policies were confidential and could not be disclosed under the firm's partnership agreement.

Simon waited for his heart rate to subside a few beats before rereading the letter more slowly. He remembered that Case, Maxwell & Shine was a mid-sized Boston law firm specializing in litigation that enjoyed a good reputation. The letter to the hearing officer was signed by Helena Peck and her picture on her firm's website showed a middle-aged woman with long, straight, blond hair, blue eyes, and a winning smile. Peck was a partner in the firm specializing in employment matters.

Simon considered the strategy of refusing to furnish the hearing officer with requested information. Francis McPhee would have it in for the respondents while the case was before him. No doubt he would deny the motion to dismiss Meredith's case. Still, it took some stones to flat out refuse a request made by a presiding hearing officer.

Simon made several copies of the letter and e-mailed a copy to Philly. Carpenter was off exercising, so Simon left a copy of the letter on his desk. Rachel had spread out papers on the conference room table as she researched minority stockholder rights, and Simon decided that an interruption was in order. "Check this out," he said depositing her copy of the letter in front of her.

Rachel read the letter through, looked up, and read it again. "Wow," she said.

"My sentiments exactly."

"Eventually, we're going to get the information about Pinkerton's two-year evaluation policy," Rachel said. "These new lawyers have to know that. I wonder why they're digging in their heels."

Simon shrugged. "Pinkerton must think disclosure of the policy is worse than losing Meredith's case. What else could be going on?"

"Where is Carpenter when we need him?" Rachel replied.

"At the gym," Simon said. "Who would have figured him to turn into an exercise nut?"

"Gotcha!" Herb said in a whisper. He slipped his camera into the side pocket of his windbreaker, left the modest protection of the entryway to the Esplanade Condominium complex, and began walking quickly in the opposite direction of the parking garage. As a precaution he had dressed in black, but as he picked up his pace, he realized that it probably didn't matter whether he was seen. He had taken a risk camping out by the entryway, but it paid off—he had gotten a clear photograph of Gwen Cantor and Stephanie Manley emerging from the parking garage, holding hands and laughing. The camera he had borrowed for the occasion had an incredible zoom lens, a lightness-darkness resolution feature that made any night shot appear as if in broad daylight, and a timer mechanism that recorded the day, hour, and minute of the photograph. It had taken him ten evenings to obtain the photograph he had just taken, and for the moment, the futility and frustration of the previous nine were fading fast.

Meredith Sweeney would be pleased with the photograph, but not with the rest of his news. The twelve other women who had left the Pinkerton firm had refused to talk with him about sexual harassment.

37

Philly idly rubbed her belly and contemplated next moves in Martina Glass' personal injury suit. Logical next steps dictated that she or Simon take the depositions of the two guys who had accompanied Fred Dunn to the Salem Stampede hockey game. The defendants could be counted on to take the depositions of Jeremy and Mary Rhodes, the couple who observed one of Dunn's friends tossing Dunn a bag of peanuts, which he reached for, causing him to fall over a railing and land on Glass. The Rhodes' testimony would help Glass' case against Dunn but would probably bolster the hockey team's position that Glass' injuries were caused solely by Dunn. There was no getting around the fact that Glass' case was weakest against the defendant best able to pay for her injuries—the hockey team. Dunn's assets were negligible.

Glass' best case against the Salem Stampede was to claim that the team's security was close to nonexistent, that railings in the arena were too low to prevent a fan from falling, that the team had not posted warnings against standing or leaning over railings, and that the team had no effective way to monitor fans' consumption of alcoholic beverages. On the last point, Barney Freedman and Herb McCauley had gone to a Salem Stampede game and Herb had reported that without hassle, he had bought and consumed eight beers.

Glass' case forced Philly to consider each defendant's ability to pay. She wanted one-on-one time with Carpenter to assess trying to settle the case with either defendant. Simon had brought in the case and probably should be part of the discussion. But Philly decided on alone time with the geezer before adding Simon to the mix.

"Lunch time," Philly heard Sarah call out, followed by the *thump, thump* of Daisy's feet. 'Another country heard from,' she thought as she set her computer on Sleep.

38

"*You* open it!" Rachel said, tossing the envelope from the Worcester Superior Court to Simon. "It's got to be the decision in Fay Richardson's case against that scumbag ex-boyfriend. I can't bear to look at it!"

Simon shrugged and slit the envelope. He was seated at the workstation in Philly's office, across the room from Philly's desk, which Rachel had claimed this morning. "As you know, Carpenter says there are two ways to do this. Go to the last page and get to the bottom line or read the decision through. *You* decide."

"Oh, God!" Rachel exclaimed, and Simon worried that she'd hyperventilate. Was he some kind of freak because he wasn't sharing in her nervous excitement?

"Go to the last page," Rachel directed, a note of desperation in her voice. "I can't take the suspense."

The last page was numbered seventeen. Simon quickly determined that Judge Murray had made the preliminary injunction Fay Richardson had obtained against Al Townsend and Rita Stout permanent; the billboard would have to stay down. "We won," he said, handing the decision to Rachel.

"Thank God!" Rachel said, slightly breathless.

With the bottom line known, Rachel's demeanor abruptly changed. She began reading the decision without her previous nervousness. "Oh, *this* is good. The judge found that Townsend was not a believable witness. Townsend testified that he had friends but the one friend he named—Sam Goodyear—was barely an acquaintance."

Simon wondered whether he'd be a more effective or less effective advocate if he brought Rachel's strong emotions to a case. Less effective, he suspected.

"Oh, and listen to this! Ms. Richardson cannot be second-guessed for feeling threatened by Mr. Townsend. Mr. Townsend had in fact threatened the woman he had previously lived with."

While Rachel read on, Simon studied the other envelopes she had dropped at his workstation. One bore the letterhead of the Massachusetts Commission Against Discrimination.

Rachel continued reading. "And then it says, 'I find and rule that Mr. Townsend and Ms. Stout's first amendment claims are without merit. Mr. Townsend's billboard posting was a personal attack directed against Ms. Richardson that wrongfully accused her of being a killer. Although fully aware of Massachusetts and federal law relating to abortion, both Mr. Townsend and Ms. Stout refuse to recognize the established right of a woman to choose when it comes to an abortion decision.'" Rachel looked up and smiled before resuming her review.

Simon slit the envelope from the MCAD. Hearing Officer McPhee's ruling was short and direct: "The respondents' motion to dismiss is denied. Material facts are in dispute and the respondent law firm has willfully refused to comply with a Commission order to provide the Commission with relevant and material information."

"Oh my God!" Rachel let loose. "He awarded Richardson one hundred and fifty thousand dollars for the intentional infliction of emotional distress. This is a total victory!"

Simon was cheered by the possibility they would be paid for their legal services. He returned to observing Rachel. She was again smiling as she concluded her initial read of the judge's decision. "This is great," she said. "I'll let Philly know and then I'm going to call Fay."

"Here's something else that's great," Simon said, presenting her with a copy of the MCAD order. "We're two for two today. I'll call Meredith."

Simon had been unable to reach Meredith. He had just concluded his message telling her that the motion to dismiss her case had been denied when Carpenter buzzed his intercom informing him of an incoming call from Helena Peck. It took Simon a moment to place the name with Meredith's case.

"Hello, Ms. Peck. Simon Jeffries."

"Thanks for taking my call."

"My pleasure. What can I do for you?"

"As you know, my firm will be taking over the representation of the respondents in the Sweeney case that's before the MCAD. I'm calling to explore with you whether the case may be settled."

Simon paused and not just for effect. He was taken aback my Peck's overture after Carpenter had warned that the Pinkerton firm would fight Meredith's case to the death.

"In theory, any case may be settled. Frankly, I haven't given any thought to whether this was one of those cases."

Peck paused. "We don't know each other," she finally said. "You haven't a clue as to whether you may trust me, and I certainly don't have a clue as to whether I may trust you. But I'm reaching out to you on the settlement subject because I believe that this may prove to be the only time a settlement may be possible."

"I don't follow you," Simon said.

"You haven't been practicing as long as I have but I suspect that you've already come across clients who would rather fight than settle. Pinkerton, Ashley & Rosewood has a reputation that I assume you are aware of. They are no-holds-barred litigators so you can imagine their mindset when *they've* been sued. I'm new to the case. I spent a fair amount of time going through the Pinkerton files and then I provided my client with a frank appraisal of the situation and a recommendation or two. As a result of that discussion, I am authorized to explore settlement possibilities with you. My authority to discuss settlement may end in an hour but currently it's in place."

When Peck had referred to his limited years of practice, Simon felt he was being talked down to. But after she'd had her say, he reconsidered. Peck probably *was* dealing with a difficult client and had advised the client that settlement may be in its best interests, notwithstanding its natural inclination to battle to the bitter end. "I'm listening," he said.

"Do you have a demand figure?" Peck asked.

"No." Simon was able to answer truthfully. "Did you call with a specific proposal in mind?"

"Actually, I did. It's not a proposal that I have discussed with my client, but it is a proposal that I'm prepared to recommend."

Simon stayed silent.

"Here's my thinking," Peck said. "Ms. Sweeney was a third-year associate making one hundred and forty-five thousand a year in base salary. Her bonus after her second year was fifteen thousand dollars. What I have in mind is a two hundred-thousand-dollar settlement on money. Also, the parties would come to a mutual agreement on a letter from the firm that Ms. Sweeney could use in connection with seeking another job. I don't want to call it a letter of recommendation, but the letter I have in mind—and I've drafted my share of this kind of letter—would make the point that Ms. Sweeney satisfactorily performed her duties at Pinkerton."

Several moments went by before Simon realized that Peck was now waiting him out. "How would the letter deal with Ms. Sweeney leaving the firm?"

"It wouldn't," Peck replied. "Inquiries to Pinkerton about Ms. Sweeney would be directed to a designated individual who would say, if asked, that Ms. Sweeney's departure from the firm was a mutual, amicable decision. Ms. Sweeney could inform prospective employers that that was the case. The letter I have in mind would identify the individual in charge of fielding inquiries about your client."

Simon found Peck's proposal reasonable and wondered whether he was missing something. If Meredith accepted Peck's proposed deal, she'd put some money in her pocket and would not be dogged by a previous firing.

"This comes as a surprise so I'm not going to answer you," Simon said. "Obviously, I'll discuss what you've said with Ms. Sweeney."

"Excellent. One more thing. My approach to settlement discussions of this type is to cut to the chase when it comes to money as opposed to starting out with a low offer. Pinkerton may think what I've proposed to you on money is excessive. But I tried to come up with a dollar figure that was fair and reasonable in my opinion."

"I'll keep that in mind. Thank you for calling."

'The gang's all here,' Simon thought, as Philly's face appeared via Skype. He and Rachel and Carpenter were seated together in Carpenter's room facing his computer screen. He had sent his partners an e-mail memo outlining Peck's proposal. "Meredith is going to ask for our recommendation. I'd like to hear from each of you."

"What do *you* think?" Philly asked.

"I'm inclined to accept the offer," Simon said, "but would try to do better on the money."

"Why?" Philly asked.

"I think Meredith would be fairly compensated. She'd be able to provide a suitable letter from her most recent employer. Plus, she could move on and put all this behind her."

"What do you think Peck advised Pinkerton?" Carpenter asked.

"I think she told the firm that their policy on two-year negative evaluations could be trouble for them once it got out," Rachel said. "I think she advised that the policy would be discovered if Meredith's case was litigated and that the policy's disclosure would be embarrassing."

"I agree," Carpenter said. "Pinkerton might have some monetary exposure if an associate was fired because of a negative two-year evaluation. And as Rachel said, the embarrassment factor would be huge. This would be so all over the Internet even I couldn't miss it."

"Are they trying to buy Meredith's silence on the two-year policy?" Philly asked.

"Something like that," Carpenter said. "They know that we know the policy exists. They don't know how we learned of the policy. Sweeney doesn't have personal knowledge of the policy."

"I don't like the idea they're trying to buy Meredith off," Rachel said. "That sucks."

Carpenter favored Rachel with a hard stare. "Personally, I'm thrilled when a defendant wants to buy off one of my plaintiff clients." Carpenter turned toward Simon. "When Peck said there was a brief window to settle the case and her authority to settle could disappear in an hour, I think she was indirectly delivering the message that once the policy became public, there was no reason for Pinkerton to settle. On the sexual harassment claim the firm will probably take its chances on the she said—she said situation."

Simon silently applauded Carpenter. He had a way of looking at cases from an angle that wouldn't have occurred to him. "What's our plan? he asked.

"You and Rachel need to have a heart-to-heart with Sweeney," Carpenter answered. "I'm okay with you recommending that she take the settlement. It *is* a reasonable offer and there's something to be said for your friend being able to put this behind her. But tell her we think we should try to increase the payout."

Simon sat in the visitor's chair in Philly's office, and Rachel was behind Philly's desk. Meredith was on speaker phone and the first thing she had said was a heartfelt thank you for their successfully defending Pinkerton's motion to dismiss her case. Simon had just finished relating her former law firm's settlement proposal, had underscored that the proposal was not a formal offer, and had then explained their firm's recommendation that the proposal be accepted, subject to further negotiation on money. Meredith fell silent and when Rachel seemed about to break the silence, Simon held up a hand to stop her.

"To be honest, I never expected this," Meredith said. "I think you guys are right—the offer has to do with the two-year policy of negative evaluations. They don't want that to get out."

Simon shook his head when Rachel again appeared poised to comment.

"I'm conflicted," Meredith said. "On the one hand, I have this overwhelming sense of relief at the thought of the case being over. On the other hand, I want those bastards to pay and to never treat any associate the way they treated me."

"Pinkerton will never publicly acknowledge its two-year negative evaluation policy if it doesn't have to," Simon said. "But reading between the lines, I don't think the firm will ever employ the policy again. My guess is that Peck read them the riot act on that."

Meredith again fell silent. Simon had no idea whether her combative nature would lead her to reject whatever deal Pinkerton put on the table.

"Fuck!" Meredith exclaimed.

"You don't have to make a decision this moment," Simon said, "and we recommend that you don't. Think about it and get back to us. Take a few days if you have to."

"I don't want to think about it," Meredith said. "I'm sick to fucking death of thinking about it. Three hundred thousand. Tell them we have a deal if the money goes up to three hundred thousand and not a penny less."

Simon focused on the 'not a penny less.' "I don't think you should draw a line in the sand on money at this point. I think that's a mistake."

"That's my position," Meredith declared.

"I think Simon's right," Rachel said. "If three hundred thousand is your bottom line, we'll probably have to propose a higher number."

"No. You can tell this woman what she told you. You can tell her the three hundred thousand cuts to the chase and it's a bottom-line figure. Tell her that you're not going to waste her time by starting out with a higher figure and then negotiating. Tell her the three hundred thousand is what it will take to make the case go away."

"I don't think you should make this decision without sleeping on it," Simon repeated. "Let's talk tomorrow."

"Fine. We'll talk tomorrow. But I'm not changing my mind."

"One other thing. Call Herb McCauley and have him tell that former Pinkerton lawyer how the MCAD motion to dismiss played out. The guy went out on a limb for you."

"Good point," Meredith said.

"I was afraid of this," Simon said after Meredith disconnected.

"Maybe Pinkerton will take the offer," Rachel said.

Simon shrugged. He doubted the firm would accept Meredith's demand figure. Pinkerton might be willing to throw more money in Meredith's direction but not enough to meet her bottom line. "And then again, maybe not," he said.

April

From Meredith's Playlist

"Jungle Love"

Steve Miller Band

39

"I told you that I wasn't going to say another word to you," Wilson Finch barked.

Paul held his phone away from his ear, forcing himself to be civil. "I get that all the time," he said, opting for a light tone that would probably further piss Finch off. "I'm doing you and your brother a favor by calling you. I would like the two of you to come down to the stationhouse in Cambridgeport and look at some photographs."

"What kind of photographs?"

"I'm not going to answer that question. All I'm going to say is that the photographs are graphic. It's important that the two of you look at them."

"Fuck off."

"That's very grown up. Let me explain what's going to happen if you and your brother refuse to cooperate. A grand jury is likely to be the next group that takes a look at the pictures. Once the grand jury gets a look at the photos, I think the odds are about one hundred percent the grand jury will have questions for you and your brother. You've probably seen enough TV shows to know that you can plead the Fifth Amendment and not answer the grand jury's questions. That'll be up to you. If you take the Fifth Amendment in front of the grand jury, we both know what that's going to look like to the jurors regardless of what the law says."

"Do what you have to do. I'm not saying another fucking thing."

Paul paused several beats. For whatever reason, Finch hadn't hung up on him. "There's one more thing. On the back of each photograph there are the initials 'LFLS.' We believe you and your brother know what they stand for and that one of you wrote those initials. Ultimately, we'll get a handwriting sample from each of you. You and your brother might be able to spare yourselves a lot of trouble if you cooperate with us. But if you both want to continue to act like assholes, that's your prerogative. We know that one of you contacted Social Security for your father's address."

"Are we suspects in a crime?" Finch asked.

"In my view you are," Paul said, wishing he hadn't been asked the question.

"Then I guess we need a lawyer."

"That's your call. Here's my phone number," Paul added and rattled off the digits. "I won't do anything until next week. Let me know before Friday if you've changed your mind on the cooperation front. I'm going to ask you to relay this call to your brother. My partner would prefer not to call him."

"All right," Finch said with undisguised bitterness. "I'll let him know."

Paul set down his receiver amazed that Finch had agreed to anything.

Waiting for his call to be put through to Helena Peck, Simon remembered Carpenter's final thoughts as to his approach: "When a client draws a line in the sand, the lawyer's job is easy—don't cross the line even if the line is in the wrong place."

"Good afternoon, Mr. Jeffries."

"Good afternoon." Simon gathered his thoughts. "The proposal you put forward is acceptable in principle with the exception of the dollar figure you had in mind. If the dollar figure were three-hundred thousand and your client were to go along with what you outlined, we would have an agreement in principle."

Peck didn't respond immediately. Simon wondered whether she had seriously believed her initial proposal would be accepted as is. She might regard her own notions of fairness as beyond reproach and not subject to dispute.

"I believe I went out on a limb with the two-hundred-thousand-dollar figure," Peck said. "I wanted to put forward a figure that exceeded a year of compensation for Ms. Sweeney. I anticipated having a hard time selling that figure, but I was prepared to give it a go. I don't think your counter proposal on money is reasonable and, even if I did, I doubt it would be acceptable to Pinkerton."

"I understand," Simon said. "You made a proposal and I've responded. The ball is in your court. As between us, I decided to follow your lead. Rather than come back to you with a figure that was even higher than the one I just mentioned, I've come back to you with the figure that *will* bring this case to a close. I don't believe I will be given authority to settle below the figure I mentioned to you."

"I see." Peck paused. "Well, maybe I'll be pleasantly surprised and your number will be accepted. I don't think that will be the case, but stranger things have happened. Perhaps I hadn't fully considered that I might not be the only one with a challenging client. I didn't get a feel for Ms. Sweeney in reviewing Pinkerton's files."

"No comment," Simon replied.

"None expected. Thank you for getting back to me so promptly. I'll take this to my client and get back to you."

Simon set down his phone wondering whether Meredith could be moved off her position. She had been adamant on the $300,000 when she called this morning. "I've slept on it," she'd said, "and not a penny less. Fuck them."

Simon recalled the probably apocryphal story about a divorce settlement going awry when the couple seeking to carve up assets in the millions couldn't agree to the disposition of an ashtray valued at less than a dollar. People drew lines in the sand over items whose location on either side of the line made no difference in the long run. He couldn't shake the feeling that it was more important for Meredith to put her case behind her than to extract more dollars from Pinkerton. Meredith likely would have no trouble finding another high paying job if she had a neutral but essentially favorable letter from Pinkerton. Financially, she'd be better off accepting Peck's proposal and landing a job immediately than fighting on and struggling to get a new job because of not being easily able to explain her leaving her only employer after law school.

Simon moved Meredith's case file to the back of his workstation. 'Think positively,' he told himself. Maybe Peck *would* be pleasantly surprised.

"This is a tough one," Carpenter said after Philly had gone through her concerns about obtaining a meaningful dollar recovery in Martina Glass' lawsuit.

"Which is why we're talking," Philly replied.

Carpenter recalled several cases in which he was forced to settle for short dollars even though liability was clear. There wasn't a damn thing a plaintiff's lawyer could do about a judgment-proof defendant.

"Tell me again what assets this guy Dunn has," Carpenter requested.

"He's literally got nothing. He lives at home, makes slightly above minimum wage in the moving business, and had slightly under five hundred dollars in a checking account when he answered interrogatories about his assets."

'Judgment-proof,' Carpenter thought. "Who's paying for his lawyer?" he asked.

"I don't know."

"What are the chances the team will settle?"

"I haven't explored that option."

Carpenter recalled Philly describing how she had defeated the Salem Stampede's motion to dismiss Glass' case. "Didn't the judge buy your argument that Dunn falling on Glass was no different than a ceiling tile falling on her? You argued that a fan had an expectation of safety attending a sporting event and that a fan would never expect to be crushed by another fan."

"I did argue that. I was surprised that the judge bought it. The judge is a nasty, sarcastic guy."

"If we approach the hockey team to settle, that's what we're going to argue."

"Agreed."

"There needs to be a meeting with Glass," Carpenter said. "I'll sit in if you want."

"Yeah, I'd appreciate that."

"Set it up. How's the pregnancy?"

"So far so good. I'm eating like crazy and the nausea has gone away. Once again I'm going to be a goddamn blimp."

"But a sweet and adorable blimp."

"Very funny. Thanks for listening."

"Don't mention it. That's what I'm here for."

40

Philly had brought her laptop to the living room so she could keep an eye on Daisy and Rosalind. Sarah had a doctor's appointment and Isabella was at work. She felt exhausted watching the two little ones interact. How the hell did Sarah do it day after day? Rosalind was now walking after a fashion. She could stand up by herself and keep erect by holding onto a piece of furniture. But every so often she would forget herself and start after Daisy, keeping her feet going for several steps before crashing. Daisy was currently stacking small building blocks. Rosalind had one of the blocks in her mouth.

With no real expectation of getting any work done, Philly began to list the depositions that needed to be taken. She had decided to take charge of the depositions in Martina Glass' case. Today, if it was the last thing she did, she was going to schedule depositions of the two guys who had accompanied Fred Dunn to the Salem Stampede game. The hockey team's lawyer, Wayne Martin, had already scheduled depositions for Jeremy and Mary Rhodes, the couple who had seen the incident, and Philly would defend those depositions.

Her partners were also in deposition hell. Carpenter was scheduled to defend Clyde Atkins' deposition. He had assigned Simon the task of deposing Atkins' sister, Mary Ellen Pines. Carpenter hadn't decided whether to take the deposition of Clyde's brother, Malcom, or of the patriarch of the family. The siblings' father had been listed as a witness for the defendants.

Daisy began to jabber nonsense. She had a few recognizable words, but a lot of it was still a sort of word-like nonsense. Rosalind listened intently, as if she understood her. Philly could feel that the two little ones were going to be best friends in much the same way their mothers were.

It was a bright sunny morning and nearly two hours until lunch. She went over to the girls for diaper checks. "You guys are good to go. We're going out. Time to take a walk and play in the park."

At the word "park," Daisy got to her feet and made a beeline for her jacket hanging from a hook in the front entryway. Rosalind crawled after her. In short order Philly wiggled each girl into a jacket, commandeered the stroller for Rosalind, and donned a sweatshirt for herself. "And we're off," she announced, thinking that she was about to experience the best part of her day.

Paul took a call from Anthony Cianno, a Cambridge criminal lawyer with a well-deserved reputation. Cianno, a former prosecutor, had taken over a criminal law practice manned by Simon Newsome, an unorthodox criminal lawyer and somewhat of a legend who had practiced law as a sole practitioner. The two had worked together for three transition years before Newsome eased into retirement. Paul had seen Cianno in court on one occasion and had been impressed. He had wondered how he would fare if Cianno ever had occasion to cross-examine him.

"I've been retained by Wilson Finch and Edwin Finch," Cianno said after pleasantries had been exchanged. "I need a week to review their situation and I'm calling to ask that you keep the status quo until I get back to you."

Paul couldn't fault the Finch brothers for lawyering up. After all, he'd told Wilson that he and his brother were suspects in a case. Still, the prospect of locking horns with Cianno was dispiriting. "That's not unreasonable. Get back to me in a week."

"Would it be possible for me to take a look at the photographs you want my clients to view?"

Paul wanted the Finches' initial reaction to the photographs to be free of outside influences. "I'm not inclined to do that."

"Is there anything else you can tell me about what's going on?"

"I'd like to leave it at what I told your clients. I'm sure they filled you in."

"They did," Cianno replied. "But I don't have a handle on what's going on. It's all a little vague."

"Everything I could say I've relayed to your clients. There's nothing else I can add at the moment."

"Okay," Cianno said. "Thanks for your time and I appreciate your letting me have a week to look into this."

When Cianno rang off, Paul searched out the criminal lawyer on the Internet. Cianno looked to be in his early fifties. His photograph showed a dark-complexioned man with dark eyes, wavy black hair, and a strong chin. It wouldn't be long before he got to know the guy better.

41

A Law School Dean and a Law School Professor

Simon was taking a walk. After completing an outline for Mary Ellen Pines' deposition, he decided he needed a change of pace. He wasn't an outdoors type, but being outside on this glorious, sunny day brightened his mood. The sky overhead was a relaxing shade of pale blue with wispy clouds moving in slow motion, responding to a faint breeze. He had cut through the Boston Common and had commenced circumnavigating the Public Garden, when his cell phone sounded. He didn't recognize the number and thought briefly of letting the call drift to voice-mail. This was his time, he thought, before remembering Carpenter's admonition that free time was a luxury a practicing lawyer never got to enjoy.

"This is Simon."

"Mr. Jeffries," came a booming voice that Simon recognized but couldn't place. "I'm glad I reached you. Do you have a moment?"

"Who *is* this?"

"So you don't recognize my voice?" came the surprised response.

"Should I?"

"I would say so. We had our share of legal arguments."

Simon stopped walking and concentrated. The voice was tantalizingly familiar. And then it came to him. "Professor Jamison?"

"Very good. Although these days I only teach one evidence class. I insisted on the one class as a condition of being recently named Dean of Students. I like to keep my hand in teaching and, as you know, evidence is my course of choice."

Simon hadn't been aware of his former professor's new position. "This is a surprise."

"I'm sure it is," Jamison replied. "Let me get to the point of my call. Your illustrious alma mater has been sued. The school is considering engaging one of the large downtown firms to defend it. But I have requested the dean to consider other options."

Simon was shocked. He had taken Jamison's evidence class as well as a seminar Jamison taught on litigation techniques, and the two of them were constantly sparring, largely because, for the hell of it, Simon simply liked to mix it up with the man. There were times when Jamison gave way to dramatic eye rolling upon seeing Simon's hand in the air, but Simon had always felt that the professor, underneath his acerbic manner and wickedly cutting barbs, enjoyed their battles.

"What's the suit about?" Simon asked.

"Would you and Ms. Boyle be free this evening for dinner?"

"I'll need to check with Rachel."

"I suggest you do that. If at all possible, try to clear your schedules. I think you'll be interested in what we have to say."

"We?"

"Yes, we. Dean Stockman will be joining us."

"I'll call you back," Simon said. 'So much for exercise,' he thought, as he made a U-turn back to the office.

Dean Stanley Stockman's corner office on the sixth floor of the Spenser School of Law in Boston had the cozy look and feel of a well-stocked library in a country estate mansion. During law school, Rachel had never set foot in the office and she doubted Simon had either. Dean Stockman was a large man with a booming voice and a garrulous air, but beneath his bonhomie was a shrewd administrator whose efforts had closed the reputation gap between Spenser School of Law and the tier of Boston-area law schools trailing Harvard Law School. These days, Rachel was seldom greeted with the "I-never-heard-of-it" response when she revealed where she had gone to law school.

Stockman directed them to high-backed maroon leather chairs arranged around a small conference table. As they approached, Professor Adam Jamison rose from one of the chairs and offered a smile that was genuinely warm, neither mocking nor belittling, as was typically the case in law school. Shaking Jamison's hand, Rachel struggled to look him in the eye. When taking his evidence course, she had continually lived in fear of being called upon and humiliated by the professor's questions. Jamison wasn't physically prepossessing. He was short, plump, and stoop-shouldered. But the man's acerbic barbs could be devastating, and he seemed to enjoy taking students down a peg.

"Always nice to see distinguished graduates," Stockman said, and it took Rachel a moment to register that the dean was talking about her and Simon.

"Let me get to it," Jamison said. "I told Simon that our law school has been sued but I provided no details. The school is being sued for fraud and misrepresentation by a small firm that presents itself as a public interest law firm. The plaintiffs are three law school graduates who have been unable to land a job. The complaint alleges that Spenser School of Law falsely promised incoming students that it placed the majority of its students in legal positions, and never identified the difficulties in finding a legal job. The complaint alleges that the school's claimed job placement percentage is false. The complaint alleges that our placement department has been wanting and basically useless. The plaintiffs have filed a motion to certify the case as a class action. They want damages for pain and suffering and want all tuition payments returned to them." Jamison glanced at the dean. "I believe that I have cogently summed up the allegations in the thirty-five-page complaint."

"Are the allegations true?" Simon promptly asked. "Did the law school misstate job placement results?"

Jamison laughed. "It's good to see you haven't changed, Mr. Jeffries. Always direct and to the point. The answer is..."—and here Jamison imitated a drum roll on the arms of his chair which didn't seem to sit well with the dean— "yes and no."

"What's your defense?" Simon asked.

"Context, Mr. Jeffries," Jamison said. "The promotional document that states that the majority of graduates were placed in legal positions was published in 2008 and hasn't been updated. At the time of publication, fifty-one percent of graduates responding to a survey were working in a legal-related field. In later years, the percentage figure dropped to approximately forty-nine percent."

"Why wasn't the promotional document revised?" Simon asked.

"Take a few wild guesses," the dean said. "In no particular order try money, inertia, and other priorities. Add to those the lousy economy. We have never promised any incoming student job placement."

"You can add another factor contributing to the reduction in job placements," Rachel said, remembering vividly her own experience trying to find legal work. "The school's placement office *was* basically useless in my case."

"But you two are partners in a boutique litigation practice," the dean proclaimed in a manner that Rachel found off-putting. It was as if the dean were somehow taking credit for their landing jobs.

"Do you have any idea what Simon and I went through?" Rachel said with heat. "Simon had to wait tables for two years, and I had to settle for a paralegal job during that time."

"But you persevered," the dean said with his previous enthusiasm still in evidence.

"We were lucky," Simon said. "If we hadn't been on the law school's faculty-student disciplinary committee, we never would have been noticed by the lawyer who ultimately contacted us and fed us some real legal work. He's one of our partners now. I didn't stop waiting tables until late last year."

Jamison was studying them with interest. Rachel wanted him to get to the punch line—why were they here?

"Your alma mater intends to vigorously defend the lawsuit," Jamison said. "The question becomes, who will represent us? Historically, one of the large Boston firms has represented the law school on all matters requiring outside counsel. In this instance, I've prevailed on the dean to consider engaging Spenser graduates to carry our banner."

Jamison smiled at her, and Rachel realized that she'd been staring at him open-mouthed. Jamison knew his rules of evidence and was reputed to be brilliant, but clearly the man had taken leave of his senses if he was seriously considering engaging two recent graduates to defend the law school's reputation and money.

"Forget representing the law school for a moment," Simon said. "If we were witnesses in the case, our testimony would probably be harmful to the law school."

"You have a point," Jamison conceded. "But the dean also has a point. You *have* persevered. Each of you—as your firm's website boasts—contributed to million-dollar verdicts last year. Frankly, Ms. Boyle, your involvement in a jury trial surprised me. As I recall, you never said a word in my class and lived in fear that if I called upon you, you would be required to speak. I never doubted that Mr. Jeffries' voice would be heard in a courtroom. But I remember your final examination in evidence, Ms. Boyle. I gave you one of the highest grades I have ever awarded a student. I never doubted that you would be heard from although I suspected it would be through the written word."

Rachel couldn't believe that Jamison recalled her evidence exam. True, she had graduated *summa cum laude,* but had felt on leaving the law school that she hadn't left a mark, had gone unnoticed except to be cited at graduation for achieving highest honors.

"Did the 2008 date appear on the law school's reference to placing the majority of its graduates?" Simon asked, and Rachel was struck by Simon's focus on the case they were being considered to defend.

"Yes," the dean replied.

Rachel now felt calm and began to address the law school's legal problem with Simon's serious attention. "What, if any, other facts give you concern about the case against the law school?"

Jamison and the dean exchanged a look that Rachel couldn't read. The dean frowned and cleared his throat.

"The point you made comes to mind," the dean said. "You're right. Our placement office has not always been effective, and our promotional materials say that placement services will be provided to graduates. We think that situation is turning around. However, there was a period of time when the placement office was not all it should have been."

"Promotional materials suggest that the law school measures up to other law schools in the area," Jamison added. "There's some language noting that Spenser is a recent addition to the excellent law schools in the Boston area. In terms of faculty, I believe that Spenser does measure up to other schools. But in terms of placing graduates in law-related jobs, Spenser lags behind other law schools."

"The truth is," the dean said in a subdued tone, "many of our students were rejected from other Boston-area law schools. College grade point averages and law board scores of our students are below the grade point averages and board scores of students at other law schools."

"You might consider Spenser a safety school," Jamison said. "Students apply to Spenser out of fear they will be turned down by other schools. For many of our students, those fears are realized."

Rachel recalled her own bitter disappointment at not getting accepted by another Boston-area law school. Her grades had been good and she had done well on the law boards. She had applied to Spenser almost as an afterthought and, as it turned out, it was the only law school to accept her.

"Even though neither of you has directly said so, I assume we're being considered to represent the law school," Simon said. "My question is, why us? Obviously, this is an important case for Spenser. Why not use the large, downtown firm you typically use?"

"The dean is inclined to go with that firm," Jamison said. "I believe that Spenser needs to make a statement in this case, and what better way to make that statement than by defeating the lawsuit with recent graduates as counsel?"

"Why us?" Rachel repeated Simon's question.

"You tell me," Jamison replied. "You need to convince the dean. The dean is less interested in making a statement than winning the case."

"Because we're good," Simon said while Rachel was trying to think of a response to Jamison. "The lawyers who are our partners have given us responsibility we never would have had in a large firm. We've been in court and we think we can handle ourselves. Our partners have more trial experience and they're available to us. If you hired us, they would be actively involved in the case. We're a team."

"We would not look favorably on being triple billed," the dean said. "What is your hourly rate?"

Rachel was shocked when Simon rattled off a figure that was a hundred dollars higher than the rate they usually charged.

"That's much less than what a partner would charge at the large firm we use," Jamison said. "In fact, the senior partner of that firm who would likely defend us charges well more than twice the hourly figure we just heard."

Jamison was grinning, but the dean was not. Jamison had told them that the dean was the audience they needed to pitch. "There are a few other points we need to make," Rachel said. "First, we edit our bills, and no client has ever complained about our fees or that we were piling on hours. Second, and more important, we've gotten in the habit of winning our cases. That's no guaranty we'd be successful defending Spenser. But we're not chopped liver."

The dean's neutral expression caused Rachel to put herself in the administrator's position. If he selected relatively inexperienced lawyers and Spenser lost the case, he might be second-guessed out of his job. The safe, conservative course for the dean was to hire a large, well-respected firm and let them deal with the case. In the dean's position, that is probably what she would do. Jamison's leanings had more to do with a kind of poetic justice than sound business judgment. Still, it would be beyond satisfying if Spenser could prevail in the lawsuit being defended by recent grads.

There was a knock on the door and a dolly bearing food was wheeled into the office by a man wearing an apron and chef's hat.

"I said we'd feed you," Jamison said, "and we intend to do just that. It'll give us more time to get acquainted."

"Great," Simon said. "I'm starved."

Jamison made no motion to rise. "I want to tell you both something before we dine. I've had occasion to mention this to the dean, but I want you to hear it from me." Jamison paused. "I could be teaching at one of our better-known competitors, but I turned them down which was not in my financial interests, something my wife reminds me of from time to time. But I've never regretted my choice, and I'll tell you why. There are young men and women who have what it takes to be attorneys but for some reason will never be accepted at most law schools. Perhaps you two are cases in point. Spenser offers those young men and women an opportunity to realize their potential. The dean is correct: the paper qualifications of our students don't measure up to the paper qualifications of the students accepted by our competitors. But I've never believed that paper qualifications were a valid predictor of lawyer competence and success." Jamison glanced at the dean, whose look remained inscrutable, and then rose. "Let's eat," he concluded.

Simon had insisted they stop for a drink. They were seated at the bar in a fashionable restaurant that catered to a young crowd, and Rachel was content to let her mind idle amidst the background noise.

"I want that case," Simon said determinedly after downing a healthy slug of scotch.

After Jamison had painted Spenser as a school of opportunity, Rachel shared Simon's desire. The professor's short speech had struck a nerve and she wanted to prove him right. "I don't think the dean will agree to hire us," she said, voicing her primary concern.

"You may be right," Simon said glumly. "He didn't strike me as a risk-taker."

"We need to ask Carpenter and Philly what else we can do to sell ourselves."

Simon nodded. "You know, my college grades sucked, and I didn't exactly distinguish myself on the law boards. I will always be grateful to Spenser for giving me a chance. It would be nice to give something back to the school."

"Especially at a hundred dollars an hour higher than our usual charge," Rachel said.

"I don't know why I said that," Simon admitted. "It just came out."

Rachel sipped at her beer. "To this day I don't know why I didn't get into another law school. I was smart, goddamn it."

"You're still smart," Simon said. He glanced at his watch. "It's after ten o'clock," he announced as he took out his cell phone. "Fuck it, I can't wait. I'm calling Carpenter."

"It's late," Rachel pointed out. "This can wait until morning."

"No, it can't," Simon said.

42

Simon finished his e-mail to Stockman and Jamison and paused before pushing SEND. He had followed Carpenter's lead and kept it short and sweet. This morning, Philly had independently proposed Carpenter's approach, so Simon figured it probably was the way to go: Thank the two administrators for meeting with them and considering them for representation. Confirm the firm's desire to represent Spenser. Wish the law school luck in the litigation regardless of whom the school selects to represent it.

Simon smiled as he recalled last night's call to Carpenter. Carpenter had been surprised by the late call but quickly found his bearings. "No shit!" he'd exclaimed when Simon related how he had goosed up the billing rate he and Rachel charged.

Carpenter's read on the situation was that Jamison was in their camp. Carpenter didn't think there was anything else that could be done to talk up their accomplishments. "Let this guy Jamison work on the dean," was Carpenter's advice.

Simon saw no reason to delay and hit SEND. 'It's out of my hands,' he thought.

Philly closed her eyes and focused on the flurry of depositions that had concluded in Martina Glass' personal injury case. Sarah had taken the girls outside, and she had the house to herself. She was tempted to blow off work, get on her bike, which had been given a spring tune-up but had yet to be used, and go off on a short adventure. Outside it was warm but not humid, a clear day perfect for cycling. Unfortunately, work beckoned. She didn't want to let her partners down.

Philly opened her eyes and took out a fresh notepad. On balance, she was pleased with the deposition results. She had decided to put off meeting with her client until the depositions had been concluded, and she was glad that she did.

Now only Glass remained to be deposed. But the depositions that had concluded gave her a better feel for Glass' chances at trial.

The defendants had deposed Jeremy and Mary Rhodes. Mary had ignored all of her instructions and offered a rambling answer to nearly every question. But when all was said and done, Mary Rhodes hadn't budged as to what she had seen: Fred Dunn had fallen over the rail in front of his seat while reaching for a bag of peanuts tossed to him by one of his friends.

Jeremy Rhodes' testimony gave Philly hope that the Salem Stampede could be held to pay more than nominal damages. Jeremy had counted the number of beers Fred Dunn had consumed—four, one more than the posted three-beer limit per person—and in a phlegmatic tone had expressed his opinion that the monitoring of fans' beer intake left a lot to be desired. Over the years, Jeremy claimed to have observed fans being served beer who'd had trouble walking and talking. It had made Philly think that the way to the Salem Stampede's pocketbook was through the bloated stomachs of beer drinking fans. Jeremy had once been told by a beer vendor that the markup on beer exceeded 50%, a figure confirmed by the Salem Stampede's answers to interrogatories. It would be easy to paint the hockey team as an organization motivated by greed as opposed to fan safety.

Deposing Dunn's friend Jerry Lynch had been an exercise in futility. Lynch may not have been as dumb as a doorknob, but nothing he said at his deposition elevated his intelligence over that of any inanimate object. Lynch had sat next to Dunn and claimed not to have seen or heard anything out of the ordinary. Lynch didn't see Dunn fall, didn't hear Frank Madden say anything about being a quarterback throwing Dunn peanuts instead of a football, and couldn't recall how many beers Dunn had consumed but believed it was at least one. During the deposition, Philly had entertained doubts as to whether Lynch was conscious during the hockey game. For the hell of it she asked him who won the game. Lynch couldn't remember. She asked him to name any player on the Salem Stampede and Lynch drew a blank. Lynch couldn't remember whether, during the game, he had consumed food or beverages but owned up to probably having one beer.

Frank Madden, Dunn's other friend, appeared to have suffered a memory lapse of his own, although not as severe as Lynch's. In response to questions from Wayne Martin, the Salem Stampede's lawyer, Madden stated that he had left his seat to go to the men's room, but he couldn't recall buying a bag of peanuts let alone tossing a bag in Dunn's direction. He returned to his seat to see Dunn fall over the guard rail but couldn't say how that occurred.

Martin had gone after Madden methodically. First, he had a series of photographs marked as a deposition exhibit.

"Mr. Madden, the parties have stipulated that the photographs in this exhibit I've handed you were taken where Mr. Dunn landed on the plaintiff just after the accident. Please take a look at the third photograph in the sequence."

Madden desultorily turned over photographs. "I've looked at it."

"What do you see in the lower right-hand corner of the photograph?"

"It looks like a bag of peanuts, but I can't be sure."

"This bag of peanuts that you're not totally sure of—is it open or closed as far as you can tell?"

"I can't tell for sure."

Martin next had a document marked as another deposition exhibit.

"Mr. Madden, the parties have stipulated that this exhibit is a true copy of the police report that was made as a result of Mr. Dunn falling on Ms. Glass. Please read aloud the fourth sentence that begins with the words, quote, 'The contents on the floor where the victim was injured include...'"

Madden squinted and held the document close to his face. "The contents on the floor where the victim was injured include an empty plastic glass that smelled of beer, pieces of popcorn, a torn paper napkin, and an unopened bag of peanuts."

"Thank you, Mr. Madden. I'll ask you again. Isn't it true that you tossed an unopened bag of peanuts to Mr. Dunn and he fell when unsuccessfully reaching for it?"

"No," Madden said with little force.

"No further questions," Martin said.

Ward had no questions for Madden, but Philly did.

"What bar did you stop at before attending the Salem Stampede game?" Philly led off.

Madden lowered his eyes. "I don't remember the name of the place," he said in a small voice.

"Where was it located?"

"It was one of those sports bars across from the arena."

"How many beers did you have there?"

"I don't remember."

"It was more than one, correct?"

"Yeah, probably."

"Isn't it true that you had three beers because you, Mr. Dunn, and Mr. Lynch each bought a round?"

Madden's eyes widened; he was looking at her as if she was clairvoyant, and Philly had to work to maintain a hard stare. She had drawn on her own drinking days for inspiration for her last question. Years back, sitting in the Brighton bar called Shredders, she and the other regulars had often bought each other a round.

"I guess so," Madden said.

"You had a buzz on when you showed up for the game, correct?"

"I was feeling pretty good," Madden said with a note of pride.

"And then you drank more beer at the game, right?"

"Yeah."

"If you hadn't had more beers at the game, wouldn't your throwing a bag of peanuts to Fred Dunn have been more accurate?"

"Maybe… wait a minute! You're trying to trick me."

"Objection!" Ward shouted.

Philly had made a note to herself after the Lynch and Madden depositions—neither of Dunn's friends saw him get pushed.

Philly thought, 'What the hell?' and phoned Wayne Martin. As a plaintiff's lawyer she shared Carpenter's view that it was important for a defendant's lawyer to initiate settlement discussions. But for every rule there had to be an exception and Martina Glass' case struck her as an exception.

"To what do I owe the pleasure?" Martin said when he got on the line.

"Is your client open to discussing settlement?" Philly got to the point.

"Depends what you have in mind."

"I need to talk with my client, but what I have in mind is six figures and the first number isn't a one."

"I don't think settlement discussions would be productive," Martin replied straightaway.

"I appreciate your directness. It struck me that your client may have exposure when it comes to its beer policy. Representing a plaintiff, I don't like to initiate settlement discussions, but I thought it was worth a call to you to explore the subject."

"Mr. Dunn injured your client and my client's position is that it is not responsible for what Dunn did."

"I'm not so sure about that," Philly countered. "My client paid your client money and wasn't kept safe."

Martin laughed. "I guess you're back to your ceiling tile analogy. That may have worked with the judge on a motion to dismiss, but I don't see it working at trial."

"I would disagree."

"We're having this discussion because Dunn is basically a deadbeat. We both know that. My client isn't about to cough up big bucks because the guy who caused your client's injuries is judgment-proof."

"Of course I've considered Dunn's ability to pay a judgment," Philly acknowledged, seeing no reason to play coy over an obvious fact of life. "I simply believe that the way my client was injured leaves your client exposed. Martina Glass wasn't struck by a hockey puck. She was crushed by an inebriated fan."

"Besides cheering loudly, there is no evidence Dunn was drunk."

"Again, we disagree."

"That's what trials are for."

"Is there an amount you would consider recommending to your client?" Philly asked.

"There is, but it would be substantially less than six figures."

"Okay, thanks for taking my call."

Philly set down her phone and dialed Martina Glass' number. A client meeting could no longer be avoided.

Simon had been fantasizing about appearing in front of a jury on behalf of Spenser School of Law when his phone sounded.

"Simon Jeffries."

"It's Helena Peck. Do you have a moment?"

"I do."

"The only issue separating us is money," Peck began. "My client is willing to settle for two hundred fifty thousand dollars. It is not willing to accept the three hundred thousand figure you stressed was necessary to resolve the case. Off the record, I was pleased that the firm was willing to consider a substantial six-figure offer. You may remember that the six-figure number I previously mentioned to you had not been presented to the firm."

"I'll relay what you said to Ms. Sweeney and get back to you promptly. I don't expect the figure to be accepted but stranger things have happened."

"I hope you will recommend the firm's monetary offer," Peck urged.

"For all you know I may have recommended the first figure you mentioned to me."

"I doubt that," Peck said. "All right then; get back to me once you talk with your client."

Simon set down his phone, rose from his desk, and went to see Carpenter.

"I think Meredith should accept the offer, but I'm convinced she'll be too stubborn to bend," Simon concluded his summary. "Any advice?"

Carpenter took out his calculator and the jotted down some figures. If Pinkerton accepted Meredith's offer, she would walk away with $200,000 and the firm's fee would be $100,000. If Meredith accepted Pinkerton's $250,000 offer, she would walk away with $167,500 and the firm's fee would be $82,500.

Carpenter used his computer to locate the time records for work done for Meredith to date. Had they billed for their time on an hourly basis, the total would have been just under $40,000. The lion's share of that time had to do with defending Pinkerton's motion to dismiss Meredith's complaint. Private investigator costs totaled a little over $2,000.

Carpenter turned back to face Simon. Simon's distress seemed genuine and he wondered whether his partner's agonizing had to do with his knowing Meredith.

"I don't like adjusting any fee down, but Philly and I have had occasion to reduce our take on a contingency fee. So there is a way to get Meredith what she wants—or to get her closer to what she wants. If she took the Pinkerton offer, and we lowered our fee from eighty-two thousand five hundred to fifty thousand, that extra thirty-two thousand, five hundred would bring Meredith's take away to the two hundred thousand she wants. So far, on a billable hour basis, we've put in a little under forty thousand on her case, so we wouldn't be taking a hit really—just making less than we could. I might be willing to do some kind of fee adjustment, but everyone would have to agree on how much it was."

Carpenter labored to keep a straight face at Simon's obvious relief.

"I thought of that but didn't know if it was right to bring it up. I'd be willing to adjust our fee. What did you have in mind?"

"I'm not willing to lop the whole thirty-two thousand, five hundred off our fee. But I'd be willing to reduce our fee by half of that—sixteen thousand two hundred and fifty."

"That seems fair," Simon said. "Because it's Meredith we're talking about, I probably would agree to take a bigger hit. Maybe the whole thirty-two thousand, five hundred. Anyone else, probably not. I really think Meredith needs to put this behind her and I think Peck did her best to make that happen."

"I wouldn't agree to reduce our fee to fifty thou," Carpenter said. "Your friend needs to understand that this is real life and you don't always get what you want."

"I understand," Simon said. To Carpenter he still looked tortured.

"Talk to Philly and Rachel," Carpenter said. "If they're on board, talk to Sweeney."

"Okay."

"I have a feeling about this case," Carpenter said. "If we go to trial, I think we're going to end up somewhere around the figure Peck has put on the table. Peck will make out because she's being paid hourly. But we'd be into this case for hundreds of thousands of dollars in billable hours."

"But we'd get attorney fees," Simon said.

"Right, provided we win."

"I think we will win," Simon replied. "I never thought I'd be saying this because I like a good fight, but this is one case where I think it would be best for Meredith if she walked away."

Carpenter decided no matter was too obvious not to be mentioned. "Don't get into talking about reduced legal fees unless Sweeney rejects the Pinkerton offer. Those should be separate discussions separated by at least a day."

"I already figured that out," Simon replied.

Simon steeled himself to call Meredith. Rachel had offered to sit in, but Simon decided to make the call alone: Meredith was looking to him to take the lead in her representation and it was time to act like he was in charge.

"We have a counteroffer," Simon said when Meredith got on the line, and he proceeded to spell it out.

"The answer's no," Meredith said with a finality that Simon had anticipated.

"I heard you loud and clear," Simon replied. "But we have a recommendation for you, and you need to hear it." He consulted his list of talking points and proceeded to touch on each one.

"The answer's still no," Meredith said.

"So be it," Simon said, trying for a neutral tone that didn't reveal his disappointment. "What's your thinking? I'm interested because but for thirty-two thousand, five hundred dollars, you're getting what you want."

"It's not really the money," Meredith said. "It's what the money represents. To me, a three hundred thousand recovery represents something that those bastards will feel. That was the figure I came up with when you first talked to me about what that lawyer proposed. The figure hasn't changed."

Simon decided that arguing with Meredith would be futile. "Suit yourself," he said. "I have my instructions. Frankly, I believe two hundred fifty thousand sends as much of a message as three hundred thousand dollars, but you're the client."

"That's right I am. You've made your point and I know you're trying to look out for me. I appreciate all that. This is just something I have to do."

"As I said, I have my instructions."

43

Paul gestured to one of the empty seats at a conference table in their captain's office. There was no other reasonable place to hold a meeting of this type. The Cambridgeport station of the Cambridge Police Department had formerly been a school that had been rehabbed to serve law enforcement. Officer desks occupied a large open area that didn't offer privacy. The interrogation rooms were simply unsuitable for a meeting with an attorney.

Tony Cianno took the designated seat and regarded his surroundings. "This station never changes."

"You asked for a meeting without your clients present," Evelyn said, and Paul observed her eagerness to get down to business. After living with the Finch case for months, the prospect that some light would be shed on the mess had them both ratcheted up a notch.

Cianno eyed Evelyn for a moment. "So that's the way it is," he said. "No small talk. Fair enough." He opened his briefcase and extracted a plain brown paper bag.

"You want my clients to view some photographs, correct?"

"Correct," Evelyn confirmed.

"So far, you will not permit me to view the photographs until my clients see them."

It wasn't a question, but Evelyn said, "Correct again."

"I have photographs in this paper bag," Cianno said, shaking it. "I propose that we simultaneously exchange photographs. I'll show you mine if you show me yours."

Paul saw Evelyn's irritation rising. Cianno must have noticed her reaction but his expression remained neutral.

"That's not something we're prepared to do at this time," Paul said.

"May I ask why?"

Paul shook his head. "No. It's simply the way we want to proceed in this case."

Cianno sat still for a long moment. Paul entertained the thought that he would return his bag of photographs to his briefcase, get up, and leave.

"Very well. I will show you the photographs I have brought with me provided that you make no copies and I leave here with all of them. Do we have a deal?"

Evelyn gave a barely perceptible head shake, but Paul overruled her. "Deal," he said.

Cianno removed the photographs from the bag, cleared some surface area, and began to lay out the photographs one at a time so they were facing the detectives.

Paul's breath caught as he viewed the first photographs to be revealed. They looked identical to the photographs that were found in Daryl Finch's bedroom. Perhaps they were identical. Paul counted eighteen photographs. He turned over the first displayed photograph and observed the letters LFLS.

"Where did you get these?" Evelyn demanded.

Cianno ignored her question. He searched in his briefcase and withdrew a sheet of paper. "You may keep this copy," he said, passing the paper across the table.

Paul held the document so Evelyn could read it with him. It was a copy of an ad run in a newspaper. "*Wanted. Young boys aged 8 to 10 to pose for photographs of a graphic, disturbing nature. Parental consent required. Parental presence during the photo shoot required. Payment to be provided in the amount of $750. Approximate time of photo shoot 1 to 2 hours.*"

Evelyn silently fumed beside him. Paul put her funk out of his mind and began to rearrange the pieces of the Finch puzzle. Reassembled, the pieces told a unifying story.

"LFLS," Paul said.

"Aren't you going to take a guess what they stand for?" Cianno asked.

"No," Paul said.

"Life father, like son," Cianno replied.

Paul paused, made a show of assessing the answer. "Was the old man that much of a prick?" he finally asked.

"His sons thought so."

"Do they have the names of the boys who posed?"

"They do."

"We'll need that information."

"First, I need you to tell me where you're headed," Cianno insisted.

"Fair enough. I'll get back to you."

"Are we done?" Cianno asked.

"Shit!" Evelyn muttered.

Paul ignored his partner. He took his time replaying the story to see if it still hung together. "I wouldn't have figured the old man would be so upset by the pictures," he finally said.

"But he was," Cianno said. "Imagine getting one or two every month."

"Are you saying the sons weren't like the father?" Paul said, thinking of Heather Finch.

Something Paul took for concern flashed briefly in Cianno's eyes, but the change in the lawyer's expression was so fleeting that Paul wondered whether it had occurred.

"When it came to these boys in the photographs, it was not 'like father like son.'"

Paul digested the defense lawyer's comment. Paul assumed that Cianno knew what had gone on between the siblings; the lawyer would have demanded to be informed of anything of a criminal nature that could rear up and bite his clients. The Finch brothers, if they were smart, would have informed him of what had gone on. And Cianno was too experienced to provide any information that would call into question his clients' conduct toward their sister.

"Now we're done," Paul said, rising and extending his hand.

Cianno shook hands, gathered the photographs, and left the office without another word.

"Motherfucker!" Evelyn let loose after the lawyer shut the door.

"What's eating you?"

"Are you buying all this shit?"

Paul was. "It makes sense," he said. "We'll check it all out to be sure, but it makes sense."

"Shit!"

"Enough already with the attitude!"

"I can't believe all the time we put in."

"So what? The important thing is to get it right. If there's no crime, there's no crime."

Paul watched Evelyn simmer down. Her reaction was inappropriate even if she had taken a blow to the head in the line of duty.

"Sorry," Evelyn said.

"Apology accepted. Just don't do it again."

"That's quite a story," Philly said.

"Yeah, it is," Paul said.

Paul rarely talked about his cases, but this was one case that he'd continued to fill her in on. Philly thought of the sister living far away, always concerned her brothers might come after her. "Are you or Evelyn going to circle back with the sister?" she asked.

Paul snuggled closer. Philly loved ending a day this way—love-making, cuddling, talking about whatever in the dark.

"I don't think so," Paul said.

"What are you going to do next?"

"I'll talk it over with our captain. If he agrees, I'll call the sons' lawyer and tell him if his story checks out, we won't be pursuing the matter. I'll ask him to send me copies of all the photographs tied to a list of the kids who posed. And I'll want a parent contact for each kid."

"What was going on with Evelyn?" she asked.

"I'm not totally sure. I think she wanted to throw someone in jail. She's not going to get her wish."

44

Simon had let two days go by before he called Meredith. This time he wanted Rachel with him.

"Rachel's here and you're on speaker," Simon said when Meredith picked up. "I haven't called Peck back because we've been kicking your situation around some more."

"There's nothing to kick around," Meredith replied. "I thought I was clear."

"You were clear," Simon acknowledged. "We know you have a contrary view, but we continue to believe Peck's offer is fair and should be accepted. If you do change your mind and accept her proposal, we will reduce our legal fee by sixteen thousand, two hundred and fifty dollars. That means you would recover monetarily close to what you would have recovered if your offer had been accepted less the investigator costs we advanced."

When Meredith didn't respond immediately, Simon hoped she was working a calculator, checking his math. If she was crunching numbers, it meant she was considering what he'd said.

"For me," Meredith said, "it's always been more about what Pinkerton had to pony up than what I put in my pocket. I appreciate what you guys have offered to do. But I still want Pinkerton to pay three hundred thousand to make the case go away."

Simon had prepared himself for Meredith's response. Rachel looked shocked.

"Hi Meredith. It's Rachel. May I say something?"

"Sure."

"I know you want to make a point. I understand that. In all honesty, I think you will have made your point if you accept Pinkerton's offer. I don't think the point you will have made will be made any better if Pinkerton paid two hundred and fifty thousand, three hundred thousand, or six hundred thousand."

"I don't see it that way," Meredith interjected.

"I know you don't," Rachel said. "But hear me out. I totally disagree with you that this is not about what you put in your pocket. This is all about what you put in your pocket. Before Simon and I started practicing with our partners, I thought more like you. I thought that money wasn't the end-all and that scoring a moral victory was important. I no longer believe that to the extent I used to. When you represent a lot of plaintiffs, as we do, you learn that what has lasting impact on a plaintiff's life is the dollars the plaintiff puts in her pocket."

"What alien took over your body?" Meredith said.

"I haven't even gotten to my most important point," Rachel said. "There's something to be said for putting this matter behind you and moving forward. I'm probably contradicting myself because I just told you what you put in your pocket was what was important. But in this case, I think moving on is even more important. Think about what your life is going to be like if you have to live with this case 24/7 for months, or even years. Is that how you want your life to be?"

Simon realized he should have had Rachel with him during his first phone conversation with Meredith.

"I don't think I can bring myself to yield on this," Meredith said.

"You're wrong there," Rachel quickly countered. "It's amazing what you can yield on. I swore to myself I would never set foot in a courtroom, let alone get in front of a jury. Now, if you believe our website, I'm some kind of hot-shot litigator. People have it in them to focus on what's really important and to make their life better."

"Okay, I get what you're saying," Meredith said.

"Just the same, I'm going to spell it out anyway," Rachel said. "You need to get out of your own way. You've drawn a line in the sand at three hundred thousand. You need to consider erasing that line and drawing a new line."

When Meredith rang off, Rachel asked, "How did I do?"

Simon could never have spoken to Meredith the way Rachel just did. "You did great," he said. "But you know what she's going to do, don't you? She's going to say no."

"We'll see," Rachel said. "You can never tell."

Simon's line rang and he picked up.

"It's Dean Stockman. Do you have a moment?"

"I do, Dean. Rachel's with me and I'm going to put you on speaker. Give us a moment."

Rachel had been working at Philly's desk. She got up, moved the visitor's chair to Simon's workstation and offered him what she hoped was a reassuring smile. Simon rarely showed upset or disappointment, but she was certain he'd be crushed if Spenser didn't select them for representation. She'd pointed out that even if the law school opted for former graduates to take on the case against it, they might not be the ones.

"We're all set, Dean," Simon said.

"Professor Jamison has worked me over big time," the dean said. "As you might expect, he can be very persuasive. It must have to do with all the nitpicking he does about evidentiary issues. I have some questions for you. First, do you have the resources to handle the case? There will be a lot of paper and a lot of discovery. You have a small firm and I have to consider the possibility you will be overwhelmed by the documents."

"We can handle paper," Simon quickly replied.

Rachel regarded Simon's answer as too glib. "We've been involved in a number of cases that had a lot of paper," she said. "For example, the first case we worked on with our other partners involved the representation of a finance company that was in trouble with a regulatory board. There were hundreds of loan documents that had to be reviewed. Simon and I and one of our other partners dealt with virtually all of the paperwork."

"I see," the dean said. "Have either of you ever been involved in a case such as the suit brought against the law school?"

"No," Simon responded reluctantly.

The dean fell silent. Simon squirmed in his seat. Rachel anticipated that the dean would make a decision before he rang off; the administrator wouldn't have called them if he hadn't been entertaining the thought of hiring them.

"Send me an engagement letter," the dean said. "You're not hired until I sign it but the fact that I'm asking for it should tell you the direction I'm leaning. I want to sleep on this decision a little longer."

"We're grateful for your confidence in us," Simon said, grinning broadly.

"I haven't officially hired you yet," the dean qualified.

"A mere formality," Simon replied, and Rachel was relieved when the dean laughed.

45

Jeannie Smith was setting up her stenographer equipment in the conference room. Mary Ellen Pines' deposition in Clyde Atkins' case was scheduled to begin in ten minutes. Simon tried to focus, but distractions gnawed at him. Meredith hadn't gotten back on whether she would accept Pinkerton's monetary offer. Dean Stockman had yet to sign the engagement letter that had been sent to him by e-mail. Simon wished that these matters had sorted themselves out before this deposition.

"Am I going to enjoy this?" Smith asked.

"Since I don't think *I'll* be enjoying myself," Simon replied, "I don't see any reason for *you* to enjoy yourself."

Smith grunted. "Spoken like Carpenter. Heaven help you."

Benjamin Learner, Mary Ellen Pines' attorney, had been objecting to nearly every question, and this tactic had had one beneficial effect. Simon was now pissed off and focused. Learner's objections were unnecessary; they had stipulated that his objection rights were preserved.

Simon took a moment to regard Pines. She was smug and had come across as if her deposition was a nuisance that she was deigning to tolerate. She was dressed in a conservative blue business suit and, as was the case when she had appeared in court, she was impeccably turned out. The upswept curl to her blond hair looked like a pipeline that a surfer would find enticing. As in court, she wore bright red lipstick and heavy black eyeliner. She struck Simon as the sort of woman who would join a country club and play tennis as if her life depended on the outcome.

Simon introduced Pines' 2011 personal financial statement as a deposition exhibit and directed her to the net-worth line. "Is it true, Ms. Pines, that you and your husband are strapped for cash?"

"Objection," Learner said. "What does 'strapped for cash' mean? Your question is vague and unintelligible."

"Did you understand my question?" Simon asked Pines.

"Not really," Pines replied, taking the cue from her lawyer.

"Do you and your husband live paycheck to paycheck?"

"I wouldn't say that," Pines said with a note of hostility.

"Would it be correct that your liquid cash at the end of 2011 was slightly under fifty thousand dollars?"

Pines studied her financial statement. "That's what it says here."

"Is it true that over the last five years your liquid cash has decreased?"

Pines paused, favored Simon with an angry stare. "I believe that's right."

"Given this decrease over time, at what point in time do you project your liquid cash to run out?"

"Objection," Learner said. "Answer the question if you can?"

"I've never made such a projection."

"Are you concerned your liquid cash will run out?"

"Not particularly. I'm sure we'll make do."

"Why are you sure you'll make do?"

Pines leveled another sullen stare in his direction, and Simon realized that she didn't like to be pressed on the details behind any assertion she made.

"We can always find ways to economize if necessary."

"Economize on what?"

"I don't know," Pines sputtered in irritation. "I suppose food, entertainment, things like that."

"Is it true that if you were able to put some of the money that your brother, Clyde Atkins, the plaintiff in this case, was receiving from the business in your own pocket, you wouldn't have a need to economize?"

"Objection," Learner said.

"I haven't done any calculation if that's what you mean."

"That's not at all what I meant. Please read back my question," Simon requested Smith.

Pines settled into a funk after the question was read back to her. "I suppose the more money I was able to take from the business, the less I would need to economize. But that's not anything I was counting on."

"Where will the next payment for your son's private school come from?"

"Objection," Learner said.

"How dare you," Pines flared.

"Answer my question," Simon said slowly, drawing out each word and keeping his tone even.

"We have the cash to make the payment."

"Is the cash you are referring to the liquid cash we just spoke about?"

"Yes."

"As we sit here in 2012, is the liquid cash currently available to you less than the liquid cash that existed at the end of 2011 as shown on your personal financial statement?"

"Yes," Pines said grudgingly.

Simon opted for an abrupt subject change. "What are the specific things done by Clyde Atkins that you contend were not in the best interests of your family business?"

"He routinely took positions that were contrary to the financial best interests of the company."

"Please give me an example," Simon requested.

"He didn't want to charge for follow-up repair work even if an initial repair had been done correctly."

"Did the company ever not charge for follow-up repair work?"

"No."

"Did you and your brother Malcolm outvote Clyde on that issue?"

"Thankfully, yes."

"Can you give me any other example of Clyde Atkins acting contrary to the financial best interests of the company?"

"I mentioned this in the affidavit I filed in court. He wanted us to take a loss on a snowblower model we had purchased."

"Are you talking about a snowblower called the Snow Blaster, model number AZ9500?"

"Yes."

"Did the company ever stop selling that model?"

"No."

"Is this another instance in which you and your brother Malcolm outvoted Clyde?"

"Yes."

"What was your and Malcolm's response to Clyde's contention that the Snow Blaster was dangerous?"

"We didn't buy it. Clyde mentioned some consumer report article, but he wouldn't accept the fact that there was no recall ordered on the product."

"Did you read the consumer report article?"

"No."

"Do you know whether Malcolm read the article?"

"No. You'll have to ask him."

"Did your company ever sell all of its stock of Snow Blasters?"

"No."

"How many were left unsold?"

"Twenty-nine."

"Were salesmen and saleswomen in your company instructed to push the Snow Blaster model to customers?"

Pines glanced briefly at Learner. "Our sales staff is instructed to sell all products in stock."

"Was your sales staff given any special instructions to sell Snow Blasters?"

"That's possible."

"Did you give company sales staff any special instructions to sell Snow Blasters?"

"I don't remember. I might have."

"Did any customers point to the consumer report article as a reason for not wanting to buy the Snow Blaster?"

Pines sat rigidly in her chair. "I think a few might have mentioned the article."

"Did anyone in your company try to downplay the article because of there not having been a recall?"

"I don't know."

"Did your brother Clyde provide a copy of the article to you and Malcolm?"

"I think he did."

"Then why didn't you read the article?"

Simon met Pines' stony stare with a smile and her expression further hardened.

"I didn't see a reason to read the article."

"When Clyde provided you and Malcolm with a copy of the article, did he mention that the Snow Blaster had had occasion to blow up?"

"He might have."

"Is it correct that despite hearing of the machine exploding, you still didn't see a reason to read the article?"

"Yes. I already explained about the lack of a recall notice."

Simon realized that it had been a while since Learner had objected to a question. "Besides not wanting to charge for repeat repairs and not wanting to sell Snow Blasters, what else did Clyde do that you regarded as not in the best interests of your company?"

Pines shifted in her chair. "I can't think of anything else at the moment. Those were the main things I was concerned about."

"What do you want to do with the money that will no longer be paid to Clyde?"

"Objection!" Learner intervened. "What do you mean by 'you?' Do you mean Ms. Pines? Do you mean the company?"

Simon directed what he hoped was a withering stare in Learner's direction. "What do you personally want to do with the money that will no longer be paid to Clyde?"

"I haven't decided."

"When will you decide?"

"Probably when this case is over. As you know, the Board of Directors held a meeting and voted to terminate Clyde's contract without cause. He'll be paid for sixty days and, after that, as the court ordered, the money he would have been paid will be set aside in a bank account."

"Before the judge ordered the money set aside in a bank account, what did you want to do with the money that would have gone to Clyde?"

"I'm not sure I ever came up with a decision on that."

"Did Malcolm ever express to you what he wanted to do with the money?"

"He may have. I don't remember one way or the other."

"Who is performing Clyde's duties at the company?"

"I am."

"Have you increased the hours you devote to the business since Clyde stopped working at the business?"

"I would say so."

"How has the company's business fared since Clyde stopped working?"

Pines directed a glance toward Learner and quickly refocused on Simon. "I would say there's been no real change. There might have been a slight dip in sales."

"If your company hired an individual to perform the functions previously performed by your brother Clyde, would you anticipate paying that individual more or less than Clyde had been paid?"

Pines paused. "I can't say for certain, but I would anticipate paying someone less."

"Over the last ten years would you describe your relationship with your brother Clyde as cordial?"

Pines sighed, her exasperation evident. "'Cordial' is not the word I would use."

"What word would you use?"

"We put up with each other, but I don't think either of us particularly likes the other."

"Would you use 'cordial' to describe your relationship with your brother Malcolm over the last ten years?"

"No. My relationship with Malcolm has been pretty much the same as my relationship with Clyde."

"Over the last ten years how would you describe the relationship between your brothers?"

"For God's sake!" Pines exclaimed, sending an imploring look Learner's way. "I don't know. It seemed to me they put up with each other."

"Did you and your siblings spend holidays together over the last ten years?"

"I can recall a few occasions when that happened. We didn't make a habit of it."

Simon reflected that the family dynamic among the siblings described by Pines was pretty much in accord with Clyde Atkins' assessment.

"Before Clyde's lawsuit, is it true that you and your brother Malcolm determined to send your brother Clyde a letter terminating Clyde's employment with the company?"

"Yes."

"Why wasn't the decision to terminate Clyde's employment brought up at a Board of Directors meeting?"

"Objection," Learner said with some force.

"I really couldn't tell you. It didn't seem necessary. The two of us had had it with Clyde's indifference to the financial wellbeing of the company."

"Before the letter terminating Clyde was sent, did you and Malcolm meet together to discuss that action?"

"Yes."

"Was anyone else present at the meeting?"

"I think our father may have been present for part of it."

Simon made a notation on his notepad. This bit of information was new.

"What did your father say during the meeting?"

"I don't recall."

"What do you recall about your father's involvement at the meeting?"

Pines paused and drummed her fingers on the conference room table. "I recall that he was in favor of removing Clyde."

"How did your father express his being in favor of removing Clyde?"

"Now that I think about it, I believe he said something like, 'If Clyde is being irresponsible, then you have to do something about it.'"

"Why wasn't Clyde at that meeting?"

"He wasn't invited."

"Where did the meeting take place?"

"At my father's house."

"When the meeting was set up at your father's house, was your father told that a purpose of the meeting was to consider terminating Clyde's employment with the company?"

"I think I mentioned that to my father."

"Why was the meeting scheduled at your father's house?"

"I thought it was a good idea so my father wouldn't have to travel."

"Before the recent Board of Directors meeting you previously mentioned, when was the last time the company's Board held a meeting?"

Pines emitted another audible sigh. "I don't know. Probably years ago."

"The corporate records that you and your brother provided in discovery show that the last meeting of the Board of Directors occurred in 2007. Are the corporate records correct in that respect?"

"I suppose so."

"Did you regard Board of Directors meetings as unnecessary following the Board meeting in 2007?"

"I guess I did to some extent. The three of us worked together and we typically talked about problems without having to schedule a formal meeting."

"Before terminating Clyde before Clyde's lawsuit, did you talk with Clyde about the problems you and Malcolm had with him?"

"No."

"Who is paying for Mr. Learner's legal services?"

"Objection!" Learner said.

Simon had Smith read back his question.

"The company is," Pines said.

Simon consulted his deposition outline. He had covered the ground he needed to traverse. But since Pines and Learner had bugged him, he couldn't bring himself to end his questioning.

"When I asked about paying for private schooling for your son, you became visibly upset. Why was that?"

"Objection!" Learner said.

"Christ!" Pines muttered under her breath.

"You were wrong," Jeannie Smith said as she packed up her stenographer gear following the conclusion of Mary Ellen Pines' deposition.

"In what way?" Simon asked.

"I enjoyed myself."

"I'm glad somebody did."

"Stop being so grouchy. I think you did an okay job. That woman was a tough customer. She came across as pushy, demanding, and wanting her own way. I don't think a jury will like her."

"Any other impressions?" Simon asked.

'I'm guessing here," Smith said, "but I'd bet this woman is a stronger person than her brother Malcolm. You might want to take Malcolm's deposition or start off with Malcolm at trial."

Smith had a point. Mary Ellen Pines had probably led the charge to oust Clyde from the company. "Any other observation about Pines?"

Smith closed her carrying case. "No matter what she says, I think money is a big deal to the woman. Being part of a profitable company and not being able to save any money has got to gall her."

Simon had come away with the same impression.

"And you didn't ask her about her social life. Is she a member of a country club? Does she go to the theater? Does the family have a boat? Where does the family vacation? Things like that."

"Where are you going with this?"

"Geez, you're the lawyer," Smith said. "What if this woman is trying to keep up appearances while her money dwindles away? She struck me that way."

"I'll keep that in mind," Simon said. "The thing is, her financial statement didn't show any country club dues or list a boat as an asset."

"So you believe the financial statement?" Smith asked, smiling and raising her eyebrows.

"I guess I did," Simon said.

"Aren't you the trusting sort!"

46

Meredith's cell phone number appeared on Simon's caller ID. He motioned for Rachel to join him.

"Hi, Meredith. Rachel's with me. You're on speaker."

"I'm glad you're both there. I'm not going to keep you in suspense. I've decided to take the deal. Get this done fast before I change my mind."

Simon felt relieved. He didn't care why Meredith had changed course but since Rachel was sure to ask her, he figured he'd beat Rachel to the punch. "Do you care to share your thinking with us?"

"Rachel was right. I need to focus on landing a job and making a fresh go of my career. Fighting Pinkerton would have made both those goals more difficult. And it is a lot of money."

Rachel grinned broadly. Simon was thankful he didn't take her up on the side bet she had proposed as to Meredith's decision.

"We'll get on it and call you back," Simon said.

"I want to thank you both. I'm sure I wasn't the easiest of clients."

"Don't mention it," Rachel said, employing Carpenter's standard response.

"Did you guys ever figure out what was going on with that woman—Stephanie Manley?"

"Our partner, Carpenter, has a theory," Simon said. "McCauley's photograph of Manley and Gwen Carson suggests they're an item. Carpenter thinks that Manley called Carson after McCauley contacted her. He thinks that Carson put Manley up to approaching McCauley."

"As a theory," Meredith said, "it makes a kind of sick sense. But if they were an item, why did Carson come on to me?"

"Maybe they have some kind of open relationship," Simon replied.

"Jesus!"

"No more small talk," Simon said. "We've got a call to make."

Rachel not only wanted to be present when Simon spoke to Helena Peck, she also wanted to do the talking and try to get more money for Meredith. "I don't like it," Simon said. "What if Peck pulls the offer off the table?"

"We're not going to reject her offer," Rachel said.

"She could still pull the offer off the table. Pinkerton could direct her to do that. We need to talk to Carpenter about this. I don't want to screw this up."

"I ran this by Carpenter," Rachel said. "He thinks there's some risk but not a lot of risk."

"Shit!" Simon exclaimed. "You're trying for poetic justice of a kind after all. You're a hypocrite."

Rachel didn't look offended. "Come on. I'll do the talking."

"What's gotten into you?"

"I'm working on being more assertive. Josh has given me a few tips. I really think this is something that makes sense to do."

"I've got a bad feeling about this," Simon said as he dialed Peck's number.

"I hope you have good news for me," Peck said when she picked up on her line.

"We have news," Simon said. "You're on speaker because my partner Rachel Boyle is with me. Rachel will report to you."

"Hi, Ms. Peck. We appreciate everything you've done to try to resolve this case informally. I can tell you that if your client adds sixteen thousand, two hundred and fifty dollars to the last figure you mentioned, we have a deal in principle on all issues."

"So you're rejecting my client's offer," Peck said.

"Not at all," Rachel said. "I didn't say a thing about rejecting your client's offer. What I did say was that if the amount I mentioned was added to the figure you previously communicated, there would be a resolution of all issues."

Peck fell silent. Simon couldn't stand the suspense. Peck would have to get back to them but first she'd have to talk with Pinkerton representatives. Another week would go by before this got resolved and Meredith, rightly, would want to know why there was a delay.

"What an odd amount," Peck finally said. "You wouldn't be reducing your fee by any chance, would you?"

"Why would we do that?" Rachel responded, and Simon was surprised at how much his partner was enjoying this back and forth. "Don't lawyers take an oath that they won't reduce an earned fee under any circumstances?" Rachel added.

"Very funny," Peck said. "I'll have to go back to my client."

"We would like to hear back from you today if at all possible," Rachel said.

"I'll bet you would," Peck said. "I'll see what I can do."

"That went well," Rachel said, when Peck dropped off the line.

"I've got a bad feeling about this," Simon replied.

"I thought I was the pessimist," Rachel said.

Simon had ignored a voice mail message from Meredith who plainly wanted to confirm that Pinkerton's offer had been accepted. It was now after five and he and Rachel were the only ones in the office. He disliked leaving Meredith hanging but had no choice. He was about to shut down his computer when he noticed a new e-mail in his Inbox from Dean Stockman. There was an attachment to the e-mail that signaled good news.

"Rachel!" Simon called out. She had retreated to Carpenter's office for some privacy, but they had left their doors open and he hoped she had heard his shout.

Dean Stockman had countersigned the engagement letter, the first engagement letter Simon had signed on behalf of the firm. A copy of the court complaint and other pertinent documents would be delivered first thing tomorrow morning.

Rachel entered Philly's office. "You called?"

"Dean Stockman hired us. Infuckingcredible!"

"All right!" Rachel shouted. "This is great." She moved to Simon's workstation and gave him a hug.

"Tomorrow we're going to be swamped," Simon said.

"Stop complaining. You got what you wanted."

"So I did," Simon said, thinking, 'Just be careful what you wish for.'

Simon's line rang and he picked up the phone. "Simon Jeffries."

"Helena Peck."

"Hold on. Rachel's here so I'm putting you on speaker."

"Are you two joined at the hip?"

"Simon should be so lucky," Rachel said.

"We have a deal," Peck said.

"Excellent," Simon said. 'Thank God,' is what he thought.

"If I said my client wouldn't agree to more money, what would you have done?" Peck asked.

"We would have accepted your previous offer," Rachel said.

"I think the two of you played a dangerous game here," Peck said. "I might have called to say no to the additional money and to inform you that my client's previous offer was now off the table."

"You might have," Rachel said, "but you didn't. And we all know one reason you didn't is that your client's policy on negative two-year evaluations is beyond contemptible. We sensed that largely through your efforts your client understood the harmful repercussions if that policy became known. The further proposal made to you wasn't overreaching. If you had to sell it, we're appreciative of your efforts."

Simon again felt that he was seeing a new side of Rachel.

"That's an impressive speech, Ms. Boyle, but I meant what I said. If you tried to obtain more for your client without her consent, you were asking for trouble. If you ask for trouble often enough, trouble is sure to find you."

Rachel was unrepentant. "You've made your point," she said to Peck. "Who's taking the first shot at settlement documents?"

"I'll do that," Peck said. "You'll receive drafts including a draft of the firm's letter commenting on your client's employment at Pinkerton. Let's try to wrap this up in a week."

"Thank you," Rachel said.

When Peck rang off, Simon regarded Rachel. "I think Peck was right," he said. "I don't think we should have played that little game without consulting Meredith. Frankly, I'm surprised Carpenter didn't object."

"I think we were okay so long as we didn't reject Peck's offer."

"I disagree. Meredith told us to accept Peck's offer. We were playing with fire. This was plain dumb. If Peck had withdrawn her offer, how would you feel?"

"Lousy," Rachel admitted.

"'Lousy' wouldn't begin to describe it for me. We could have been in real trouble here if the deal blew up."

"Peck's an experienced litigator," Rachel pointed out. "She knew exactly what game we were playing. She could have said—but she didn't—that if she went back to Pinkerton with the request for additional money, there was a good chance her previous offer would be pulled off the table."

Simon wasn't mollified. "In the future, I'm going with my gut. But right now, I'm going to return a call to Meredith."

47

Paul had never been able to warm up to his captain on a personal level, but he respected the man. Jacob Woods was a short, spare man with a salt and pepper buzz cut and a complexion so dark his face seemed to be made of weathered, dried out leather. Paul had let Evelyn deliver the briefing on the Daryl Finch case and Captain Woods heard her out without expression.

"Outside of the brothers abusing the sister, there's been no crime committed by either of the brothers in connection with the kids in the photographs," Woods summed up.

"That's our conclusion," Paul said. "Evelyn interviewed three of the parents whose kids sat for photographs. The stories checked out."

"All right," Woods said. "I don't want to hear about this fiasco anymore. We've spent enough time and money chasing our tails."

"I could take another run at the sister," Evelyn said. "Maybe she can be persuaded to press charges."

"I don't recommend that," Paul said, irritated that Evelyn had raised the subject. "The sister plainly wants to stay lost. The brothers were teens when it happened. I think we'd be chasing our tails again."

Evelyn stared at her hands. Paul couldn't figure why she wouldn't let go of the case.

"I agree," Woods declared. "This is over. If the sister reaches out to us, that's another story."

Paul held the door for Evelyn as they exited the captain's office. When they returned to their desks, he decided to confront her.

"I didn't appreciate your trying to keep this matter alive. What the hell is going on?"

Evelyn met his gaze. "The brother I met was a creep and it sounded like the brother you met was no better. I don't like to see guys like that get away with anything."

"The captain was right," Paul said. "Heather knows where to find us."

"I don't see it that way."

"Then open your eyes."

Sitting down in the Boston office conference room, Philly felt dispossessed. Her office had been totally taken over by Rachel and Simon. If she ever managed to return to work full-time, they would need a bigger office. There was no way Carpenter would share his space.

Carpenter led her other partners into the conference room. Philly realized that it had been a long time since the four of them had sat down together. The geezer looked good, which in his case meant less cranky than usual. And Carpenter hadn't mentioned his cancer in a while, which had to be a good thing. "So here we are," she said, "the proverbial motley crew."

"You're looking good," Rachel said to Philly. "Are you showing yet?"

"I'm showing weight gain," Philly replied. This pregnancy was tracking her first one—she was eating like crazy.

"We've got Meredith coming by in an hour," Simon said. "I'd like to get started. There are a couple of things I want to discuss."

"I'll start," Philly said. "Martina Glass' case. I met with Glass and she doesn't want to settle for small dollars with the Salem Stampede. The case is going to go to trial. Simon and I will handle the trial."

"How's Glass doing medically?" Carpenter asked.

"Pretty good," Philly said. "She's pretty much recovered."

"What were her medical expenses?"

"A hundred and fifty thousand."

Carpenter frowned. "I think the case is a winner," he said, "but I don't see a big score here."

"Agreed," Philly replied.

"Let's move to Meredith," Simon prompted, and Philly sensed that this was the case Simon wanted to focus on. "The paperwork is done. Thanks for so quickly reviewing what Helena Peck sent over," he said to Philly and Carpenter.

"Did Sweeney look at the papers?" Philly asked.

Simon nodded; he looked tense and uncomfortable. "She wanted to know why she was getting more money than we had talked about previously and I said we'd explain it to her when we met. Her getting more money is what I really want to talk about. I don't think we should have tried to get her more money without talking to her first and getting her approval."

"What's the problem?" Carpenter prodded.

"The problem is that Meredith directed us to accept a settlement offer and we didn't follow her instructions. Instead we tried to get her more money. We should have gotten her approval to do that. We risked having an offer taken off the table that we were instructed to accept."

"Rachel talked to me about this," Carpenter said. "My view was that as long as you didn't reject the offer, there was nothing wrong with trying to do better for Sweeney. The other attorney—Peck—never said the offer might be withdrawn if you came back asking for more money."

"That doesn't matter to me," Simon responded. "I think if we're going to disregard a client's instruction, we need to talk it out with the client first. If the offer had been retracted, we would have been up shit's creek. When Peck went back to Pinkerton with the new dollar figure, Pinkerton could have been pissed and withdrawn its previous offer."

Philly was surprised that Rachel was the one who had taken the aggressive course. "I think Simon has the better side of this," she said. "It worked out, but if it hadn't, the fallout would have been miserable."

"After talking with Carpenter, I thought the approach made sense," Rachel said.

Carpenter was sitting still, staring off into space, his jaw muscles working. "I forgot two important rules," he said, his focus returning to their gathering. "I forgot the 'sleep at night' rule. You don't want to do anything that's going to make you lose sleep. Simon clearly wasn't able to sleep over this."

"I was trying to be more aggressive than I usually am," Rachel said, but she didn't look put out by Carpenter's change of heart.

"What was the other rule?" Simon asked.

Carpenter exhibited what for him passed for a smile. "The most important rule," he said. "Clients are mean-spirited shits who will turn on you in a second. If we had screwed up what Sweeney thought was a done deal, she could have come after us."

"That's probably true," Simon said. "But it's also that a client needs to be able to trust us. Even if it works out, a move like we made chips away at the trust, and maybe at a client's willingness to refer us to someone else."

"For the future," Philly said, "let's follow Simon's lead. A client's clear instruction gets followed unless the client is consulted and approves an alternative approach."

Philly paused a beat to see if there was a dissenting vote. There wasn't. Even Rachel was on board. "What's next?" Philly asked.

"Spenser School of Law," Rachel and Simon said together and immediately started laughing.

"Congratulations on landing this case," Philly said. "Especially at a higher than usual rate. We could use a meaty billable-hour case."

Simon nodded toward Rachel who cleared her throat. "Simon and I have gone over the complaint and the plaintiffs' discovery requests. Dean Stockman had been concerned about our ability to handle the mass of paper this case will generate. He was right to be concerned. It's enormous."

Carpenter had brought a notepad to the meeting and was poised to write.

"The plaintiffs want to see the law school's records on students for the last five years. They've requested documents for the last five years as to job placement efforts by the law school on behalf of students past and present. They also want to see all records going back five years relating to students' employment both within and outside law."

"The school is concerned about the confidentiality of student records," Simon said. "There's likely to be personal, confidential information contained in each student's file."

"Which means a lawyer needs to go through each student's file before anything is handed over to the plaintiffs," Carpenter observed.

"Right," Simon confirmed. "We're talking about hundreds of files and some of the files are fairly thick."

"Simon and I may need some help going through records," Rachel said.

"Also, the law school would prefer to have student records reviewed at the law school," Simon added.

Carpenter wasn't going to bury himself searching through records. With her pregnancy and the law school wanting to keep possession of student records, Philly couldn't be much help, either. "What do you want to do?" she asked.

"We haven't quite figured that out," Rachel said.

The room fell silent. Philly hoped that the firm hadn't bit off something it couldn't chew.

"There's always Meredith," Simon said.

"The gang's all here," Meredith said as she took a seat in the conference room.

Philly took the moment to size up their client. There was no denying that Meredith had presence, a confident bearing and a penetrating gaze. If she was relieved that her case had settled, you couldn't tell from her expression. Philly couldn't figure out what was missing and then it hit her. The young woman was about to sign papers entitling her to a major payday, but she was exhibiting no sign of joy or excitement at the prospect.

"We've looked over the papers and we think they're in order and ready for your signature," Simon said. "You've had a chance to review them. Do you have any questions?"

"Just one. What's with the extra money?"

Simon nodded to Rachel.

"We explored getting you a little something extra," Rachel said, "and it worked out. Our legal fee is as we previously agreed."

"I'm getting what I would have gotten if my proposal had been accepted."

"Correct," Rachel confirmed.

"Your legal fee should apply to the extra amount you obtained."

"No," Simon said. "We're not going to change our arrangement."

"Why are you being so generous?"

"We're being fairly compensated," Carpenter intervened. "The matter's closed."

"Okay," Meredith said. "I want to thank you all for everything. I'm very grateful."

"Don't mention it," Carpenter said.

Meredith's thanks seemed genuine, but Philly was still puzzled by her lack of positive emotion. It wasn't every day that you got to put a six-figure check in your bank account.

"Are you okay?" Rachel asked, and Philly believed that Rachel had picked up on their client's lack of enthusiasm

"I think I'm having trouble processing all this. I can't believe it's over."

"That's only natural," Rachel said.

Philly was picturing what it would be like to work with Meredith if they brought her in on the Spenser School of Law case. She didn't doubt that the young woman was smart. But would she fit in personality wise?

"Enough of this chit chat," Meredith said. "Where do I sign?"

Philly was ready to leave when Rachel poked her head into the conference room. "Patrick Lassiter is on the line," Rachel announced. "He asked for you. You can take the call here."

"I want you to sit in," Philly said. "Put him on speaker." If Lassiter was going to appeal Judge Murray's decision in Fay Richardson's case, he didn't have much time left to do so.

"Hello, Mr. Lassiter. Rachel Boyle has joined me for this call so you're on a speaker phone."

"Thanks for taking my call ladies. I wanted to let you know that I'll be filing an appeal from Judge Murray's decision. However, I have talked with my clients about not appealing the decision if the matter could be settled."

"What did you have in mind?" Philly asked.

"I would recommend to my clients dropping the appeal if your client would agree to waive damages."

'I'll bet you would,' Philly thought as she observed Rachel vigorously shaking her head. "I'll relay this to Ms. Richardson," Philly said, "but I'm not going to recommend it. I believe that Ms. Richardson will not waive her monetary award. What I would consider recommending is that she waives a portion of interest if payment is made promptly."

"Then I believe an appeal will be necessary," Lassiter said.

"Appeal away," Philly replied. "I'll get back to you one way or the other, but you might want to assume that the proposal you made will be rejected."

"Is there a reduction from the damage award you would be willing to recommend?" Lassiter asked.

"I'm not going to answer you," Philly said, "and since you've been at this longer than I have, you know why. That said, if your client puts a serious monetary offer on the table, my belief is that it will receive serious consideration."

"What do you mean by serious?"

"That's for you to figure out."

"I guess we're done," Lassiter said, and the line went dead.

"What a piece of shit," Rachel exclaimed.

Philly sat still. "We may have missed a trick," she said. "Maybe we should have tried to put liens on Townsend's and Stout's property. Assuming they have property. I need to get going. Would you talk to Carpenter about this call and whether we should be going after property?"

"Okay."

"Remind Carpenter that that the monetary judgment is against Townsend and Stout individually, and against Stout's billboard company."

Rachel nodded, jotting down a brief note.

"I'm out of here," Philly said, and headed for home and Daisy.

48

Carpenter had long ago concluded that introspection was not his strong suit and that, more likely than not, any attempt at self-analysis would produce a conclusion that was off the mark. So he was reasonably certain that his current satisfied state was not to be trusted. Yet he couldn't ignore feeling reasonably content. His life with Maxine in the new condo had settled into a routine he liked. Each gave the other space and he enjoyed the time they did things together. Maxine was at the end of her consulting work and would be fully retired from the practice of law at the end of the year, but he didn't foresee Maxine demanding more of his time when her free time increased.

Weeks had gone by when he hadn't given his cancer a thought. If stable blood tests were the best he could hope for, then he'd settle for stable. His oncologist, Dr. Specter, had been right about one thing: exercise was helping to mellow him out. Feeling physically tired helped him sleep. Monthly personal trainer sessions with Camellia Kim probably weren't necessary, but he enjoyed them and had resolved to keep them going.

Plus, Viagra worked. Once he got over embarrassment and filled the prescription, he no longer had to worry about keeping it up and keeping up with Maxine. Win-win!

And so far, he liked the partnership arrangement that began the year. He had gotten used to having Rachel and Simon around. The more they were around, the more he liked them. With another pregnancy on the horizon, Philly would largely continue to be a ghost, but so what? She managed to keep up with work and while he found Skype a frustrating way to communicate, it at least provided the illusion of in-person interaction.

Carpenter studied the firm's active case list. For billable hours, they were dependent on two cases: Clyde Atkins' lawsuit against his siblings, which was coming up for trial, and the Spenser School of Law case brought in by Simon and Rachel. Simon's spur of the moment decision to ask for a high hourly billing rate for representing the law school would be a big help.

Martina Glass's personal injury suit was also coming up for trial, but unless something changed, she wasn't likely to obtain a judgment that would produce much, if any, money. He made a notation on his notepad to give further thought to how the hockey team could be held liable.

Lastly, there was Fay Richardson's case. Barney Freedman and Herb McCauley had determined that Rita Stout owned her own home. Rachel would try to seek an attachment on the property so there was an outside chance the firm would be paid for its services to Richardson.

Carpenter thought about the small number of active, billable hour cases sustaining four lawyers. In the past, he'd be beating himself up over the lack of business. But for the moment, he wasn't upset. If the Spenser School of Law case was the paper monster described by Rachel and Simon, they may have lucked out and secured the proverbial cash cow. He made a further notation on his notepad to get involved in the law school litigation from the outset.

His phone sounded causing him to start.

"Carpenter."

"Hi," Maxine said. "What are the chances of you coming home early for a walk and some fun, in that order?"

"The chances are good. It's as if you were reading my mind."

"I'd say we have a real crime this time," Evelyn said.

It was early evening and they were standing in the living room of one of the large Cambridge mansions tucked into the maze of one-way streets south of Huron Avenue. Paul agreed with Evelyn: there was no question that a robbery had been committed. He motioned for the lead officer on the scene to join them.

Thomas Hampton and his partner had responded to the 911 call and had forced entry when the doorbell and vigorous knocking produced no response. He had found the owner of the house, Grace Mansfield, locked in a closet off the front entryway. Mansfield's personal care attendant, Simone Moorhead, had been bound and gagged and found lying on the floor of the living room. Mansfield, her daughter Eva, and Moorhead were in the dining room. Before questioning the trio, Paul wanted some more details from Hampton.

Hampton was tall and muscular with flaming red hair. Paul had worked with him once before and found him to be competent and reliable.

"The daughter, a Mrs. Eva Tibbens, called 911 after unsuccessfully trying to reach her mother by phone a number of times," Hampton said, consulting his notebook. "The daughter was worried because her mother is homebound and has an attendant with her 24/7. The daughter told the dispatcher that she was going to go to her mother's house, but it would take her a while to get there. She wanted a cruiser to stop by the house."

"We can see the mother's in a wheelchair," Evelyn said. "What's her illness about?"

"ALS," Hampton replied. "It's pretty bad. She can't speak. She's got to write things down and show them to whoever she needs to talk to."

"How long did it take you to respond to the dispatcher's call?" Paul asked.

"About ten minutes. I tried the bell and knocked hard on the front door. I had my partner walk around the house and when he came back and reported nothing unusual, I used my nightstick to knock out a glass panel on the front door and I was able to open it."

Paul listened carefully as Hampton detailed his discovery of the two victims. "I felt bad for the mother," Hampton concluded. "She was petrified but she couldn't talk about it."

Paul imagined the older woman imprisoned in a closet, shrouded in darkness, powerless to call for help. It was not a pretty picture. "Was the mother gagged?" he inquired.

"No."

"When did the daughter show up?" Evelyn asked.

Hampton again consulted his notes. "About a half hour after we arrived."

"Do we have an idea what was taken?" Evelyn next asked.

"About ten thousand dollars in cash, some jewelry, and a painting that's supposed to be valuable."

"That's a fair amount of cash," Paul observed.

"We didn't ask about the cash," Hampton said. "We figured that was something you'd want to cover."

Paul nodded. Hampton had used good judgment. "Time to meet the cast of characters," he said, leading the way to the dining room, where the daughter was encouraging her mother and the caretaker to have some tea and cookies, apparently trying to help them take their minds off the ordeal they experienced.

Paul paused in the entryway. He knew little about ALS except that it was a wasting disease. Muscles gave way and the body shut down. Jane Mansfield was holding a cup in both hands and painstakingly bringing it to her lips. Her hands trembled. She was painfully thin. Her skin had that papery look he had noticed on some elders. The white hair that framed her face and curled up at the nape of her neck, looked recently styled.

The woman in white, rubber-soled shoes no doubt was Mansfield's attendant, Paul theorized. Simone Moorhead looked to be in her thirties. She was solidly built, tall, with a round face and dark eyes. Eva Tibbens, Mansfield's daughter, was wearing jeans, a white blouse, and running shoes. She nervously eyed the teacup her mother was holding.

Paul cleared his throat and introduced himself and Evelyn. There was no objection to his asking a few questions, and he directed Evelyn to interview Moorhead in the living room. He sat down next to Tibbens and across the table from Mansfield. Tibbens promptly rose and fetched a small notepad and pen for her mother. When Mansfield settled her cup in its saucer, Paul asked his first question.

"Did you get a look at who did this?"

Mansfield nodded before picking up the pen and beginning to write. Her efforts were slow-going and Paul hated himself for thinking this was going to take all evening.

When Mansfield turned the pad so it faced Paul, he read three words: *man, mask, gun.* He was seldom treated to such succinctness when interviewing a witness. "That's very helpful," he said, meaning it. "Did you see what happened to Ms. Moorhead?"

Mansfield shook her head.

Paul consulted his notes and read off the list of stolen property provided by Hampton. "How did you determine what was taken?" he directed at Eva Tibbens.

"The first thing we did was check the cash drawer in the study," the daughter responded.

"The cash drawer?"

"Mom likes to have money on hand, and she had made a large cash withdrawal to make gifts to grandchildren. I went to her bedroom and noticed jewelry was missing. I also noticed a painting had been removed from the study."

"Ten thousand dollars is a lot of money to have on hand," Paul said neutrally.

"Let's just say that Mom is very generous when it comes to grandchildren. She spoils them and there's no stopping her. Which is not to say my brother and sister and I haven't tried. She refuses to write checks; gifts to the grandchildren have to be in cash."

Mansfield was far from repentant. She smiled at Paul and he wondered what it would have been like to have grown up with a grandparent able to lavish expensive cash gifts.

"When my partner finishes up with Ms. Moorhead, I'd like to see the study," Paul said.

Evelyn consulted her notes. Simone Moorhead had responded to the front doorbell and, on opening the door, had been confronted by a masked gunman.

Her description of the intruder hadn't been helpful. Dressed in black, the robber had been average in all respects: height, weight, build, tone of voice. The voice was a man's voice, and it occurred to Evelyn that if the home invader had remained silent, Moorhead might not have been able to identify the person's sex. The intruder seemed to have knowledge of the house. Moorhead was told to wheel Mansfield into the entry hall closet and place a chair angled against the doorknob to secure the closet. Then the intruder ordered Moorhead to the living room where he produced cord and duct tape to hogtie her. He placed a gag in her mouth. Moorhead had heard his footfalls on the first floor and on the stairs. She estimated his time in the house at thirty minutes. The intruder had left by the front door. While tied up, Moorhead had heard the phone ring numerous times.

"How many people knew that Mrs. Mansfield had a fair amount of cash in the house?" Evelyn asked.

"I did," Moorhead said. "I handled the withdrawal from the bank. She may have mentioned it to her daughter, but I'm not sure. Ms. Tibbens is the daughter who lives nearest to her and she visits often. They also talk on the phone a lot."

"I thought Mrs. Mansfield couldn't speak."

"That's right. But she can type. She uses this service. She types out her side of the conversation and the service reads it to the other person on the line."

"What's the name of that service?"

Moorhead frowned in concentration. "I think it's called Living Voice Solutions. There's a business card next to the phone in the study."

Evelyn studied Moorhead. The woman had been through a traumatic event but seemed reasonably together. "How are *you* doing?" she asked.

"I'm a little numb," Moorhead replied. "I think it's all going to sink in later."

"How long have you been caring for Mrs. Mansfield?"

"About five months."

"How's that working out?"

Moorhead paused. "It's becoming more difficult."

Evelyn pocketed her notepad. "Let's join the others."

In the study, Mansfield's daughter pointed to the place where the stolen painting had been hung. Then she explained the household connection with Living Voice Solutions. It was a clever arrangement. Mansfield would type her part of a phone conversation and an employee of the company would read what had been typed to the other person on the line. "Is what your mother types saved anywhere?" Paul asked.

"The company saves typed conversations for at least thirty days," Tibbens explained. "There's no backup in the house."

"Did you and your mother have a phone discussion mentioning the money she had in the house?" Evelyn said.

Tibbens was standing behind her mother's wheelchair and gave her mother's shoulder a gentle pat. "Yes. Mom mentioned she had withdrawn money and would shortly be sending gifts to grandchildren. I told her she was going overboard when she mentioned the size of the gifts, but Mom asked what the point of saving the money was? She wanted to make her grandchildren happy."

"How valuable was the stolen painting?" Paul asked.

"I'd guess fifty thousand. It was one of those situations you read about. Mom and Dad bought the painting years ago at an antique place in Maine because they liked it. Later on, they had it appraised and it turned out to be valuable."

Paul asked the next logical question. "Was the value of the painting ever mentioned in a discussion you had with your mother when she was typing her answers?"

"You know, I think that did come up fairly recently. Mom's personal attorney is aware of her condition and suggested that all her possessions be inventoried and evaluated so that he can do some tax and estate planning. I thought that was a good idea and I was encouraging Mom to move on it. I think I mentioned the painting as an example of something she owned that had probably gone up in value since the last time anybody checked. She typed that she would get around to it."

"When your mother does her typing, is she typically alone?" Paul asked.

"No, Simone is usually around to help out."

"Anything else?" Paul asked Evelyn when she looked up from her note taking.

"No, not for the moment."

"Thanks for your help," Paul said. "We won't trouble you any further. We'll probably be contacting the phone service. We would appreciate it if you'd call the company tomorrow and tell them not to destroy any typing your mother did."

"Do you suspect them?" Eva Tibbens asked, sounding incredulous.

"Let's just say we suspect everyone but have no suspects," Paul replied. "We know the way out."

49

Philly had been taken aback when Carpenter said he would be stopping by her house. Now that he was seated at her dining room table, she remained nonplussed. Typically, he wouldn't opt for a face-to-face meeting unless he had something important on his mind. Often, importance equated with unpleasantness. If there was something serious for the two of them to discuss, Carpenter, in all likelihood, had given no consideration to the kids factor. Sarah wasn't around this morning and, it being morning, Daisy and Rosalind were operating at high energy levels, making adult discourse—let alone concentration—a challenge. Daisy was constantly active in the adjoining living room and Rosalind, whose walking remained a hit-or-miss adventure, was falling down repeatedly as she tried to keep up. With the kids on the loose, Philly doubted they'd get anything done.

Carpenter produced two lollipops from his shirt pocket and Philly shook her head. "Sugar is not what they need," she said, noting his disappointment. But immediately her partner's expression turned positive as he extracted a can of Play-Doh from each of the side pockets of his suit jacket. "Girls," he called out and soon he had Daisy and Rosalind each balanced on a knee and working the mustard colored contents of the cans.

"Don't let them put it in their mouths," Philly warned, and Carpenter nodded. "I've got this," he said.

"To what do I owe the pleasure?"

"I want to go over cases."

"Then I should have come to the office. The kids are a distraction."

"A welcome distraction," Carpenter said. "Go over your witnesses in Martina Glass' case."

Philly forced herself to concentrate. Carpenter was showing Daisy how to roll out the Play-Doh into a thick, spaghetti-like strand. Rosalind tried to imitate her older friend but couldn't get the hang of it. Soon Carpenter was working Rosalind's hands, his wrinkled, hairy fingers guiding her motions.

"Witnesses," Carpenter prompted, and it finally sunk in for Philly that he was serious about making this a working session. "Simon will start with Martina's direct testimony. Second up will be her doctor. Simon will also take him."

"Next?" Carpenter asked, and Philly had to acknowledge that the girls had calmed down.

"Mr. and Mrs. Rhodes, the couple that saw one of Dunn's friends toss him a bag of peanuts. I'll do their direct. Lastly, I'll put McCauley on, and he can tell about ordering beer at Stampede games."

"Why not add the guy who threw the bag of peanuts to Dunn as a defendant?"

"He's probably also a deadbeat and it might delay the trial."

"I'd do it anyway."

"Sure, why not? Why not have two deadbeats instead of just one?"

"Good job," Carpenter said softly to the girls, who were still focused on making Play-Doh snakes.

"The Rhodes and McCauley will testify about the lack of warning signs in the arena," Philly added. "There were no signs saying, 'Stay in your seat at all times' or 'Don't lean over the rail in front of you.'"

Carpenter nodded. "Play that up. I'd also beat to death the beer sales. If Dunn and his buddies claim they didn't overdo it on the beer, I'd bet a jury is going to think that a bunch of young guys were probably getting wasted. We're talking about a hockey game for God's sake."

"Got it," Philly said.

Rosalind released her Play-Doh snake and began to squirm. Carpenter lowered her to the floor and she staggered off toward the living room where she lay down on the floor. Then Daisy eased off his knee and plopped down beside Rosalind holding her Play-Doh snake. Rosalind glanced at the snake and closed her eyes. Daisy followed suit.

"I'd say you're ready," Carpenter said. "Beer and no signs. Beat those two themes to death. Those are the avenues to get at the Salem Stampede."

"Are you going to attend the trial?"

Carpenter shrugged. "Probably not. I've got the Atkins trial to gear up for. We're going to be fighting for Simon's time."

Philly agreed. The Atkins case and its billable hours had to take priority.

Carpenter changed the subject. "Now we've got the Spenser School of Law case. The law school is looking to Simon and Rachel to lead the way, but we need to be involved. I've been trying to sort out our roles."

Not for the first time, Philly marveled at the way Carpenter always found time to take a big picture view of any litigation matter. She hadn't considered what she and Carpenter should be contributing.

"I think we need to monitor our partners," Carpenter said. "I don't want them making big strategic decisions without our input. We've got to come up with a way to exercise control over the case while letting them run with it."

"Don't you think Simon and Rachel wouldn't hesitate to ask us for advice?"

"I'm not sure," Carpenter said. "Simon in particular has a lot of emotion invested in the case and clearly wants to be in charge."

Daisy and Rosalind were now lying on their backs asleep. Philly motioned for Carpenter to look at the girls. "Cute," he said.

Carpenter was looking at her expectantly. Philly fought to put the girls out of her mind and think about how the Spenser litigation would unfold. "We need to be briefed on the discovery," she said, knowing that neither of them would wade through the documents. "Maybe even daily."

"I like that," Carpenter said. "Let's schedule a time for that every day. How about four o'clock?"

Philly thought of approaching dinner time. Isabella and Sarah would be present, but the two hours preceding dinner were chaotic. "Make it three-thirty."

"Done. I'll e-mail Simon and Rachel. I think the four of us are in agreement that we should try to prevent the plaintiffs from getting their hands on personal information in students' records."

Philly perceived a two-edged sword situation. "If a student had lousy grades or lousy professor evaluations, that kind of evidence might explain why the student didn't get a job."

"Shit!" Carpenter muttered. "Good point. Let's you and I each take a look at three records in detail and get a handle on what we're dealing with."

Philly nodded. "What did you think about Simon suggesting that Sweeney be brought in to help with discovery?"

"The first thing I thought about was money," Carpenter confessed. "We'd bill her out, but we'd have to pay her. Then I thought about hiring someone we just got through representing. There's something off about that."

"Yes and no," Philly said. She had thought about using Meredith and, except for wondering whether there was a personality fit, didn't have a negative reaction. "If it's true that Sweeney is as smart as Rachel, then we may want to use her. This case is going to drift toward the time when my pregnancy is going to get in the way of what I can do."

"All right," Carpenter said with some misgivings in his tone. "I'll keep an open mind on Sweeney."

"Do you think we have any shot at getting the case dismissed?" Philly asked.

"I've thought about that," Carpenter answered. "I don't think that the judge will consider a dismissal motion until the plaintiffs have had discovery. But if we can show that the law school didn't put out any false information, I think there's a chance we can get some of the case thrown out."

Rosalind began to whimper. "Another country heard from," Philly said. She and Carpenter had snatched thirty minutes of uninterrupted time. Daisy removed her thumb from her mouth and reached over to touch Rosalind's cheek. Rosalind settled down. "In fifteen minutes, it's snack time. You're staying."

"I wouldn't miss it," Carpenter said. "This has been productive."

50

They were in the conference room with piles of paper spread out on the table. Five boxes of documents delivered by the law school had yet to be opened.

"Do you think Carpenter and Philly are going to take over this case?" Simon asked.

"No," Rachel replied, surprised by the question. "The dean has made it clear that he wants the trial conducted by graduates of the law school. Just because they want to be informed about discovery doesn't mean they want to conduct the litigation."

"I wonder," Simon said in a soft voice.

"I don't wonder," Rachel said. "I think they want to make sure we win the damn case."

Simon pushed the stack of paper in front of him toward the middle of the table and leaned back in his chair. "This is all a little overwhelming," he said.

So far in their professional relationship, Rachel was typically on the receiving end when it came to pep talks. She couldn't remember a time when she felt the need to give Simon a boost. "The amount of paper doesn't bother me," she said. "You know we're going to get through it. We just need to be methodical and not try to do everything at once." She remembered something Josh had said to her about tennis. When you fell behind in a match, it was important to focus on each point and avoid thinking about how the match was going overall.

Rachel pointed to the unopened boxes delivered by the Dean's office. "We're not going to open those boxes today," she declared. "Our objective is to make it halfway through the documents on this table."

"I need to know what's inside the boxes," Simon said. "We need to get a handle on what we're going to have to deal with."

"No." Rachel noticed Simon's surprise at the forcefulness of her pronouncement. "Those boxes will be here tomorrow. We can't do everything at once."

"I need to know," Simon protested.

"Look, Simon, when you're right, you're right. I shouldn't have dealt with the offer to Meredith the way I did. But I'm right this time. You're just going to drive yourself crazy if you don't back off a bit. We have time. We're going to need extensions to file an answer to the complaint and to reply to discovery, and we'll get the extensions. We don't have to go nuts over this case."

"I'm already nuts over this case."

Living Voice Solutions' office was in Somerville, occupying a second-floor suite in a five-story office building located on a side street about a half a mile from the city center. Evelyn had decided to cold call the business. She had a signed, notarized letter from Grace Mansfield authorizing her and Paul to have access to Mansfield's phone call records.

Evelyn entered without knocking. She was confronted by a receptionist desk manned by a large black woman who glanced at her briefly and then continued typing. Behind the woman was open space filled with six desks joined together in pairs so that the occupants faced each other. Two women faced each other at one of the workstations and a man sat alone at another station. The third station was unmanned. Behind the workstations was a vacant, small office with an open door.

The typist said, "May I help you?" without looking up or slowing down. Evelyn placed the woman in her fifties. She wore rings on every finger but her thumbs. The jewelry had no effect on her typing.

"I'd like to speak to the person in charge."

"You're looking at her," the woman responded, still not shifting her gaze from her work.

"I'm Detective Rodriguez with the Cambridge Police Department." She paused, waiting for a reaction or at least a slowing of the woman's typing, but there was no change in her expression and, if anything, the pace of her typing picked up. "I'd like to look at the call records of one of your clients, Grace Mansfield. I have a letter from Mrs. Mansfield giving us permission and I believe her daughter let you know about this."

"I'll be with you in a second. I'm almost done and I'm on a roll."

There was no name plate on the typist's desk. With no place to sit down, Evelyn felt foolish hovering over the woman. The three people at the workstations wore headphones. Each was facing a computer.

"Okay, that's done. Sorry to keep you waiting. My name is Rhonda Stone. We got a call from Mrs. Mansfield's daughter, Eva. Let me see that letter you mentioned and some identification."

Stone wrote down the information on Evelyn's badge and took her time reading the letter before excusing herself and going to the office in the rear of the suite. She returned with a file folder and resumed her seat at the reception desk. Stone began to rifle through the file folder until she came upon the document she was searching for. "This is sad," Stone said, turning the file document and the letter so Evelyn could see them. "She signed a contract with us two and a half months ago. Look at the deterioration in her signature."

Stone was correct. The signature on the authorization letter was made in awkward, shaky strokes. If you didn't know Mansfield's name you might not have been able to decipher it.

"I'm not going to give you a hard time," Stone said. "This file I have is our business file. We save the typed client's side of phone conversations for thirty days but since we don't tape the calls, you won't get anything of what the person Mrs. Mansfield was talking to had to say."

Stone worked the computer at her desk. "You're in luck. We've got records saved for forty-five days. If you want, I could put them on a thumb drive for you."

"That would be very helpful. Also, I'm going to ask you not to destroy any call records relating to Mrs. Mansfield."

"We can do that. I'll put an instruction on the file so nothing gets removed. There we go." Stone rummaged through her desk and produced a thumb drive that she unwrapped and inserted into her computer. "This will take a minute. You mind I ask you something?"

"Why don't you ask. Then I'll tell you if I mind."

"What's this about?"

Stone had been cooperative, but it didn't follow that she needed to reciprocate. Still, on balance, Evelyn didn't see a downside to mentioning the crime.

"Mrs. Mansfield was robbed. We're looking at any information that bears on what was taken."

"Do you think someone here made use of something Mrs. Mansfield typed?"

"I'm not saying that happened. But it occurred to us that it could have happened."

Stone's gaze had yet to turn hostile or leery. The woman was being helpful and appeared to have nothing to hide.

"We thoroughly screen the people who work here," Stone said in an even tone. "What you're suspicious of is something that we've thought about. We advise clients not to type information on highly confidential matters but, frankly, once a client uses our service for a while, that warning doesn't get heeded. It's as if they get comfortable and forget our employee is on the line. In this case, I'm not particularly worried. Mrs. Mansfield always insisted that her typing be handled by Maria. Maria would respect any confidences Mrs. Mansfield typed. I'm sure of that."

"Maria?" Evelyn asked.

"She's right over there," Stone said, pointing to one of the women manning the workstation at which both desks were occupied. "Maria Gomez. When she finishes her call, why don't you talk to her? It might save you a trip back here."

Evelyn regarded Maria Gomez across the expanse of the two facing desks that had previously been unoccupied. Gomez looked to be her age. She was short, slim, and dark-complexioned. Her long, dark hair was clipped in place with a gold barrette, and she wore a wedding ring, a thin gold band that was loose on her ring finger. Gomez's eyes had opened wide when Stone had introduced Evelyn as a police officer, and she still seemed uneasy.

"I explained to Ms. Stone that we're investigating a robbery at Mrs. Mansfield's house," Evelyn began, making no effort to put Gomez at ease. "While you were finishing up your call, I had a chance to look at the recent messages Mrs. Mansfield typed for you to pass on. Did you ever discuss any of her typed messages with anybody?"

Gomez's eyes again opened wide and her shocked expression struck Evelyn as genuine.

"No, I would never do that. Miss Stone has made it very clear that we are not to discuss what is typed with anyone."

"What about your husband?" Rachel pursued. "Do you mean to say that you've never discussed anything typed with your husband?"

Gomez lowered her eyes and fidgeted in her seat. "I told my husband a funny story once," she said, keeping her eyes averted. "This did not come from Miss

Mansfield. Another elderly woman typed about her cat getting stuck in a tall tree. When the firemen came to rescue the cat, the cat moved up higher on the tree and fell. The firemen had a safety net ready in case the fireman climbing after the cat fell from the tree, but it was the cat that fell. The cat bounced off the safety net and landed back in the tree."

Evelyn stared at Gomez. The woman had to be serious; the anecdote was not one she was likely to have made up.

"I thought it was funny," Gomez said. "I imagined the cat flying back up into the tree with its hair fluffed out like you see in cartoons."

Evelyn struggled to maintain a stern look: the image of a bouncing cat *was* funny. "Recently, Mrs. Mansfield typed about having money in her house that she was going to use to send gifts to her grandchildren. Did you ever discuss that with anyone?"

"No," Gomez said. "I would never do that."

"Did you ever discuss with anyone any artwork that Mrs. Mansfield mentioned she had at her house?"

"No," Gomez repeated.

"Okay," Evelyn said. "Thank you for your time. Is there a home telephone number I can reach you at if I need to talk to you further?"

Gomez provided the information and quickly retreated to her previous workstation.

"Got what you need?" Stone asked as Evelyn made to leave.

"Yes and no," Evelyn replied.

"Isn't that always the case?"

"Discovery report," Philly said, her image appearing via Skype on the computer mounted on the conference room table.

Rachel nodded to Simon to field the question, sensitive to his need to be front and center on the Spenser School of Law case.

"We've gotten through a chunk of the documents the law school delivered," Simon began. "We've gone through all documents relating to the school's placement office for the last five years."

"What are we talking about?" Carpenter asked.

"What aren't we talking about?" Simon said in what Rachel found to be a beleaguered tone. "Phone records for one. There are also contact logs noting contacts *from* third parties to the placement office, and contacts *to* third parties by the placement office. It's hard to tell whether the contact reports actually picked up all contacts."

"My guess is that they don't," Rachel said. "Whether a contact got recorded seems to be a hit or miss proposition. There are gaps in the contact logs. Sometimes a week goes by without any contact recorded. Then you run into a stretch where there are multiple contacts every day."

"Then we have promotional materials talking up the law school," Simon continued. "These documents put in plugs for the law school's faculty and students stressing that both are of high quality."

"Do these documents make any claims about placing students in jobs?" Philly asked.

"No," Simon replied. "They try to sell the school by saying that graduates have received a first-class legal education."

"I'm thinking we probably have to turn over the phone records, these contact reports you mentioned, and the documents trying to sell the law school," Philly said. "I don't see how the documents can hurt the school except for maybe the contact reports. You need to find out whether all contacts were recorded."

"We've made a note to do that," Rachel said.

"We've also made it through the documents that relate to graduates' employment," Simon said. "A lot of this information comes from questionnaires that are sent to graduates yearly. The response rate to these questionnaires is about sixty percent."

"Is this the information that the law school relies on for its statistics on graduates finding legal employment?" Philly asked.

"Pretty much," Simon responded.

"I want to understand this," Carpenter said. "When the law school says fifty-one percent of graduates found law-related jobs, does that mean fifty-one percent of the sixty percent returning questionnaires found law-related jobs?"

"That's the way we understand it," Rachel said.

"Does the law school explain that its fifty-one percent success rate is based on those responding to questionnaires?" Carpenter next asked.

"Yes," Simon said. "There's a note explaining that the fifty-one percent figure is based on graduates responding to a survey conducted by the placement office."

"Then the law school was disclosing the source of its figure," Carpenter observed.

"That's correct," Simon replied.

"So far so good," Carpenter said, but it struck Rachel that he was waiting for a bad news punch line.

"We've gone through the paperwork concerning the staffing of the placement office," Simon continued. "The placement office has never had more than one full-time employee. Until 2005, the position was not full-time. When the placement person is on vacation, calls to the placement office are forwarded to a secretary in the dean's office. We don't know for sure, but it seems to us that the calls remain in limbo until the placement person returns from vacation. We'll follow up on this with the dean."

Carpenter was frowning and Rachel noticed that Philly's Skype-blurred features appeared troubled.

"We've looked at the resumes of the people employed in the placement office since 2005," Simon resumed. "Not one of the employees had any placement experience with law schools, or even placement experience generally. For example, the person currently running the placement office used to work in the human resources department for a mid-sized computer company. She handled employee complaints, medical plan issues, and retirement plan matters."

Carpenter broke out of a momentary funk. "Refresh my memory on what the law school said about its placement office."

"And I quote," Simon said, holding a brochure that he and Rachel had gone over. "'Graduates of the Law School are assisted in finding law-related employment by an experienced and knowledgeable placement office.'"

"From what you've told us, the *experienced* part may be stretching it," Carpenter said.

"There's on-the-job experience," Rachel said, presenting what she thought might be the only way to spin the available information that might help the law school. "I'm going to meet with the woman currently in charge of placement. We'll let you know how that goes."

"*Knowledgeable* also seems questionable," Carpenter said, referencing the other featured adjective in the law school's brochure.

"We should be able to tell in short order whether the current placement department head is knowledgeable. We're hoping that she is."

"Hope springs eternal," Carpenter said with only moderate sarcasm. "What other documents have you waded through?"

"We've made a start on some of the students' files," Simon said. "We want to do a little more work before reporting to you on that. Also, I've made copies of three of the files so that you can look at what we're dealing with."

Carpenter was staring at the ceiling, his jaw muscles working, a faraway look in his eyes. "When you talk to that placement person," he said, "make sure you ask her about any orientation she went through."

Rachel made a note to do that.

"I think we're done," Simon said. "Anything else? No? Thanks," he concluded, and it seemed to Rachel that Simon had come to terms with Carpenter and Philly providing input, maybe even welcomed their involvement.

"Don't mention it," Carpenter said.

May

From Meredith's Playlist

"We Are Young"

Janelle Monae

51

Carpenter suddenly had paper to wade through—specifically, the three student files of recent Spenser School of Law graduates assembled by Simon. If the daily discussions on discovery were to be helpful, he and Philly needed to promptly follow through on what they said they would do.

Simon had selected the files of a male 2010 graduate who had yet to land a law-related job; a female 2009 graduate who was working as a paralegal in a medium-sized commercial law firm; and a 2011 female graduate who had yet to find a legal position. Carpenter took his time going through each file, making notes as he did so. He quickly concluded that he was reviewing records of three individuals whose law school careers were basically as undistinguished as his own. The most recent Spenser graduate had a grade point average in the middle of her class; the earlier graduates ranked in the bottom third of their classes. While in law school, only the most recent graduate had engaged in an outside activity that involved the law; the woman had participated in a volunteer clinical program that helped a Boston legal services office deal with landlord-tenant disputes.

Carpenter concluded that he wouldn't hire any of the graduates. There was nothing about any of them that stood out or showed potential. He thought back to the time he hired Simon and Rachel to help him with cases while Philly was pregnant with Daisy. When he offered them part-time work, he hadn't known anything about their law school records. He'd been impressed with their oral comments as members of a Spenser School of Law faculty-student disciplinary committee that was addressing whether one of his clients, a student at the law school, had failed to report another student for cheating on an exam. Simon had not given an inch in opposing a professor who asserted that his client had violated the law school's honor code by not reporting the other student. Rachel had focused on the language of the honor code and had interpreted the code in a commonsense way that helped his client. Carpenter realized he'd been lucky. It turned out that both Simon and Rachel had what it took to be lawyers. But he had hired them on nothing more than subjective impressions based on each of them being able to articulate a supportable, defensible position. Maybe the three recent graduates he had just considered were equally capable of rising to the occasion, but nothing jumped out at him that they would.

Carpenter was interested in what Philly made of the three student files. He'd try to talk to her before the next discovery call. For the moment, his inclination was to provide the files to the plaintiffs who were suing Spenser. Let the plaintiffs make the case that the three students were qualified to be hired for a legal position. Maybe Spenser needed an expert witness, someone with experience with legal job placements who could testify that there was no compelling reason to hire Spenser's unplaced graduates for a legal position. But use of such a witness was a two-edged sword. The testimony of such an expert would undercut Spenser's assertion that all of its graduates received a top-flight legal education and were employable.

"Here's something," Evelyn said.

Paul looked up from the report he was writing. Evelyn was looking at him with a complacent smile on her lips that bothered him. "What?"

"Emilio Gomez, Maria Gomez's husband, has a record. He's done time. One conviction was for breaking and entering. Another was for receiving stolen goods."

"I thought you believed the Gomez woman when she said she never discussed Mansfield with anyone."

Evelyn shrugged. "I did. Now I'm not so sure."

"What was that word you used to describe Maria Gomez?" Paul asked, thinking back to her briefing him on her visit to Living Voice Solutions. "You said she was an innocent, right, that there was something childlike about her and that she looked shocked when you asked whether she'd ever discussed Mansfield with anybody."

"Maybe she's a great actress," Evelyn said. "She married a guy who is no innocent."

"Maybe she's telling the truth," Paul said. He began to wonder whether Evelyn was taking a harder look at the Gomez woman because she was Latina.

"Okay," Evelyn said, "maybe I'm reaching. But this is the most logical explanation for what happened. Maria Gomez tells her husband that this defenseless old lady has ready cash in her house, and they have a short window to relieve her of it before she mails it to her grandchildren. Then the husband does what he knows how to do: he robs the place."

"You were convinced that the Gomez woman was telling you the truth," Paul pointed out. "Plus, the owner of Living Voice Solutions was fully cooperative. I'm okay with your questioning Gomez's husband. But there is another explanation for what happened."

"What am I missing?" Evelyn said, favoring him with a hard stare.

"We both think that someone might have made use of the typed information that cash was in the house. There's another person who knew about the cash—the Moorhead woman, Mansfield's attendant."

"But she was attacked and tied up," Evelyn protested.

"So what?" Paul replied. "What if Moorhead has a boyfriend with a criminal record? Would that change your thinking?"

Evelyn's jaw clenched and her stare remained hard. "I think that's a reach," she said.

"Maybe, maybe not. You need to keep an open mind here. At the moment, I'm not ready to lock in on anyone."

Evelyn drummed her fingers on her desktop. "I'm going to pay a visit to Mr. Gomez. Maybe I'll tail Moorhead for a bit."

"Sounds like a plan."

Carpenter was the only one in the office. Philly was at home. Simon was at the courthouse library. Rachel was looking at files at Spenser School of Law and was using the school's law library to research the school's opposition to the plaintiffs' class action motion. He couldn't remember a time when the four of them were so spread out that a dial-in number was necessary for them to converse. Philly had suggested not having today's discovery call, but Carpenter had insisted, remaining convinced that they needed to confer daily on the law school case.

Once everyone had joined the call, Carpenter started. "Philly and I reviewed the three Spenser student files you copied for us. We think it's okay to provide the information to the plaintiffs. But you may want to redact the graduates' names. See if the plaintiffs will agree to that." Carpenter paused, gathered his thoughts. "We thought about getting an expert witness with experience in placing lawyers but decided against that approach. If the expert testified that the three graduates we reviewed were unqualified to secure law-related employment, that would undercut the law school's claim that its graduates received a topnotch education that made them employable."

There was silence for a long moment which Simon broke. "What's going on here?" he asked.

"What do you mean?" Carpenter demanded.

"It sounds like you two are making decisions without us," Simon said.

Carpenter aimed for an even tone, trying to mask his irritation. "Listen, Simon, that's not what's going on at all. The two of you are going to litigate this. That's a given. I think one of us should be in the courtroom, but I don't feel strongly about that. Anything we talk about we're presenting to you. If you want to hire an expert on placing law graduates, fine, knock yourselves out. We just told you why we think that's a bad idea."

"We appreciate your help," Rachel said, and Carpenter sensed she was trying to smooth things over.

"What's new on your end?" Philly asked.

"The current head of the placement department is Molly Grant," Rachel said. "She received an orientation from the woman whom she replaced and from Dean Stockman's personal secretary. As far as I can tell, the orientation pretty much focused on the placement department's filing system and electronic records. Grant is young and eager and anxious to do a good job. She's networked with her counterparts at other law schools and she claims she has a good handle on what she needs to do. She started work last September at the start of the school year."

Carpenter read between the lines: Spenser School of Law had hired someone who was bright and energetic but lacked experience.

"When Grant is away, the contact logs we talked about aren't always kept current. Dean Stockman's personal secretary has her own work to do and doesn't always follow up listing placement department contacts."

"So there really are gaps in those records," Philly observed.

"Correct," Rachel confirmed.

"Simon and I have finished looking through each of the boxes of placement department documents sent over by the dean. Several boxes contain brochures from law firms most of which are in Boston. There are also scores of documents showing open positions that go back for years."

"Is there a placement bulletin board at the law school?" Philly asked.

"There is," Rachel said. "Also, if you go to the law school website and click on the placement department, you can find information about job openings that have come to Grant's attention."

"Has Grant ever gotten a graduate a job in the law?" Carpenter asked.

"Yes," Rachel replied. "I asked her about that, and she said she played a big part in several graduates landing jobs with law firms."

"What exactly did she do?"

"She put together an alphabetical file card system listing open positions that is also available electronically on her computer," Rachel explained. "Any student or graduate who contacts the placement department gets entered into her system. She records what the person's interests are. Let's say John Doe contacts her and says he's interested in a small firm that specializes in litigation. She would go through her job opening listings and send John Doe information about small firms interested in hiring a litigator. These leads produced three placements. Grant has the thank you e-mails to prove it."

"Where was this woman two years ago?" Philly said glumly.

"Simon and I talked about that," Rachel responded. "One concern we have is that the plaintiffs are going to point to the things Grant has done and ask why those things weren't done earlier."

"That's a problem you can't dwell on," Carpenter said. "The law school can always say it had to juggle priorities and that recently the placement office has received more attention. A defendant can't let a lawsuit prevent it from improving something that needs improvement."

"What's next?" Philly asked.

"We're going to take a hard look at the files of the three named plaintiffs," Rachel answered, and Carpenter became concerned that Simon hadn't said a word for a long while. "Depositions might be next."

"Send copies of those files to Carpenter and me," Philly requested, and Carpenter was pleased that she was also making demands for information about the case.

"Are we done?" Simon asked.

"Yeah," Carpenter said.

"We're busy," Rachel said.

"But are we happy and making money?" Carpenter queried.

"You need to be busy first," Rachel said, and Carpenter found he had nothing to add to that.

52

Judge Clarence Ford regarded the lawyers before him as if they were beneath his contempt. He was one of the senior members of the bench, tall, lean, and unsmiling. He had the reputation of treating lawyers similarly, without favoritism, and that would have been fine, Carpenter once remarked, if he didn't treat all lawyers like shit.

"I remember this case," the judge said without enthusiasm from his perch on the bench as he studied the joint pre-trial memorandum that had been submitted for this pre-trial conference. "This is the case where Ms. Piper—now Ms. Sullivan, it appears—compared the defendant, Fred Dunn, to a ceiling tile that fell on the plaintiff. Why hasn't this case been settled? The defenseless plaintiff was nearly crushed."

Philly willed herself to be invisible. She noticed that Wayne Martin, the Salem Stampede's lawyer, was sitting perfectly still as if lack of motion would cause him to escape the judge's notice. William Ward made the mistake of clearing his throat, and the judge's eyes lighted on Fred Dunn and Frank Madden's attorney.

"I'll start with you, Mr. Ward," the judge said. "You represent the ceiling tile who fell on the plaintiff. You also represent Mr. Madden, who allegedly tossed the ceiling tile a package of peanuts. Why haven't your clients paid the plaintiff to make this case go away?"

"Mr. Dunn is not a ceiling tile," Ward replied with some force, and Philly remembered that Ward had not been present at the hearing last year on the Salem Stampede's motion to dismiss Martina Glass' case.

"That's your opinion," the judge snapped. "A jury might well conclude that your client is a large ceiling tile who should have remained fixed in his place instead of reaching for bag of peanuts thrown by your other client."

"A jury might also conclude that Mr. Dunn did nothing inappropriate and was pushed," Ward retorted, and Philly had to respect Dunn's lawyer for not backing down. "Also, Mr. Madden denies throwing anything to Mr. Dunn."

"Any other comment on settlement?" the judge asked. "Too bad," he continued when no one said anything. "Silence may be golden, but not in this instance. I suppose we need to set a firm trial date and get this case disposed of. How about the fifteenth of next month?"

"I'd prefer a date two to three months out," Ward said.

"I'll bet you would. Is that agreeable with the plaintiff?"

"No," Philly said. "I'm pregnant and I want this case moved. Next month is fine."

"Pregnant," the judge repeated in a tone that suggested the condition was foreign to his experience. "Well, in that case, the show must go on. Next month. The fifteenth. No continuances."

"Thank you, Your Honor," Philly said.

"Don't thank me," the judge retorted. "Getting what you wish for isn't necessarily a good thing." He glared at the three lawyers. "Do yourselves a favor and work this out. Next case."

"What is with that guy?" Ward asked when they had repaired to the corridor outside the courtroom.

Philly shrugged and kept silent. She had gotten what she wanted, and she didn't think much of the judge belittling getting what you want. Besides, as a bonus, the judge had put in a not-at-all subtle dig at the defendants to settle the case.

"Why doesn't your client throw a bucket of money the plaintiff's way and put us out of our misery?" Ward asked Martin.

"Bite me," Martin replied, and it struck Philly that Judge Ford's crankiness was contagious. "Have your clients throw half a bucket of money at the plaintiff and I'll make sure my client considers throwing in a half bucket of its own."

"No can do," Ward said, shaking his head. "My clients have no money. A judgment against them has as much value as a piece of toilet paper."

"Somebody's paying *you*," Martin retorted.

"One of the great mysteries of life," Ward replied with a devilish grin. "People with no visible means of support somehow find a way to pay their lawyers. God, this is a great country!"

"Nice chatting with you guys," Philly said, and she started to move toward the elevators.

"Wait a second," Ward said. "What would it take to settle this case?" he asked. "It's a hypothetical question considering my clients are broke, but I'm curious."

Philly returned to her adversaries. "I'm not turning over a settlement card to a party who claims he's broke," she told Ward. "Mr. Martin is free to reveal our settlement discussions if he chooses to. I'm not going to play your game."

"That's not very collegial," Ward replied. "I'll attribute that to your condition and hormones."

"Bite me," Philly said, employing Martin's phrase, which brought a smile to the hockey team's lawyer's face.

"Why can't we all just get along?" Ward deadpanned.

"You think this is funny?" Philly raised her voice. "This judge is going to bury the drunken louts you represent. And as for *your* client," she said, turning to Martin, "serving beer to already drunk fans is going to sink its ship."

"That never happened here," Martin responded.

"Where were you when Mr. and Mrs. Rhodes gave their depositions? Asleep?"

"I've had it with you guys," Martin fumed as he made his getaway.

"That goes for me too," Philly snarled as she took off after Martin, who, when he saw her following, headed for the stairs and not the elevator.

"I suppose coffee is out of the question," Ward called out.

Carpenter completed his first review of the law school files of the plaintiffs suing Spenser School of Law. On separate sheets of notepaper, he made notes under each plaintiff's name summarizing pertinent facts.

Tina Farrell had been unable to find a law-related job since her graduation from Spenser in 2007. She ranked in the top third of her graduating class. During law school, she had not engaged in any extracurricular activities. She had sent out resumes to law firms, government agencies, and businesses offering in-house counsel positions. Since graduation she had been granted six interviews. She had passed the Massachusetts bar exam on her first try. Spenser's placement office had offered her nothing constructive in the years following graduation with one exception: Molly Grant had met with her and had come up with suggested changes to her resume. Currently she was working as a secretary for an insurance company. She was still paying off law school loans.

Felix Hennessey graduated from Spenser in 2009 ranking in the bottom half of his class. He had never received a course grade higher than a C. Like Farrell, he had not been involved in any extracurricular activity during law school. He had passed the Massachusetts bar exam on his third try. After passing the bar, he began sending out resumes to law firms but had yet to be granted an interview. Molly Grant had met with him and routinely sent him job opening opportunities that came to her attention. Currently he worked for a car dealership as a salesman paid on commission.

Marlon Gold graduated from Spenser in 2010 and had passed the Massachusetts bar exam on his first try. Like Hennessey, Gold graduated in the bottom half of his class. His preferred legal job was with a government agency or a business that had an in-house counsel legal staff; private practice did not appeal to him. He had sent out more than a hundred resumes and had yet to be interviewed for any position he had applied for. During law school, he had participated in a student prosecutor program during the first semester of his senior year but had dropped out of the program after a month. He had not been employed since graduation and was already in default on his law school loans.

Carpenter wrote a question on his notepad: *Why didn't the plaintiffs go out on their own?* He didn't have an answer but thought the question a legitimate one. If confronted with the brick walls that loomed in front of the Spenser plaintiffs, he wouldn't have sat on his ass waiting for a change in his fortune that would land him a legal job. He would have gone out on his own and hustled to make a go of it, taking court-appointed cases if worse came to worst.

Philly had gone out on her own, which was how they'd met. She had gotten nowhere applying to law firms for a job. She'd worked her way through law school and hadn't distinguished herself academically. Still, she'd had the guts to open up her own office. He remembered the time during the first year they began to seriously work together when she had confessed that she wasn't making it financially. Her solution wasn't to give up the law; instead she'd considered taking on court-appointed criminal cases to make ends meet.

Carpenter made another notation on his notepad: *Some people have what it takes to be a lawyer, others don't.* The observation was trite, but it was also true. The plaintiffs struck him as individuals who might not have lasted had they obtained a job in law. Maybe in defending the Spenser suit, they should look at whether graduates who landed a law-related job after graduation kept the job. Someone graduating from law school might think law was for him, but actually practicing law might provide a wakeup call that he was in the wrong line of work. Carpenter wondered whether on some level, the Spenser School of Law case involved what it took to become a practicing lawyer.

Carpenter wrote the word "Loans" on his notepad. The plight of the two plaintiffs saddled with law school loans bothered him. Back in his day, law school tuition was in the four figures. Today, tuition probably set a student back ten times that much. The two plaintiffs who had borrowed money to go to law school were probably in the hole for six figures. Even if law school debt was a common fact of law student life today, those two plaintiffs might elicit sympathy because of their inability to land a job to pay back Spenser's high tuition.

Underneath the word "Loans," Carpenter wrote the word "Depositions." Simon and Rachel needed to discover personal details of each plaintiff's life. What made each decide on law school? What did each plaintiff do before applying to law school to determine whether a career in law suited him or her? What did each plaintiff understand was the likelihood of landing a law school job?

Carpenter envied Simon and Rachel. They had an opportunity to display creativity in coming up with a defense for the law school. If only he had graduated from Spenser.

Patrick Lassiter was angry. "We were talking settlement," he nearly shouted at Philly over the phone. "Then you go behind my back and get an attachment against Rita Stout."

Philly was in her home office and needed to get downstairs to help Sarah out with the kids. "Don't give me that," she said testily, deciding to make short work of Lassiter. "You know damn well you can go before Judge Murray and move to dissolve the attachment on Stout's house. Besides, when we last talked settlement, I told you my client probably wouldn't give up the damage award. There was nothing close to a real settlement discussion."

Lassiter didn't respond immediately. Philly doubted that he wanted to show his face before Judge Murray.

"My clients are prepared to offer fifty thousand to settle the damage issue," Lassiter said.

Philly did some rough calculations. Her firm's attorney fees might equal that sum. "I'll relay that proposal. But I'm going to recommend it be rejected. I don't know this, but if your clients want to avoid pursuing an appeal of Murray's decision, they're going to have to put six figures on the table."

Lassiter again paused. "Please get back to me on my proposal," he requested in what Philly regarded as a more conciliatory tone.

"Okay," Philly said.

53

Emilio Gomez was of average height with a lean, hard body. Evelyn couldn't take her eyes off the tattoos of black snakes that slithered from the sleeves of his blue, short sleeve shirt down to his wrists. She'd caught him before he started his mechanic shift at a full-service garage in Somerville. When she'd identified herself, Gomez had glared at her for a long moment before hissing, "Not here." He had led her to the front of a nearby warehouse that looked abandoned.

Gomez didn't look like a man Maria Gomez would choose to marry. Unless, of course, she had misjudged Maria as an innocent.

"We're investigating a robbery at a house your wife had phone contact with as part of her job," Evelyn explained. "Has she ever talked to you about her customers?"

"What does this have to do with me?" Gomez protested. "Maria has her own job."

"The crime we're looking at is a crime you've done time for."

Gomez bristled, fighting to keep his cool. "That's right, I did do time. That's in the past. This has nothing to do with me."

"That's not for you to decide," Evelyn said. Gomez already was pissing her off.

"Do I have to talk to you?"

"No."

"Then I'm not going to talk to you."

Gomez started to walk off. Evelyn understood a heavy hand wouldn't work on him. "You'd be helping your wife if you'd answer a few questions," she called out.

Gomez stopped, and paused without looking back. Then he turned around and walked back to face Evelyn.

"I'm only talking to you to help Maria. She's my life. Make it quick. I've got to punch in."

"Has your wife ever talked to you about her customers?"

Gomez shook his head. "She says she's not allowed to. I can talk to her about what I do, but she can't tell me anything about what she does."

"Does Maria bring papers home from work?"

"Papers?"

"You know, copies of things she works on at her office."

"No," Gomez said. "One of the things we like about our jobs is we don't bring work home. When we leave for the day, we're done."

"Do you know the house where the robbery took place?"

"Like I told you, I don't know shit about a robbery or anything else."

"Did Maria tell you that we questioned her?"

Gomez averted his eyes. "Yeah. She said some cop talked to her about one of the people she helped on the phone. But she never told me what it was about."

"And you didn't ask?"

"Why the fuck would I ask? It didn't concern me."

"But it concerned your wife. Weren't you interested?"

Gomez glowered at her. Evelyn had no doubt that the man could be dangerous.

"Maria would have told me anything I needed to know. If she didn't say anything specific, I figured it was something I didn't need to know about, or she couldn't tell me about."

Evelyn found Gomez's last response unconvincing.

"Do you keep up with anyone you did time with?"

"That's my business. We're done here."

"You better sign in so you're not late. But you better get it through your head that we're not done."

Rachel edited Spencer School of Law's answer to the three former graduates' lawsuit as well as a request to delay the hearing on the plaintiffs' motion to certify the case as a class action until the law school responded to discovery and had taken the plaintiffs' depositions. Then she attached the drafts to an email to her partners. She couldn't recall a time when she had been this busy with paperwork.

Simon was also stressed with work. In addition to dealing with the Spenser lawsuit, he was gearing up for next month's trial in the Martina Glass case. Plus, he was helping Carpenter prepare for trial in the Atkins case. Trial in the Atkins case had been delayed because of the large caseload in the Suffolk Superior Court business litigation session, but the case could be heard at any time.

Rachel stood up and stretched. For the first time in a long time she felt that her professional life was submerging her personal life. Josh had proposed that they move in together and she'd agreed. But she hadn't had time to join Josh to search for an apartment. It would be a mistake to leave the choice to him. Besides, she didn't want to send a signal that where they first lived together wasn't important to her.

Rachel sat back down at Philly's desk and put her head down on her arms. 'So this is what being burned out feels like,' she thought. She wanted a short nap before the late afternoon conference call on the Spenser case. So far, the calls made her feel that she and her partners were working effectively as a team. When the four of them were working in their own silos without interacting, she would forget how much she enjoyed their company.

"Hey, sleepyhead!"

Rachel looked up to find Carpenter staring at her and she felt herself reddening as she straightened in her chair.

"This is embarrassing. I think I dropped off for a moment."

"You okay?"

"I'm beat."

"Then finish your nap. I'll wake you up in time for our Spenser call."

"No, I..."

"A nap," Carpenter interrupted. "I still outrank you for a little while longer. This is an order. Finish your nap."

The door closed and Rachel set her head back down on Philly's desk. Then she sat back up. She'd take Carpenter's advice but first she needed to make a call. Tonight, she and Josh were going to look at apartments.

Rachel woke with a start and checked her watch. She had dozed for only twenty minutes. There was still plenty of time before the call with her partners and she decided to use the time to check out their adversaries in the Spenser School of Law case.

The Blaisedell Group billed itself as a public interest law firm specializing in cases that would bring about meaningful reform to disadvantaged people. Located in Brooklyn, New York, the firm listed twelve attorneys on staff. Christopher Blaisedell, the firm founder, had graduated from New York University School of Law twelve years ago. After brief stints with the Office of the United States Attorney in New York and a non-profit law reform institute, he founded his own group. His firm website photograph showed a serious young man with black hair and blue eyes, a strong chin, and half-moon eyeglasses. The Blaisedell Group would typically employ local counsel to assist them in non-New York litigation. That had been the approach in the Spenser case; they had engaged a two-person litigation firm in Boston—Shapiro & Morales—as their local counsel. The small Boston firm had been in business for less than two years.

Rachel printed out the names of the cases brought by The Blaisedell Group against law schools. It would take time, but she believed it was necessary to obtain the court pleadings in the similar cases and perhaps to consult with the lawyers defending the suits. According to The Blaisedell Group's website, some of the suits had settled for substantial damages; however, specifics were missing, which indicated that the settlement agreements had to be kept confidential. She didn't believe that Dean Stockman would consider settlement. This was a case that would be tried.

Carpenter asked to take the lead for this scheduled Spenser call and it quickly became clear to Rachel that he didn't want to talk about discovery. Simon had arrived for the call from the Spenser law library, where he was drafting jury instructions for the Glass case, and Philly joined the call through Skype. Rachel wondered if either of them was as surprised as she was that Carpenter wanted to spend the call on overall strategy.

Watching Carpenter consult an outline, Rachel realized that the strategy session was necessary. To date, she and Simon had been immersed in the minutia of the litigation and hadn't taken the time to view the case from thirty thousand feet.

Rachel began to take notes. She underlined Carpenter's point to examine whether law school graduates kept at the job of finding work as a lawyer, or ultimately abandoned law. The answer to that question bore on whether the plaintiffs could prove actual damages.

Carpenter next pointed out that somewhere on the Internet were studies gauging lawyers' satisfaction with their profession. He recalled that over time, lawyers were becoming increasingly dissatisfied with the practice of law. When it came to the private practice of law, the emphasis had switched from practicing a profession to making money. Carpenter wondered if the plaintiffs were aware that lawyers in increasing numbers regarded the legal profession negatively.

Carpenter speculated that there had to be studies on what traits were necessary to be a successful lawyer whether in private practice or in some other role. He thought it worthwhile to learn what those traits were, and Rachel agreed. Perhaps the plaintiffs simply didn't have what it takes to be a lawyer. It would be interesting to ask each plaintiff what he or she had done to determine whether law really was the right career choice.

Carpenter wanted each plaintiff to be asked whether he or she had ever made an investment of money in a business or stocks. He didn't care how the question was answered. But if the question was answered yes, he proposed follow-up questions seeking to discover the research that had been done before the investment was made. Had similar research gone into the decision to go to law school? Rachel jotted down another area of inquiry: "What analysis did each plaintiff undertake before deciding where to go to college?"

Rachel glanced at Simon. Simon wasn't taking notes but he was paying attention. His eyes were fixed on Carpenter and his expression was serious.

Carpenter suggested a focus on the economy. Wasn't a major issue of the 2008 election that the economy had tanked? Numerous articles noted that the economic downturn had affected law firms. Large firms, in particular, had implemented hiring freezes and had let lawyers go. He recalled reading about some firms withdrawing offers that had been made to first year associates. The plaintiffs needed to be questioned about their knowledge of how the economic downturn was affecting legal jobs. Rachel didn't want to interrupt Carpenter, but she made a note to ask Molly Grant whether applications to law schools had gone up as graduates sought to improve their education while riding out the lousy job market during the economic downturn.

When Carpenter finished going through his outline, Rachel had made six pages of notes. It was disheartening to leave a meeting with a long to-do list, but she felt invigorated. This strategy session had been fun. Even Simon, who seemed to be in some kind of funk recently, looked recharged.

"There's one other thing," Carpenter said. "I initially didn't think this was such a great idea because we represented her. But I think we ought to reach out to your friend Sweeney to see if she's willing to help us with research and discovery. We've got two trials coming up in short order and I don't want to shortchange them. If she's agreeable, we need to clear it first with the dean."

Simon stared at Carpenter with his mouth open.

"We could use the help," Rachel said, amused by Simon's surprise since he had mentioned Meredith as a potential source of help.

"I agree," Philly said.

"Sure, why not," Simon said without any real enthusiasm as far as Rachel could detect.

I read through the answer you drafted in the Spenser case and your request to delay the hearing on the plaintiffs' class action motion," Carpenter said to Rachel. "I liked what you came up with. I've got a few changes that I'll get to you first thing tomorrow."

"You'll have my edits tomorrow as well," Philly added.

"I haven't had a chance to look at it," Simon said.

Rachel gave voice to the concern she'd been entertaining. "What happens with Simon if the Glass and Atkins cases are scheduled for trial at the same time?"

"I shoot myself," Simon said.

"We'll figure that out if and when the time comes," Carpenter said. "In the worst case, one of us will jump in. Since we're a law firm, we're going to act like one. That means we're there for each other."

Carpenter paused and his gaze settled on Simon. "I'm thinking, Simon, that there's too much on your plate. Rachel and I can take a shot at the jury instructions in the Atkins case. And who knows? Maybe Ms. Sweeney can lend a hand. You've got to speak up if you're stretched too tight."

"I can handle it," Simon said, an edge to his voice.

"I don't doubt that," Carpenter said. "But you don't have to drive yourself nuts. That's the point I'm trying to make."

"I said I can handle it," Simon retorted, and Rachel wasn't sure she believed him.

After the Spenser case conference call, Carpenter loaded up his briefcase with file folders and announced that he was heading for the gym. Rachel sat at Philly's desk and for a brief moment experienced a panic-induced paralysis. There were so many tasks she had to deal with that choosing one left her unable to act. Simon entered Philly's office, plopped down on the chair in front of the extra workstation, and emitted a deep sigh, which Rachel took as a signal as to what should be her priority.

"Do you want to talk about it?" Rachel asked.

"What?"

"What's bugging you."

"I'm fine. There's nothing to talk about."

"Carpenter picked up that everything's *not* fine," Rachel pointed out.

Simon didn't reply. He stared at the computer screen in front of him that he had yet to turn on.

"I'm your friend, Simon. You can talk to me."

Simon continued to stare at his computer screen. He had yet to turn around and face her. Rachel decided to wait him out. She took out a fresh notepad and started a new to-do list.

"Okay, maybe I'm a little down at the moment."

Rachel looked up. Simon had turned his chair around and was looking at her with a hangdog expression. Rachel nodded but didn't reply. She wasn't about to push him further.

"Part of how I'm feeling has to do with Frank," Simon said, coloring. "This long-distance relationship stuff truly sucks."

Rachel couldn't remember the last time Simon had taken time off to visit Frank Stevens at Wesleyan or Frank had made the trip north to Boston. It had to have been well over a month since they'd seen each other.

"Frank asked me whether I thought our relationship was working," Simon continued. "I told him it wasn't ideal, what with living apart, but I wanted it to work. We left it like that but I'm pretty sure he wants to see other guys."

"You don't know that," Rachel said.

"I can tell that's what he's thinking."

"But you haven't asked him."

"I'm afraid to," Simon admitted. "Besides, it's something I need to ask him in person, and when the hell am I going to get a chance to do that? As it is, I feel guilty that I'm not doing more on the Spenser case."

Rachel inventoried what had gotten Simon down. There was one thing she could give him that could help—time.

"This weekend, you are going to drive down to Wesleyan Friday afternoon and not return until Sunday night. You are not to take any work with you. That's an order."

Simon emitted a derisive snort. "That's not going to happen. I have too much to do."

"The only thing I want you to do before you go is give me your comments on the answer I drafted in the Spenser case. I'll take the first crack at the jury instructions in the Atkins case. The rest of the Spenser case can wait."

Simon lowered his eyes. "If I do what you want, I think I'll feel even guiltier than I already feel."

"Well, fuck you," Rachel said with some heat. "I absolve you. You're going and that's all there is to it."

Rachel had figured her rare use of the f-word would wake Simon up but instead he continued to look downcast, and her heart went out to him.

"I'm being selfish," Rachel said. "I need you here and happy. *We* need you here and happy. Get things with Frank squared away. From where I sit, that needs to be your first priority."

Simon smiled for the first time. "You're not being selfish, you're being nice."

"That's me, nice."

54

There were times when Evelyn wondered whether everyone ended up living in Somerville at some point in their lives. Simone Moorhead lived in the city in an apartment near Maria Gomez's apartment. The two women might have passed each other in the street countless times, unaware of their common connection. Eva Tebbins had confirmed that Moorhead would not be on duty this weekend; an agency caretaker would be looking out for Grace Mansfield through Sunday night.

It was five o'clock on a Friday evening and Evelyn was on her own time, parked across the street from Moorhead's apartment building. There was no way Paul would authorize overtime for tracking Moorhead, even though he was the one who suggested her as a possible suspect. Besides, she didn't want Paul to know what she was up to. If it led to something, hopefully he'd conclude she'd showed initiative.

Moorhead arrived at the building at a quarter past the hour and in another fifteen minutes was out the door. Evelyn got out of her car and followed, keeping a healthy distance between them. There was a bounce to Moorhead's step and Evelyn figured that the woman was relishing the expanse of free time before her. It couldn't be easy catering to Mansfield's needs 24/7.

Moorhead was heading to a row of trendy eateries not far off. When she checked her watch for the second time, Evelyn suspected that she was meeting someone.

The French restaurant that Moorhead entered couldn't be cheap. Evelyn didn't break stride as she walked past the front door, but still she took in white tablecloths and napkins, tall wine and water glasses. And Moorhead locked in an embrace with a tall man whose back was facing the front door.

Evelyn paused at the next intersection and thought about her next move. She saw two possible options for monitoring the French restaurant: a deli that had stools facing the street and a bar that had several tables for two facing the street. She opted for the bar. It was easier to nurse a drink than a sandwich. She crossed the street and headed back the way she had come.

Simon tried to remember the line from the Pink song, the one that went something like you were on the right track if passion was there. Frank had arranged for his roommate to be gone and they had his dorm suite to themselves. Frank hadn't wanted to talk or eat and the urgency of his lovemaking swept away the rehearsed speech that Simon had worked on during the drive down to Wesleyan. Following Rachel's advice, he hadn't brought any work along for the ride.

"Nice to see you too," Simon said when his heart rate returned to something resembling normal.

"I needed that," Frank said. "We needed that."

Frank had provided a lead-in and Simon debated whether to take it. He was spent, hungry, blissfully lightheaded—all signs he wouldn't be thinking clearly. 'What the hell,' he thought. Rachel was right: this was priority number one.

"What was on your mind when you asked me whether our relationship was working?" Simon asked, and the sound of Frank's breathing stopped.

"I don't know. Maybe I was feeling down. This not seeing each other for weeks on end is… I don't know… frustrating, maddening, pick a word, any word."

"Frustrating and maddening tell the story," Simon replied. He decided to be direct. "Are you having doubts about the two of us?"

Frank turned to face him, and Simon realized that this was the first time he had seen pain in Frank's eyes.

"I don't have doubts about us," Frank said. "But the situation we're in leaves a lot to be desired."

Simon had thought back to his early college years. It was the first time he felt that he could be himself, and it was a heady, liberating sensation. He couldn't shake the feeling that he was depriving Frank of that discovery experience.

"Do you want to see other guys?"

Frank closed his eyes briefly as if trying to block out the question. When Frank's eyes opened his pain was still there.

"Not particularly," Frank said. "But if we're being honest with each other, I've thought about it."

"Thought about it?"

"This guy came on to me. When he did, I thought about it."

"What stopped you?"

"Shit!" Frank erupted. "This is like the third degree!"

"We need to talk about this," Simon persisted. "What stopped you?"

"What stopped me? You. Me. I don't know."

"Not seeing each other for stretches is going to continue. Right now, the work demands on me are intense. It's not always going to be like this, but for the moment, I feel like I don't have time to breathe."

"But here you are," Frank pointed out.

"You can thank Rachel for that. She pretty much ordered me down here to talk to you. Being apart has been bothering me too and she picked up on it."

"What are we going to do?" Frank asked.

Simon remembered his ill-advised night with Meredith and Frank's reaction to that situation.

"We're going to keep seeing each other when we can," Simon said. "As for you, if anyone hits on you and you want to take him up on it or you want to hit on someone else, go for it."

"Are you serious?"

"Yes, I am," Simon said, meaning it. "I just don't want to know about it. And for God's sake, be careful."

"What's going on here?"

Simon choose his words with care. "Part of it has to do with our age difference. College should be a time for experimentation and discovery, and I don't want to deprive you of that. Part of it has to do with your agreeing I could contact that woman I told you about to see if her offer was still open. Maybe those aren't the best of reasons but they're all I've got."

"We're not breaking up, right?" Frank questioned.

"Right."

"If I do anything, I'm going to tell you."

Simon shook his head. "I've already told you I don't want to know."

"I wouldn't feel right if I didn't tell you," Frank insisted. "And what you said goes for me, that goes for you too."

"That's very noble of you," Simon said, "but I'm not in the market. At the moment, I've found my market."

"Would we be living together if I was going to school in Boston?"

"That would be my choice," Simon replied.

"This is a lot to take in," Frank said, sighing.

"Food is what I need to take in. Let's get out of here. My treat."

Frank made no move to leave the bed. "Why is everything so fucking complicated?"

"Because, as Carpenter likes to say—and I'm quoting him directly—'nothing is fucking easy.'"

55

A College Professor

For the moment, Philly had the conference room to herself. She had left Brighton early to beat the traffic and was the first to arrive at the Boston office suite. She rubbed her belly and wondered how big she would be when it came time to try the Martina Glass case. At this morning's spinning workout, she hadn't even made a pretense of keeping up with Isabella. She had maintained a moderate pace with moderate resistance and had seldom pedaled standing.

When she announced last night in an e-mail that she had scheduled today's early morning meeting with a potential new client, Simon questioned whether they had the ability to take on a new case that might require an immediate court appearance, Rachel thought that the case sounded interesting, and Carpenter had gotten straight to his point, in italics: "*We don't turn away potential new business.*"

On balance, Philly sided with Carpenter; referrals were uncertain, and they'd be foolish to pass up the opportunity. Also, the potential new case had been a referral from Daniel Spring, a teachers' union representative in the Boston school system who had been the source of several referrals. She wanted to stay in Spring's good graces.

"How are you feeling?" Rachel said, entering the conference room. She was followed by Simon, who nodded his greeting.

Philly sized up her young partners. Each looked worn out but neither looked defeated. Rachel appeared determined and Simon's previous funk had been replaced by his cool reserve.

"I'm feeling good," Philly declared.

"Sorry, I'm running late," Carpenter said, taking a seat at the conference room table. Of course Carpenter had voted for trying to take on another case, Philly reflected; first meetings with potential clients were what he lived for.

"What do we have?" Carpenter asked, and Philly filled the group in on what Daniel Spring had reported to her.

Brendan O'Day looked surprisingly chipper for a man who had just been fired. Philly guessed O'Day was in his early forties. He had a close-cropped red beard, straggly red hair worn long, and green eyes that sparkled. He was tall and thin and assessed the lawyers facing him with a confident air that bordered on pugnacious. He looked so thoroughly Irish that it was almost a shock when he spoke without an accent.

"I didn't expect to meet the entire law firm," O'Day said after introductions had been made.

O'Day must have visited their website. Philly opted for honesty. "We're currently extremely busy. We all want to hear what you have to say so we can best allocate resources to help you if you decide to hire us. Daniel Spring filled me in on what happened, but we'd like to hear it from you."

"I'm on the faculty at Baywater State College here in Boston. I teach English and I'm the faculty advisor to the student newspaper, the Baywater Bugle. There was an organized, publicized rally on campus to protest violence against women. Approximately three hundred people attended. Some of the speakers were rape victims. One of those rape victims introduced herself by name. The Bugle's lead article reported on the rally and the article included the name of the speaker who had identified herself at the rally. That touched off a shit-storm."

"Did you approve the article before it was run?" Rachel asked.

"I did. The editor showed it to me and asked me whether it was okay to use the rape victim's name. I said that there was nothing to prohibit using the name because the individual had publicly given it. I said that the article didn't have to include the name and it was the editor's decision."

"Did the editor ask you for a recommendation?" Rachel next asked.

O'Day frowned in concentration. "No."

"What would you have said if asked for a recommendation?" Rachel continued.

"I'm not sure. I probably would have opted not to include the name, but I can't say that for sure."

"What was the shit-storm?" Simon asked.

"The dean of the college claims he got over a hundred calls protesting the violation of the rape victim's privacy rights. He called me into his office along with the student editor of the Bugle and demanded that the rape victim's name be deleted from the online version of the article. The student editor refused, and I backed her up. The dean said I was fired and he told the student editor that if the name wasn't removed from the article in the next two hours, he—the dean—would have it removed. The student editor told him to fuck himself and I told him he'd be hearing from a lawyer." O'Day paused. "I believe that qualifies as a shit-storm."

"What happened to the online version of the article?" Philly asked.

"The dean had the name deleted."

"What's the position of the rape victim?" Simon asked.

"She made a statement that she preferred for her name to be removed from the online article. What she didn't say is why she identified herself in the first place."

"Was the editor disciplined in any way?" Philly asked.

"I don't think so. Her name is Helene Bridge. She's already fired off a tweet that's making the rounds claiming the dean has violated the Bugle's right to freedom of the press."

Carpenter joined the discussion. "Let me get this straight. You backed up the editor on not deleting the rape victim's name from the online version of the article and the next thing that happens is the dean fires you. Did the dean provide any explanation for firing you?"

"No."

"Why didn't he just remove you as the Bugle's faculty advisor?" Philly wondered aloud.

O'Day again shrugged. "This is just my opinion, but I think the dean didn't like it when I refused to back him up against the editor. I would describe the dean as arrogant and as a man who doesn't take kindly to anyone not caving in to his authority."

"Are you tenured?" Simon asked.

"No."

"Do you have a contract?" Carpenter followed up.

"I have a letter of appointment to a tenure track position. That's about it."

"What have your performance reviews been like?" Rachel asked.

"Good. I'm a lively teacher. Students like me. I try to get them to think and my methods aren't always conventional."

"You're here seeking potential legal representation," Philly said. "What is it you want a lawyer to do for you?"

"Do you really have to ask?" O'Day said with a sneer. "I want my fucking job back. I want the dean's sorry ass hauled into court. He fucked with the wrong guy. I'm on tap to teach a summer school class and I want to teach the goddamn class."

Even before this outburst, Philly had concluded O'Day would be a handful as a client. His confirming her assessment gave her pause, but a new case was a new case and there was no such thing as a model client.

"We can try to get you your job back," Philly said, "but there's no guaranty that we'll be immediately successful. You have some legal claims available to you and one of them is a first amendment claim. To go to court and try to get a court order putting you back in the classroom will require us to draft a complaint and a legal memorandum, and to put together affidavits in support of your position. Are there any students or faculty members who will back you up?"

"I'm sure Helene will be helpful. I can probably come up with some other students. Faculty support is another thing altogether. Baywater State's faculty is largely made up of cowards who probably don't have what it takes to stand up to the dean. I'll ask around, but I don't have great hopes when it comes to the faculty."

Philly informed O'Day of the firm's billing rates and the need for an engagement letter. She noticed that O'Day didn't blanch when she ticked off the hourly fees. When O'Day didn't ask how much the initial court proceeding would cost, she decided to ask for a $5,000 retainer.

O'Day handed over a business card after writing on the back of it. "Use my home e-mail to send me a copy of the engagement letter. I'll let you know whether you're hired by noon tomorrow."

Philly returned to the conference room after showing O'Day out and was greeted with three serious expressions one of which—Simon's—was unmistakably glum. There was one item she needed to get off her chest.

"I know I should have talked with you before mentioning a retainer, but I wanted to try to get a read on whether O'Day would be a deadbeat."

"You did the right thing on that when he never asked about the cost of going to court," Carpenter said.

Philly realized what was weighing Simon down—he was overworked. Rachel probably was in the same boat but was more willing to grin and bear it.

"I'm thinking you and I deal with this if he engages us," Philly said to Carpenter. "I'll bring in Daisy if I need any backup on my end."

Philly's attempt at a light tone didn't resonate with her younger partners.

"I don't understand why the rape victim identified herself in the first place," Rachel said. "I wonder if she got a good look at the guy. She must not be concerned that her attacker may come after her."

Philly jotted down a reminder to search for information about the rape.

"We're being overrun by deans," Carpenter groused. "There's the dean at Spenser and now maybe this Baywater dean."

Carpenter's griping was welcome to Philly. It was like old times.

"I'll do the complaint if we get the case," Philly said to Carpenter, falling back on what had been their typical division of labor. "You deal with the affidavits."

"Sounds like a plan," Carpenter said. "We've got a lot of plans in play. What about the Sweeney woman? Has anybody talked to her?"

"I got sidetracked this weekend," Simon said sheepishly.

"I forgot," Rachel admitted. "I was working on a draft of jury instructions for the Atkins case, which I'll send around after this call."

"No time like the present," Carpenter said. He took charge of the conference room phone and put it on speaker. Simon read off the number from his cell phone contacts.

"Hello."

"Ms. Sweeney," Carpenter replied. "Your lawyers have got you on a speaker phone. The Gang of Four is all here."

"To what do I owe the pleasure?"

"First things first," Carpenter said. "How are you?"

"Still unemployed, but happy. I've got a few leads, but the truth is I'm relaxing and taking my time. The money helps. The pressure's off."

"Excellent," Carpenter replied. "Are you interested in doing any freelance legal work?"

"Are you offering me a job?"

"If you're interested, we're offering just what I said—freelance legal work. We'd pay you for your time at a rate to be negotiated. We would only want to pay you for time we billed out, so you may end up putting in hours that you don't get paid for. What do you say?"

Meredith didn't say anything. "What would I be working on?" she finally asked.

Carpenter paused a beat. "There is one case that will require your immediate attention, and a second case that may require your immediate attention if we are hired by a potential client. For the first case we need to run your involvement by the client, but I don't anticipate a problem. But before I tell you what we're dealing with, I need you to assure us that you will say nothing about these matters to anybody regardless of whether you decide to help."

"Agreed," Meredith said.

"Let's start with your alma mater," Carpenter said, and he quickly summarized the Spenser and O'Day cases. "So, what do you think?" he wrapped up.

"You had me at Spenser School of Law. I'm in."

"We haven't talked money yet," Carpenter reminded Meredith.

"What did you have in mind?"

"Hold on a minute," Carpenter said, before muting the line. "I'm thinking we pay her one hundred fifty an hour and bill her out at two hundred. I know it's a lot less than your hourly rates," he added, nodding at Simon and Rachel, "but she's not a partner here or even an employee and I'm inclined to keep her billing rate low. The law school will be getting a bargain for any work she does."

"Works for me," Philly said, and Simon and Rachel nodded agreement.

"We went offline for a moment," Carpenter said before relating the proposal.

"Well, I have to say that's a fraction of what I was billed out at Pinkerton, but I'm still in," Meredith said. Simon breathed a sigh of relief.

56

Meredith was to report to him at noon and Carpenter wondered how he would deal with her coming aboard and depriving him of something he treasured beyond all measure—his privacy. There was simply no room for a third lawyer in Philly's office, so he had been forced to step up to the plate and let Meredith occupy his personal domain. Already he was thinking of routinely directing her to one law library or another to minimize her intrusion. But no matter how much research she accomplished off-site, she was going to need a home base for a lot of the work that was headed her way.

Simon had gotten Dean Stockman's approval to have Meredith work on the Spenser case and to hear Simon tell it, the dean was thrilled: the more Spenser alums involved, the better. Brendan O'Day had signed the engagement letter Philly had sent to him and had passed on the names of two students who were willing to help his cause: Helene Bridge, the editor of the Baywater Bugle, and Brad Counsel, the student body president. The retainer was being sent via overnight mail.

Carpenter tried to think through the assignments he would be unloading on Meredith but kept being distracted by the two computer geeks who had appropriated a section of his office to set up a workstation for her. A new PC, monitor, and printer were in place on a computer table positioned across from his desk. An adjustable chair faced the screen. Meredith would need some sort of a filing cabinet, but Carpenter decided she could use a storage box for starters.

Watching the computer guys leave his office, Carpenter wondered whether this was the last time for a long time when he would be truly alone.

Meredith thought of the stark differences between Pinkerton, Ashley & Rosewood and the four-person partnership that was now throwing work her way. At Pinkerton, she'd had her own office, access to paralegals, and a shared secretary to do her bidding. Even the support staff workspace at Pinkerton with plush carpets and modern furnishings was several cuts above the lawyer offices she had seen in Carpenter's three-minute tour of the Milk Street suite. Here she would be working at a narrow computer table in the office of an elderly lawyer who didn't look pleased by the arrangement. She was disappointed that neither Simon nor Rachel was around to welcome her. Still, taking notes as Carpenter outlined her first assignment, she didn't think that she'd taken a step backwards in her career. There was the possibility she was trying to sell herself, but there was something about the small firm that made her believe she was going to be counted on.

"Have you ever drafted a legal memorandum supporting a request for an injunction?" Carpenter asked.

"No," Meredith had to admit, and was taken aback by Carpenter's shocked look that suggested he couldn't imagine what she'd been doing at Pinkerton for more than two years.

"I've made copies of three memoranda that were used in other cases. Rachel drafted one of them. Use these as models. You've got Philly's rough draft outline of the complaint we're going to file for Mr. O'Day that outlines his legal claims. You need to find case law support for those claims."

Meredith nodded. She'd be holed up in a law library but vowed to produce a work product in the next twenty-four hours if it killed her. When she looked up from her note taking, Carpenter was staring at her as if taking her measure.

"We're very pleased you're able to help us," Carpenter said, softening for the first time since Meredith had sat across from him in the visitor chair at his desk. "Rachel and Simon have spoken highly of you and we're giving you two interesting assignments right off the bat. Any draft you produce needs to be sent to the four of us. That might seem like overkill, but it's just the way we do things. If you get bogged down on this O'Day case, call me. I don't want you wasting time going down blind alleys."

Not exactly the welcoming speech she had received on joining Pinkerton, Meredith reflected. But it would do.

Evelyn looked across the expanse of their joined desks. Paul was working on a report to their captain and his concentration was total. Evelyn had her own paperwork to complete but knew that she wouldn't be able to focus until she had briefed Paul on the Mansfield robbery. She feigned reviewing the papers in front of her and waited for Paul to finish his report.

"Do you want to talk to me?" Paul said without looking up, and Evelyn couldn't figure out how he knew she was waiting for him to come to a stopping point.

"I don't want to interrupt you."

Paul put down his pen. "Interrupt me. You're not going to be productive on anything else until you do."

"I followed Simone Moorhead, the caretaker. It was evening. She met a guy at a fancy restaurant. Afterwards they went back to her place. I followed the guy when he left the next morning."

"So you pulled an all-nighter."

It wasn't a question, but Evelyn nodded. "It won't be the last. Anyway, he walked back to his place—also in Somerville—and then he got in his car and drove to work. I ran the license plate. The guy she met is Dennis Wilbur. He's got a record. A ten-year-old conviction for breaking and entering, and a twelve-year-old bad check conviction. He works for a Waltham building supply company in the company's business office."

Paul set his elbows on his desk and rested his chin in his hands. "Who would have figured it?" he said. "Each possible female suspect is running around with a guy with a record."

Evelyn had noticed the irony but hadn't dwelled on it long. "What about searching the Gomez apartment and Moorhead's and Wilbur's apartments?"

"Talk to the assistant DA who worked with us on the liquor store robbery a couple of months back. She seemed to have her head screwed on right. Let's also think if there's a way to flush one of these folks out without having to go the warrant route."

"What do you have in mind?"

"I don't know," Paul admitted. "The stolen painting is something the thief is going to want to move. I'm wondering what we can do to help that along."

"I'll think about it," Evelyn said, struck by the notion that Paul never made it easy.

"Nice work," Paul said, before turning back to his paperwork.

57

"You look like hell," Carpenter said.

Meredith was too tired to care what she looked like. She had worked in the Spenser law library until eleven last night and had finally finished a draft of the legal memorandum required in the O'Day case at four in the morning, which she e-mailed to Carpenter.

"This isn't bad for your first time dealing with an injunction memorandum," Carpenter continued, waggling her work product in her direction.

Meredith reflected that on this, the second day of her new contract job, she was the recipient of two firsts: an insult on her appearance and a compliment on a work product. But maybe Carpenter hadn't insulted her appearance. Maybe he was being observant and expressing concern that she looked a wreck.

"Bring your chair around here," Carpenter said, and once Meredith was seated next to him behind his desk, he began to go through the changes he had made to her memorandum draft. She fought off her lethargy and paid attention. Myriad red ink markings were on every page she had produced.

"Some of these markups reflect my personal preferences as to wording. I have a way I like to express certain things, which doesn't mean that the way you worded something is wrong. Maybe I'll win you over to the way I like to say things, maybe I won't. I went through this with Philly years ago when she had to go to court for the first time. Consider this a learning experience."

Meredith nodded. As she read through Carpenter's edits, she had to acknowledge that his changes improved the memorandum. He seemed to have an aversion to adjectives and adverbs.

"You did a good job on irreparable harm," Carpenter said. "You can't get an injunction unless you can show irreparable harm, and you made O'Day seem like he'd been put through the circles of hell. I've toned it down a little but not too much. And I like the cases you found that hold that a first amendment violation is itself irreparable harm."

'I could get used to this,' Meredith thought. 'Meaningful feedback. Go figure.'

When they finished reading through Carpenter's edits, he waved Meredith back to the visitor's chair position.

"Here's what I want you to do," Carpenter said. "I want you to go home and take a long nap. Then rewrite the memorandum and circulate it to the four of us. I'm almost done with the affidavits and when I send them out for comment, I want you to make suggestions. The rule here is that no suggestion is stupid. Even if you make a stupid suggestion—and someone will probably tell you if you do—sometimes a stupid suggestion leads to an idea that isn't stupid."

'Here's another first,' Meredith thought. At Pinkerton, she had never been asked to comment on a partner's work product.

"Nap time," Carpenter said. "Nice job."

"Thanks," Meredith said, unable to stifle a yawn.

Philly rubbed her belly as she turned pages in her trial notebook. She and Simon were seated at her dining room table, and from the backyard Simon heard Philly's daughter and the younger child, Rosalind, squealing with delight under Sarah Fergusson's watchful eyes. "Are we ready?" Philly asked.

"I am," Simon said. "The truth is I want this over with. I need to be spending more time on the Spenser case."

"I'm thinking Martina's trial will take three to four days," Philly said. "Rachel will hold the fort in the Spenser case. Meredith will be available to her. Besides, the other side has given you more time to file your answer and respond to discovery."

Simon nodded. He had hated calling Christopher Blaisedell to ask for lengthy extensions, but there had really been no choice. Dean Stockman had not commented on the delay, but Simon sensed that he wasn't pleased. Stockman was probably second-guessing his decision to farm the case out to a small firm.

Simon found his focus drifting, the laughter of the little girls claiming his attention. Was he going to be one of those gay guys who never had children in his life? Did he even want children in his life? The path of least resistance was to let the practice of law take over his life, providing the ready excuse that he had no time to even think about kids. Simon tried to imagine him and Frank dealing with a baby. Frank would be the warm and cuddly parent.

"It's been a while since our last trials," Philly observed, and Simon saw that she was watching him intently, had perhaps picked up on the fact that his mind was wandering.

"I just want the trial to start," Simon said. "At the end of last year, we had those two jury trials coming back to back but there wasn't much else going on. Now there's a lot going on. I think once the trial starts, I'll feel better. I'll be forced to put the distractions aside."

Philly frowned. "That's one way of looking at it." She closed her trial notebook. "How about staying for lunch? If you're lucky, the little monsters will keep the food to themselves."

Simon pictured food smeared on Daisy's and Rosalind's faces. The image was both gross and intriguing. "Thanks. I wouldn't miss it," he said, striving for a convincing tone that he didn't completely feel.

58

Meredith was perched on a bench in the first row of the visitors' seating directly behind the plaintiff's counsel table occupied by Carpenter and Philly, trying not to let her nervousness show. On this occasion she was more on edge than she'd been when arguing motions for Pinkerton clients. She felt a personal investment in Brendan O'Day's case, a feeling that had rarely surfaced with the cases assigned to her at Pinkerton.

O'Day sat next to her, glaring at Judge Priscilla Burgess, who was taking her time reading through the papers that had been thrust upon her. At the defendants' counsel table sat a trio of lawyers from the Boston firm of Levin, Tarlow & Smith, a large firm not quite the size of Pinkerton but nonetheless one of Boston's biggest. Meredith focused on the youngest Levin lawyer, an earnest looking man with glasses who was filling the role she had played at Pinkerton: the role of the associate who had done the lion's share of the grunt work and was being permitted to sit at the counsel table—the grownups' table instead of the kids' table—while partners did the arguing.

"Interesting case," Judge Burgess said, looking up from her reading. She was a short, slim, forty-something woman with blond hair cut short and a thin face with prominent cheek bones. "Why shouldn't I put the plaintiff back in the classroom?" the judge addressed the defendants' counsel table. "The plaintiff has been recognized as a capable teacher both by students and in performance reviews. His firing seems unrelated to his teaching function."

Stephen Larson, the senior Levin attorney, rose to his feet. Meredith reflected that Larson would have fit in perfectly at Pinkerton. He was a tall, thin, middle-aged white man with a self-assured air, a calm manner, and a hard stare. He was wearing the dark blue suit favored by Pinkerton litigators.

Larson addressed Judge Burgess. "The plaintiff refused to obey a direct order from the dean of Baywater State College and was terminated from his position for that disobedience. Dean Walter Sternman's affidavit makes the foregoing abundantly clear. The plaintiff has no right to his position under contract or anything else. He was basically an employee at will who could be terminated for any reason or no reason."

"I would disagree with you there," Judge Burgess responded. "The plaintiff couldn't be let go because of his skin color, his sex, his age, or his national origin, among other things. And the plaintiff makes a persuasive case that he could not be terminated for exercising first amendment rights applicable to freedom of speech and freedom of the press."

Larson shook his head. "The dean made the proper judgment that any first amendment rights—and we submit there are none in play here—could not be used to violate the privacy rights of a rape victim. The first amendment claim is a red herring."

The judge turned to Carpenter and Philly. "What does the plaintiff have to say in response?"

Carpenter rose which caught Meredith off guard. Philly had brought in the case and Meredith had simply assumed that Philly would be arguing today.

"Any right to privacy—and we submit there is none in play here—cannot trump self-evident first amendment rights that are paramount in this case."

Meredith felt a rush of excitement at Carpenter's articulating one of the legal arguments she had written.

"The rape victim who spoke at the rally identified herself by name. The student newspaper printed the information that the speaker made public. There is no allegation that the newspaper article contained an untrue statement. The article is factually correct. The plaintiff properly left the decision to publish the article with the rape victim's name to the student editor and, as his affidavit attests, regarded the dean's instruction to delete from the online version of the article the name that had been made public as blatant censorship. In short, the plaintiff defended the student editor's editorial decision as protected by freedom of the press."

The judge studied Carpenter for a long moment. "The defendants cite a discussion with the rape victim in which she states that she preferred to have her name deleted from the online version of the article. She mentions that she is sure she can identify her assailant and is concerned that her assailant will now have an easier time finding her. Doesn't that suggest that there is a privacy right in play here that the dean was within his rights to respect?"

"No," Carpenter said without hesitation. "You can't un-ring a bell. The rape victim put her name in the public domain. Why she did so is not relevant. That she did so is relevant. While she may have a preference as to what she would like done after she voluntarily identified herself publicly, first amendment principles trump whatever after-the-fact preference the individual came up with."

"Would you agree, Mr. Larson, that it is odd for an individual desiring to protect her privacy to fully identify herself when she had no reason to do so?" the judge asked.

"Perhaps," Larson said. "But while we don't know her motivation for doing so, we do know that the dean acted in accordance with the second thoughts that the speaker later voiced. It's fair to say that the dean anticipated the speaker's second thoughts that she wished her privacy to be protected and respected. The dean cannot be faulted for taking action that the speaker ultimately endorsed."

"Did any other newspaper print the name of the rape victim?" the judge inquired.

"Not that we're aware of," Carpenter acknowledged, and Meredith knew that he was relying on her Internet search for his response.

"What about you, Mr. Larson? Are you aware of the rape victim's name appearing in print anywhere else?"

"No, Your Honor, but to be frank, our office has not done an exhaustive search."

The judge frowned. "I'm trying to think of a reason why this victim identified herself. It makes no sense if she were truly concerned about keeping her identity secret."

Carpenter and Larson said nothing. Meredith wondered whether the judge was going to rule on the injunction request immediately after oral arguments concluded.

"Don't we need testimony from the rape victim?" the judge asked.

Carpenter's "absolutely" overlapped with Larson's "no."

The judge smiled. "Well, I suppose those responses were predictable." The judge then sat back in her chair and closed her eyes.

Meredith was now certain that the judge would rule from the bench.

Judge Burgess opened her eyes and sat straight in her chair. "Here's my ruling," she announced. "I'm going to grant the plaintiff's motion for a preliminary injunction because I find on the record before me that the reason for the plaintiff's termination was his support for a student editor's decision to publish a factually accurate news story. The plaintiff regarded the editor's decision as freedom of the press protected activity, and I am satisfied that this is a viable legal claim. When it comes to irreparable harm, I conclude that the plaintiff has the best of it. He is harmed if he is not permitted to teach his classes and the college is not harmed if he is permitted to teach. The plaintiff's teaching abilities are not in question. Plus, if the plaintiff does not teach, his students suffer harm, as one of the student affidavits before me makes clear."

Meredith glanced at O'Day. He sat beside her tense and worried. Hadn't he realized that he'd prevailed?

"Mr. Larson," the judge said. "You are free to take the deposition of the rape victim and, upon doing so, if you discover information you believe would warrant a different decision on my part were I to consider it, I will entertain an emergency motion by the college to vacate the injunction I have just entered."

Philly and Larson's colleagues were writing feverishly. Meredith reasoned that Larson had nothing to lose by taking the rape victim's deposition. The judge was basically telling him that was what the college needed to do to get her to change her mind.

"Any questions?" the judge asked. "No? Very well, the court is now in recess."

Meredith stayed in the background as Carpenter dealt with O'Day's questions. She tried to maintain a neutral expression but found herself breaking into unexpected smiles. Of course she might now be suicidal if the judge had ruled against O'Day. But for the moment she was caught up in the joy and satisfaction of having contributed significantly to a winning effort.

"I didn't follow what the judge was saying at the end," O'Day said. "Why would she change her mind after a deposition of the rape victim? What does that deposition have to do with anything?"

"We have to remember what bothered the judge," Carpenter replied. "She couldn't understand why a rape victim who wanted to protect her privacy would reveal her name. Frankly, I'm also in the dark. So maybe the judge has in mind that this victim gave her name for a reason and that once the reason is known, she might reconsider her ruling."

"Shit," O'Day muttered. "That means the college would be stupid not to take the deposition. They've got nothing to lose and everything to gain. This will just drag on for bloody ever."

"Cheer up," Carpenter said. "You just won a round. Be thankful."

"This is costing me," O'Day said.

"Well, on this occasion you got what you paid for," Philly reminded him. "Why do you think the victim gave her name?"

"I don't have a fucking clue," O'Day said, glowering.

Meredith remembered what Carpenter had said about there being no such thing as a stupid idea. But surely he didn't mean floating a radical idea in the presence of a client. She'd hold her peace until O'Day departed.

"The gang's all here," Carpenter said, as he signaled for a waiter. Meredith was pleased to be included. Carpenter had called Simon and Rachel on his cell phone, informed them of the O'Day decision, and suggested a celebratory lunch. They had rendezvoused at a waterfront restaurant that Carpenter promised served mouthwatering sandwiches, which Meredith received as welcome news—she was starved.

"This is on the firm," Philly announced. "We've earned it."

When Carpenter ordered a beer with his meal, Meredith hesitated following suit but then thought, 'What the hell?' She had helped win a case, she had six figures in a savings account, and she was happy.

As they waited for their food, Carpenter took charge. "We need to get Meredith's head into the Spenser case." He motioned toward Simon and Rachel. "When you two go back to the office, tell her where to start."

"She needs to start with the documents Spenser has to turn over in discovery, especially the student files," Rachel said. "I've got a plan for that."

"Good," Carpenter said. "Is there anything any of us can do to help with the Glass case?" he asked Simon and Philly.

"We're good," Philly said. "Simon and I want the damn thing over with. It feels like it's been hanging around forever."

After their orders were served, they ate for a time in silence. Meredith tried to slow down but she was famished.

Philly nodded at Meredith. "For the record, I'm a recovering alcoholic so I don't drink. I wanted to get that out of the way."

Meredith hoped her surprise didn't show. "Okay, thanks for letting me know."

"Any thoughts about the O'Day hearing?" Carpenter asked Meredith.

Meredith was grateful for the beer. It made it easier to broach her crazy idea. "I've got a theory on why the rape victim gave out her name."

"No shit," Carpenter said. "I'm all ears."

"It's because she wanted to," Meredith said, and then she spelled out her thinking.

Meredith couldn't read the four partners' expressions, even Rachel's, which was a surprise since in the brief time she'd been interacting with her, Rachel was an open book. She now wished that she'd kept her mouth shut. Carpenter—or perhaps it would be Philly—was going to tell her she was nuts and any progress she'd made in gaining the partners' confidence was about to be set back to zero.

"That is twisted, devious thinking," Carpenter said with a stare Meredith found menacing. "But it makes a kind of sick sense."

"If Meredith's right," Philly joined in, "what the hell do we do about it?"

"Shouldn't we be asking how her theory can be used to help O'Day?" Rachel asked.

"If Meredith's right," Simon said, "I think helping O'Day means doing nothing."

"I agree," Philly said.

"If the rape victim is deposed would you bring my theory up?" Meredith asked.

No one answered for a long moment.

Carpenter broke the silence. "Probably not. But we all need to think about that."

Meredith drained the rest of her beer. She hadn't been laughed out of the restaurant. 'I could get used to this,' she thought.

Philly sought out her sponsor, Melanie, before tonight's AA meeting began in the basement of Saint Sebastian's Church. Recently, she had kept to a two-nights-a-week schedule, but that was about to change.

"I'm about to start a trial," Philly explained, "so there's a good chance I'm going to miss a few sessions. I wanted to give you a heads up."

Melanie didn't reply for a long moment and Philly found her sponsor's stare and serious expression uncomfortable.

"I'm glad you told me," Melanie said. "I would have been worried about you."

Philly was surprised at Melanie's reaction. Usually her sponsor gave her a lecture about priorities the moral of which unfailingly was that nothing—even a trial—was more important than meetings. But tonight Melanie seemed almost mellow. Her sponsor was painfully thin, intense when it came to AA meetings, and oftentimes nervous. But at this moment she appeared laid back.

"I thought you'd be giving me a lecture and assorted grief," Philly said.

"I can if you want," Melanie replied, and Philly tried to remember when, if ever, Melanie had joked with her.

"I'll pass," Philly said. "You seem different, more relaxed."

"I'm feeling good," Melanie said.

"But why are you going easy on me?"

Melanie shrugged. "I'm trying to lighten up a little. Charlie made me a sponsor for someone else and we had a talk. He encouraged me to put myself in the position of the person I was trying to help. I remember last year how stressful it was for you to be doing one of your trials. And here you are pregnant again. I figured I didn't have to add to your stress."

"Thanks," Philly said, knowing she was looking at Melanie dumbfounded.

"Besides, I think you've been doing good. You've been coming to meetings regularly, and it looks like you've gotten by that bad spell at the end of last year."

"Thanks," Philly repeated. "Whoever got you as sponsor is lucky."

Charlie brought the meeting together. Philly was pleased that his appearance hadn't changed; there were some constants in her life that she wanted to remain in place. Tonight, Charlie's Hawaiian shirt was bright yellow; coconuts dotted the i's in the word Hawaii spread in purple across his chest. His ponytail was neatly tied off. When Charlie asked if anyone wanted to start tonight's discussion, Philly volunteered.

"How do you know when you have things under reasonable control?" Philly asked. "I was telling Melanie that I have a trial coming up, and you can tell by looking at me that my pregnancy is moving right along. I should be freaking out, but that hasn't happened, and I can't figure out why."

"Are you doing anything differently?" a man in a Red Sox cap questioned.

"Not really. My law partners have been supportive, but they always have."

Charlie broke the silence that followed. "I don't want to throw cold water on the way you're feeling but, speaking for myself, I don't think there's been a time when I felt I was in control of everything in my life. This disease we have has me constantly looking in the rear-view mirror to see what's sneaking up on me. It's a hell of a way to live. But this place you're in now? Enjoy it, give thanks for it, and try to keep it going."

Philly did feel that Charlie had thrown cold water on her upbeat mood. But then she remembered what Charlie had said in the past about how with a drinking problem, you were never out of the woods. According to Charlie, when you thought you had gotten on top of your problem was the time to worry in earnest.

"When we get to the good place where Philly is at now, and we've all been there," Charlie said, "we need to keep putting one foot in front of the other and try to soldier on. Just keep that rear-view mirror clean. Objects appearing *are* nearer than they seem."

"How was the meeting?" Paul asked.

Philly didn't answer right away. She was caught up in the sensation of Paul's hand moving over her belly and hoping for a response inside her.

"Good. Charlie's message remained the same. Stay vigilant because you're never going to be totally cured."

"Charlie's right," Paul said, moving closer to her on their bed. "Listen to the man."

"Yeah, but the way he said it this time was depressing. He made everything seem a bit hopeless."

"Maybe Charlie had a bad day. It happens."

"I was feeling positive going into the meeting, but down after the meeting. That was a switch. It's not supposed to work that way."

"Then go with the positive and the hell with Charlie."

"Easy for you to say."

"I know. It is easy for me to say. If Charlie's starting to wear thin, you could try a different meeting. Or you could talk to me. I'm an upbeat guy."

"Very funny," Philly said. "I'm beat. But if you're such an upbeat guy, tell me something to put me in a good mood before I drop off."

"I'm in awe of you," Paul said. "You're my heroine. I can't imagine dealing with a pregnancy and a big case at the same time."

"That's why men don't get pregnant. They're wusses. They'd never survive."

"No disagreement here. Will you be able to slow down once this trial's behind you?"

"I'm going to try. But who the hell knows? Any second thoughts about learning the sex?"

"No," Paul said. "I'm still okay with being surprised."

"Any preferences?"

"There's a part of me that's hoping for a boy. Then I think about Daisy and Jennie and a girl starts sounding very good."

"If it's a girl, you're really going to be outnumbered."

"I can live with that."

59

Judge Clarence Ford empaneled a jury after the lunch recess and then proceeded to dismiss the jurors for the day promising that opening arguments would commence first thing the next morning.

"That judge was a real sourpuss," Martina Glass said as they left the courthouse. "Is he always like that?"

"That's his reputation," Philly said. "He's one of those judges who likes to give everyone a hard time."

"I didn't like him," Martina said firmly.

"Got a minute?" Wayne Martin called out heading their way.

"I'll take this," Philly said. "Keep Martina company," she told Simon before turning to meet the Salem Stampede's lawyer.

"Three hundred thousand," Martin said when they were face to face.

Philly couldn't identify anything in the case that was new or different. Maybe the Salem Stampede was anticipating negative publicity if the case went to trial and was picked up by the press. Maybe the hockey club feared the case could jeopardize its liquor license. Whatever was behind the hockey club's change of heart, Martin didn't appear discomforted by the fact he had gone back on a line he had drawn in the sand that he would never offer six figures in settlement.

"I'll talk to my client," Philly said. "Thanks for taking another run at settlement."

"Your client's here," Martin said, pointing to where Glass and Simon sat on a bench. "Have your talk now. I'll wait."

"Is this offer just for your client?"

"Correct."

"We have a new settlement proposal from the hockey club," Philly said after joining Simon and Glass. When she mentioned the figure, Simon's eyebrows rose but Glass showed no reaction.

"What changed their mind?" Glass asked.

"I don't know," Philly admitted. "Sometimes the prospect of a trial causes a defendant to increase a settlement proposal."

"What do you think I should do?"

Philly hesitated. She was not afraid to make a recommendation but preferred to have Carpenter weigh in on her reasoning.

"Hold on a minute," Philly said, and she moved off to have some privacy as she called Carpenter.

"Carpenter."

"It's Philly. The hockey club has offered three hundred thou."

"No shit!"

"I'm going to recommend the offer be accepted, but I thought I'd check with you first."

"I agree," Carpenter said. "She's over her injuries. There are no permanent damages, even though she was seriously hurt. True, rehab took a while, but a jury could find the whole thing was the fault of that guy Dunn and his friend."

"Okay, we're on the same page. Thanks."

"Good luck."

Philly rejoined Glass and gave her recommendation. She went through her reasoning and Glass still showed no reaction.

"I think they're scared," Glass said. "I'd rather go to trial."

Simon rolled his eyes. Philly focused on their client. "That's your right, of course. I wouldn't say the hockey club is scared. I think the club is assessing the cost of trial and maybe the publicity that would come from a trial. But you need to understand that if a jury finds that your injury was Dunn and Madden's fault, you could get nothing."

Glass seemed unmoved by Philly's caution. "I want to talk this over with my husband and my friend you met last year. I don't want to make a decision right now. I feel too rushed."

"That's fine," Philly said. "I don't want you deciding anything if you feel pressured. But you do need to decide tonight so I can let the hockey club's lawyer know. I'll tell him you need to think about it."

Glass nodded. "I'll call you tonight."

"What does she need to think about?" Simon asked when Glass was out of earshot.

"Beats the hell out of me. I'm still trying to figure out why the hockey club went as high as it did. They have a decent chance of pinning all this on Dunn and Madden."

Philly saw Wayne Martin moving to join them. "Here's another guy who's going to wonder what our client is thinking."

Meredith arranged the contents of one legal-sized file box on a table in the Spenser School of Law placement office thinking that the papers being arrayed chronicled the hopes and dreams of dozens of would be lawyers. What advice would she provide law students based on her nearly three years practicing law? Her two-plus years of experience at Pinkerton suggested that "Be careful what you wish for," was suitable advice. But after a brief time working with Simon and Rachel and their partners, "Don't lose hope" seemed a fair alternative message.

Rachel had come up with a one-page information form that she wanted completed for each student who had been at Spenser for the past five years.

Rachel envisioned a spreadsheet that would permit trends and patterns to be extracted from the data. Dean Stockman had agreed to hire someone to input the data. The form asked for obvious information: class rank, grade point average, extracurricular activities, success or failure at finding a law-related job. But there were less obvious blanks: past work experience with decision-making responsibilities, public speaking experience, letters of recommendation.

Meredith checked her watch and went through a student folder, filling out the form when she came to a relevant bit of information. Twelve minutes, she noted after concluding her run through. That meant five folders an hour. Which ensured that she would be saddled with this task for weeks on end.

Before dinner, Philly snuggled on her bed with Daisy, rubbing her stomach, when her cell phone sounded. William Ward was calling. "To what do I owe the pleasure?" she greeted the lawyer for Dunn and Madden.

"I'm instructed to offer one hundred thousand dollars to settle the case against Dunn and Madden. If the case goes to trial and they lose, you can chase them for what they owe."

Philly took a deep breath to focus. "Who's putting up the money?"

"That's none of your business."

Ward had a point. "I'll get back to you," she promised. "Will you be at this number?"

"Unfortunately, yes."

"Do you think Glass will come to her senses and agree to settle?" Carpenter asked when Philly reported Ward's offer.

"I don't know," Philly said. "I'd consider not having our contingency apply to this recent figure if it would get her to agree."

"I don't like doing that, as you know," Carpenter said. "But to put this case behind us, I'll go along."

"Then I've got some phone calls to make."

60

Judge Clarence Ford smiled. He was the only one in his chambers sporting a pleased expression. Martin and Ward had objected to meeting with the judge, but Philly had heeded Carpenter's instruction to have all counsel present when Martina Glass' case was reported as settled. "From everything I've heard," Carpenter had said last night, "I wouldn't trust William Ward at all."

"I want to commend you all," the judge said. "I've said from the beginning that this is a case that should be settled. You may have thirty days to complete the paperwork."

"Thank you, Your Honor," Philly said, as she led the procession of lawyers from the judge's chambers. Simon brought up the rear, his thoughts already switched to the Spenser School of Law case.

"Was Glass happy?" Simon asked as Philly drove them back to Boston.

"Only when I told her that if she took the deal, our fee would be waived on the hundred thou put up by Dunn and Madden. Madden's parents are rich and decided to bail him out, but they weren't going to bail him out if the case got tried and they paid for Ward's legal fees."

"How do you know this?" Simon asked.

"From Martin, the hockey team's lawyer. Martin demanded the information as a condition of the Salem Stampede keeping its three hundred thousand on the table. Martin also learned from Ward that Dunn's mother was paying Ward's legal fees for her son."

"We got lucky by bringing Madden in as a defendant," Simon said. "Right now it feels anticlimactic."

"But good anticlimactic," Philly reminded him.

Evelyn was getting ready to leave the station for the day when her phone rang. She answered it, said "yes" several times, and thanked the caller. When she looked up, she was smiling. "We got a nibble," she said.

Paul shared his partner's excitement. "Let me guess," he said. "The home aid's boyfriend, Dennis Wilbur, right?"

"Right," Evelyn confirmed. "He's using a different name but Wilbur's cell phone number."

"You're using Marvin Binder, right?"

"Right."

"Well, Binder owes me. I know he's been convicted of receiving stolen goods, but I can't remember whether the goods included art."

"Some art but mostly other things. Marvin is eclectic."

Sometimes Evelyn's choice of words surprised Paul. If he polled the squad room, he doubted he'd come up with anyone else who knew what eclectic meant. In the Mansfield robbery, Evelyn had showed initiative. Once the assistant district attorney she'd consulted didn't believe there was enough evidence to obtain a search warrant, Evelyn had gone through the list of informants, focused on Marvin Binder, who owed Paul a favor, and had set up a fake buy.

"You did a nice job on this. Knowing you, you're probably going to hang around now and obsess about this case."

"Not tonight," Evelyn said, sporting a loopy grin. "I've got a date."

"Good for you. Anyone I know?"

"You've talked to him, but I wouldn't say you know him."

Evelyn was enjoying his puzzlement. "Who are you talking about?" Paul gave way to his curiosity.

"Horace Benson."

Paul recognized the name but couldn't place it. "The name's familiar."

"He's the officer from Omaha that helped us out earlier this year. He wants to see for himself the stuck-up assholes who live in the northeast."

"No shit!"

"I'm duty bound to show him professional courtesy."

"I'd say you look up to the task."

61

Carpenter cursed his luck. If he had left his office five minutes earlier as he had intended, he would have missed the call from Benjamin Learner. Now he had to listen to the lawyer who represented Mary Ellen Pines and Malcolm Atkins deliver whatever unpleasant news Learner had been saving for the end of the workday.

"What can I do for you?" Carpenter said without enthusiasm.

"If your client was bought out, would the litigation go away?"

Carpenter was caught off guard. He hadn't figured out a way to settle Clyde Atkins' suit, so he had pretty much dismissed settlement from his mind. Perhaps the imminent trial date in the case had caused Learner's clients to try to come up with a settlement proposal.

"I don't know," Carpenter responded. "I suppose if the buyout figure was high enough, my client would consider it. But this is not something we've discussed. Did you have anything specific in mind?"

"Two years' annual salary."

Each sibling had earned $250,000 a year. That meant the defendants' proposal was for $500,000.

"Are you talking a lump sum or payment over time?"

"Lump sum," Learner replied.

"I take it you want me to run that by my client."

"I do. Get back to me when you have a response."

"Just to be clear, we're talking five hundred thousand."

"Correct."

Carpenter couldn't predict Clyde Atkins' reaction. "Would your clients be willing to be bought out for the same figure per person?" Carpenter had no idea whether Clyde Atkins could come up with a million dollars, but he figured he might as well come back at Learner—talk was cheap.

"I tend to doubt it," Learner said. "But if that's something you want me to run by them, let me know after you talk to your client."

"Okay, I'll be back to you."

Carpenter debated whether to delay contacting Clyde Atkins until tomorrow. With the start of trial imminent, that was probably a bad idea. He'd have to call Maxine—late for dinner again.

June

From Meredith's Playlist

"Cream"

Prince

62

Clyde Atkins sat across from Carpenter and Rachel in the conference room with a stoic expression. Last night when Carpenter had relayed Learner's offer, Atkins had replied with a laconic, "I'll think about it," and had made an appointment to meet this morning.

"Do you have a recommendation?" Atkins asked.

Carpenter's knowing he'd be put on the spot had done nothing to shed light on the advice he should impart. Rachel was inclined to accept the proposal because she was concerned that the language in Atkins' employment contract might leave him with nothing following a trial.

"Before I answer your question, I have a question of my own. If you could pick the way this case would sort out, what would you pick that's realistic?"

"The truth is I'm conflicted," Atkins responded without hesitation. "There's a part of me that's enjoyed not dealing with my sister and brother these past months. They're both pains in the ass. But there's also a part of me that wants revenge for the way they treated me. I'm torn."

"Do you want to continue being a part of the family business?" Carpenter pursued.

"It depends what day you ask me."

"If you could buy out your brother and sister for a million dollars, would you do it?"

Atkins shrugged. "That's a lot of money. I suppose I could borrow it, which is probably what my siblings are going to do if I take their offer. I don't know. At this moment, probably no. I'm thinking that trying something new is the way to go for me. Why are you asking me whether I'd buy Mary Ellen and Malcolm out?"

"I raised that with their attorney," Carpenter explained, and he proceeded to fill Atkins in on that part of his discussion with Benjamin Learner.

"Mary Ellen and Malcolm would never sell." Atkins sighed. "I don't think I would buy them out for that kind of money."

"In that case," Carpenter said, "I'd recommend taking their offer. You believe there's life for you after the family business. You've indicated that your siblings have nothing but the family business. You're not interested in buying them out. Plus, you might end up with nothing if the case goes to trial." Carpenter nodded toward Rachel.

"As you know," she said, "we've been able to obtain an injunction on your behalf that requires your siblings to hold in escrow the money that would have gone to you as salary after sixty days. But there's no guaranty that money will end up with you."

Atkins looked conflicted, a far cry from the sardonic man Carpenter had met in a sports bar.

"I just don't see myself giving them the opportunity to say they got the better of me."

"Why would you say they'd be getting the better of you?" Rachel asked. "When they hand over a check to you for five hundred thousand dollars, they'll probably feel like the money's coming out of their hide which in a sense it would be. Every month that they pay back the money they borrowed to buy you out, will remind them what they paid you."

"When do I have to make a decision?" Atkins fretted.

"Sooner rather than later," Carpenter said. "The latest from the court clerk is that the trial could start next week. You can't sit on this."

"Shit!" Atkins exclaimed. "Before you called last night, I was actually looking forward to the trial."

Carpenter kept his peace. Any person looking forward to twelve strangers deciding the next turn his life would take had to have a fucking screw loose.

"You got a minute?"

Rachel looked up from Philly's desk to observe a tired, disgruntled Meredith leaning against a door jamb. "Sure."

Meredith flopped onto the visitor's chair at the front of Philly's desk, her poise and forceful presence nowhere in evidence.

"This has got to be the worst assignment I've ever had," Meredith complained.

Rachel opted for mollification. "Thanks for doing it and hanging in."

"Talk about tedious work! I no longer give a shit what happens to any of these Spenser graduates. They can rot in hell for all I care."

"I know you don't mean that."

"Then a lot you know!"

"Did you come in here just to complain?" Rachel asked, which produced a withering glare from her former law school classmate.

"I guess I did," Meredith said after a while, offering up a sheepish smile.

"Have you found anything?"

Meredith sighed and slumped in her seat. "Have I found anything?" she repeated. "I haven't organized anything so I'm not totally sure. I'm basically brain dead. But I do have some impressions."

Rachel had been the architect of the information form Meredith was working with and felt personally invested in what Meredith came up with. "Give me an example of an impression."

"An example," Meredith repeated, making a visible effort to focus. "Okay, here's an example. If you were in the bottom third of your graduating class at Spenser, you can pretty much kiss a law-related job goodbye."

That made sense to Rachel. Spenser was not an upper echelon law school so a student who couldn't distinguish himself or herself at Spenser was not likely to receive serious consideration from an employer.

"If you were in the bottom half of your graduating class, close to the halfway line, getting a law-related job is pretty much hopeless but not impossible."

Another conclusion that made sense in Rachel's opinion. A private law practice would not want to risk putting a Spenser grad in the bottom half of his or her class up against someone in the bottom half of the class at a bigger name, more prestigious law school.

"There seemed to be little interest in any graduate who didn't participate in outside activities or who didn't have a favorable teacher recommendation."

Rachel hadn't participated in any outside activity while in law school. She'd been so quiet in her classes that she'd been unable to summon up the nerve to ask a professor for a letter of recommendation. Her fear had been that the professor would have no idea who she was.

Rachel decided on a pep talk. "In case you need reminding, what you're doing is important. Spenser put out some promotional materials stressing the importance of outside activities. We can use those materials to beat up on any plaintiff who never took up an outside activity."

"Whatever," Meredith groused. "Right now, I don't want to talk about it."

Rachel checked her watch. Josh would have set aside her dinner and she was ready to leave the office and spend some time with him. But sometimes, she reflected, you had to take one for the team. "How about a drink?" she asked.

"Now you're talking."

Rachel smiled at the first sign of life Meredith had displayed since entering her office. "I'll be right with you. I need to make a call."

63

On the first floor of the Brighton house, Sarah Ferguson was organizing Daisy and Rosalind for a trip to a nearby park. In her second-story home office, Philly had turned on her computer and was staring at the home page trying not to think about what task needed her attention next. What she really wanted to do was nothing, sit where she was and let the cool morning air wash over her. She started when her phone rang.

"Philomena Sullivan."

"It's Patrick Lassiter."

Philly took a moment to regroup. She had put Fay Richardson's case out of her mind during the preparation of the Glass case. She and Lassiter had agreed to push back the hearing on the attachment Rachel had obtained on Rita Stout's house while they explored settlement. So far settlement discussions had gone nowhere.

"How are you?" Philly asked as she tried to shift mental gears.

"I'm fine," Lassiter said in a tone that suggested otherwise. "You said that a six-figure proposal needed to be put on the table to make this case go away. Would, in fact, one hundred thousand dollars do the trick?"

Philly had never imagined presenting Richardson with a six-figure proposal. "That's an encouraging number," she said neutrally. "I just finished preparing for a trial that suddenly settled and there are some things I need to attend to. I'll let Ms. Richardson know of this discussion and I hope to get back to you shortly."

"I'll be looking forward to your call."

Philly set down her phone. She opened the firm's billing file on the Richardson case and studied the billable hours spent on the litigation. She and Rachel and Simon had done the lion's share of the work. The billable time totaled seventy thousand dollars. "Crap," Philly muttered. How could you recommend a settlement offer where most of the settlement proceeds would go to you? Maybe Carpenter had a solution.

"I just can't bring myself to accept their offer," Clyde Atkins said.

Carpenter moved his phone away from his ear. "Ultimately the decision to settle is yours. We've made our recommendation and you've made your decision. I'll call your siblings' lawyer and give him the news."

"I know the reasons you gave for settling make sense," Atkins said, and Carpenter wondered whether their client was now trying to talk himself out of the decision to go to trial. "Shit!" Atkins muttered. "This truly sucks."

"Here's another way to think about this," Carpenter said, drawing on an approach he sometimes used with clients. "We've advised you that after a trial you could walk away with nothing because your employment contract can be terminated without cause. Think about how you'd feel if that happened, if you walked away with nothing and ended up with an overall loss because of legal fees."

"I'd be pissed," Atkins finally said.

"It's a question of degree," Carpenter replied. "How pissed?"

Atkins again fell silent. Carpenter recalled Meredith Sweeney abandoning what she wanted and accepting the Pinkerton firm's settlement offer. The Atkins case was more complicated because it involved family and God only knew how many stored-up childhood grievances.

"Fuck!" Atkins exploded.

"I see you've moved beyond shit."

"Very funny."

"Why don't you take some time to think about it?" Carpenter advised.

"Tell me one thing," Atkins said. "If you were representing my brother and sister, would you be advising them to pay me anything?"

It was a fair question and Carpenter didn't like being on the receiving end of it. But he had an opinion—didn't he always?—and Atkins was paying for the privilege of hearing it.

"In Benjamin Learner's position, I'd be concerned that you got an injunction. But the language of the contract you signed is clear and works against you. I would probably advise your siblings to try to settle the case for small dollars because you can never predict what will happen in a trial. I definitely wouldn't have told them to put a five hundred thou figure on the table."

"I appreciate your honesty."

"That's what I'm here for—brutal honesty. Call me back later. I've got to run."

When Carpenter set down his phone he didn't run anywhere. He remained seated at his desk and resolved to freshly consider why Benjamin Learner had made a $500,000 offer to settle the Atkins case. He was mentally kicking himself for not thinking about that earlier. Learner was an experienced litigator and had a big firm behind him. Did Learner truly believe that his clients would lose big bucks if the case went to trial?

Carpenter tried unsuccessfully to think through what he was missing. Maybe the explanation was as simple as the siblings being willing to pay a premium to get Atkins out of their lives. Then again, maybe pigs could fly.

Looking at Rachel and Meredith across the conference room table, Simon knew he should be upbeat because the two women had the Spenser case under control. Yet there was no mistaking the unease he was feeling. Was it because he'd viewed himself as indispensable when it came to the suit and now had to face the prospect that he was not? While preparing the Glass case, he had envisioned a mountain of work that needed to be done in the Spenser litigation, but listening to Rachel's update, he realized that the mountain was a molehill at best.

"So there you have it," Rachel concluded. "We owe Meredith big time. She slogged through the boxes of student documents that we'd been avoiding."

Meredith smiled at the compliment and Simon wondered how it had been for her to take direction from Rachel. Neither woman seemed put off by Rachel's being a partner who outranked Meredith. If anything, the women seemed to have bonded.

"It's good to have you back," Rachel said to Simon. "You're going to have to take over for me while the Atkins case is tried. Although the defendants have put a settlement proposal on the table."

"Let's get back to the Spenser case. I have to admit feeling left out. You've got things under control."

Rachel and Meredith exchanged a glance that Simon couldn't read.

"If you're worried about getting back into the swing of things, we have just the word for you," Rachel said.

"What word is that?"

"Depositions."

Somerville Police Department detective Eric Brand was being a good sport. Paul and Evelyn were on his turf because they didn't want to use a Cambridge location, but he was letting them take the lead. Paul made a mental note to praise Brand to his superiors if the operation went as planned. They were sitting in an unmarked car, Evelyn behind the wheel, Brand in the passenger seat, Paul in the rear. The East Somerville apartment where they had arranged for Marvin

Binder to set up shop was across the street; they had a clear view of the front door. The meet was scheduled for nine tonight, which was five minutes away.

"Why's Binder being so cooperative?" Brand asked. The Somerville officer was a big guy who Paul pegged to be about his own age.

"It comes down to the fact that he owes me," Paul said, prepared to offer the details if Brand pressed, which he didn't. Paul had collared Binder in a small-time fencing operation in which Binder had been a middleman. Maybe it had been the guy's slight build and mousy appearance; Binder had struck him as harmless, a down-on-his-luck loser who had drifted to a life of crime because it was easier than obtaining legitimate work. Paul remembered going with his instincts, promising Binder he would recommend a reduced sentence if Binder would help him on a future occasion. He had kept his end of the off-the-record bargain by cajoling a young assistant district attorney to go easy on Binder, and so far, on the Mansfield robbery, Binder was repaying his debt.

"Does Binder know anything about paintings?" Brand next inquired.

"Probably not," Paul admitted. "But he got the word out that he had a buyer who was interested in anything and everything to do with art."

"So why aren't we going after anyone and everyone who contacts him?"

Brand's question was a fair one but, because he didn't know the Somerville officer, Paul was uncomfortable answering it. Still, he couldn't lie to the man. "It's not part of my arrangement. Binder has turned down a few inquiries. He's putting his neck out and I don't want to go beyond what I asked him to do."

"Been there," Brand said, and Paul found his unease lessening.

"Showtime," Evelyn said. "There's Wilbur."

There was a light over the front door of the apartment building. Wilbur was carrying a package. He looked about before pressing a buzzer and quickly disappeared into the building when the door opened.

Evelyn led their procession to the front door, which was opened by Brand's inside officer as they approached the threshold. "Secure the back of the building," Brand directed the officer and the man hurried out the front door.

"I'll take the front door," Brand said when they assembled in the lobby. "I don't mind," he added.

"We appreciate it," Paul replied as he and Evelyn made for the stairs.

Binder's apartment was on the third floor. Outside the unit, Paul held up his key so Evelyn could see it and drew his weapon. Evelyn already had her weapon out. "Follow me," he whispered as he turned the key.

The door opened onto a small living room where Paul expected Binder would be examining the painting Wilbur had brought along. The door opened easily, silently, but no one was in the living room. He heard a noise from the small bedroom to their right and motioned in that direction. Evelyn nodded and moved to the side of the closed bedroom door, which suddenly opened and shielded her from view. Binder appeared in the doorway with a gun pressed against his temple, Wilbur holding him steady by the back of his shirt.

"You need to put your weapon down now," Wilbur said, "or this asshole is going to die."

Paul hesitated. Then he knelt slowly and carefully placed his weapon on the floor.

"This asshole knows less about art than I do," Wilbur said with a sneer as he turned his weapon on Paul and shoved Binder forward. "I knew this was a set up the moment he opened his mouth."

The bedroom door hit Wilbur in the side of the head with such force it knocked him to the floor. Then, not taking any chances, Evelyn delivered a brutal kick to Wilbur's head that left him motionless.

Paul had to make an effort to stop from shaking. As he had lowered his weapon, he'd pictured Wilbur taking him down.

"What the fuck! You didn't tell me the guy would have a gun!" Binder wailed.

Paul took a deep breath. "Relax. You did a good job. We're even. Get out of here. Tell the officer in the lobby to come up."

"I could have been killed!" Binder squawked before he left the apartment.

"You all right?" Evelyn asked.

"Not really."

64

Isabella pedaled like a madwoman, but Philly was just going through the motions. She had ratcheted down the resistance on her bike, content for her legs to make lazy circles. She had planned to skip this morning's scheduled spin using her advanced pregnancy as a ready excuse but, for some reason, she had woken at six, couldn't get back to sleep, and saw no reason not to exercise. The large glass of orange juice she'd had before getting on her bike had gotten her baby to stir. The baby's kicks had their own irregular rhythm. It would have been something if the baby's kicks matched the beat of "Baba O'Riley" sounding from her boom box.

"Thanks for keeping me company," Isabella said after slowing her pace.

"Sorry I can't keep up," Philly responded. Already it was getting hot and sticky outside and she didn't see herself lasting much longer.

"It doesn't matter," Isabella said. "I don't like doing this alone."

"Sweeter" kicked in and Isabella picked up her pace. Philly moved her hands from the handlebars and settled them on her belly. She could feel the baby's kicks under her right hand.

The back door opened and Daisy and Rosalind let loose shrieks as they made for the backyard. Paul followed holding a steaming coffee mug and gave her a wave. "Raul's made breakfast," he announced.

"I'm going to stop," Philly told Isabella. "We'll keep an eye on the kids."

Paul set up two folding lawn chairs on the grass and Philly was grateful to take a load off. "Hey you," she said to Paul.

Paul reached out and took her hand. "Do you have time for a quick, serious discussion?" he asked.

Paul's question gave Philly a jolt. "Serious discussion" were the words she and Philip had used to preface a talk that was important. "Sure."

"Last night, Evelyn and I solved a robbery. You were asleep when I finally got home. It was that case I've been telling you about where a painting was stolen in what looked like an inside job."

Philly nodded, remembering the last time Paul had filled her in.

"The thief took a hostage and pointed a gun at me. He said he'd kill the hostage if I didn't put down my weapon. The hostage was a petty crook and for the briefest moment before I put down my gun, I considered telling the thief to fuck himself and firing at him. Evelyn came to my rescue and took the thief down."

"God! That sounds horrible."

"When it was over, I almost lost it. There was an instant when I pictured the guy shooting me and leaving you all alone. I did the right thing by putting down my weapon, but the fact that I thought about risking the hostage's life by engaging in a gun battle to be with you is scary as hell."

Philly didn't say anything. She hadn't dwelled on the dangers of Paul's job. She knew that police officer marriages often disintegrated because the spouse couldn't live with the danger inherent in the officer's job. Did not constantly worrying about Paul coming home alive everyday mean she didn't love him enough? That was bullshit. She was crazy in love with him.

Paul was staring at her, waiting for her to voice a reaction. Philly tried to put the girls' happy laughter out of mind and concentrate. "You love your job, right?"

"Until last night I did."

"But even with last night you love your job, don't you?"

"Yeah. It's what I've always wanted to do."

"Then you can't stop being a cop. I was just thinking that maybe I was a lousy wife because I've never obsessed about the risks you take on the job. I think subconsciously I've put those risks out of mind because I know being a cop is what you want to do. I know you try to be careful. I don't want to be the reason you stop doing something you love."

Paul didn't respond immediately, and Philly saw his genuine distress.

"It's shaken my confidence," Paul said in a soft voice. "I never doubted my instincts until now."

"Does the department have counseling available?" Philly asked.

Paul nodded. "I thought of that. I'm still thinking about it."

Daisy and Rosalind scurried to them and held out dandelions. "Thanks," Philly said, accepting the offerings and then watching the girls return to search the backyard grass.

"I think you should stop thinking about it and talk it through with a professional," Philly said. "Remember how you stayed on my case about forgiving the teenager who ran down Philip? You were right about that. You need to act here. That's my opinion."

"Thanks for listening," Paul said, but Philly couldn't tell whether a weight had been lifted off his shoulders.

Paul had been relieved that Evelyn had the day off—he had wanted time to himself—so he was surprised to see her in jeans and a white T-shirt advancing toward their desks with a blue-eyed, blond-haired mountain of a man by her side wearing an identical outfit.

"This is Horace Benson," Evelyn said, grinning broadly. "I wanted to introduce you."

Benson had a vice-like grip, but it was Evelyn who claimed Paul's attention. The woman was giddy, a state she'd never exhibited.

"What brings you from Omaha?" Paul asked.

"That would be your partner. I had a fair amount of vacation time due me, she's carved out some time to entertain me, and I've missed your partner."

Paul grabbed a chair from a neighboring desk that wasn't in use. "Take a load off."

"We've got to run," Evelyn said, remaining standing. "We're going to do touristy things today."

"Did Evelyn fill you in on last night's adventure?" Paul asked Benson.

"She did," he said with undisguised admiration.

"I want to thank you again," Paul said to his partner. "You saved my ass."

"You would have done the same for me. How are you doing this morning?"

Paul realized that Evelyn was checking up on him. Introducing him to Benson had been a convenient cover.

"Better," Paul said. His morning talk with Philly had helped. He had scheduled a session for late afternoon with the psychologist on call to the department.

"Good," Evelyn said. "You look better."

"I never had a gun pointed at me without my own weapon handy," Benson said. "I hope it never happens to me. I can't even imagine how I'd react. Glad you're okay."

Paul knew he'd have a better handle on "okay" after his afternoon counseling session.

"Take the deal," Clyde Atkins said over the phone. "I've changed my mind."

Carpenter wasn't surprised by Atkins' turnabout. He leaned back in his chair. The office air conditioning was on, but couldn't overcome the day's suffocating humidity, and he could feel his shirt sticking to his back.

"Let me ask you something," Carpenter said.

"I don't like the sound of that," Atkins replied. "I thought you'd be jumping up and down with joy because I'd seen the light."

"Yeah, I'm ecstatic. Can't you tell?"

"What's going on?"

Carpenter had woken this morning at five and had known at once that returning to sleep was out of the question. He'd been wrestling with Atkins' situation without success ever since he'd gotten out of bed.

"I'm trying to figure out why your siblings are putting five hundred thousand dollars on the table," Carpenter said. "It was not something I would have done, as I told you. I would have proposed a lesser amount—a significantly lesser amount. So why are they offering a generous number right off the bat?"

"I have no idea," Atkins responded.

"Neither do I," Carpenter admitted. "But there is a reason to put a high number out there."

"Like what?"

"To make sure you take the offer."

"Well it worked. I'm going to take the offer. I agree with you that the offer's generous."

"Which still doesn't explain their generosity," Carpenter said. "The only thing I can think of is that your siblings believe the family business is more profitable than you think it is. Was there any business prospect that could have come through that they know about and you don't?"

"I guess that's possible," Atkins said after a long pause. "I just can't imagine what it could be."

Carpenter voiced an idea that had come to him at six in the morning as he had started on his second cup of coffee. "Maybe your company is about to become an exclusive dealer for some new, hot-shit, snowblower model."

"I can't imagine anything like that..."

Atkins broke off, became silent, and Carpenter wondered whether he had struck a nerve. "What?" he asked.

"It's probably nothing," Atkins said. "It just made me think of something. There is a snowblower model that's top of the line. The manufacturer, PowerArm, doesn't have an exclusive dealer anywhere in Massachusetts. My father knows the president of that company, Martin Schuler. When he was in charge of our business, he tried to get Schuler to cut a deal making us the exclusive distributor in eastern Massachusetts. Even when my brother and sister and I started managing the business, my father would periodically take a run at Schuler to try to do a deal."

"I want details," Carpenter said. "I want every name and phone number you have on this outfit. And while you're at it, I want phone numbers and e-mail addresses for your father."

"Are you trying to tell me I shouldn't take the deal?" Atkins asked.

"I'm trying to tell you to hold that thought."

Paul would have preferred a male psychologist. His preference was irrational, probably sexist. Maybe it had to do with too many women in his life: Philly, Evelyn, Jennie, his ex-wife, Daisy, Rosalind, Isabella, Sarah Ferguson—everywhere he looked was a woman. He and Philly didn't know the sex of their baby, but Paul knew; they were going to have a girl.

With the exception of Raul, there were no men in his life outside of work. And Raul wasn't much of an exception. They got along, liked each other up to a point, but Raul wasn't a guy he could bare his soul to. Like it or not, he was going to have to open up to another woman.

Samantha Gray had been working with the department for about six months after a short, intensive search to fill her position. Paul didn't know anything about her. Officers had been in sessions with her, but no feedback had filtered back about her or her work.

Gray's eyes matched her name. Paul guessed she was about his age. She had long brown hair that fell below her shoulder line. They were seated in facing chairs and Paul was surprised that she had no pen and paper within reach.

"I did a little research on you," Gray began. "I hope you don't mind. I suppose you know your reputation is excellent. The word is out you're an up-and-comer."

"Don't believe everything you hear."

"I don't. But in your case, I'm prepared to make an exception. How can I help you? I'm sure you know that anything we talk about remains confidential."

Paul nodded. "My partner and I had an adventure last night."

"I overheard some talk about that. It must have been a scary moment."

"It was," Paul said and, once he got those words out, he replayed the evening from beginning to end, leaving nothing out.

Gray didn't say anything when he finished his account. Instead, she stood up and began pacing in a small area behind her chair. She was taller than Paul expected, and she made a striking figure striding back and forth in a tailored black pants suit.

"Aren't you supposed to be writing this stuff down?" Paul asked.

"That's not necessary," Gray replied, and she proceeded to throw back at him, word for word, about a minute of his narrative.

Paul opted for silence. Gray continued to pace as if he wasn't in the room. Maybe, like Evelyn, she needed to be in motion to sort through a problem.

Gray returned to her seat. "Have you talked to your wife about how you're feeling?"

Paul recounted his sit down with Philly this morning, again leaving nothing out. When he finished, Gray's response was to rise and continue her pacing. The longer she paced, the more curious he became as to what she would say.

Without warning Gray promptly resumed her seat. "There are some professional things I need to say to you and I'd just as soon get them out of the way. If I drift into psychobabble you need to tell me. Agreed?"

Paul nodded. He wondered about the extent of Gray's prior experience with law enforcement agencies.

"You have been through a traumatic event. I have colleagues who would say it is the type of event that could be a cause of PTSD. At the moment, I wouldn't go quite that far, but there is no denying that the event you experienced last night was traumatic. You had serious, legitimate concerns you'd be shot. Having doubts and anxiety following such an event is common and can be therapeutic. Are you with me so far?"

"I think so."

"Your thoughts turned to your wife and soon-to-be-born child. Tell me a little about your marriage and home life."

Paul went through his first marriage in short order and spent a longer time describing how he had met Philly and was drawn to her immediately. Gray listened without expression, but this time Paul had no doubt she was retaining every word.

"Thank you. That's extremely helpful. The thing that needs to be said to you has already been said to you by your wife. I don't know you very well and that's something I'd like to change. But everything I've heard about you paints a picture of a smart, caring, and brave officer with considerable abilities and great potential. Law enforcement is your chosen profession. It is a profession with serious personal risks. I believe that you found yourself in a stressful situation that suddenly brought home to you how much you would lose if something were to happen to you. Your wife, in turn, has tried to bring home to you that you need to do your job without being tied up in knots thinking about what you have to lose. Of course that's easier said than done. But I believe it is what you need to do."

Paul took his time digesting Gray's last comments. "Is there anything you can suggest to help me come to terms with thinking about what I have to lose?"

"Yes," Gray said. "I can talk with you and I would recommend that we have three more sessions and see where we are then. I can also remind you of how you responded during last night's—what did you call it?—adventure? You were struck by what you had to lose and yet you responded as a police officer should have responded in that situation. In other words, your professional instincts and professionalism took over. You briefly thought about using your weapon, but you ended up putting your weapon down. Given the way you responded, I don't believe that concerns about how you will react in the future should be weighing you down. Does that help?"

The way Gray had put things did provide comfort. Paul felt some of the pressure and worry he'd been experiencing ease. "Yeah, it does."

65

Philly called Carpenter first thing in the morning, hoping he had stuck to his practice of arriving at the office early. She wasn't disappointed. She relayed Patrick Lassiter's proposal in the Richardson case and the number of hours they had spent on the litigation.

"One approach is not to settle," Carpenter said. "The one hundred thousand dollars would save the defendants fifty thousand plus interest. Interest is running at twelve percent. Do you see Richardson walking away for thirty thousand?"

"I don't really know," Philly admitted. "It doesn't seem right to me that that's all she gets. I began to think about reducing our fee."

"Are you thinking we'd split the hundred grand?" Carpenter asked.

"Yeah, pretty much," Philly owned up.

"I'm okay with that," Carpenter said promptly. "If the case is appealed and we have to do a brief, that's just more legal fees that Richardson would have to pay."

"This is really another contingency case, isn't it?" Philly asked.

"That seems to be our specialty."

"Your father has been in frequent contact with Martin Schuler over the last three weeks," Carpenter informed Clyde Atkins by phone. "We're talking twenty phone calls," he added, referring to the information sent to him by fax by Barney Freedman and Herb McCauley."

"No shit!" Atkins exclaimed. "How did you find this out?"

"I can't tell you and you don't want to know."

"This means my brother and sister have a deal with PowerArm Equipment. Those fuckers! A deal with PowerArm could be huge."

"How huge?"

"I'm guessing here," Atkins said. "I could see this adding over three hundred thousand to our company's yearend bottom line."

"Then your brother and sister would have new income to pay you off," Carpenter said.

"And my father's take would increase as well. Everybody wins except me."

"That's one way to look at it," Carpenter said. "Another way to look at it is that you win as well. Without this new business, you wouldn't have seen the generous offer that's been made to you."

"But didn't my brother and sister have an obligation to tell me about this?" Atkins complained. "I'm still a director of the company and a stockholder."

"I'm not sure," Carpenter confessed. "I could have some research done on that. But putting that aside for the moment, there are several ways to play this."

Carpenter began writing key words on his notepad, trying to keep up with his thinking. "First, you could simply accept the offer on the table. You could do that without telling your siblings what you know, or you could do it and tell them what you know."

"Why would I accept the offer?" Atkins demanded indignantly.

"We can talk about that but let me finish. Second, you could reject the offer with or without an explanation."

"That's what I want to do," Atkins said.

"Third, you could tell your siblings what you believe has occurred with this PowerArm outfit and demand more money."

Carpenter waited for Atkins to react, but his client didn't say anything. Maybe this was an option that hadn't occurred to Atkins.

"Fourth, we could move ahead with the trial and subpoena in all records of calls and e-mails between your family and PowerArm. A jury might find that your siblings and father were being underhanded and stick it to them."

"That sounds good."

"Or," Carpenter went on, "you could go to trial and end up with nothing."

"That would truly suck."

Carpenter wrote the word "settlement" on his notepad. "Typically, when a party makes a settlement offer, the offer can't be introduced into evidence. So a jury would never hear about the five hundred thousand offer. You might have an argument that your brother and sister concealed a business opportunity from you, but I'm not sure they had a duty to let you know because it's unclear as to your father's role."

"There's a downside to every good side," Atkins said moodily.

"Here's something else to think about," Carpenter said, wary of overloading his client's circuits. "I'd be willing to bet that at the moment, there's no signed deal. If your brother and sister learn we're onto them about PowerArm, they'll probably say your father's been working on it, but nothing is final yet. I don't have a clue what this guy Schuler—PowerArms' president—would say. Schuler's another wild card."

"I don't know what to think," Atkins said dispiritedly.

"Here's what I recommend," Carpenter said. "Let me have some research done and call you back."

"Okay," Atkins said. "Here's something for *you* to think about. Remember when you asked whether I would pay a million dollars to buy out my brother and sister? I told you no. If I had known about a deal with PowerArm, I would have said yes."

"Where's Daisy?" Carpenter asked. He was sitting in the office suite's conference room, flanked by Rachel and Meredith, and Philly had just come into focus on Skype.

"You miss her," Philly said with exaggerated, cloying sweetness. "Aren't you sweet!"

"Forget I asked," Carpenter grumbled as he made a concerted effort to ignore Rachel's giggling. "I want your two cents on this," he said, then proceeded to update Philly on the Atkins case. "Rachel and Meredith have done some quick research and I'll let them fill you in."

"We couldn't find anything directly on point about whether the brother and sister were required to tell Atkins about the PowerArm opportunity," Rachel began. "A corporation's officer or director can't take a business opportunity away from the corporation and use it for himself. But I don't think that rule applies to the situation we're dealing with. In this case, the father might say he's trying to bring a business opportunity *to* the corporation. He'd probably also say he's been working on a deal with PowerArm for years and there's no certainty there will be a deal. The siblings will probably say they knew their father was working on the opportunity, but their father hadn't reported anything definite."

"Then what was the basis for the five hundred thousand offer?" Philly asked.

Rachel shrugged and Carpenter fielded the question. "They'll say they decided to pay a premium to get rid of Atkins because they weren't getting along and they wanted him totally out of the picture."

Philly frowned in concentration.

Carpenter felt like pieces of a jigsaw puzzle were being moved around on a table without any hope of meshing. Then he remembered what Atkins last said to him.

"Here's something I forgot to mention. Atkins said he would have been willing to buy his brother and sister out for a million bucks if he knew that there was a deal with PowerArm. What if Atkins were to make a counteroffer? His counteroffer would be to buy out his siblings for one million dollars subject to his negotiating and finalizing a deal with PowerArm."

"Isn't that rejecting his siblings' offer?" Rachel asked.

"No, technically it would be a counteroffer, without accepting or rejecting the offer made to him," Carpenter replied. "Benjamin Learner is aware I might be making a counteroffer. Plus, it would give the other side something to think about. They'd have to think about how Atkins learned of discussions with PowerArm and what he was going to do with that information at trial."

Philly smiled. "I like that. But what would Atkins do with the information at trial?"

"Damned if I know," Carpenter replied. "Maybe we'll think of something when the time comes."

"The old wing-and-a-prayer strategy," Philly said.

"Nobody talked like this at Pinkerton," Meredith said.

"When is this case being tried?" Philly asked.

"The trial should already be over," Carpenter said. "But the clerk keeps calling to push it back. We'll probably get short notice out of the blue to be in court the next day."

"Hey, Carpenter," Philly said. "I've got a surprise for you."

Carpenter found Daisy and the other little girl—Rosalind—waving at him and sporting sloppy grins.

"Say hi," Philly prompted.

"Hi," Daisy said.

"Hi yourself," Carpenter responded. "What do you think of my idea?"

Philly whispered to her daughter.

"Yes," Daisy said.

"Then it's a go," Carpenter declared.

Carpenter was tired, cranky, and generally out of sorts. 'So what else is new?' he thought as he dialed Benjamin Learner's number. He had spent more time on the phone with Clyde Atkins then he had wanted to, but the back and forth had been useful and he had come away from the exchanges with a respect for the man's intelligence and business acumen. Atkins was convinced a counteroffer was low risk because his siblings would never sell.

"I'm sure you're calling to accept my clients' offer," Learner said when he picked up his line.

"Actually no," Carpenter said, relishing the moment. "I'm calling to make a counteroffer."

"Not what I expected, but let's hear it."

"My client proposes to buy out your clients for one million dollars, payable in equal five hundred thousand dollar amounts with the first payment coming upon the signing of a settlement agreement and the next payment coming a year later."

There was a long pause.

"I'm writing," Learner said. "I don't think my clients will accept any offer to buy them out, but I'll present your proposal to them."

"Excellent," Carpenter said. "There is one more thing. My client mentioned to me that the father of our clients was trying to get the business of a company known as PowerArm. We'll find out about that at trial but since we're seriously talking settlement, I'm going to ask you to check in with your clients and get back to me where things sit with PowerArm. The one million figure I mentioned is contingent upon my client being given an accurate update on PowerArm that he finds acceptable."

"PowerArm," Learner said. "Is that two words?"

'If Learner's playing dumb, he's doing a good job,' Carpenter thought. "One word, capital A."

"Got it. I'll get back to you."

Carpenter put down his phone and assessed Learner's response to his counteroffer. He started with the premise that Learner was as smart as he was—it was a mistake to underestimate any opposing lawyer. In Learner's position, he would not have recommended a $500,000 offer to Clyde Atkins *unless* he knew about PowerArm money coming through in the near future. That said, it remained a possibility that Mary Ellen Pines and Malcolm Atkins had insisted on the $500,000 offer without telling Learner about PowerArm. If Learner had known about PowerArm before their just-concluded call, Carpenter had to admit that his opposing counsel was a consummate actor.

66

Rachel sat in the visitor's chair in Carpenter's office and watched as he puzzled over his phone before finding the "speaker" button.

"Ms. Boyle is with me," Carpenter said. "I assume you're calling to accept my client's counteroffer."

Benjamin Learner's laughter sounded unforced to Rachel.

"Nothing like having my words thrown back at me," Learner said. "But to borrow a page from your book, my answer is no. Instead I have a revised offer to you. Six hundred thousand dollars."

What passed for a smile on his part briefly crossed Carpenter's features. "What's going on with PowerArm?" he asked.

"As you said, you'll find out at trial. I can tell you that Mary Ellen Pines and Malcolm Atkins have had no contact with PowerArm. I can also tell you that their father has."

"We need to stop dancing around," Carpenter said. "If there's a contract with PowerArm, the value of the family business increases. So what's the status?"

"As we speak there is no contract. When you put the father on the witness stand you can ask him about the probability of a contract. I have nothing further to say on that subject. And there's one other thing. The counteroffer you made is rejected. Pines and Malcolm Atkins will not sell their stake in the business for any amount. Although I suppose they might relent if an obscenely large sum was dangled under their noses."

Learner seemed to be enjoying himself. Rachel believed that Carpenter had failed to put his opponent on the defensive by bringing up PowerArm. Still, Carpenter's reasoning was sound—the defendants would not have offered to buy Clyde Atkins out at $500,000—now $600,000—unless a contract with PowerArm would be in place.

"Under your proposal, what happens to the Atkins money that's been put in escrow?" Carpenter asked.

"I mentioned that to my clients. They propose to split it fifty-fifty."

"I'll get back to you," Carpenter said, and he abruptly hung up the phone.

"Does this mean another round of phone calls with our client?" Rachel asked.

"Yes, it does," Carpenter confirmed.

"There has to be some sort of oral understanding on the terms of a PowerArm contract for the siblings to be offering the kind of money they're offering."

"That's my working assumption," Carpenter said.

"What if the siblings paid our client and then PowerArm didn't sign a contract?" Rachel asked.

"Not our problem," Carpenter replied.

"This is getting interesting," Clyde Atkins said on Carpenter's speaker phone. "Maybe this PowerArm possibility is worth more than I figured. Maybe I should call the president of PowerArm and ask him point-blank what's going on."

"If the guy's in bed with your father, I don't think he'll take the call," Carpenter said.

"You may be right," Atkins replied. "Martin Schuler works in New York. Does that mean we can't subpoena him for trial?"

"Yes," Carpenter said. "But we could ask for a trial delay while we try to take his deposition in New York."

"I don't want to drag this on," Atkins said. "There's nothing to prevent me from starting up a competing business, is there?" he asked.

"There's no non-compete agreement in any of the papers you provided us," Rachel said, "so there's no reason why you couldn't start your own business."

"But then again," Atkins continued, "maybe I've had it with snowblowers and leaf blowers and chain saws."

Carpenter put a finger over his lips. Rachel nodded to show she understood. Atkins was at a decision stage and Carpenter had obviously decided to wait him out.

"Take the offer," Atkins said.

"What's your thinking?" Carpenter asked, and Rachel shared his curiosity.

"It's my vote on one of the major issues of today," Atkins said, laughing.

Carpenter frowned in puzzlement. "What are you talking about?"

"I'm voting that global warming is real. Snowblowers may prove to be a hard sell if we have a couple of warm winters like this past one. The warm winter didn't hurt us this year because of the October blizzard. People bought snowblowers in December and January. They rarely got to use them. But they bought them. I'm betting that for this winter and the winter after that it's going to be a different story."

67

A Recent Law School Graduate

As she waited for her meeting to begin with a Beacon Street headhunter firm, Meredith was conflicted. On the one hand, she needed to find a job with another firm. On the other hand, she entertained the hope—or perhaps the fantasy—that Simon and Rachel's firm would make her an offer to join them as an associate even for a trial basis. The four partners were an odd group and working with them over time might prove trying. But on the positive side, she was struck by the way they interacted. Each of them felt free to say anything to the others. No suggestion or idea broached by one was dismissed out of hand by any of the others. And then there was Rachel: working with the other three had transformed her into a woman who, while not exactly fearless, was confident and poised and apparently skilled in litigation. If Rachel could blossom after a couple of years with the other three, Meredith believed her own skills and potential would go through the roof after a year or two working with all of them.

Meredith thought about going for drinks with Rachel a while back. Clearly, Rachel had provided her drink invitation after picking up on Meredith's frustration going through Spenser documents. Meredith remembered being dead tired and then perking up after a second drink. She'd talked Rachel's ear off, cataloging her gripes about her Pinkerton experience, speculating wildly on where the hell she would finally end up as a lawyer, even bemoaning the fact of no man or woman in her life. Thinking back on that evening, she couldn't recall anything that Rachel had said. Rachel must have picked up on the fact that she simply needed to vent.

A young woman reported to the receptionist and then claimed the waiting room seat next to Meredith. They exchanged weak smiles and Meredith thought nothing more of the woman until she heard her sobbing. The woman was younger than her and, surprisingly, taller. She had long, straight, black hair that was held by a clip at her neck and then descended over her back. Meredith rummaged in her purse and found a mashed packet of tissues, which she offered up. The woman reached for the tissues and Meredith observed bloodshot blue eyes and high cheekbones. "Thanks," the woman whispered after dabbing at her eyes.

"Aren't you supposed to cry *after* your interview when you learn getting a job is hopeless?"

The woman smiled through her tears. "You don't know the meaning of hopeless."

The woman was right. Even after being let go by Pinkerton, Meredith had never believed that her legal career was over and done.

"Are you a lawyer?" Meredith asked.

The woman nodded. "Not officially. I have to take the bar exam but I'm pretty sure I'll pass."

Meredith introduced herself and then fished out a business card that listed her home address and phone number. "I'm working from home at the moment. I parted ways with a law firm, and I'm basically trying to start over again."

The woman accepted the card without reading it, sighed, and made an effort to gather herself. Meredith had hoped that her own candor would prompt the woman to explain her situation but that didn't appear to be happening, so she prodded her gently. "I've told you my tale of woe. What's *your* story?"

"I don't really want to talk about it," the woman said.

"I don't think that's going to work," Meredith said. "Aren't you going to have to spill the beans when you get interviewed here?"

That question brought on another crying jag, which only increased Meredith's curiosity. "It's true we don't know each other," she said, "but I'd be glad to listen if you need someone to talk to."

The woman blew her nose and again wiped at her eyes. "I am so screwed," she said.

Meredith thought about the work she had done reviewing the records of Spenser graduates. When it came to wannabe lawyers, the screwed outnumbered the non-screwed.

"Ms. Sweeney!" the receptionist announced. "They're ready for you. If you'll come with me, please."

"Give me a minute," Meredith said, studying the woman next to her. "What's your name?" she asked.

"What's it to you?" the woman responded.

Meredith resolved not to be dismissed easily. "I'm told these interviews take about an hour. I propose that whichever one of us finishes up first waits for the other. I'd like to have coffee with you. A while back, I thought I was screwed big time. It didn't work out that way in the end. You're never as screwed as you think you are."

The woman didn't respond. Meredith figured that she'd made her pitch and headed for the receptionist.

"Noreen Clark," came from behind her. "My name is Noreen Clark."

Doris Keane and Fred Avery claimed they'd been successfully placing lawyers for twenty years. Placing lawyers probably qualified for hazardous duty pay; the two middle-aged headhunters looked weary and their upbeat smiles seemed forced.

"Thank you for filling out our questionnaire," Keane said. "You state that your objective is to be placed with a law firm as a civil litigator. Have you ruled out everything but private practice?"

"Pretty much," Meredith said. She'd concluded that working for any governmental body was not for her. The prospect of working as an in-house counsel was a turnoff. Criminal law held no interest for her. Despite bitching and moaning about life at Pinkerton, she had liked civil litigation, and was convinced that she could be good at it.

"Why did you leave Pinkerton, Ashley & Rosewood?" Avery asked.

"It was a mutual decision. As you know from the firm's reference letter, I performed satisfactorily."

Keane and Avery exchanged a glance. "That's not particularly enlightening," Avery said.

"It didn't work out. Moving on was best for me and the firm. That's all I'm going to say about it."

"That may raise eyebrows at any firm we send your name to," Keane said.

"Then that's the way it will have to be."

"It's a tight job market, as you know," Keane went on. "I'm simply saying that avoiding anything that might create a question in a prospective employer's mind is to your advantage."

Meredith had no idea why Noreen Clark was screwed, but it now occurred to her that she might be equally screwed even with a neutral letter from Pinkerton. "You've made your point and I trust that I've made mine. Let's move on."

Another glance passed between the headhunters.

"What draws you to civil litigation?" Keane asked.

Meredith took in a deep breath and slowly let the air out. She needed to hear what these people had to say. They stood to make money if they could place her; what did it matter if greed was their motivation?

"I'm competitive by nature and litigation is a form of competition," Meredith began. "I like arguing. I like brief writing. I think I'm good at those tasks. Plus, winning something in court provides a rush. Of course, losing's another thing altogether."

"What would you say your weaknesses are?" Avery asked, confirming there would be no good cops at this interview, only bad ones.

"I'm strong-willed and opinionated, which are not always good things. I don't find it easy to change my mind and admit that I'm wrong, but I'm working on that. Sometimes I have a hard time having a superior follow through on something I've worked my tail off to complete." Meredith paused. "I think that covers it."

"Do you regard yourself as a team player?" Avery asked.

Meredith realized that her answer to that question had changed with recent events. "Yes," she said, "but back when I started at Pinkerton, I'm not sure that I always was."

"Have you been doing any law-related work since leaving Pinkerton?" Keane asked.

Meredith nodded. "I've been doing some contract work for a boutique litigation practice."

"Would that firm provide you with a reference we can use?"

Meredith considered what the firm's reaction might be at the prospect of losing her. "I think they would give me a reference, but I haven't decided whether I will ask them for one."

Keane and Avery exchanged another glance. That was three glances by Meredith's count. Three strikes and you should be out, she reflected. She'd give them a five-glance maximum. Two more exchanged glances and they *were* out.

"Do you have any problems with the hierarchical structure of large law firms?" Avery asked.

As she thought about her answer, Meredith knew one thing for certain: glance number four was on its way.

Meredith returned to the reception area to find Noreen Clark sitting in the same chair. "Does this mean you haven't been interviewed yet?" she asked.

"No," Clark said standing. "I've been interviewed. Let's just say my interview was shorter than yours."

Meredith made a snap decision. "I don't know about you, but something stronger than coffee appeals to me right now. My treat."

"You don't have to twist *my* arm."

Meredith steered them into the first non-disgusting bar they came to and directed them to stools at one end of the bar. She didn't feel like sitting at a table; in the mood she was in, putting up with the discomfort of a raised stool with no back support seemed preferable to a table for two. This way she and Clark could stare grimly at their reflections in the mirror behind the bar and never have to look at each other directly. Time would tell who had the grimmer tale to tell; however, the brevity of Clark's headhunter interview suggested that Clark would come out ahead.

Meredith opted for scotch and Clark chose bourbon. They sipped at their initial drinks until they were gone, and Meredith signaled for another round.

After their second drinks arrived, Meredith broke the ice with, "My interview sucked."

"Mine took twelve minutes," Clark said.

"That's probably a record," Meredith acknowledged. "I have to say I'm curious about what's going on with you."

"First, what was that business about you being screwed over and coming out okay?"

Meredith told her everything except the name of the firm she had worked at, the terms of her settlement agreement, and the amount she had received in settlement. Clark, of course, could unearth the Pinkerton name on the Internet, but Meredith wasn't about to provide it.

This time it was Clark who signaled the bartender for another round. "I should probably eat something," she said when the drinks were delivered.

Meredith rose from her stool lightheaded. She approached the bartender and returned to their seats with peanuts and pretzels. For a time, they ate in silence.

"I don't even know where to begin," Clark said.

"Where did you go to law school?" Meredith asked.

"Sloan-Webster School of Law."

Meredith knew the law school. It was in the same class of law schools as Spenser: a lower tier, small institution that probably was a candidate for the same kind of lawsuit that Spenser had been hit with.

"I take it you graduated in May and are studying for the bar exam?"

"Right. I was in the top five percent of my class and had done really well at an internship with a legal service organization. I received an offer from a mid-sized litigation firm in Boston at a starting salary of ninety thousand. The offer was withdrawn when the firm received a copy of my transcript."

"Why?" Meredith asked, now totally engaged.

"My law school accused me of plagiarism. If you were to see my transcript, you would see a notation that I was guilty of plagiarism. There's also a letter in my law school file that says I was guilty of plagiarism."

Meredith debated a matter of seconds before asking the next obvious question. "Did you do it?"

"No," Clark said in a tone that suggested to Meredith her companion was doing better with booze than she was.

"What happened?"

"Why am I even telling you this?"

"Because you need help and I might be able to give you that help or find it for you."

Clark mulled that over as she licked the salt off a pretzel stick. Meredith didn't know whether she would have opened up to a stranger, but she hoped that Clark would.

"What the hell," Clark said, sighing. "I was doing an article that was supposed to be published in one of the law school's journals, the one on health care. I was critiquing the legal arguments that had been made before the Supreme Court on Obama's health care reform law. Obviously, this was before the Supreme Court made its just issued ruling. The article was supposed to come out before the ruling."

Clark started in on another pretzel. "Just before I was supposed to hand in a final draft of the article in Mid-April, my laptop became infected with some kind of virus and crashed. I lost everything: the article, my research notes, you name it. I was stupid. I never backed anything up. I remembered sending my now ex-boyfriend a copy of the nearly finished article attached to an e-mail. He remembered getting the e-mail and he said he downloaded the article but had never read it except for the title. But when I broke up with him, he must have taken it hard because he said he deleted all my e-mails and the downloaded article. He said he couldn't locate the deleted article and he wasn't aware of any backup he could search."

"How did this turn into a plagiarism situation?" Meredith asked.

Clark sighed. "You're not going to believe this. I found a fairly early draft of my article which I must have printed out. When I handed it to the journal editor, I explained the situation. I specifically told her that my computer crashed and that I was only able to locate the early draft I had given her. I explained that footnotes were missing, and a lot of text was missing as well. I specifically told her it wasn't ready for publication, and that I couldn't meet the deadline for handing in a finished article. I explained that I wouldn't be able to run down missing footnotes and text in time."

"Did you ever finish the article?"

"No. But the editor treated the early draft I gave her as a final draft and informed the dean's office that I appeared to have plagiarized works that I didn't cite. Under the law school's rules, plagiarism only applies to a final draft, not to any initial draft. When I told the editor that the article I gave her wasn't final, I wasn't thinking about plagiarism. But after she notified the dean's office, I looked at the rules and confronted her. She wouldn't talk to me. She said to take it up with the dean's office."

"I have to say that what this editor did sounds ridiculous," Meredith said.

"That's what I thought," Clark said with some heat. "But then I had several interviews with an assistant dean of students. At the first interview, I told her about my computer troubles and that I hadn't submitted a final draft. At a second interview, the assistant dean told me that she had interviewed everyone involved and that it was clear to her that I had plagiarized portions of the article without attribution. She wouldn't listen to me when I repeated that what I had given the journal editor was not a final draft. You just had to look at the article to know it wasn't a final draft."

Meredith found anger cutting through the booze haze she'd been experiencing. Clark's legal career was dead in the water. No law firm would ever hire an individual targeted for having plagiarized something. Why take the risk? No wonder the headhunters made short work of her: there was no way a headhunter would waste time searching for a placement for an individual who had been branded with a scarlet P.

In Clark's position, Meredith wouldn't take the law school's decision lying down. Clark needed a lawyer and probably couldn't afford one. There was nothing to prevent her from taking Clark on as a client except acquiring malpractice insurance. Now that she thought about it, did she need her own malpractice insurance for the work she was doing for Carpenter and his partners?

"Why would the editor lie about what you told her?" Meredith asked.

"Because she's a vengeful shit," Clark said. "We don't like each other. The short version is I was pissed that I didn't get the editor position and I told her that during an argument we had. I outperformed the woman who got the job. I had better grades and I write better."

Meredith wondered if there was more to the story. "What's the name of this editor and what's your ex-boyfriend's name?"

"Caryn Wheelwright and Kevin James."

Meredith wrote down the information.

"So, do you agree that I'm screwed?" Clark asked.

"For the moment. But moments pass. Here's the plan. First, you're going to give me your contact information. Second, you and I are going to get some real food and continue to get liquored up. Third, I'm going to think about what you've told me and maybe run it by some people in this firm I'm doing some contract work for. What do you say?"

"It's three steps ahead of what *I've* been up to," Clark said as she fished a piece of paper out of her purse and started to write.

"Any further thoughts about our first meeting?" Samantha Gray asked.

Over the last few days Paul had been thinking of little else. The notion that to be the police officer he wanted to be meant constantly putting his ass on the line and risking everything he held dear took some getting used to even though it should have been obvious from Day One. Gray was observing him without expression. They were seated in the same facing chairs as at their last meeting. Again Gray had no paper or pen.

"Here's what I don't understand," Paul said. "While I was married for the first time with a kid I adore, I was never troubled by thoughts of what I had to lose. And I had the same things to lose: a wife, a child, a family. And I had some close calls. Maybe not as close as this last one but close enough. So why did this all strike home this time around? I mean, I've always been aware of the dangers of the job."

"I don't have an answer for you," Gray said, and Paul felt a rush of frustration; he'd been hoping to receive direct insights that would explain what he was feeling.

"That's not to say I don't have some thoughts on the subject," Gray continued. "For one thing, you're older now, pushing forty, right?"

Paul nodded. The notion that his life was half over was another reality that was hard to come to terms with.

"Think of your reaction to what happened in the hostage situation as being related to a developmental stage you're going through. You're older, more mature. You're starting what you may think of as a second family. You're at a different place in your life than you were at during your first marriage. Is this helpful?"

"I'll have to think about it. Are you suggesting that I'm now more aware of my mortality?"

"Yes," Gray said.

"Are older cops more conflicted?"

"I'd agree that *thoughtful* older cops *migh*t be more conflicted."

Gray had just provided the directness he had been looking for. "How do thoughtful older cops resolve this kind of conflict?"

"Some of them do and some of them don't," Gray replied. "In my opinion, the ones that do resolve the conflict successfully come around to the view that your wife suggested you take. You need to do your job without nagging doubts about what you have to lose. It comes back to that in my view."

Paul realized he was not back to square one. Thinking of his reaction as stemming from a developmental stage in his life was helpful. He was no longer a young guy who thought he was invincible.

"I'm also thinking that starting a new family has to do with your reaction during the hostage situation. Tell me how you're feeling about your new family."

Paul uttered the first thought that came to mind. "Excited. I think I'm in some denial about how big an adjustment it's going to be. We have this communal living arrangement that seems to be working, but a new baby is going to require changes."

"Tell me about the communal living arrangement."

Paul described the home ownership agreement that with Philly's lead, had been worked out with Raul and Isabella and Sarah. His previous doubts about their arrangement were gone; the arrangement was beneficial.

"Your wife sounds like a remarkable woman."

"She is. She's battled demons of her own and has emerged stronger. She's amazing really."

"What do you mean she's battled demons of her own?"

Paul described Philly's drinking and how she had come to deal with it. Recounting this part of their history left him with a tightness in his gut.

Gray fell silent, seemed to be thinking through something that had struck her.

"I wonder whether you think you'd be letting your wife down if you went about doing your job," Gray finally said, "because you wouldn't, you know."

"What? I don't understand."

Gray repeated what she had just said and continued. "If something had happened to you during that hostage situation, your wife would have been left alone, pregnant, much as she was when her fiancé was killed. I could be wrong, but I think that notion was working on you maybe subconsciously. Your wife strikes me as a survivor. If something happened to you, she would soldier on. It wouldn't be easy, but she would. When she told you to do your job, I think she was reassuring you that she would persevere no matter what happened to you."

Paul felt a lump in his throat. The tightness in his gut increased.

"I've given you enough to think about. We've got two more sessions before we decide whether to proceed further. So, until next week..."

68

Simon and Rachel were having lunch in the conference room and Meredith decided now was as good a time as any to approach them. "I ran into a woman who needs a lawyer," she said as she took a seat next to Rachel and across from Simon. "Do you have a moment?"

Rachel held up her hand as she washed down a bite of sandwich with water. "Let me get Carpenter."

Carpenter followed Rachel into the conference room sporting what Meredith regarded as a deeper scowl than usual. "What is it with lawyers?" Carpenter grumbled as he took a seat next to Simon.

"What?" Simon asked.

"We just got served with motions to dismiss Brendan O'Day's suit against Baywater State," Carpenter groused. "Now we've got to deal with that shit."

"It could be worse," Rachel said. "It's billable-hour work."

Carpenter muttered something that Meredith couldn't make out. "What's this about somebody needing a lawyer?" he snapped.

"I ran into a woman who needs help," Meredith said.

"So why don't you help her?" Carpenter said. "Why are you talking to us?"

Meredith felt herself coloring. "Maybe I will help her. But I'm interested in hearing whether she has a case."

"Everybody has a case," Carpenter said. "The problem is that most everybody has a losing case. Are you talking to us because you think you might want to refer the case here?"

Carpenter was nothing if not direct, Meredith reflected. "I thought about that. I'm not sure what I'm going to do."

"Should we patch Philly in?" Carpenter asked Simon and Rachel. "There are a few things I want to touch base with her on."

"Good idea," Rachel said. "Let's see how she's doing."

Carpenter whipped out his cell phone and poked away. "Skype, now," he barked. "That is if it's convenient." He paused. "Okay, ten minutes."

"Hi," Daisy said in a soft voice after some off-camera prompting.

"Hey, cutie," Carpenter greeted the toddler. He loved her fine black hair, which Philly was letting grow long. And those gorgeous blue eyes were going to have guys sniffing around her before she hit her teens. "Tell your mommy that Meredith has a potential new case situation she wants to discuss. But before we get to that, I have some housekeeping I want to get out of the way. I'd just as soon talk to you as to your mother."

Daisy began to squirm and then disappeared from view. Immediately Philly was visible. "You scared her off with housekeeping."

"Very funny," Carpenter said. "I was just telling everybody that we have to deal with dismissal motions in the O'Day case. Today I'm disbursing funds from the Glass case settlement. So that case is over. Finally, the paperwork is done on the Atkins case settlement. That should be signed in the next couple of days and Atkins will get paid. Another case bites the dust."

Carpenter attributed the following silence to Meredith's presence. If Meredith weren't around, he and Philly would be bringing up the need for more business. The Spenser case was the biggest case they had going for them and it was not a case that four lawyers could bill for. The frenzy of activity that had recently beset them was now a thing of the past.

"What's this about Meredith coming up with a potential case?" Philly asked.

Meredith began to fill them in. At first Carpenter jotted down a few key words but, in short order, he simply listened, wondering what he was missing, trying to understand why the Sloan-Webster School of Law had lowered the boom on a third-year student who, as far as he could tell, had done nothing wrong. He didn't like the fact that computers were involved, which put him at a major disadvantage. But these days you couldn't take three steps without bumping into a computer or e-mail or the goddamn Internet.

"I felt so sorry for her," Meredith concluded her account.

"What do you think you can do for this Clark woman?" Carpenter said to Meredith, immediately wishing that he hadn't come across as his typical challenging self.

"She needs to have her school record cleaned up," Meredith said. "It contains false information that will irreparably damage her career. She needs to get an injunction."

"What are her legal claims?" Philly chimed in.

Meredith colored slightly. "I haven't totally worked that out. But her school record is defamatory. The false school record is interfering with her right to earn a living. Maybe she has a contract claim insofar as she paid money for a legal education so she could practice law and is being prevented from pursuing that livelihood due to the false statements in her record. And maybe she has a claim that the law school tortiously interfered with her contract with the firm that hired her and later withdraw its offer. Lastly, she can claim that the law school's investigation was inadequate because she never got to confront the journal editor."

Carpenter thought Meredith's legal theories were reasonable.

"Are the journal editor and Clark enemies?" Simon asked. "It strikes me this journal editor went out of her way to screw Clark."

"They don't like each other," Meredith replied, and she filled the group in on what Clark had told her.

"Can Clark pay for legal representation?"

"I didn't really get into that," Meredith acknowledged sheepishly. "I doubt she can afford a lawyer. She mentioned that she was stuck with a bunch of student loans."

"If there's no clear way to recover attorney fees," Simon said, "then you could be working for nothing if you take her case and she can't pay you."

"I never really had to deal with the business aspects of the law while I was at Pinkerton," Meredith acknowledged. "I guess I've got a lot to learn."

"What are you going to do?" Carpenter decided to press.

"I guess I have to talk further with Clark." Meredith paused, her expression troubled.

"What's bothering you?" Carpenter asked.

"Is this the kind of case you guys would take?"

Philly laughed. "We'd have an earnest, somewhat contentious discussion. There are those of us who would opt for common sense and vote not to take on a case where we wouldn't be paid. Then there are the bleeding hearts like me who would say we have to help the woman. We'd also give consideration to taking the case on a contingency basis, but we'd take a hard look at that. So far Clark is out a ninety-thousand-dollar offer of employment and probably out about ninety thousand dollars in useless tuition payments. I'm assuming a year's tuition is at least thirty thousand."

"More," Simon and Rachel said together.

Meredith looked unsettled and Carpenter realized that they had probably added to the uncertainty she'd already been experiencing. 'Welcome to the practice of law,' he thought.

"By the way," Meredith said, "when I do work for you guys, do I need my own malpractice insurance?"

"You do," Carpenter said. "It just gets better and better, doesn't it?"

July

From Meredith's Playlist

"Criminal"

Fiona Apple

69

Paul had dropped off almost as soon as his head hit the pillow, but Philly found her mind racing. The July Fourth barbecue combined with Daisy's birthday party had turned into an all-day affair. Paul and Raul had had to make additional food and charcoal runs when most everyone ignored the afternoon hours listed on the e-mail invitations and stayed through the early evening.

Her parents had driven up from Fall River and when she saw them, Philly was conscious of how much they had aged. She hadn't seen them since the previous Thanksgiving and they seemed to have lost a step or two. The same could be said for Philip's parents who were unnaturally subdued as if burdened on their granddaughter's birthday by more than the reminder of the son they had lost.

Two of her former drinking buddies had shown up without having sent an RSVP. Rainey, who she had hooked up with for a time, and his girlfriend, Monica, had married and moved to Roxbury. Monica revealed that she had just found out she was pregnant. Mace, who was largely responsible for dragging her off to AA had taken Philly aside, asked her if she was staying off the booze, and left when Philly had confirmed she was.

The most unexpected news of the day had come from Raul and Isabella. The two had kept their wedding low key and private, getting hitched before a justice of the peace. But Philly noticed the wedding bands, had asked the couple "What gives?" and had received shy smiles in return. "We finally got around to it," Raul said, and his offhand manner seemed okay with Isabella.

And Paul's partner, Evelyn, had come by as well, giving Philly a chance to personally thank her for saving his life. Evelyn was not what she'd expected. The woman was beautiful with enough don't-mess-with-me attitude to make Philly wonder how Paul dealt with her on a day-to-day basis. Evelyn came alone and left early, clearly putting in an appearance to cover herself with her boss.

Meredith came alone and had surprised Philly by spending a fair amount of time with Daisy and Rosalind, almost as if she wanted to find out what spending time with little kids was all about, sprawling on the grass with the two little girls who played with wooden blocks and fuzzy animals.

Carpenter, Rachel and Simon came with their significant others. Philly couldn't remember seeing Carpenter so relaxed. When he made time to interact with Daisy and Rosalind, his smile was more than his usual grimace.

Daisy survived the day without a nap and Rosalind slept for only an hour after lunch. The girls had gotten Daisy's birthday cake all over themselves and Raul had been the one to literally hose them down.

Philly thought about next year's July Fourth celebration. Maybe by then the baby inside her would be standing by holding onto something. Daisy would have a vocabulary. Rosalind would be speaking a word or two. And the older generation would have moved further into decline.

Philly closed her eyes and ran her hands over her belly. She felt movement which, she took for a sign that all was well.

70

Ideally, Philly would be meeting with Fay Richardson face-to-face. There was a lot to be said for eye contact when it came to a discussion crucial to resolving a pending case. But leaving Daisy was inconvenient, traveling to Boston unthinkable, and waddling around with an enormous belly near impossible, so Philly had decided a phone call would have to do. She took her time answering Richardson's questions about Patrick Lassiter's proposal to settle her billboard case for $100,000 if there was no appeal.

"Do you think they would win their appeal?" Richardson asked when Philly began to wonder if she would run out of questions.

"In my opinion, no. But I need to stress that's only my opinion. I think we have the better side when it comes to arguing whether Judge Murray's decision should be upheld."

Richardson fell silent. Philly looked out her office window at a clear, cloudless day and longed to stretch out on a recliner.

"You said it could take over a year for the appeal to be decided," Richardson said. "Interest would be running during that time, right?"

"Right," Philly confirmed. "At twelve percent."

"I really don't want to have to think about this for more than another year," Richardson said. "It seems I'm giving up a lot of money if I agree to what they want. I'd be giving up fifty thousand dollars plus interest. If I take their deal, I'd be walking away with fifty thousand dollars only because you would give me a break on legal fees. But if I don't take the deal, I'd have to pay you legal fees for the appeal."

"My suggestion is that you take some time and think about your options. Maybe you could sound out your friend Selena Boyd for her opinion."

"She'd tell me to fight them to the bitter end," Richardson said. "I know Selena."

"I still think you should talk to a friend or family member about the case."

"Okay, I will. I'll call Selena. I really appreciate what you're willing to do about your legal fees."

"Don't mention it," Philly replied.

Carpenter had just concluded a meeting with Rachel and Meredith when his phone rang. He had given them specific assignments in connection with the motion to dismiss Brendan O'Day's case and regarded it as an eerie coincidence that O'Day was now on the line. He assumed that O'Day had questions on the motions to dismiss his case and so was taken aback by his client's first question.

"Do you have a TV?"

"At home, yes, but not here in the office."

"It'll be noon in an hour," O'Day said. "You need to be by a TV for the noon news."

"What's going on?"

"Rather than have me explain, it'll be easier if you just watch the news. Then we'll talk."

Carpenter didn't appreciate a cryptic client, but he suspected that O'Day would not be more forthcoming.

"Before you watch the news, take another look at the newspaper article run by the Baywater Bugle. Sorry, but I've got to run."

Carpenter reread the college newspaper article focusing on the paragraphs that mentioned the woman who had identified herself at the rally protesting violence against women. Audrey Quinn had been one of the final speakers at the rally. "I'm Audrey Quinn and I was raped and beaten a little over a year ago," was how she had introduced herself. Quinn related that she was certain she could identify her attacker and that she had provided his description to an artist working with the police department who had created an excellent likeness. She bemoaned the fact that since her attack and notwithstanding her description of the rapist, the police had no leads in the case. Quinn ended her brief remarks with an exhortation to women to fight back when attacked. She confessed to not having fought back as hard as she could have because her assailant had a knife. In retrospect, Quinn believed that she'd made a mistake.

Carpenter remembered Meredith's theory of why a victim of an attack would identify herself at the rally. If Meredith was correct, the noon news would be sensational.

By noon, Carpenter had everyone in the office with him, seated in a bar on adjacent stools before a TV angled downward directly in front of their seats. Carpenter had only ordered a round of beers after extracting a promise from the bartender that he would turn to a news channel at noon. The only detail he'd provided to his colleagues was O'Day's request that they watch the noon-time news.

At two minutes before noon, Carpenter signaled the bartender, who changed the channel from sports to news causing a number of patron groans.

"Good afternoon, everyone," an anchorwoman said with one of those well-modulated voices that made Carpenter think of robots.

"We start off with our developing lead story which involves a shooting in the South End that may turn out to be a case of self-defense. Mary Naismith is on the scene reporting live. Mary!"

"Thank you, Tanya. Police are releasing few details as their investigation is ongoing. There are unconfirmed reports that a man was killed in the course of a home invasion. The occupant of an apartment is said to have used deadly force when the shooting victim, armed with a knife, entered her apartment and attacked her. There's a twist to this story, Tanya. There's a further unconfirmed report that the shooting victim assaulted and raped the homeowner over a year ago. That crime had gone unsolved, although the woman had provided a detailed description of her attacker to a police sketch artist. Recently, the woman spoke at a rally condemning violence against women. At the rally, the woman urged all women to learn self-defense and to resist an attacker with force. This is a fast-moving story, Tanya, and I'll be passing along updates as we learn more."

"Thank you, Mary. Excellent work. Turning now to national news..."

Carpenter gave a short wave to the bartender. Then he turned slightly on his bar stool to observe his colleagues at a loss for words. Rachel, in particular, seemed stunned by what she had just seen and heard.

"My crazy idea isn't looking so crazy anymore," Meredith said.

"No it's not," Carpenter agreed. "But how does it help O'Day if the woman who identified herself at the rally did so deliberately to provoke a second attack from the man who raped her?"

Carpenter wasn't surprised that there were no immediate responses to his question. Although he had guessed the gist of the news story, he had drawn a blank on how O'Day could benefit from the fact that the Quinn woman had used the rally to draw out her previous attacker.

"Were speakers at the rally told not to use their names?" Simon asked.

"That's a good question," Carpenter said. "I'll ask O'Day."

"Baywater State College and the student newspaper were used," Rachel observed. "This woman probably trained to fight and to shoot a gun."

"How did you come up with this theory?" Carpenter asked Meredith.

"The woman's response to her name being used in the student newspaper article seemed off. She wasn't irate that her name was used. Instead she said something tepid like she would have preferred that her name was not mentioned in the online version of the article. She also stressed that she could identify her attacker. All that made me think that she had put her name out there deliberately."

"If the woman was deposed, do you think she would own up to deliberately giving out her name?" Simon asked.

"She'd be nuts to do that," Rachel said. "The police might conclude that her shooting her attacker was premeditated and had nothing to do with self-defense."

Carpenter jotted down two notes on the napkin beside his beer. Did the dead man match the description of the attacker provided by the Quinn woman? Did Baywater State College prohibit rally speakers from giving their names? With any luck, the first question would be answered yes, and the second one no.

Meredith stayed late, waiting for everyone to leave the office so she would have some privacy for her call to Noreen Clark. Carpenter was the last to leave and he gave her the fisheye, which she no doubt deserved. He had to know she had no work to do that required her to stay late. She had assembled Spenser files at her workstation for show.

"I'm getting back to you, as I said I would," Meredith said when Clark picked up her phone. "I reviewed your situation with the lawyers I'm doing some contract work for. Without going into great detail, there seemed to be a consensus that you have a case. If it's true that you didn't plagiarize anything, then your law school record contains false information, which is harming you when it comes to obtaining a job. In fact, the false information has already harmed you because your job offer was withdrawn."

"That sounds positive," Clark said.

Meredith had never talked legal fees with a potential or actual client. She took a deep breath and decided to tackle the issue head-on.

"As you know, lawyers charge for their services. Are you able to afford to pay for legal services?"

"Not really," Clark said. "I mentioned my law school loans to you. I'm doing some temp secretarial work to pay for room and board. Basically, I'm broke. I was counting on the job offer to help me start paying back the loans."

"Then that's going to be a problem," Meredith said. "When I went over your situation with other lawyers, nobody was able to come up with a theory where you could recover legal fees if you won your suit."

"What about a contingency fee arrangement?" Clark said. "I lost over a hundred grand in tuition payments because of this plagiarism bullshit."

"That's a possibility," Meredith replied, "and I want to give it more thought. As I explained to you, I'm also looking for a job and I have to be careful about making professional commitments. For example, I don't want to be in a position where I take on a case and a firm that hires me wants nothing to do with it. Also, I'm factoring in that you could lose the case without further documentation you had nearly finished the article."

"Would the lawyers you talked with take my case?"

Meredith chose her words carefully. "I'm not sure. None of them proposed doing so but I didn't flat out ask them if they were interested in taking your case on."

"I need to protect my reputation and career. If you or these other lawyers won't help me, I need to find someone who will."

Meredith admired Clark for coming on strong. The woman was correct about needing to take immediate action.

"I need to think about this a little more," Meredith said. "I'll call you back tomorrow with a decision one way or the other."

"Okay," Clark said. "That sounds fair."

Meredith set down her phone. Her real reason for putting Clark off was different. She was going to accept Clark's case and the only question in her mind was whether to give Carpenter and his firm a chance to take the case over. Maybe she could get a referral fee if Clark recovered damages. She was flying blind—the practicalities of running a law practice were never taught at Spenser.

Meredith realized there was one further thing she could accomplish tonight and placed a call to Herb McCauley.

"This is Herb."

"Hi, this is Meredith Sweeney. Am I calling too late?"

"Not at all. How are you?"

"Pretty good all things considered. I'm doing some contract work for Carpenter and Philly's firm which has been mostly fun."

"Good for you."

"Do you guys know any computer experts? There's this case I might take on where I may need one."

Herb laughed. "Barney and I are computer illiterates. For some of the work we've gotten into we needed to go on Facebook. Setting up a Facebook account just about did us in."

"I'm pretty clueless about computers as well. I'm looking for someone who knows about retrieving deleted documents."

"When Barney and I were with the Cambridge Police Department, we worked with a guy who's got a kid who's supposed to be pretty good with computers. I can't think of the kid's name, but he likes to be called Flash."

"Flash?"

"Yeah, Flash. The kid's a nutjob, but he's supposed to know his stuff. His father's last name is Nestor. I'll e-mail you the kid's first name and a phone number."

"Flash?"

"I wouldn't sell him short based on his nickname. If you're lucky, the kid might talk to you."

"Okay, thanks" Meredith said. 'Flash?' she thought.

71

"I've done some nosing around with help from Helene Bridge, the student newspaper editor," Brendan O'Day told Carpenter on the phone. "As far as we can tell, Baywater did not tell any speaker at the rally not to identify herself."

Carpenter digested this information and decided to share obliquely a fact that he had learned from Barney Freedman and Herb McCauley. "I want you to imagine for the moment that the intruder that Quinn shot matches the police artist sketch that was put together from information provided by Quinn."

"Okay. Where are you going with this?" O'Day asked.

"Also imagine that since she was attacked over a year ago, Quinn obtained a license to own a nine-millimeter Glock pistol and practiced with the weapon for months at a firing range."

"Where did you learn all this?"

"Who said I learned anything? I'm simply asking you to use your imagination."

"All right, play it your way. So what?"

"So one might infer that Quinn deliberately identified herself so that her attacker would try to silence her."

"And she'd be ready," O'Day added.

"Something like that."

"That's a bit twisted," O'Day said.

"Yeah, it is. The rally that was reported in the newspaper was sanctioned by Baywater State College, right?"

"Right. The dean's office gave permission and it was well publicized. I remember seeing posters announcing the rally all over campus."

"I've been trying to think of a way to play this information to get the college to bring you back."

"What information?" O'Day questioned. "I thought I was supposed to be imagining things."

Carpenter laughed. "Point taken. What I've come up with is telling the college's lawyer that if we file a response to the college's motion to dismiss, that response is going to include a defense that the college contributed to Quinn shooting her attacker by failing to prohibit rally speakers from identifying themselves."

"That strikes me as a stretch."

"I agree. I can't think of anything else."

Carpenter decided not to break the silence on the other end of the line.

"I'd say go for it," O'Day finally said. "As far as I can tell, I don't have anything to lose."

"That's what I was thinking."

Carpenter studied Stephen Larson's photograph on the website maintained by his firm. The lead counsel for Baywater State College and Dean Walter Sternman had the unruffled, serious look that was de rigueur for litigators these days. Carpenter remembered his opponent from the previous court hearing—a tall man, all business, quick on his feet. There was no right way or wrong way to approach an opposing hard-ass lawyer. Carpenter opted for being a harder ass.

"Thanks for taking my call," Carpenter said after penetrating the defenses of an administrative assistant who had seemed poised to request a DNA sample before passing him on to her boss.

"What can I do for you?"

"I want you to give consideration to rehiring Brendan O'Day."

"That's not going to happen," Larson said dismissively. "We're confident the motions to dismiss that were recently filed will be allowed."

"I'll bet you are, even though an injunction was entered against your client," Carpenter replied.

"Is there a point to your call?"

Carpenter counted out five beats in the hope that Larson would perceive his delay in responding as a sign Larson had him on the run. "Silly me. I was thinking I'd take the high road and try to spare your clients some embarrassment. But since you're pissing me off, fuck your clients."

"I have no idea what you're talking about." Larson said icily.

"Of course you don't, because you're coming across as a rude, arrogant prick. But I'll tell you this. When we file our responses to your frivolous motions, I'm going to make sure the media gets hold of this case. Then your clients can start fielding questions about why they failed to instruct the people who spoke at the rally to remain anonymous. They can also answer questions about how a woman who spoke at the rally used the rally sponsored by your clients to kill someone."

"You've lost me," Larson said, and Carpenter wondered whether it was his imagination that his adversary sounded less sure of himself.

"I tried to be nice, but since you clearly prefer to be a prick, I'm not going to explain a goddamn thing to you. What have you been doing, sitting on your ass all this time? Surely you've read about the recent shooting!" Carpenter waited five more beats. He had no doubt that Larson *had* sat on his ass when it came to looking hard at the rally giving rise to O'Day's case. "It's obvious from the motions you filed that you don't have a fucking clue that the woman who identified herself at the rally did so deliberately. And God only knows why you never took up the judge's suggestion to take her deposition instead of moving to dismiss O'Days case."

Carpenter slammed down the phone and couldn't stop from grinning. It had been a while since he had ranted and raved at a fellow attorney. It had felt good to let it rip.

"What's up?" Philly said.

Carpenter missed seeing Philly on Skype. Or maybe it was Daisy he missed. Either way, lately, ordinary phone calls to Brighton were a letdown.

"Any thoughts on that case Meredith told us about? I thought she was fishing around to see whether we were interested in her offloading the case."

"Yeah, I had the same impression. We'd have to take it on a contingency. If we were busier, I wouldn't be excited about taking it on. But we're not busy so I think we should consider it."

"That's the way I came out," Carpenter said. "Getting paid off on the Glass case was nice for all of us. Also, Atkins owes us a fair bit for the billable hours we put in. But after that, the Spenser School of Law case is pretty much it."

Philly didn't respond right away. Carpenter strained to hear sounds from the little girls, but only picked up Philly's breathing.

"It may be good for Meredith to run with a case on her own," Philly said. "It takes some getting used to, as I well remember."

"So where are you heading with this?"

"I think we should leave it up to Meredith," Philly explained. "If she approaches us again, we can tell her we'll take the case. If she decides to keep the case, I don't mind being there for her in a backup role the way you were there for me when we started working together."

Carpenter remembered that during those early days of their collaboration, he would bitch and moan whenever Philly sought advice, but always ended up helping her. "I'm okay with all that," he said. "I like Meredith. I'm always going to be impressed with the way she figured out what was going on with the Quinn woman in the O'Day case."

"I like her too," Philly said. "What are we going to do about new business?"

"Damned if I know. How are you feeling, by the way?"

"I'm feeling big and ungainly and that makes me cranky."

"So everything's as it should be."

"Yeah," Philly said. "I guess that's right."

Tina Farrell was arguably the plaintiff in the Spenser case most qualified to obtain a law-related job. Simon watched Rachel and Meredith review the third iteration of the outline he had prepared for Farrell's deposition. They were in the conference room leaning toward each other, working off the same document. They seemed to be able to read each other's mind; one would point to a line and without a word passing between them, the other would nod and make an edit. Women, Simon decided, were definitely spooky.

As the women worked, Simon revisited the most recent conference call with Philly. It had struck him that their firm needed new business. It was unsettling to think that he, with an assist from Rachel, was responsible for bringing in the case that was likely to sustain them over the short term. Without the Spenser litigation, their firm would be hurting. Other than that, Brendan O'Day's lawsuit was the only billable-hour case in the office and that case might settle if Carpenter's hard line against Baywater State College was successful.

Despite these business worries, Simon had no doubt that he'd made the right decision joining Carpenter, Philly, and Rachel. They were a team and he liked and trusted them. They were there for each other. Philly was a case in point. There was no question that when her pregnancy ended, she'd be out of action for a time dealing with her new baby. But she would continue to share in every dollar the firm made, and Simon knew that neither he nor his other partners would begrudge her that benefit. There had been no discussion about this subject, but the conclusion was simply a given. Besides, Philly being Philly, she would do whatever she could working from home.

Rachel pointed at the deposition outline with her pen, drawing a laugh from Meredith. "He can't spell but he has other good points," Rachel said, looking up briefly and favoring Simon with a smile.

Simon needed no reminder that a lot was riding on the Spenser case depositions he was about to take. There was the case itself; discrediting and tearing down the plaintiffs was necessary to prevail in the litigation. But beyond the case, a successful result in the litigation might mean more business from the law school.

"When's the first deposition?" Carpenter asked, entering the conference room.

"Next week," Simon replied.

"Are you all set?"

"Once Rachel and Meredith get through with me, I should be."

"Good. Let me know if I can help."

"I'm glad you popped in," Meredith said. "I've decided to take on that case I told you about. But I was wondering whether I could ask you guys to take a look at the complaint I come up with."

"That's not a problem," Carpenter said. "Look at the O'Day complaint for starters. I'll flip you some other complaints we've drafted."

"You'll soon see that Carpenter doesn't like adjectives," Rachel said. "Adverbs are another no-no."

"I think I figured that out already," Meredith said.

"Congratulations," Carpenter said. "This is your first case on your own after Pinkerton, right?"

"Right," Meredith confirmed.

"Here's one thing you can count on," Carpenter said. "You'll never forget your first time."

72

As she sat on her spinning bike, Philly marveled that her belly reached the handlebars. When she pulled up on the pedals, her knees grazed the bottom of her belly. Were she to raise her seat and push it forward, her enormous belly would sit atop the handlebars. To her right, Isabella was pedaling like a woman possessed. "You need to put in an appearance soon," she instructed her belly, and mercifully Isabella was too caught up in her speed work to have heard. "What Doesn't Kill You" sounded from her boom box. Philly doubted that another month and a half of pregnancy was going to make her stronger.

As her legs moved without any significant resistance on her bike, Philly's thoughts drifted to firm business or, more precisely, to the lack of firm business. Were she and her partners in the same precarious position as the plaintiffs in the Spenser case? Without the Spenser case, they would be hard pressed to take future draws. Could the plaintiffs in the Spenser case really be faulted for not going out on their own and hanging up a shingle? If she and Carpenter, established lawyers, were worried about making a go of it, what did that say about the prospects of law school grads with no track record? She needed to caution Simon about deposition questions that focused on the failure of a Spenser lawsuit plaintiff to go out on his or her own.

"What are you thinking about?" Isabella asked. She had slowed her pace and was putting in some recovery time.

"I was thinking about something Carpenter often says. He says in the legal business you get to enjoy a success for about fifteen seconds and then you have to go out there and figure a way to do it again."

The chip on Stephen Larson's shoulder must have been at least partially dislodged. Carpenter was surprised by the civil tone of Baywater State College's lawyer as they made introductory small talk.

"Again, thanks for taking my call," Larson said. "I've reviewed our last discussion with my clients and you may have a point. It's not the only way to view the situation, however."

If Larson had a different way to view the situation, Carpenter wanted to hear it, but he held that thought.

"Would your client agree to a thirty-day suspension?" Larson asked.

"Is that with or without pay?"

Larson hesitated. "Without pay, but perhaps that is open to some negotiation."

"I'll ask my client," Carpenter responded, "but for purposes of this call you may assume that the answer is no."

"Is there a settlement that would be acceptable to your client?"

"I honestly don't know," Carpenter said. "But if you're interested in what I'd be prepared to recommend, I'm thinking of something along the lines of my client being rehired and paid as he would have been paid, all references to this matter being permanently deleted from his personnel file, and the college defraying his legal fees."

"Your client wouldn't be giving up anything under that scenario," Larson pointed out. "Is he prepared to make any concessions?"

"I don't know," Carpenter replied. "I just told you what *I'd* consider recommending."

"Why don't you confer with your client and let me know whether something along the lines of a brief suspension would resolve this case?"

'Because that would be a waste of time,' Carpenter thought. "Okay," is what he said.

Carpenter set down his phone, leaned back in his chair, and put his feet up on his desk. He decided not to talk with O'Day until tomorrow. Let Larson simmer.

Flash was not what Meredith expected. For one thing, the guy was gorgeous. Broad shoulders tapered down to slim hips. His black look—black jeans, black T-shirt, black vest, black running shoes—suited him and didn't come across as an affectation. A black rubber band pinched off a two-foot-long ponytail. His blue eyes rarely blinked. The only thing off about Flash was his actual name—Raymond Nestor. No wonder he preferred his nickname.

Previously, on the phone, Meredith had filled Flash in on Noreen Clark's situation and had asked if he could help. His response had been to request a face-to-face meeting, claiming he didn't trust phones. Now, facing him across the office suite's conference room table, Meredith repeated her question. "Can you help?"

"A couple of things up front," Flash said, ignoring the question. "I charge one hundred dollars an hour for my time. I expect to be paid in cash. I do not expect to receive a 1099 form. Do you have a problem with any of that?"

Meredith foresaw a brief meeting. "I've got a problem with everything except your hourly rate. I wish you'd told me about these conditions when we talked."

"I'm telling you now," Flash said evenly, his blue eyes locked on hers.

Meredith wondered why Flash was still seated at the table after she had rejected his terms. But had she rejected them? No; she'd merely acknowledged problems with his conditions. The guy had just about admitted that he was a tax cheat.

"Are you a businessman?" Meredith asked.

"What kind of a question is that?"

"It's a straightforward question that I would like you to answer." She had caught Flash off guard. Maybe keeping him off balance was the way to get him to do what she wanted him to do.

"Yeah, I'm a businessman. Why else would I be here?"

"Then act like a businessman," Meredith said in a clipped tone. "The two investigators who gave us your name know your father. They put in a good word for you. Out of respect for them, I'm not going to do anything that's not on the up and up when it comes to taxes."

"On the up and up," Flash repeated. "I'm trying to think of the last time I heard someone say that."

Meredith decided to push. "You're getting a 1099 if you get hired. And paying you in cash is a pain in the ass so that's out."

Flash leveled an appraising look in her direction. Meredith hoped she had piqued his interest.

"Yeah, I might be able to help," Flash said.

"What about the 1099 and payments in cash?"

"Those items are negotiable."

For the moment, Meredith was willing to assume that Flash would back down on his previous demands. "What can you do to help?"

"I'd like to look at Clark's computer and at her ex-boyfriend's computer. Maybe Clark can bring her computer to his place and I can look at them there."

"What are you hoping to accomplish?"

"If Clark's computer did get hit with a virus, the most recent draft of the article may be lost. I want to see for myself."

"What are you going to do with the boyfriend's computer?"

"Hope and pray he has some backup he doesn't know about. I also want to figure out whether a document recovery tool might bring back the recent draft."

Meredith nodded, not understanding what Flash intended to do. She considered Clark's reaction to Flash's requests. Clark really didn't have other options.

Flash slid a business card across the conference room table. Below the word "Flash" was an East Cambridge address.

"I'll talk to Ms. Clark and get back to you," Meredith said, realizing the meeting was over. She didn't want it to be over. She liked looking at Flash. Fortunately, there was one unfinished matter that needed resolution.

"What about the 1099 and cash payments?"

"Those are not a problem. I was just testing you."

"Yeah, right," Meredith said, and she was favored with an amused look in Flash's brilliant blue eyes.

Frank's late-night call to Simon was unexpected. They had been good about e-mailing each other and had had several exchanges during the day. "Everything all right?" Simon asked.

"Yeah," Frank responded in a despondent tone. "I need to tell you something so I'm just going to say it. I had sex with another guy."

Simon felt a hot flash of anger and it took all his self-control not to say anything. Frank's announcement wasn't unexpected. He'd told Frank that it was okay to take up with someone else. That didn't make Frank's news any less painful.

"Say something," Frank pleaded.

Simon knew that he owed Frank for giving him a free pass to make a fool of himself with Meredith. But Frank getting it on with another guy was qualitatively different from his stupidity with Meredith because Frank had hooked up with a fucking guy.

"Please," Frank said.

"I'm disappointed," Simon managed to say. For the moment, he wasn't ready to thank Frank for coming clean.

"I guess I just had to get it out of my system," Frank said. "As soon as it was over, I knew I had made a mistake. I'm sorry."

Simon thought about how for some things there couldn't be a worse time. Coming on the eve of Spenser case depositions, Frank's news would provide a major distraction for what he needed to do in his job.

"Talk to me," Frank said. "You've got to have something else to say besides you're disappointed."

"Where does this leave us?" Simon asked.

"Together, I hope," Frank answered.

Words of forgiveness stuck in his throat. Simon knew that meaningless sex happened. Maybe that was what Frank had experienced. He thought of his life without Frank in it and didn't like the picture that emerged.

"Okay," Simon said. "You're forgiven. I told you before that if you did something like this, I didn't want to hear about it. But I'm glad you told me."

Frank's sigh was hard to miss. "Thanks," Frank said. "I know this isn't like you and that girl. I was just stupid. Thanks."

"Don't mention it," Simon said. 'When in doubt,' he reflected, 'borrow a standard Carpenter line.'

73

Jeannie Smith seemed unfazed by the stares directed her way as she set up her stenographer equipment in the conference room. Simon used the delay to survey those in attendance.

Tina Farrell's appearance provided a clue as to why she had never landed a law-related job: the woman was obese. Simon was aware of articles written about discrimination directed at obese individuals, but he hadn't paid much attention to them. He'd ask Meredith to research the subject. If a person was genetically predisposed to a particular body type, it was unfair to punish the individual because of the condition. But this was America where appearances were everything and life was unfair. Farrell was saddled with attributes associated with extremely overweight people: multiple chins, a fat puffy face that made her eyes look small and beady, thick arms and legs. Simon tried to keep his expression neutral as Farrell moved haltingly toward the witness chair and used both hands on the chair arms to take a seat. But he was so taken aback by her appearance that he was fairly certain that his surprise had shown through. There was no getting around the fact that he would have to be a shit and ask her about her weight.

Christopher Blaisedell had traveled from Brooklyn to personally defend this deposition. His firm website picture didn't do him complete justice. True, it captured his long black hair and sparkling blue eyes, but it didn't show his powerful build. Blaisedell was a guy who obviously worked out. His half-moon eyeglasses gave him a serious look, but the guy was built like a brick wall.

Simon glanced behind him where Molly Grant was seated with a notepad at the ready. Rachel had described her as young and energetic, but on this occasion, she appeared nervous, no doubt thinking about her own deposition. Grant was short and trim, with brown wavy hair. Simon wondered why the head of Spenser's placement department had never mentioned Farrell's weight. Perhaps Grant thought it would be discriminatory to do so.

Meredith, plainly excited, was sitting to Simon's left poised to take notes. Simon had used much of the work she had done to formulate the approach he would take during this deposition.

"I'm all set," Jeannie Smith announced. "The usual stipulations?"

Simon and Blaisedell nodded. Smith asked Farrell to rise and Simon found it painful to watch. After Farrell had been sworn in and resumed her seat, Simon proceeded with basic background questions.

"You've stated that you were granted six interviews in your search for a law-related job. Is that correct?" Simon asked, steering his first question toward the heart of the case.

"Yes."

"Were you ever given a follow up interview?"

"No."

"Were you ever given a reason why you were no longer being considered for any of the positions you interviewed for?"

"No."

"Did you ever follow up with any of the places you interviewed at as to why you were no longer being considered?"

"No."

"Do you have any explanation for why any of the places you interviewed no longer considered you as a job candidate?"

Farrell paused for a long moment. "Not really."

"Before any of the interviews you went on, did you obtain any assistance on how to conduct yourself during an interview?"

"No," Farrell said.

"If you had been hired by any of the six prospective employers you had interviewed with, would your job duties have required you to interact with members of the public?"

Farrell looked flustered and Simon wondered whether she had figured out where his last question was headed.

"I think all of the jobs would have had me meet with members of the public. There were four law firm interviews and I would have had dealings with clients if I had been hired. And there were two government agency positions where I would have been involved in agency hearings."

Simon consulted his deposition outline. "You said that you are currently employed as a secretary for an insurance company. Is that correct?"

"Yes."

"In that job, do you meet with members of the public?"

Farrell colored slightly. "No. I pretty much report to a vice-president."

"Have you asked your superior whether the insurance company can make use of your legal training?"

"I think I mentioned something like that to my boss."

"What happened?"

"He said he would look into it."

"Did he?"

"I'm not sure."

"Did your boss ever get back to you on that subject?"

Farrell lowered her head. "No."

"Did you bring it up again?"

"No."

"How long ago did you raise this subject with your boss?"

Farrell frowned in concentration. "About six months ago. I'm not sure exactly."

Simon had Farrell's Spenser School of Law file marked as a deposition exhibit.

"Spenser School of Law provided your counsel with a copy of this document, which has been marked as Exhibit 1. Have you reviewed this document?"

"Yes."

"This is your law school file, Ms. Farrell. Did you discover anything that is inaccurate in this document?"

Farrell idly flipped through pages. "No."

"Do you believe that there is any document that should be in the file that isn't in the file?"

Simon was puzzled by the desultory way Farrell skimmed pages. He had expected a more intense scrutiny by a named plaintiff in the litigation.

"I can't think of anything at the moment."

"Did you engage in any extracurricular activities while you were a law student at Spenser?"

"No."

"Is there a reason you didn't engage in any extracurricular activities?"

Farrell shrugged. "I didn't have time, really."

"Were you employed at all during your years in law school?"

"No."

"Were you aware that other law students had time for extracurricular activities?"

"I guess so. It's not something I gave much thought to."

Simon had Jeannie Smith designate a document as Exhibit 2, and placed it before Farrell.

"Ms. Farrell, Exhibit 2 is a copy of a document that was on Spenser's website during the years you were at the law school. It's entitled 'Clinical Programs and Activities.' Have you seen this document before today?"

Farrell again shrugged. "I probably did. I don't really remember."

"Would you please read the portion of Exhibit 2 highlighted in yellow?'

Farrell sighed as she drew the document closer. "'Spenser School of Law offers a wide variety of clinical programs and activities that will enhance a student's law school experience. These programs and activities provide hands-on, practical training and are likely to increase a student's success in finding legal employment.'"

Farrell looked up without expression, as if she had shut off a part of herself to get through this deposition.

"Thank you. Would it be correct that you voluntarily made the decision not to participate in the programs and activities referred to in the paragraph you just read?"

"I guess so."

"Do you agree that it would have increased your chances of finding a law-related job if you had participated in an outside program or activity?"

"Objection," Blaisedell intervened. "Answer the question if you can."

"I don't know," Farrell said after a long pause.

"Do you agree that if all other things are essentially equal with respect to two job applicants, the applicant with extracurricular activities has an advantage over the applicant with no extracurricular activities?"

"Objection," Blaisedell repeated.

"I don't know," Farrell said. "I suppose that's possible."

After Smith marked a document as Exhibit 3, Simon asked Farrell whether she could identify the document.

"That's my current resume," Farrell said.

"Is this the form of your resume that you sent to the prospective employers who interviewed you?"

"No. Molly Grant, who's sitting behind you, suggested some changes to my resume which I made after the interviews."

"Do you see the line reading 'References furnished upon request?'"

"Yes."

"Was that line listed on the resume that you sent to the six prospective employers who interviewed you?"

"Yes."

"If one of those employers had asked you to provide references, who would you have provided as references?"

Simon was certain his last question had caught Farrell off guard.

"I'm not sure. I would probably use my boss at the insurance company."

"Were you working at the insurance company at the time you had the six interviews you told us about?"

"No."

"Then let me repeat my question. If asked, who would you have used as a reference at the time of the six interviews?"

"I'm not sure."

"Did you know any Spenser School of Law professor well enough to ask for a reference?"

"Probably not," Farrell said, reddening.

"During law school, were you outspoken in class?"

"Not really. I'd answer if a professor called on me."

"Does that mean that you typically didn't speak up in class unless called upon?"

"Pretty much so."

Simon looked over his deposition outline.

"May I have a break?" Farrell asked.

"Of course," Simon replied. "Whenever you need a break just ask. Shall we say ten minutes?"

Blaisedell left the conference room with his client. When the door closed, Grant spoke first.

"I feel sorry for her."

Meredith agreed, but she wasn't about to say so. Under Simon's persistent, probing questions, Farrell reminded her of an onion being peeled away layer by layer so that at the end of the deposition, all that would be left of Farrell was a small, round, insignificant bud.

"The woman has sued your employer," Simon pointed out to Grant.

"I know. But I still feel sorry for her."

"Get over it. If Farrell's lawyer makes you squirm when he takes your deposition, I assure you Farrell will have no sympathy for you."

Grant fell silent. Meredith scanned Simon's deposition outline. If Grant felt sorry for Farrell now, she might be overcome in the next hour.

"Did anyone associated with Spenser School of Law promise or guarantee you that you would have a law-related job upon your graduation from the law school?" Simon began after the break.

Farrell paused and Meredith sensed for the first time during this deposition that she was angry.

"No," Farrell said, "but the law school boasted about how it did a good job placing graduates with legal jobs."

Simon studied Farrell and then turned to Blaisedell. "For the record, Mr. Blaisedell, I'm going to object to your client's last answer after the word 'no' and I move to strike the answer after the word 'no.'"

"Also for the record," Blaisedell said, "the witness' answer was responsive to your question and shouldn't be stricken."

Farrell give her attorney a grateful look.

"Let's go back over your last answer," Simon resumed. "Is it correct that no one associated with Spenser School of Law promised or guaranteed you a law-related job upon your graduation from the law school?"

Anger flashed again in Farrell's eyes.

"Yes, that's correct."

"Thank you. Now let's turn to the part of your answer where you referred to the law school boasting about how it did a good job placing graduates with legal jobs. Do you recall telling us that moments ago?"

"Yes, that's what I said."

"Can you be more specific about the law school boasting?"

"It was on the school's website," Farrell replied assertively. "And I think there was something in the application documents that the law school sent out to me."

"Besides the law school's website and the application documents you just mentioned, do you recall any other source of the law school boasting?"

Farrell again frowned in concentration. "Not at this time."

Simon jotted down a note. Meredith was struck by his deliberate, persistent style.

"Let's start with the law school's website. Please tell me what the law school boasted on its website."

"It's like I said before. The school boasted it did a good job placing graduates in legal jobs."

"Did the law school provide a percentage figure as to legal-job placements?"

Farrell shrugged. "It might have. I don't remember."

"What else do you remember about the website posting that you've described as boasting?"

"Not much else."

Simon had a document marked as Exhibit 4 and handed it to Farrell. "Do you recognize this document?" he asked.

Farrell took her time reading the document. "It looks familiar," she said when she looked up.

"What's familiar about it?"

"It looks like what I saw on the law school's website."

"For the record, I'm going to identify Exhibit 4 as a copy of a Spenser School of Law website posting that existed in 2008, the year after you graduated. In the second paragraph, what does the fifty-one percent refer to?"

Farrell studied the deposition exhibit. "It refers to the percentage of law school graduates placed in legal jobs based on responses to a questionnaire."

"Now that you have studied Exhibit 4, are you able to identify it as the kind of website posting you've described as boasting?"

"It could be. I'm not totally sure."

"If this was the only type of law school website posting that mentioned graduates being placed in law-related jobs, would you agree that Exhibit 4 would be the kind of document you have told us contained boasting?"

"Objection," Blaisedell intervened.

"Please answer my question," Simon said.

"I suppose it would have to be," Farrell acknowledged.

"Would you agree that a fair reading of Exhibit 4 shows that forty-nine percent of law school graduates were not placed in a law-related job?"

"I guess so if you're just asking about the math."

"Did you consider during or after your law school education that you had a slightly less than fifty percent chance of not ending up with a law-related job?"

"Did I consider that?" Farrell asked. "I don't think I thought about it like that."

"During law school, did you consider the possibility that you would not find a law-related job after graduation?"

"I suppose it was in the back of my mind. But when I graduated in the top third of my class, I don't think I thought about that."

"Are you saying that graduating in the top third of your class entitled you to a law-related job?"

"Objection," Blaisedell said.

"I never said that."

"Then what is the relevance to your graduating in the top third of your class to your obtaining a law-related job?"

"I think my class rank helped me. I thought that graduating in the top third of my class was a plus."

"Is there anything in Exhibit 4 that you claim is false or misleading in any way?"

Farrell took her time reading over the document. Studying the witness, Meredith wondered whether Farrell was aware of the importance of her next answer.

"I don't know," Farrell finally said. "I have no way of knowing whether the percentage figure you asked me about is correct or not. Also, I couldn't tell you whether the 2008 date you asked me to read is correct. And I couldn't tell you if the law school had more up-to-date information after 2008."

Simon stared at Farrell and the witness was the first to look away. Meredith had decided what would be her next question and was pleased when Simon asked it.

"Is it correct that as you sit here today you cannot identify anything false or misleading on Exhibit 4?"

"Yes, but I mentioned things I don't know about."

"I understand," Simon responded. "Isn't it true that if you don't know about a particular fact, you cannot say that the fact is misleading or false?"

"I guess so. I mean, I wouldn't have knowledge one way or the other."

Simon took a moment to study his notes and then turned to Meredith. "I think I'm going to move on," he whispered. "I think I got out of her that she can't say she knows anything to be false or misleading."

"I agree," Meredith whispered back. "I think you did okay."

"You mentioned the law school boasting in application materials. What was the nature of the law school's boasting in application materials?"

Farrell sighed. "I don't recall the exact words. It was something like 'the law school was successful in placing graduates in legal positions.'"

"Did you save the application materials you've been describing?"

"No."

Simon had Jeannie Smith mark a document as Exhibit 5 and placed it before Farrell. "Do you recognize this document?"

Farrell took her time going thought the document. "This looks familiar, but I can't say I recall this specific document."

"What I've handed you are copies of pages from the law school application kit that was sent to individuals interested in applying for admission to the law school for the class of 2007. Please read aloud the fourth paragraph on the second page."

Farrell first read the passage silently. "'Spenser School of Law has had success placing graduates in legal positions. The school's placement department will assist graduates in finding a law-related job.'"

"Do you regard the language you just read as boasting?"

"Yeah, I do," Farrell said in a combative tone.

"During your three years at the law school, did you visit the placement office?"

"I'm sure I did."

"Do you specifically recall such a visit?"

"No."

"Did you contact the placement office during the time of the six job interviews you told us about earlier?"

"No. I contacted the placement office after those interviews fell through."

"Please describe all the placement office contacts that you can recall."

"I don't remember who I spoke to, but I said that I'd had some interviews that didn't work out and did she have any suggestions."

"What was the response?"

"As best as I can remember, I was told to check the bulletin board postings in the placement office."

"What else do you remember?"

"That was pretty much it. The placement office was useless."

"Did you visit the placement department bulletin board?"

"No."

"Subsequently to being referred to the placement department bulletin board, did Ms. Grant provide you with any assistance?"

"Yes. I called the placement department. I went in to see her and she made suggestions for rewording my resume. And she's sent me the names of firms and agencies that have contacted her about job openings."

"Has Ms. Grant been helpful to you?"

Farrell glanced in Grant's direction. "She's shown interest. But she hasn't been able to locate a job for me."

"That's not what I asked," Simon said. "My question is, has Ms. Grant been helpful to you?"

"I suppose so. Can I have another break?"

In Meredith's opinion, Farrell looked anything but refreshed following her second break. Simon continued to appear loaded for bear.

"In 2008, did anything happen to the United States economy that you are aware of?"

"I think there was a recession."

"What effect did the recession have on your ability to obtain a law-related job?"

"Objection!" Blaisedell said.

"Do I have to answer?" Farrell asked.

"If you can," Blaisedell said.

"I don't know for sure," Farrell said. "I'm sure the recession wasn't helpful to anyone trying to find a job."

"Were you aware of law firms laying off lawyers during the recession?"

"I think I read about that happening."

"Is it your understanding that it is harder to find a job during a recession than during a period when no recession is occurring?"

"Objection," Blaisedell said.

"I wouldn't say it's my understanding. I would assume it's harder to find a job during a recession, but I couldn't tell you for sure."

"Did you apply to other law schools besides Spenser?"

"Yes."

"Which ones?"

"If I remember correctly, Suffolk, BC, BU and Northeastern."

"Were you accepted by any of those law schools?"

"No."

"Was Spenser the only law school that accepted you?"

Farrell glared at Simon. "Yes."

"Did you review the national rankings of the law schools you applied to?"

"Probably. I don't remember for sure."

"Did Spenser School of Law have the lowest national ranking of the law schools that you did apply to?"

"It may have. I don't know for sure one way or the other."

"Is it your understanding that the higher the ranking of a graduate's law school, the better the graduate's chance of obtaining a law-related job?"

"Objection," Blaisedell said. "The witness can't be expected to give an expert opinion on the effect of law school rankings."

"I didn't ask for her opinion," Simon said. "I asked her for her understanding. Please read the question back," he directed Smith.

Farrell listened to the question being read back with a sour expression. "I suppose that the higher a law school's ranking, the better it is for a graduate trying to find a job."

"Why did you apply to law school?" Simon changed the subject.

"It was something I was interested in," Farrell answered in what Meredith viewed as an indifferent tone.

"Before accepting admission to Spenser, did you do any looking into whether a law career was right for you?"

"Objection," Blaisedell said. "Answer if you can."

"Could you rephrase the question?" Farrell said.

"Are you aware of any studies that conclude that lawyers are dissatisfied with their profession?" Simon asked without missing a beat.

"Yeah," Farrell said, nodding.

"Before accepting admission to Spenser did you do any looking into whether a law career would be a satisfying profession for you?"

Farrell frowned in concentration. Meredith recalled her own decision to attend Spenser. Her decision was not preceded by any effort to discover whether she would actually like law. But, as luck would have it, she did.

"I don't recall looking into that," Farrell said. "But I may have."

"Would it be correct that you have no way of knowing whether, if you obtained a law-related job, you would find the job satisfying?"

"Right, I have no way of knowing. But I sure wish I'd had the opportunity to find out. I liked law school pretty much, so I don't see why I wouldn't like doing something in law."

"But you don't know one way or the other whether any law job you obtained would be satisfying, correct?"

"Right. I have no way of knowing because I haven't been able to get a legal job. Is it okay if we take another break?"

"Let's make this a lunch break," Simon said to Blaisedell.

"Sure," Blaisedell agreed. "About how much time do you think you'll need to finish your questions?"

"I'm going to check my notes during the break. I'll let you know when we resume. Let's continue in an hour."

After Blaisedell and Farrell left the conference room, Simon turned to Jeannie Smith. "Any impressions?" he asked.

Meredith was taken aback. She couldn't recall any Pinkerton lawyer asking a stenographer for an opinion on what had transpired.

"She doesn't like you," Smith said.

"I don't care about that," Simon replied.

"You and Carpenter are a lot alike, then."

"What do you think?" Simon asked again.

"She didn't say anything that was damaging to the law school except when it came to the placement office. Is that what you wanted to know?"

Simon nodded. "Anything else?"

"You just have to look at her to know why nobody hired her," Smith said. "Are you going to get into that?"

"Of course," Simon said. "Wouldn't Carpenter?"

Simon asked his first question after the lunch break. "Have you ever consulted with a physician or person with medical training about being overweight?"

"Objection!" Blaisedell shouted. "What kind of a question is that?"

Simon regarded Blaisedell evenly; the plaintiffs' attorney was visibly pissed off. Farrell was not as irate as Meredith suspected she would be. Perhaps Farrell had seen Simon's question coming or had considered her obesity in connection with employer rejections.

"The question is pertinent because it may be that in being turned down by the places she interviewed, Ms. Farrell's appearance has influenced the prospective employers' decisions."

"This is totally out of line," Blaisedell said.

"Are you instructing Ms. Farrell not to answer my question?"

There was a moment when Meredith thought that Blaisedell would reach across the table, grab Simon by the throat, and beat him senseless. He didn't, but Blaisedell remained furious. He had a practical dilemma: if he instructed Farrell not to answer Simon's question a judge might disagree with that advice and, if that were to happen, Blaisedell would have to return to Boston to resume the deposition.

"It's none of your business whether Ms. Farrell has consulted a physician," Blaisedell said.

"You're right," Simon said, surprising Meredith. "I was trying to lead into the subject I need to cover, and I apologize for the way I did that. Let me ask you another question, Ms. Farrell and, again, I apologize. Do you regard yourself as overweight?"

"Objection," Blaisedell said with less force. "But you may answer."

"Yes."

"Are you aware of the view some people take that it is discrimination for an employer to make a hiring decision based on a person's weight?"

"I've read about that."

"Have you considered that the six places that didn't offer you employment after you interviewed with them, may have declined to consider you further because of your weight?"

"Did I consider that?"

"Yes, that was my question."

"Yes, I considered that."

"And what did you conclude?"

"I have no way of knowing why they decided not to follow up with me."

Simon leaned over toward Meredith. "I'm inclined to leave it here," he whispered.

Meredith couldn't come up with any other appropriate follow-up question. Farrell had at least considered that her weight had adversely affected her ability to land a job. That might be enough when it came to a trial; a jury might conclude that Spenser was not at fault when it came to Farrell failing to land a legal job because her obesity had held her back. "I'd also leave it here, Meredith whispered. "You got her to admit that she considered her weight. That's probably as good as we can get."

Simon nodded and straightened in his chair.

"Since law school graduation, did you ever consider opening up your own office?" Simon asked.

"I considered it, but I didn't think it was a good idea."

"Why not?"

"I didn't have any clients and I lacked experience."

"Were you aware there were opportunities to take court-appointed cases?"

"I knew about that. But criminal law doesn't interest me, and I had heard that civil case appointments such as in probate court cases are hard to get and don't pay well."

"So you considered opening your own office but decided on balance not to do so. Is that correct?"

"Yes."

Simon consulted his deposition outline for several minutes, seemingly unconcerned with the lengthy silence. When he looked up, he studied Farrell for another long moment.

"Thank you, Ms. Farrell," Simon said in the same neutral tone he had asked her questions. "That concludes my questions for you. I apologize if any of my questions caused you any discomfort, but I have a client to represent and the questions I asked needed to be asked." Simon turned to Blaisedell. "Do you have any questions?"

"No."

"Then the deposition is concluded."

Molly Grant had departed and Jeannie Smith had just concluded her questions on spelling. As she stowed her gear Smith looked at Simon. "I suppose you're going to ask me again what I think."

"Carpenter would take me to task if I didn't."

"I wouldn't hire the woman," Smith said. "She's probably not stupid but anybody wanting to hire a lawyer could probably do better."

"Harsh," Simon said. "That's what someone looking to hire a lawyer might have said about me after I graduated from law school," he elaborated.

Meredith, on the other hand, had never doubted that anyone who hired her would be getting a bargain. She tended to forget that neither Simon nor Rachel had landed a law-related job after graduating from Spenser.

"I'll tell you one thing that Carpenter wouldn't have done," Smith said. "He wouldn't have apologized for asking tough questions."

Meredith was surprised to see Simon smile.

"I did that for you," Simon responded to Smith. "I didn't want you to think that Carpenter and I were totally alike."

74

Philly was on duty with Daisy and Rosalind this morning. Maybe it had been a mistake to take the girls on her own. Yesterday she had decided that morning spinning was over until she delivered. Now she doubted her ability to spring into action if one of the girls needed immediate help. Sarah Ferguson would return from a medical appointment in two hours. But what if she suddenly went into premature labor? What if one of the girls needed rescuing? Maybe Paul would venture out of his jurisdiction, arrive in a squad car with lights flashing and the siren on.

Using her feet to avoid bending over, Philly had arranged clear plastic over a section of the living room that was not carpeted. The girls were playing with drawing paper and finger paints and were behaving themselves. Philly would call out a color and Daisy was quick to catch on and use the named color next. Rosalind ignored the color change directions. Philly prayed that this activity would take up some of the two hours before Sarah returned. A snack would eat up additional time.

When her cell phone sounded, Philly started. With Raul's help, calls to her office line automatically transferred to her cell phone. The idea was to keep her off the stairs.

"This is Philly."

"It's Daniel Spring, Ms. Sullivan. This time I remembered your married name."

"How nice to speak with you again. And thanks again for referring Brendon O'Day. That case may settle in his favor."

"I hope you don't mind, but I gave your name to a family whose son got suspended from high school."

"Of course I don't mind." Philly tried to muster up enthusiasm when all she could think about was surviving the next two hours.

"The boy was wearing a T-shirt that said, 'Jesus Loves Gays, Lesbians, and the Transgendered.' The high school principal asked him to invert the shirt and the kid said no and was sent home."

Philly silently bemoaned the fact that if the case came her way, she wouldn't be able to work on it. Over the years, the cases she had most enjoyed involved teenagers.

"I think I told you that three other lawyers and I have formed a firm," she explained. "At the moment I'm very pregnant. But even if I go into labor, my partners can handle the case."

"Excellent. And congratulations. The family's last name is Cohen. I've known Arthur Cohen for years. The son's name is Nathan."

"I hope you know how much I appreciate your keeping me in mind."

"That's my pleasure. I hope they contact you."

"Hey Daisy! Cut that out! The paint goes on the paper, not on Rosalind."

"Excuse me!"

"Sorry Mr. Spring. I'm on babysitting duty right now."

"Not a problem. I'll leave you to it."

Rosalind's arms were adorned with blue streaks, and blue smudges appeared on her forehead and cheeks. She looked kind of punk in a toddler way.

"Anyone want a snack?" Philly called out.

The girls were happily munching on Cheerios and apple slices when Philly's cell phone rang again. "This is Philly."

"Hi. It's Fay Richardson. Sorry I've taken so long to get back to you."

"Not a problem," Philly responded. She eyed the girls, who were jabbering at each other in the incomprehensible language that worked for them. They seemed reasonably content.

"I talked with Selena," Fay Richardson said. "You were right. I needed to talk this through with someone I trust."

Philly remembered Richardson predicting that Selena Boyd would advise her to fight rather than settle for the $100,000 the defendants had offered.

"You can tell them that I will not settle for a penny less than one hundred twenty thousand. If they're willing to pay that, I propose that your firm and I each take half of the extra twenty thousand. I don't like the idea of you reducing your fee so much."

Philly knew that her partners would be willing to keep to the fee arrangement she had previously proposed to Richardson. But that was a bridge to cross only if Patrick Lassiter accepted the higher figure. "I'll pass that on to their attorney."

"Do you know whether Al is contributing to the payment?" Richardson asked.

"I don't know," Philly replied. "I had the investigator look at his assets, but he found nothing significant."

"Selena wanted me to insist that Al pay at least twenty-five thousand of any settlement, but I think that's because she hates Al's guts. I'm not particularly fond of Al, but I didn't think it was worth the hassle to insist that he pay something."

"As it is, you've drawn a hard-and-fast line in the sand. The case will be easier to settle if we stay away from insisting that part of any settlement payment come from Townsend."

"That's what I thought. I'm comfortable with this. If they say no, I'm not going to regret waiting for the appeal to be decided."

"Excellent," Philly said. There was a lot to be said for a client who could make up her mind.

Carpenter startled when his phone rang.

"It's Brendan O'Day. Is this a good time to talk?"

"Yes, it is, actually. Have you considered what the college has proposed?"

"I have. I don't want to agree to a reprimand or any kind of censure such as a brief suspension. I didn't do anything wrong and I'm not about to agree to anything that permits those assholes to save face and leave something negative on my record."

Carpenter had expected this reaction. In O'Day's position, he would have been equally adamant against throwing the college and dean any sort of bone.

"All right. I'll let the other side know."

"Do you think I'm making a mistake taking a hard line?" O'Day asked.

"Not really," Carpenter replied. "The college's proposal is more reasonable than anything it mentioned previously. I don't have a feel for what the college and the dean are thinking."

"I'll tell you what they're thinking," O'Day said. "They're thinking of the shit-storm of negative publicity they'll have to deal with if it were publicly alleged that the Quinn woman used the rally to kill someone. I think you've got them on the run."

O'Day had made a fair point. Stephen Larson's about-face, conciliatory approach suggested that Baywater State and Dean Sternman were thinking about damage control. "I'll tell the other lawyer no on accepting a reprimand or anything like a reprimand. If they say no deal, we can revisit things then."

"Go for it," O'Day said.

Rachel and Simon hadn't been joking when they told Meredith that Carpenter was picky when it came to drafting complaints. Meredith wondered whether his red revisions, cross-outs, and annotations were more extensive than her originally drafted document. She'd had the same chastened feeling when Carpenter had worked over the legal memorandum she had drafted for the O'Day case. It was particularly galling that Carpenter's amendments and suggestions improved the complaint she'd drafted for Noreen Clark. Had she learned nothing in the years she had worked at Pinkerton?

Now, in addition to the complaint, she needed to put together an affidavit for Noreen Clark, an affidavit for her ex-boyfriend, Kevin James, and a legal memorandum supporting Clark's request to prevent Sloan-Webster School of Law from communicating to anyone the fact that Clark had plagiarized. With luck, perhaps she would be able to use an affidavit from Flash. Carpenter had provided her with copies of affidavits and legal memoranda that he and Philly had drafted in other cases. Looking at the work ahead of her, it finally sank in that she'd be working her ass off on documents and then going to court without being paid for any of those efforts. And if Clark lost her case, she would never be paid for the hours she'd expended. Also, since Clark was basically broke, Meredith had resigned herself to fronting the costs to pay for Flash's services.

At Pinkerton, she'd been insulated from the economic realities of practicing law. Every month a twelfth of a substantial annual salary was directly deposited into her bank account, and a yearly bonus also magically appeared. She'd accepted those monthly and annual occurrences as a given and never considered what the Pinkerton partners had to deal with to make those deposits happen. She'd been counting on the Pinkerton settlement as a nest egg. But now she foresaw dipping into those funds. She had purchased malpractice insurance, deciding on a million dollars of coverage without a clue as to whether that figure left her over or under exposed. She had ordered her own letterhead, deciding to spring for a classy paper grade that she probably didn't need. She had bought a combination printer-fax-scanner that she had yet to use. If it weren't for being paid for the work she'd done on the Spenser and O'Day cases, she would already have made inroads on the Pinkerton settlement funds.

Meredith was certain that she'd be putting in less time on the Spenser and O'Day cases in the near future. The O'Day case might even settle. She could sit in on the remaining depositions of the Spenser case plaintiffs, but she wouldn't be paid for that time. She had helped Simon and Rachel handle the first wave of Spenser case discovery, but that wave had washed up on the shore. She'd probably been naïve in thinking that a position would open up for her at Simon and Rachel's firm.

Meredith rose from her workstation in Carpenter's office and began to pace. She'd been fretting over one of the exchanges during Tina Farrell's deposition. Farrell had rejected the notion of opening up her own law practice because she had no clients and lacked experience. Meredith considered whether she was being forced into solo practice. Her recent meeting with the Beacon Hill headhunter firm had produced no leads to other employment. She'd sent out her resume to numerous Boston firms and had yet to receive a response from any of them. If she went out on her own, she could offer her services to other firms, much as she was doing with Carpenter's firm, but that strategy seemed overly risky. With business hard to come by, any law firm would resist sending work outside of the firm.

Meredith decided to get outside, clear her head, and come to terms with whether she was screwed on the job front.

75

"All right," Stephen Larson said over the phone. "My clients will agree with the terms you said you would recommend to your client. We have a deal."

'That was fast,' Carpenter thought. It had only been a few days since he had rejected Larson's proposal. "Excellent," he said, waiting for the "but."

"But," Larson said, "we'd like O'Day's case dismissed and the settlement terms to be set forth in an agreement that is kept confidential. Also, we want to cap any attorney fees at twenty-five thousand."

Carpenter hesitated only a moment. In Larson's position, he would be seeking to end O'Day's lawsuit in the way Larson had proposed. A court record was public and Baywater State College and Dean Sternman would not want a public document to show that they were admitting defeat. Some legal commentators had inveighed against settlement agreements being kept confidential as a violation of the public's right to know, particularly in cases where a settling party received public funds. But Carpenter favored living in a real, practical world where once the terms of a deal were agreed to, keeping those terms confidential was fair game.

"The separate agreement should be okay," Carpenter replied.

"What about the legal fee cap"" Larson inquired.

"I need to circle back with O'Day but I'll likely recommend it." Carpenter couldn't imagine his firm's legal fees exceeding twenty-five thousand. "Let's assume that I'll clear that with my client. Who's going to draft the settlement papers?"

"I've got an associate prepped to do a first draft. I'll get the draft over to you shortly."

"Wait for me to get back to you before you send me any drafts."

"Fair enough. Anything else?"

Carpenter took his time with Larson's question. "I want the settlement agreement to make clear that this student newspaper incident is a non-event. By that I mean your clients are to act as if it never happened and so will mine. In terms of O'Day's advancement, lack of advancement, standing with the college, this whole event never happened. Plus, we need to make clear that O'Day remains the faculty advisor to the student newspaper until his current appointment runs out. Should he apply to remain the newspaper's faculty advisor after his current term expires, my expectation is that his application will be decided on its merits with no reference to the rally or the news article."

Now Larson took his time. Carpenter wondered whether the college and dean had contemplated firing O'Day when the flap over the news article had subsided.

"I don't disagree with your request. I'll simply point out that people may nurse grudges and all the settlement language in the world isn't going to prevent them from acting shabbily."

"We do what we can do," Carpenter said, now not trusting the college and its dean. Had Larson just given him an indication that the dean might retaliate against O'Day? In Larson's position, he wouldn't have rambled on about grudges being nursed.

After hanging up with Larson, Carpenter phoned O'Day.

"So they want to keep this quiet," O'Day commented after Carpenter had filled him in on how the settlement would be handled.

"Yes, they do. I'd be doing the same thing in their position. If keeping silent about this is something you can't live with, now is the time to speak up."

"I don't like it, but I'll live with it," O'Day said.

"Good. It's time to move on. If you are asked about your lawsuit, you may say that the matter has been resolved and that you have no further comment."

"Even though I have much further comment."

"Right, even though you have much further comment. I'm serious about this. If you're not going to abide by a confidentiality provision, then don't take the deal."

"No, I'll go along, even though the college may have it in for me," O'Day said. "And thanks. I appreciate everything you've done for me."

They had assembled in the living room of Kevin James' cramped one-bedroom apartment in Jamaica Plains. Flash directed Meredith, Noreen, and Kevin to a threadbare couch and sat on the floor with Noreen's laptop. She had turned the device on and entered her password. Flash began typing and Meredith couldn't believe how fast his fingers were moving. He retrieved a device from a large black duffle bag, plugged it into the laptop, and resumed typing. He stared at the screen for a moment and then removed the device he'd installed.

"I believe the article is lost on your laptop," Flash said to Noreen. "Your laptop appears to be infected by a virus that has made it inoperable. I believe you've lost everything."

"Great!" Noreen said, sulking.

At Flash's request, Kevin turned on his laptop, entered his password, and passed the laptop to Flash. James struck Meredith as a studious type. He worked as an adjunct English teacher in a small community college in Salem. He had longish brown hair which he constantly brushed back from his dark-framed glasses and the way he stole glances at Noreen suggested to Meredith that he still cared for her.

Flash moved Noreen's laptop aside and began to type on Kevin's laptop.

After a short while he looked up. "Did you know you have Safe@HomePlate?" he asked James.

"I don't really know what it is," James responded sheepishly. "I get a bill from them yearly on my credit card and I pay it."

"It's a backup system," Flash explained. "We may get lucky."

Flash asked Noreen for the early draft of her article she was able to find and studied the document. "What are these closed parentheses for?" he asked. "They're all over the place."

"I used them to remind me to add a footnote or text," Noreen said. "I explained that to the assistant dean who interviewed me."

Flash began typing. He stared at the screen and began to nod. "I need some plain white paper," he said to Kevin and Kevin left the room.

Flash had a printer set up to the laptop when James returned with paper. "And we're off," Flash said as the printer engaged.

"Can I see?" Noreen asked after Flash had collected a number of pages.

"Not yet," Flesh said. "Be patient."

"This is killing me!" Noreen protested.

Flash ignored her and calmly stacked each page to emerge from the printer. When the printer stopped, Flash addressed Kevin. "Just out of curiosity, do you remember the title of the article?"

Kevin took a deep breath and closed his eyes. "I didn't read the article," he said, his eyes opening. "The title was something like 'An Analysis of the Legal Arguments For and Against Obamacare.'" He paused. "There was a subtitle. Something like 'Reviewing the Legal Arguments Before the Supreme Court.'"

Flash smiled. "Close enough," he said. "Noreen's title was 'An Analysis of the Legal Claims For and Against Obamacare.' The subtitle was 'An Examination of the Legal Positions Before the Supreme Court.' Did you ever look at or receive any other version of the article?"

"No," Kevin replied.

"Did you ever alter or forge a date as to when you received or deleted the article?"

Kevin laughed. "No. I wouldn't know how to do that."

Flash handed the article to Noreen and her hands shook as she began to read. Kevin moved closer to her and put a hand on her shoulder. "I don't believe this," Noreen said tearfully, and Meredith shared her disbelief.

"I counted thirty-three pages," Flash said.

"That sounds about right," Noreen said.

Meredith studied the initial double-spaced pages Noreen had finished perusing. She first came to a closed parenthesis on page 8. Once Noreen had handed her the entire article, she located the second one on page 23. The earlier draft of the article had over a dozen closed parentheses in the first ten pages.

Noreen leaned against Kevin. "Are you going to give the law school this article?" she asked Meredith.

"I need to think about that," Meredith said.

"The law school might say you updated your article after you were accused of plagiarizing," Flash said.

"But I got the article before that happened," Kevin said. "Noreen sent it to me."

"I get that," Flash said. He turned toward Noreen. "If the law school has it in for you, it might dispute you wrote what we recovered in April."

"That's ridiculous!" Noreen exclaimed.

"Here's where I'm leaning," Meredith said. "I'm leaning toward going to court to get a court order directing the law school to reverse its plagiarism finding and to notify anyone it told about that finding that Noreen never plagiarized anything. Besides, Noreen may be entitled to damages. Without going to court, I doubt the law school would agree to pay her anything."

"What do you think I should do?" Noreen asked Kevin.

Kevin reddened. He probably hadn't expected Noreen to ask for his advice. "I'd listen to your lawyer," he said, which brought a smile from Flash.

"Now," said Flash, "let's see if I can find a backup for that e-mail."

August

From Meredith's Playlist

"Somebody That I Used To Know"

Gotye

76

This time when Paul met with Samantha Gray, he felt no sense of urgency or concern. He wondered whether the meeting was even necessary and said so.

Gray regarded him impassively. "Don't confuse feeling more comfortable due to the passage of time with getting to the root causes of what led you to see me," she cautioned. "We have one more planned meeting after this, and I would like to keep to our original plan. I can't do it at our regular time, so I'll call you to reschedule."

"Fair enough," Paul responded. "But if my wife delivers, I may need a rain check."

"That can be arranged. The two of you must be very excited."

"I'd add nervous," Paul said.

"What are you nervous about?"

"The baby being healthy. I told you we'd held off learning the sex. The sex doesn't really matter so long as the baby's healthy."

"And if the baby isn't healthy..."

"I don't know. We'd just have to deal with whatever the problem was." Paul had never been a believer in the notion that misfortune only landed in the lap of a person who could deal with it. If that notion were true, he and Philly would have a healthy kid, because he doubted he'd be able to deal with a severely compromised baby. And misfortune certainly was going around. You couldn't pick up a newspaper without seeing some statistic about an infant dealing with a rare, fatal or debilitating disease that only affected a minuscule percentage of the population. All those minuscule percentages associated with rare afflictions added up.

"I've found in my practice that people you would least expect to do so, rise to the occasion. You have described to me a solid marriage. I suspect that you and your wife would be able to address any challenge that came your way."

For a moment, Paul couldn't figure out how the subject had drifted to this depressing topic. Then he remembered—his stated desire for a healthy baby.

"Naturally all parents want their baby to be healthy," Gray said. "I'm wondering whether this topic we've touched on has any connection with the reason you came to see me, which was your concern that something would happen to you and your wife would be left alone. Do you think there's a connection?"

If there was a connection, Paul couldn't easily discern it. "Both subjects concern tragedy," he said.

"That's true. But in one situation, you are the victim of a tragedy and your wife is left to cope alone. In the situation we've been talking about today, the tragedy concerns your upcoming baby. Is there a link there?"

"I'm not sure," Paul responded. "In the first situation that landed me here, I was worrying about being killed on the job. In the second situation, I'm doubting my ability to deal with a disabled baby. I don't see a connection."

"Why would you doubt your ability to deal with a disabled baby? You told me how you encouraged your wife to forgive the drunk teenager who ran down her fiancé. That incident stayed with me; it was a powerful, moving story. You have the ability to see what others need to do to get beyond a tragedy. So I'm curious why you have doubts about your own ability to do so."

Paul had no ready answer to Gray's question. Was he only now discovering that he was brave when telling others what they needed to do, but a coward when it came to what he needed to do? Would he end his sessions with Gray feeling more unsettled than before they began?

"I don't know," Paul said weakly.

"Here's what I know," Gray said as she leaned forward in the chair opposite his. "I know that you have met every professional challenge that has come your way. I know that you have met the personal challenges that have come your way. On the personal front, you had the courage to move out of a marriage that wasn't working and enter into a marriage that has been rich for you. I'm simply going to point out that based on your track record, it's a mistake to think that you will not meet any adversity that comes your way."

Paul was tempted to say 'Easier said than done,' but held back. Somehow that damn hostage episode with Evelyn had spooked him. Gray had previously said he had discovered what he had to lose. Well, he didn't want to lose anything, least of all his nerve.

"Have I unsettled you?" Gray asked.

"A little, I guess. I wasn't counting on leaving here with more things to think about than when I came in."

"That was not my intent," Gray said. "It is my intent to help you draw connections between issues and to help you use the connections in a positive way."

Gray's explanation was fine as far it went, but Paul's takeaway was that it came down to you in the end. Whether it was dealing with his job or a new kid, he had to come to terms with his fears. "It all comes down to me," he said.

"Which is as it should be," Gray replied.

77

A High School Student

"What's up?" Carpenter asked when he picked up his phone after seeing Philly's cell phone number on his caller ID.

"I want you to return a phone call I just got. It's a referral from Daniel Spring. He's the teacher's union rep who sent O'Day our way."

"I remember the guy," Carpenter replied. "Why aren't you returning the call?"

"The truth is I'm not going to be able to work on the case. I'm as big as a cow and can barely move. We can do a conference call if you really want to. But I'd just as soon you deal with it from the get-go. You can tell the guy—his name is Arthur Cohen—that I'm close to delivering and asked you to fill in."

Carpenter remembered Philly participating in work matters up to the very end when she was pregnant with Daisy. "Are you doing okay with this pregnancy?"

"Yeah, I suppose so. I'm just so damn big and I get tired easily. I guess that's got me a little down."

"No problem," Carpenter said. "I'll make the call. What's the story?"

Rachel was the first one who happened to walk past Carpenter's open office door, so he chose her to be on his call to Arthur Cohen. "Just listen," he said as he entered Cohen's number, pressed "speaker," and directed Rachel to his visitor's chair.

"Arthur Cohen."

"Mr. Cohen. I'm returning your call to Philomena Sullivan. My name's Carpenter. I'm Ms. Sullivan's partner. You're on a speaker phone so another of my partners, Rachel Boyle, can listen in. Ms. Sullivan is scheduled to give birth at any time now and she asked me to get back to you. Daniel Spring gave Ms. Sullivan a general idea of the situation with your son, Nathan, and she filled me in. Why don't you give me further details and we can tell you whether this is something we can help you with."

"I was really hoping that Ms. Sullivan would be on this call."

Carpenter put aside Cohen's insensitivity to Philly's situation. "That's really not possible at the moment. Mr. Spring informed her that you were looking for prompt action. At Ms. Sullivan's request, we thought it best to contact you immediately."

"Very well," Cohen said resignedly. "You're right—this is about my son Nathan. Nathan wore a T-shirt to high school that got him suspended at the end of the last school year. I do need to address this before the new school year starts."

While Carpenter listened to Cohen's account as Rachel busily took notes, he was struck by how little it took to divert educators from their primary task. When he was in high school, students weren't allowed to wear jeans or T-shirts. Nowadays, they apparently could wear whatever the hell they wanted. He had his doubts about whether a strict dress code improved education. Teenagers, whatever they were required to wear, would think about sex more often than not. Maybe T-shirts should be banned from school *unless* they conveyed a message, the more controversial and outrageous the better, to distract teens from thinking about getting laid.

According to Cohen, the principal of the Edward Gibbon High School in West Roxbury believed a T-shirt announcing Jesus' love for anyone who was not a heterosexual was offensive and insensitive to people who believed in Jesus, was insensitive to people who didn't believe in Jesus, and crossed the line between church and state. In a meeting with Cohen and his son toward the end of the last school year, the principal, Bryson March, was concerned that the T-shirt in question would disrupt school discipline. Cohen pointed out that his son had worn the T-shirt for two days without incident before an assistant principal, policing the corridors, noticed the T-shirt message by chance.

"Is your son gay?" Carpenter asked.

"If we hire you, you can ask him," Cohen replied.

"How long was Nathan suspended?" Rachel asked.

"Three days. Then he went back to school without the T-shirt."

"What is it you envision a lawyer doing for you?" Carpenter asked.

"Nathan wants to be allowed to wear his T-shirt to school."

"Do you want to sue?" Carpenter clarified.

"If that's what it takes, yes," Cohen confirmed.

"Ms. Sullivan and I have had our share of cases involving students and teachers," Carpenter said. "We're interested in your son's case. If you decide to hire us and you wish to bring suit immediately, then Ms. Boyle and I will handle the matter. It's just not practical for Ms. Sullivan to take the lead at this time."

"And, of course, we would have to meet with your son," Rachel pointed out.

"I'll talk it over with Nathan. I'm not sure how he's going to react when he learns that Ms. Sullivan isn't available."

"We look forward to hearing from you," Carpenter said. "Let us know one way or the other what you and Nathan decide."

"This sounds like a fun case," Rachel said when Carpenter ended the call.

"What would Jesus do?" Carpenter asked. "I guess we'll have to take his deposition to find out."

It was a warm evening and Maxine had wanted to eat outside. They were at a seafood restaurant they liked that was within walking distance from their condo. The outside eating area was in the back of the restaurant bordered by tall hedges that blocked out the views of streets and neighboring buildings and dulled the sound of passing traffic. Their glass-topped table reflected the yellow flames of two candles set in the middle of the table. Carpenter would have preferred a little more light, but he had to admit the setting was restful.

"Are you aware that you've been in a good mood for a while now?" Maxine observed. "You're still crabby, but it's a different kind of crabby. What gives? Who made off with the old crabby guy I've come to know and love?"

"I'm trying to change the way I look at things," Carpenter admitted. "If I was my old self, I'd be silently worrying about the lack of cases we have. But I'm trying to look at the lack of work as a positive. I get to spend more time with you. I get to work out. I'm trying to relax."

"Well, I have to say I like this new Carpenter," Maxine said.

Carpenter didn't respond. He liked his new self and didn't want to jinx it.

"Let's plan a trip," Maxine said. "I'm thinking of Europe, someplace on the ocean."

Carpenter realized that he couldn't point to work as an excuse not to travel. During his marriage, work had been his readymade justification to shoot down travel plans. Now he had partners who could, in a pinch, step into the breach for him, assuming there was enough work to create a breach to step into. "Sounds good," he said.

"You're being far too amendable," Maxine said, fixing him with a probing stare. "I was expecting a month of bitching and moaning from you."

"This is the new Carpenter, remember? My only concern is Philly going into labor and being out and my not being around."

"Let me think about that," Maxine said. "Fair point."

Their entrees were served and they ate for a time in silence. Carpenter sipped at his beer thinking that he didn't have enough money stashed away to seriously consider retirement. There was a time not too recently when he had convinced himself that retirement was never going to be an option; instead he was going to be one of those guys who limped into his office, even in his eighties, because practicing law was the only thing he knew how to do. Now, in this serene evening setting sitting across from Maxine, with guttering candles casting light and shadow this way and that, he could, for the first time, picture a different exit strategy.

"Well, it appears I was wrong," Maxine said. "I actually believed you when you said you were trying to stop thinking about work. But then you go and zone out the way you used to do, and I have to believe you were thinking about work. Is that what you were thinking about?"

"How about Spain or Italy?" Carpenter said.

78

Arthur Cohen and his son, Nathan, looked nothing alike. The father was tall, thin, and pale. Nathan was dark-complexioned, short, and compact. He sat slouched in his conference room chair across from Carpenter, Simon and Rachel.

"Is there anything you want to say to us?" Carpenter asked Nathan.

"Not really. My father told me he filled you in. There's not all that much to tell really."

"Was there a reason you wore the T-shirt to school?" Carpenter asked.

"Yeah. I thought it looked cool and I liked the message. There are a bunch of Jesus freaks at the high school who think anyone who's not straight deserves fire and brimstone. I thought the T-shirt presented a better view."

Rachel wrote down Nathan's last answer. Carpenter showed no reaction to Nathan's short speech. Simon wondered if Nathan's stated reasons for wearing the T-shirt were true.

"I asked your father whether you were gay, and he told me to ask you," Carpenter resumed. "Are you gay?"

Simon hadn't pegged Nathan as gay, but given the way the teen began smirking he was no longer sure.

"I don't think that's anybody's business including yours," Nathan said. "I don't see what my sexual orientation has to do with anything."

Simon glanced at Arthur Cohen. The father seemed to be unconcerned with the subject of his son's sexual orientation.

"You're right about one thing and wrong about another," Carpenter said. "You're right that your sexual orientation is nobody's business. You're wrong if you think your sexual orientation has nothing to do with why you're meeting with us today."

"I don't follow you on that last bit," Nathan said.

"Then let me spell it out for you," Carpenter said in a tone that suggested he had already lost patience with the teen. "Given the message on your T-shirt, your legal claims, if you decide to sue, are affected by your sexual orientation. For example, if you are gay, you may have a claim that you were being singled out for suspension from school because you're gay. You might want to claim that a student wearing a T-shirt proclaiming that Jesus loves heterosexuals would not have been suspended for wearing it."

"I'm bisexual," Nathan said, and Simon thought of Meredith. He had a good handle on his own internal wiring and could comprehend the internal wiring of heterosexuals. Notwithstanding the night he had spent with Meredith, bisexuality was something he had never been able to wrap his mind around.

"There was no reference to bisexuals on your T-shirt," Rachel said.

"So?" Nathan challenged.

"I'm simply stating a fact," Rachel said, a slight, uncharacteristic edge to her voice.

"From a legal point of view, tell us what you want, Nathan," Carpenter said.

"I want to go to school wearing my T-shirt whenever I want."

"Your father explained that you may attend school so long as you don't show up in the T-shirt," Carpenter said. "So if you want to wear the T-shirt at school beginning when school starts up again, you're going to have to get a court order permitting you to do so. That means filing a lawsuit, going before a judge, and trying to persuade the judge to enter an order allowing you back in school wearing your T-shirt."

"What are the odds of getting a judge to do what I want?" Nathan asked.

"I'd say the odds of you getting what you want are less than fifty-fifty. I say that because if I were the judge, I would probably not issue an order allowing you to immediately wear the T-shirt. As a judge, I would probably wait until I heard evidence during a trial before I issued a ruling. A trial probably wouldn't occur until after the upcoming school year was over."

Neither father nor son showed any visible disappointment at Carpenter's answer. Simon found Arthur Cohen's silence mystifying.

"I would like to sue," Nathan declared, and again Simon discerned no reaction to this pronouncement from the teen's father.

"If we took on this case, we would expect to be paid on an hourly basis for our work." Carpenter said. He then listed the partners' hourly rates and Simon was surprised to hear Carpenter add an extra twenty-five dollars to his rate and Rachel's.

"Please send an engagement letter to my attention," Arthur Cohen said, passing over a business card to Carpenter. "Nathan and I will discuss the matter further, and I'll be getting back to you."

"Excellent," Carpenter said. "Thank you for meeting with us. Feel free to call with any additional questions."

"When did our billing rates go up?" Rachel asked when Carpenter had returned to the conference room after showing Arthur and Nathan Cohen out.

Carpenter resumed his seat. "I think it was the moment those two struck me as odd ducks. Did anything strike you as unusual about this meeting?"

"Not really," Simon said. He considered Nathan and his father slightly peculiar and somewhat hard to read but, in terms of a client interview, the just concluded meeting seemed about par for the course.

"The father didn't have much to say, and he did strike me as odd," Rachel said, "but he made clear that he would be the one getting back to you."

"He also struck me as odd," Carpenter acknowledged, "although I don't know exactly why. And I always get concerned when a potential client is told what legal work will be required to help him and he never asks what the legal work will cost. Also, we didn't get a question about whether Nathan could recover legal fees."

"Maybe the father's loaded," Rachel said.

"It's the rich guy who's the first to ask about legal fees," Carpenter said. "That's probably why the guy is rich."

"How come you didn't bring up a retainer?" Simon asked.

"Because unlike Philly in the O'Day case, I missed a trick," Carpenter admitted. "If the father gets back to me, I'll bring it up. I'm thinking of a modest retainer, maybe six thou."

"Divisible by four," Rachel noted.

"You can't go wrong there," Carpenter said.

79

"What's all that noise?" Patrick Lassiter asked when Philly picked up her cell phone in the living room. Daisy and Rosalind were having a giddy moment as they careened about the room at different speeds, both shrieking happily. Philly was in no position to chase after them and had no intention of trying to calm them down. At this point in her pregnancy, her best coping mechanism when she was alone with the kids was to let them wear each other out.

"I'm on babysitting duty," Philly said. "Plus, I'm very pregnant and don't have the energy to tell my charges to keep it down."

Lassiter didn't respond immediately. This was the moment when Fay Richardson's case was either going to go away or linger on for several years. Lassiter hadn't been happy when she had presented him with Richardson's $120,000 bottom line.

"We have a deal," Lassiter said, breaking the pause. "I'd like the case dismissed with prejudice and mutual releases executed that include a confidentiality provision. The dismissal would only be filed once payment was made to your client."

"That sounds reasonable," Philly said. "Why don't you get started on the documents? I'll confirm shortly."

"All right then," Lassiter said. "I'll get to work."

Philly set down her phone and thought about Richardson's case. Before contacting Richardson, Philly wanted to check in with Carpenter. If the settlement went through, there would be a nice infusion of cash to the firm. She needed to ask her partners whether they wanted to give Richardson a further break on attorney fees but, whatever was decided on that issue, a payday was in the offing. 'Every little bit helps,' Philly thought.

80

Meredith needed a break from finalizing the court complaint and accompanying affidavits she would be filing on behalf of Noreen Clark. The work was laborious, largely because for Flash's affidavit, she needed to explain in plain English the technical steps Flash had taken. Simon's deposition of the second plaintiff in the Spenser School of Law case, Felix Hennessey, provided her with a welcome diversion from Clark's problems.

Christopher Blaisedell must have used Tina Farrell's deposition to brief Hennessey on the questions he was likely to be asked; however, in Meredith's opinion, Hennessey had yet to give any indication such witness preparation had taken place.

It was easy to feel sorry for Hennessey, a large, shambling man with a florid complexion and enormous ears. Hennessey had graduated in her class, but Meredith couldn't recall ever seeing him during her three years of law school, and neither Simon nor Rachel remembered him from their law school days. Hennessey was currently selling used cars on commission. He had graduated in the bottom half of his class and had yet to be granted an interview by any of the law firms he had applied to. It had taken him three attempts to pass the Massachusetts bar exam.

Under Simon's questioning, Hennessey conceded that his job hunting success might have been greater if he had participated in an extracurricular activity during law school, agreed that those graduating in the top half of his class had a greater likelihood of landing a law-related job than he did, and admitted that no one associated with Spenser had promised him that he would obtain a law-related job upon graduation. In addition, Hennessey had no idea whether he would be happy with any law-related job he managed to obtain. When asked why he applied to law school, Hennessey replied that he thought it would be "cool" to be a lawyer like one of those lawyers you see on TV.

"Why are you suing Spenser School of Law?" Simon next asked.

"The law school hasn't really done anything to help me get a job. They were supposed to have a placement office to help you out, but as far as I can tell, that office doesn't really do anything."

"When did you first contact the placement office for assistance?"

"Less than a year ago."

"Who did you speak with?"

"Molly Grant."

"Did Ms. Grant help you in any way?"

"Yeah. She said that she had just taken over the placement department and she promised to send me job opportunities that came to her office."

"Did she do what she said she would do?"

"Yes. She's been sending me e-mails about job opportunities."

"Did you ever complain to her that she wasn't doing enough for you?"

Hennessey paused, then jerked forward in his chair. Meredith believed his awkwardness would doom him at any interview.

"Not really."

"Isn't it true that the placement department would have had difficulty placing you in a legal position until you passed the bar exam?"

"I guess that's right."

"You didn't pass the bar until last year. Isn't that what you testified to earlier?"

"Yes."

Meredith wondered where Blaisedell had come up with Hennessey. In Blaisedell's position, she would have employed plaintiff selection criteria that targeted graduates in the top half of their class, graduates that participated in extracurricular activities during law school, and graduates that had passed the bar exam on their first attempt. Yet Blaisedell appeared calm, unruffled, as one of his plaintiffs was going down in flames. Meredith considered two possibilities: either Blaisedell had something up his sleeve or the man was an idiot.

"You have one year of selling cars under your belt, isn't that right?" Simon asked.

"Yeah."

"How much did you earn in the last twelve months?"

"I don't know exactly."

"What's your best estimate?"

"Well over a hundred twenty thousand dollars."

Simon and Blaisedell were regarding Hennessey with a mixture of incredulity and respect.

"Am I correct that your earnings are pretty impressive?" Simon asked.

"Yeah, that's what they tell me. My boss says I have a magic touch. I actually know a lot about cars."

Meredith couldn't imagine a guy like Hennessey earning six figures in any law-related job he was able to land. Maybe he should be thanking Spenser for nudging him toward the correct career move.

81

Meredith reviewed the affidavits signed by Noreen Clark, Kevin James, and Flash. Carpenter had helped in finalizing the affidavits, and reading them over, Meredith believed that they presented a compelling case for Noreen to obtain injunctive relief. Flash had tried to recover the e-mail that Noreen had sent to Kevin with her article attached but had come up empty. Kevin had permanently deleted the e-mail from his laptop and the e-mail had been deleted from his e-mail backups. When all was said and done, Meredith believed that Noreen had been lucky. If Kevin had been aware of his Safe@HomePlate backup system, he might have permanently deleted Noreen's article from that source.

Meredith paused before signing her name to the complaint that would be filed on behalf of Noreen Clark. This momentous moment should have been accompanied by drum rolls and trumpet blares. Instead, she was faced with the silence of Carpenter's empty office. She signed the document and wrote out a check for the court filing fee on her newly funded business account. 'The die is cast,' she thought as she made ready to walk the complaint and supporting affidavits over to the court clerk's office.

Simon had just concluded his deposition of the third plaintiff in the Spenser case. Marlon Gold had graduated from Spenser in 2010 and passed the bar on his first try later that year. His efforts to find a government or in-house counsel legal position had gone nowhere; none of his job inquiries had produced an interview. Presently Gold was saddled with student loans that were in default. He had come across as a quintessential nerd: skinny, pale complexion, thick dark glasses, a clear plastic protector planted in the pocket of his dress white shirt.

Gold and Christopher Blaisedell had now left the conference room and Jeannie Smith was disassembling her stenographer equipment. Simon studied his deposition outline and when he looked up, he found Smith regarding him. "Any thoughts?" he asked.

"I felt sorry for the kid," Smith said. "I didn't feel sorry for the other two."

Gold inspired sympathy probably due to his sincere desire to be a lawyer. But sincerity didn't translate into ability. There was a cluelessness about Gold that was troublesome. Simon couldn't imagine Gold rising to any occasion.

"Anything else?"

Smith shrugged. "You made the same points with this kid that you made with the other two. I don't think these graduates have much of a case but what do I know? Your client's placement office didn't seem to be doing much until that woman showed up. You know who I mean—she sat in at the first deposition."

"Molly Grant," Simon supplied.

"Right. Anyway, if I was the law school, I would give this Molly Grant more resources and turn her loose."

"Thanks for sharing," Simon said, meaning it. "What?" he said, when Smith continued to regard him.

"I was just thinking about you and Carpenter. You have your own style. It's not Carpenter's, but it's effective."

"Thanks."

"Don't mention it," Smith said, employing Carpenter's standard self-deprecating phrase.

As Simon was gathering his deposition materials, Meredith entered the conference room. "Sorry I couldn't sit in," she said. "It's this damn Noreen Clark case. I'll be in court shortly trying to get an injunction."

"Not a problem," Simon replied. Meredith was energized. She paced back and forth on the opposite side of the room, obviously revved up.

"I need a break," Meredith said. "How about a fifteen-minute walk?"

It had been a while since Simon had had any one-on-one time with Meredith. "Sure," he said.

Once outside, Meredith covered ground with her long legs. Simon was working hard to keep up on a path with an upslope in the Boston Common. At least this exercise was keeping him warm. There was a fall chill in the air which reminded Simon that the daylight hours were already shrinking.

"Why is Carpenter spending so much time helping me with the Clark case?" Meredith asked without slowing down.

If their firm were busier, it was possible that Carpenter would be less generous with his time, but Simon didn't think so. "I think it's two things," he said, hoping his breathing didn't appear labored. "First, Carpenter is interested in new cases. He's always talking about how learning the facts of a new case is the best part of practicing law."

"What's the second thing?"

"Carpenter likes you."

"How do you know?"

"I don't think he'd be helping you the way he has if he didn't like you."

Meredith walked in silence for a time, her head slightly forward, her back straight, her long stride never wavering.

"I like him too, but I don't get it," Meredith confessed.

"Carpenter was the one who finally pushed us to get you involved in the Spenser case. He must have seen something he liked about you when we were representing you. Also, he was impressed with the way you analyzed the violence-against-women rally in the O'Day case. I think we all were impressed."

Meredith smiled but didn't break stride. "I owe him," she said. "He's really been helpful."

Simon was relieved when they came to a down slope. If Frank were around, he'd be getting a lecture about getting in shape.

"How are you doing?" Simon asked. "And I'm not talking about your court case."

Meredith gave him a curious, sideways look, and Simon figured she was debating whether to confide in him.

"I'm hanging in there," Meredith said. "I'm beginning to worry about not finding a job. I don't see much more work for me on the Spenser case, so I'm concerned about that. There's no man or woman in my life right now so I'm horny as hell. And I've got my first court hearing right around the corner, which you don't want to talk about."

"But you're hanging in," Simon said. "That's the important thing."

"So you say."

Simon reviewed Meredith's catalogue of concerns. "You *will* land a job," he said. "You're right about Spenser work tailing off for you. For obvious reasons, I decline to address your horniness. And I hope you *are* looking at this court hearing as an opportunity. I think you are. You're energized, whether you know it or not."

Meredith finally slowed her pace. "Thanks," she said. "I needed that."

82

Dean Stockman and Professor Jamison listened impassively to Simon's status report. Simon had no idea whether they thought they were getting their money's worth.

"Adam has read the depositions," Dean Stockman said, settling into his chair in his office's conference area. "I have to confess I haven't had time to read much of anything to do with the case. I'm going to defer to Adam as to comments."

Professor Jamison offered a cordial smile. "I thought the depositions went fairly well. I think the plaintiffs are going to have a hard time turning this case into a class action."

"We're cautiously of the same view," Rachel said, and Simon was glad to be able to defer to her on class action issues. "We think that each student's situation is different and for that reason alone there shouldn't be a class action. Also, we think we have good arguments that the plaintiffs named in the case are not appropriate plaintiffs to lead a class action case."

"Especially Mr. Hennessey," Simon added. "Rachel and I don't even remember him from our class."

"When is the hearing on the plaintiffs' class action motion? Jamison inquired.

"In a couple of weeks," Simon replied.

Jamison became lost in thought. "It's occurred to me that if you defeat the plaintiffs' motion to make the case a class action, the case might go away. With only three plaintiffs and no class, the case won't produce a big payoff."

The dean brightened at that possibility. "How's Ms. Sweeney working out?" he asked.

"She's been a big help with documents," Rachel replied.

"Are you going to move for summary judgment to try to get the case thrown out?" Jamison asked. "I think you have an excellent chance of getting the case dismissed."

"We haven't decided," Simon responded, deciding to borrow a page from Carpenter's book and downplay their client's expectations. "As you know, it's difficult to win on summary judgment, and we're concerned that until Molly Grant started running the placement office, that office wasn't particularly active. Also, we don't believe a judge will consider a summary judgment motion unless the plaintiffs have had a chance to take depositions."

Simon paused. The dean and professor seemed to be looking for a more upbeat assessment and an aggressive battle plan. He resisted telling them what they wanted to hear. "We intend to follow the path we've charted," he continued. "We've deposed each plaintiff. We'll deal with the plaintiffs' class action motion. And then we'll assess whether to try to dismiss the case through summary judgment. I'll remind you that the plaintiffs have yet to take Molly Grant's deposition or yours, Dean."

The dean nodded and when Jamison followed suit, Simon thought that the professor was doing so grudgingly. Jamison might be an evidentiary whiz, but it had probably been a while since he'd appeared in a courtroom. From the beginning, Simon believed that he had a feel for the Spenser case's themes and rhythms. Their action plan to date had been successful, and so far, they had done nothing to give their client false or overly optimistic reasons to hope for victory. He resolved to stay that course.

Simon glanced at Rachel, who favored him with a surreptitious wink. They were on the same page.

Carpenter saw a message in his Inbox from Delaney, one of his Barrister friends. That could mean only one thing—Delaney had made his prediction on whether the Red Sox would make the playoffs. According to the Barristers' rules, Delany had to fish or cut bait on a prediction before September. This year he was cutting it close to the time deadline.

Carpenter opened Delaney's e-mail. "Shit!" he muttered. Delaney had predicted that the Sox would miss the playoffs. Delaney regarded the team as inconsistent and missing whatever good karma a playoff contender needed to make it to the postseason.

In his heart, Carpenter shared Delaney's view. Still, it would have been more upbeat had Delaney deluded himself and forecast a Sox playoff run. It was stupid and unproductive to get in a funk over the prediction, but he knew that it wouldn't be until tomorrow that he began to put Delaney's negative message behind him.

September

From Meredith's Playlist

"What Do You Want From Me?"

Adam Lambert

83

Carpenter wasn't about to e-mail all his partners until he had first given Philly the news. The case referral had gone to her. Besides, he wanted to hear her voice.

Philly picked up her cell phone on the second ring. "This is Philly."

"This is your partner. How the hell are you?"

"I'm totally round."

Carpenter laughed out loud.

"That's it, laugh it up."

"I wanted to tell you this personally before I sent out an e-mail. That kid who got referred to you? Nathan Cohen? His father called to hire us. I hit him up for a six thou retainer and he didn't bat an eye."

"Divisible by four," Philly said.

"Every little bit helps. So, what's going on with you?"

"Not much. I'm trying to check in with the office early each morning to review e-mails and see whether anything's going on. It looks to me like we're slowing down."

Carpenter chose his next words carefully. "I know this is easy for me to say, but I want you to stop worrying about the amount of work in the office. Your worrying isn't going to change anything."

"Yeah, well, I can't help worrying."

"I know. But we're hanging in. The Spenser case has generated a nice flow of billable hours that's been keeping us afloat. We're not going to have a year like last year, but so what? We're hanging in."

"If you're trying to cheer me up, it's not working."

"Why would I try cheering you up? You're like me, a 24/7 grouch."

84

Meredith sat alone at the plaintiff's counsel table in Suffolk Superior Court Room 815 and tried to steady her nerves. From one perspective, her court appearance this afternoon on behalf of Noreen Clark should have been nothing to fear. She'd appeared alone in court without jitters when she worked at Pinkerton and had argued scores of motions. Yet here she was, her heart pounding, as if this were her first time in court. And in a sense it was—this time she was alone with no firm to back her up.

Meredith glanced behind her. Clark looked as nervous as she felt so, instead, Meredith turned her attention briefly to Carpenter. He had offered to accompany her to court and she had accepted. They'd discussed whether he should join her at counsel table, and he'd advised against that move. "When you represent an individual plaintiff against an institutional defendant represented by a large firm," Carpenter had said, "you want to appear alone, without backup, so that you can play the role of David against Goliath." He was probably right, but Meredith wondered whether she'd be more at ease if he were by her side.

Flash and Kevin James were also in attendance. Flash was again dressed in black. He surveyed the courtroom with cool detachment. Beside him, Kevin James looked more nervous than Noreen, her actual client.

Carpenter had joined her in reviewing the documents that Sloan-Webster School of Law would be presenting to the court. The law school would be submitting two affidavits to the judge. The first, from an assistant dean of students, Norah Warren, detailed the procedures that the law school had followed before issuing its plagiarism finding. In the second affidavit, Caryn Wheelwright, the journal editor, denied being told by Clark of computer problems and denied being told by Clark that her article submission was not a final draft. When Clark had read Wheelwright's affidavit she had reddened with anger.

The affidavits were accompanied by a legal memorandum authored by attorneys from the mid-sized Boston litigation firm of Springer, Thompson & Dash. Sloan-Webster's legal argument was straightforward: the submitted article was in plain violation of the law school's prohibition on plagiarism because portions of the article were produced without attribution to the sources from which Clark obviously borrowed. The plaintiff's claimed resurrection of a later draft article should not be credited in any way, shape, or form. Richard Dash would be arguing the law school's position, and he was accompanied by another partner in his firm and an associate. So, outnumbered three to one, Meredith *would* be in the David role against Goliath. Dash had favored Meredith with a smile when they had exchanged court papers, a smile she immediately distrusted since there had been no warmth in the man's dark eyes.

Carpenter had been helpful. He had listened to Meredith practice her legal argument and had played the role of a questioning judge. After viewing the law school's court pleadings, he had ticked off rebuttal points in a free associative discourse.

Meredith studied her one-page argument outline—Carpenter had persuaded her that more than one page was overkill—and the talking points that Carpenter had just come up with. She reminded herself that she had been hoping this day would come while she was at Pinkerton. She felt her resolve kicking in. 'Fuck it,' she thought. There was no way in hell she was going to second-guess what she had wished for.

"Court!" the court officer called out. "All rise. The court is now in session. The Honorable Judge Carmine Neal presiding."

Carpenter had never appeared before Judge Neal but had noted Neal's reputation for being strict but fair. Meredith needed fair; strict was not an issue for her. Neal had a preoccupied look as he studied the papers in front of him. Meredith guessed he was about fifty years old. He had a full, dark, closely trimmed beard, which he absently stroked as he reviewed the documents filed by the parties.

"We're here on the plaintiff's request for an injunction to prevent the defendant law school from disseminating any information to anyone that concerns the law school's determination that the plaintiff was guilty of plagiarism. The plaintiff also seeks an injunction directing the law school to retract the plagiarism charge from anyone who received it." Judge Neal looked up as if awaiting a response to his summary of the issues before the court. "We have Ms. Sweeney representing the plaintiff and Mr. Dash appearing for the defendant law school. I have five affidavits before me: affidavits from Ms. Clark, Mr. James, Mr. Nestor, Assistant Dean Warren, and Ms. Wheelwright. Ms. Sweeney, what do you say to the law school's contention that it fully investigated the plagiarism accusation and found it valid after interviewing the parties involved?"

Meredith stood, regarded the judge, and made an instant decision. If Neal was a no-nonsense type as Carpenter had suggested, there was no reason to be anything but direct.

"The statements in the affidavit of the plaintiff, Ms. Clark, and in the affidavit of Ms. Wheelwright cannot be reconciled," Meredith began. "One of those women is not telling the truth. While Ms. Clark was permitted to tell her story to law school officials, she was never given a chance to confront Ms. Wheelwright and was never told what others had said to school officials. As a matter of fact, until seeing Ms. Wheelwright's affidavit in this case, Ms. Clark had no detailed, specific knowledge of Ms. Wheelwright's fabricated story."

"Why would Ms. Wheelwright make up a story?" the judge inquired.

"I don't know," Meredith admitted. "But after seeing the made-up story for the first time today, I can tell you that Ms. Clark will use discovery to find out what Ms. Wheelwright's motivations were."

"It seems to me that Ms. Clark has more reason than Ms. Wheelwright to make up a story," the judge observed.

"Respectfully, Your Honor, I disagree. The journal article that is at issue in this case is before you. This document was an early draft of her article that Ms. Clark was able to find, and is missing footnotes and portions of text. Closed parentheses appear throughout the document and Ms. Clark, in her affidavit, states that this was a reminder to her to insert footnotes or text. The early document Ms. Clark located is plainly a draft and not a final document. These undisputed facts support Ms. Clark's version of events. The article simply cannot be viewed objectively as a final draft. Also, as the student editor of the journal, why didn't Ms. Wheelwright confront Ms. Clark and point out that footnotes appeared to be missing and that there were gaps in the text? Why didn't Ms. Wheelwright seek clarification about the closed parentheses? Confirming Ms. Clark's version of events is the draft of her article that Mr. Nestor was able to recover from Mr. James' laptop. In his affidavit, Mr. Nestor details the process he followed. Mr. James confirms in his affidavit that the article Mr. Nestor recovered was received by him as an attachment to an e-mail from Ms. Clark before she submitted the earlier draft she was able to find. That recovered document has very few closed parentheses."

"What do you say to Ms. Sweeney's various points, Mr. Dash?"

Dash rose calmly. "Ms. Wheelwright was not required to confront Ms. Clark with anything. She—Ms. Wheelwright—was familiar with the subject matter of Ms. Clark's article, did some research on her own, and concluded that the article contained materials lifted from other sources without attribution. The actions Ms. Wheelwright took are described in her affidavit. Ms. Wheelwright did the right thing: she informed the law school about what she had determined and left the matter with law school officials as should be the case. This court should not second-guess the decision of law school officials in the best position to assess the situation under the law school's rules. Moreover, the relative ease with which Mr. Nestor claims he recovered a more complete article suggests that the allegedly recovered article was recently created. On being confronted with a plagiarism charge, there was nothing to prevent Ms. Clark from immediately engaging Mr. Nestor or anyone else and producing the more complete document."

"Doesn't Mr. Dash have a point, Ms. Sweeney?" the judge asked. "Shouldn't the court defer to law school officials and the law school administrative process?"

"No," Meredith responded. "There was no meaningful administrative process afforded to Ms. Clark. As I just mentioned, she was never informed of any statement made by any person to any law school official. Therefore, she was denied the opportunity to defend herself, to confront Ms. Wainwright, or to offer specific information or data that would clear her name. The law school has falsely labeled her a plagiarizer, basically voiding her three years in law school, and making it impossible for her to obtain a law-related job to help her repay law school loans. In fact, as her affidavit points out, a job offer to Ms. Clark was withdrawn when the law school falsely informed her employer that Ms. Clark plagiarized. Ms. Clark should not be put in the position of having to grin and bear a false charge that appeared in a law school letter that resulted from an investigation that afforded her no rights."

"But if Ms. Clark did plagiarize materials, doesn't the law school have a duty to disclose that information to anyone inquiring about Ms. Clark?"

Meredith paused, glanced briefly at one of Carpenter's talking points. The judge was regarding her expectantly, and she realized that her response to his question might determine how this hearing turned out.

"Your Honor's question used the word 'if.' Therefore, my answer to Your Honor's question will also use the same word. *If*, after a hearing that includes the right to cross-examination, Ms. Clark is determined by an independent fact-finder to have plagiarized anything under the law school's guidelines which only apply to final drafts, *only then* would the law school's revealing that plagiarism be warranted. But, until that happens, the law school has no business ruining a promising legal career by airing a false accusation."

The judge leaned forward and huddled with his court clerk as they viewed the computer screen on the clerk's desk.

"I'm inclined to listen to testimony before making a ruling," the judge said as he sat back. "My calendar is free in the afternoon three days from today. I want present in the courtroom the authors of the five affidavits that are before me. I propose to treat the affidavits as direct testimony and permit cross-examination. During the next three days, I would ask the law school to agree not to communicate anything about plagiarism on Ms. Clark's part to any other person. Take a moment to think about what I've proposed. We'll recess for five minutes."

Carpenter was by Meredith's side as soon as the judge left the bench. "I've seen judges do this," he said. "I recommend that you accept his proposal. You can't very well oppose what he said given your argument that Clark needs to cross-examine witnesses. Anyway, that's what I think. You need to talk to Clark. Now."

"I'll start with you Ms. Sweeney," Judge Neal said when he resumed the bench.

"The plaintiff is agreeable to what Your Honor has proposed."

"Mr. Dash?"

"The defendant is also agreeable."

"Excellent. Two o'clock, three days from today. The court is in recess."

"So they get to ask me questions," Noreen Clark said after Meredith had again reviewed what the next hearing would involve. "That's a little scary."

They were seated in a Dunkin' Donuts near the courthouse, and after Clark had acknowledged the scariness of what faced her in several days, nobody said anything. Carpenter decided to let the silence lengthen so that the adrenalin rush from being in court would subside. The reactions of those seated at their table ran a gamut.

Clark was nervous. She had yet to drink her coffee and looked pale. In fairness, she couldn't have predicted the rapid pace of the case she had instituted. In contrast, Meredith was composed. Carpenter thought she'd handled herself well before the judge and didn't appear fazed that in a few days she'd be examining witnesses in court for the first time. Kevin James was subdued, and Carpenter wondered whether he had ever before been involved in a judicial proceeding. Flash was a whole different story. He sported a slight grin and seemed to be the only one at the table enjoying himself. Carpenter had never understood the urge to dress in black. If the intent of the fashion statement was to make a point about mystery or death, Carpenter regarded such a point as not worth making.

"I'll be in touch with each of you during the next few days to go over questions you may be asked," Meredith said. "If you think of something else you could offer that might be helpful, let me know when I call you."

"Is the law school going to have a computer expert?" Flash asked.

"I don't know," Meredith responded.

"Do you mind if I ask a question?" Clark said.

"No," Meredith replied.

Clark looked at Carpenter. "How come you're involved in this case?"

"Ms. Sweeney has done some work for my firm," Carpenter said, "and she mentioned this case before deciding to take it on. We have a working relationship and I told her it would be my pleasure to provide whatever assistance she might need."

"I see," Clark said, looking unconvinced to Carpenter.

"You can't believe everything you hear about lawyers," Carpenter said. "Sometimes we befriend each other."

Evelyn couldn't concentrate. Her thoughts kept gravitating to Horace Benson and how acutely she missed him. She believed that the feeling was mutual. The attraction was there but how could it be explained? She and Horace lived in different worlds. Evelyn saw herself as a street-smart, passionate Latina who belonged in a crazed, urban environment that didn't involve wheat, corn, flat vistas, or an inordinate number of pickup trucks. Horace lived in a state where the Hispanic population barely topped nine percent. There was white, but Horace was *white.* Talk about an Opie type! Yet she couldn't shake the notion that he was the one.

"What are you dreaming about?" Paul asked from across their joined desks.

'Shit,' Evelyn muttered to herself. Caught in the act. "I've got a lot of personal stuff on my mind. Sorry if I got lost there for a moment."

"Anything you want to talk about?"

"I don't think so. I'll sort it all out."

Paul shrugged and went back to a report he was writing.

Evelyn had her own report to complete but went on musing instead. She had toyed with the idea of moving to Omaha, but her brief time there had left her underwhelmed with the place. And Horace was such a home-grown product she couldn't envision him moving east to live. True, last spring when he'd spent time in the East, he had genuinely enjoyed himself. But it was one thing to play tourist for a brief stretch and another to settle down in a place permanently. Plus, Horace had a large family network in Omaha and its environs. She couldn't bring herself to ask him if he could see himself living on the east coast. She was afraid he'd say no.

And then there was sex. During their brief times together, they couldn't get enough of each other. When she thought of other lovers, she could recall feeling a frantic physical need for many of them. But nothing like with Horace; he literally drove her out of her mind.

Since Horace's visit in the spring, they had been on the phone nightly. She wondered whether Horace was wrestling with the question she couldn't bring herself to ask him: what were they going to do?

"Shit!" Evelyn muttered.

"Excuse me?"

"Did I say that out loud? Oops!"

Paul was looking at her with an amused grin. He had probably figured out what was on her mind but was too polite to mention it.

"Just so you know, you *can* talk to me if you want and it *will* stay between us."

Evelyn nodded. "I'll think about it."

85

Meredith had been thinking about Carpenter's observation that it was important that she sit alone at counsel table so she could play the role of David against Goliath. The problem with that advice was that she felt alone, somewhat adrift. Across from her sat Richard Dash, again flanked by colleagues; even if Dash never exchanged a word with his co-counsel, they would be there for moral support.

Judge Carmine Neal took the bench. "Let's get the show on the road. We'll start with the plaintiff. Ms. Sweeney, do you have any questions for Assistant Dean Norah Warren and Caryn Wheelwright who have submitted affidavits in this case?"

"For both," Meredith said, rising. "I'd like to start with Ms. Wheelwright."

Wheelwright kept her eyes lowered as she raised her hand to be sworn in. Her, "I do," was barely audible. Meredith took her body language as a sign of nerves. Maybe it would be possible to rattle this key witness. Wheelwright was not at all prepossessing. She was small and slight. She tightly gripped the arms of the witness chair.

Meredith decided to forgo warm up, preliminary questions. "Is it true that after you were named editor of the law school's health care journal, Noreen Clark told you that she deserved the position over you?"

The question seemed to startle Wheelwright. Meredith saw her grip further tighten on the armrests of her chair. So far they hadn't made eye contact.

"I don't recall that."

"What, if anything, did Ms. Clark say to you about your being named editor?"

"I'm not sure she said anything," Wheelwright answered, keeping her eyes averted. "I don't remember her saying anything."

"Did Ms. Clark ever mention to you that her grades were better than yours?"

"I don't recall her saying that."

"Did she ever tell you that her writing sample was superior to yours?"

"I don't remember her saying anything like that."

"Were you of the view that you deserved the journal editor position over Ms. Clark?"

"Objection," Dash interjected. "These questions are neither relevant nor material."

"Overruled," Judge Neal said. "Get to your point, Ms. Sweeney."

Meredith had the stenographer read back her last question. For the first time, Wheelwright met her gaze.

"I deserved the editor position as much as she did if not more. If she didn't like the fact I was selected, she could have taken it up with the selection committee."

"Did Ms. Clark like the fact that you were selected over her?"

"You'd have to ask her. Probably not."

Meredith sensed the judge losing patience. "Did you have a discussion with Ms. Clark when she presented you with a draft of the article she was working on?"

Wheelwright nodded, lowered her eyes.

"You need to speak your answer," Meredith said mincingly.

"We spoke. It wasn't much of a discussion."

"What was said?"

"She handed me the article and said something like she knew it was late. She may have apologized for the article being late. I told her I would be reviewing the article shortly. That was pretty much it."

Meredith consulted her cross-examination outline.

"Did Ms. Clark mention to you any computer problems she had experienced?"

"Not that I remember," Wheelwright responded, shaking her head, her gaze directed toward her lap.

"Did Ms. Clark tell you that the article was not a final draft?"

"Not that I remember," Wheelwright repeated.

Meredith received the judge's permission to place a copy of the article before the witness.

"Is this a copy of the article that Ms. Clark gave you?"

Wheelwright flipped through the pages in such a cursory way that Meredith doubted she was reading any of it. "It looks like the article."

"Did you contact Ms. Clark about footnotes being missing or inadequate?"

"No."

"Did you contact Ms. Clark about the lack of citations for certain statements in the article?"

"No."

"Did you contact Ms. Clark about apparent gaps in the article's text?"

"No."

"Is it correct that at some point you forwarded Ms. Clark's article to the dean's office?"

"Yes."

"Why didn't you discuss the article with Ms. Clark before referring it to the dean's office?"

"I thought it was something that the dean's office should handle. I had done some research on the case before the Supreme Court on President Obama's health care law. Some of the statements in the article sounded familiar to me and I did some quick research. It seemed to me that Noreen had lifted portions of other articles without citing them."

"Isn't it true that you didn't discuss the article with Ms. Clark because you wanted to get back at her for saying she deserved the editor position over you?"

Wheelwright colored. "No, that's not true."

"Isn't it true that you sent Ms. Clark's article to the dean's office because you wanted to get back at her for saying she had better grades than you and her writing sample was superior to yours?"

"No," Wheelwright responded, continuing her vice like grip on the arms of her chair.

"As journal editor, would it be correct that you have edited a number of articles?"

"Yes."

"Have you ever seen an article submitted to you that presented a lack of footnotes and a lack of text similar to those deficiencies presented in the article given to you by Ms. Clark?"

"I don't think so."

"Did you ask Ms. Clark about the parentheses that appear throughout the article she gave you?"

"No."

"What did you take those parentheses to mean?"

"I didn't think they meant anything."

"Nothing further."

"Any follow up, Mr. Dash?" the judge inquired.

Dash rose. "In contacting the dean's office or in submitting an affidavit in this case, did you act out of a motivation to retaliate against Ms. Clark?"

"No," Wheelwright said, and Meredith wondered whether it was wishful thinking on her part that Wheelwright's answer appeared to lack force.

Assistant Dean Norah Warren struck Carpenter as a consummate bureaucrat. She had yet to use the pronoun I; so far her answers were "we this," "we that," although she seemed to be the sole person directly responsible for investigating Noreen Clark's alleged plagiarism. Carpenter attributed her pronoun use to having overdosed on touchy-feely administrative management courses. Warren was middle-aged and dressed conservatively in a dark blue business suit. She wasn't old but she reminded Carpenter of an old maid. All that was missing was graying hair drawn up in a tight bun.

So far, Carpenter was impressed with the way Meredith was handling herself. For her first time in court dealing with live witnesses, she was holding her own. She didn't have Simon's flair or glibness, but she had a distinct style and, like Simon, she had presence. Her height gave her a commanding air. Also, she had something of Philly's doggedness.

"Who made the ultimate conclusion that Ms. Clark had plagiarized?" Meredith asked.

"We thought the evidence was very compelling. Ms. Wheelwright had provided us with copies of articles that contained wording similar to the wording in Ms. Clark's article."

"Who is this *we* you keep referring to?" Meredith raised her voice, and Carpenter was pleased to see that Meredith had focused on the woman's pronoun use.

"I'm sure the dean was behind me one hundred percent."

"Did the dean actually look at any of the documents you reviewed?"

Warren paused, directed a brief glance at the judge. "I don't think so."

"Isn't it true when you use the word 'we,' you're actually referring to yourself?"

"That's certainly possible."

"A moment ago, I asked who made the ultimate conclusion that Ms. Clark had plagiarized. You didn't answer my question and it's time you did. Weren't you the person who made the decision that Ms. Clark had plagiarized?"

"Yes, that was a conclusion I reached."

"Did anyone else reach that conclusion?"

"I couldn't say."

Carpenter found himself smiling as Meredith glared at the assistant dean. He tried to read Judge Neal's expression, but the man's full, dark beard made that impossible.

"Did you ask Ms. Wheelwright why the footnotes in Ms. Clark's article were missing?"

"I don't think I discussed that with Ms. Wheelwright."

The judge gave permission for Meredith to hand Clark's article to Warren. "Is this the article that you found contained plagiarism?"

Warren took her time going through the document. "This certainly looks like the article I was given."

"Since you just told us that you didn't discuss footnotes with Ms. Wheelwright, is it true that she never provided you with an explanation as to why footnotes were missing?"

Warren hesitated. "As I said before, I don't think we discussed the footnotes."

"Thank you," Meredith said in a sarcastic tone that Carpenter thought was wasted. He suspected that Warren had been inoculated against sarcasm and that her shots were up to date.

"Ms. Clark gave you an explanation for the missing footnotes, didn't she?"

"Yes."

"What explanation did she give you?"

"She said she had a computer problem that deleted the article. She said the article she handed in was an early draft."

"Did you believe Ms. Clark's explanation?"

"No. She never really backed it up."

"Did you ask her for backup?"

"I'm sure I did."

"Answer my question," Meredith demanded. "Did you ask her for backup?"

Warren paused, lost in thought. "I can't remember for sure."

Carpenter was pleased to see the judge make a note in his trial notebook.

"What kind of backup were you interested in?"

"I'm afraid I'm not a computer expert so I can't really answer that."

"Did you consult with a computer expert?"

"No."

"Did Ms. Clark inform you that the article she submitted to Ms. Wheelwright was not a final draft?"

"She said that."

"Did you believe her?"

"Not really."

"Why not?"

"The journal publication date was near and the article was submitted late. It seemed to me that this was the final draft that needed to be evaluated if the article was to be published at all."

"Isn't it true, Ms. Warren, that the lack of footnotes and text omissions are more consistent with a preliminary draft than a final draft?"

Warren paused and took a deep breath. Judge Neal was staring at the witness, which Carpenter believed was a good sign.

"Perhaps, but as I said before, the draft Ms. Clark submitted was the draft that had to be reviewed for the article to be timely published, so I considered it a final draft."

Carpenter scribbled on a piece of notepaper, folded it, and signaled for the court officer. When the officer approached, he asked the officer to deliver the paper to Meredith.

Meredith started when the court officer tapped her on the shoulder. She squared her shoulders and read the note he handed her aloud. "I move to strike everything in the witness' last answer after the word, 'perhaps.'"

Judge Neal regarded Meredith but again Carpenter couldn't read his expression. 'Beards should be banned in a courtroom,' he mused. 'Especially on judges.'

"I'm going to overrule your objection, but you've made your point," Judge Neal said.

"Did you ask Ms. Clark about the various closed parentheses that appeared in draft article you were considering?"

"No."

"Did Ms. Clark provide an explanation for the closed parentheses?"

"She said she used them to mark where she needed to add language."

"Did you believe her explanation?"

"Not really. As I said, the publication date was rapidly approaching."

"No further questions."

"Mr. Dash?" the judge inquired.

"Based on the documents that you were provided with," Dash said, "was there any question in your mind that portions of Ms. Clark's article were plagiarized under the law school's rules on the subject?"

"None," Warren said.

"Your turn, Mr. Dash. Any questions for the plaintiff or either of her witnesses?"

"Yes. I'd like to start with Mr. James."

After he was sworn in, Kevin James fidgeted in the witness chair.

"Were you and Ms. Clark in a relationship?"

"Yes."

"In your affidavit, you state that Ms. Clark ended the relationship. How did that happen?"

James cleared his throat. "Noreen was under a lot of pressure. She was writing the article this case is about. She had senior year finals coming up. Plus, she was trying to find time to study materials to help her with the bar exam after she graduated. She sent me the article we were able to rescue attached to an e-mail in early April as an example of what she was dealing with. I wanted to spend time with her and told her that. I probably wasn't as understanding as I should have been. We met for lunch and she told me that she needed to take a break from our seeing each other. I tried to argue with her, but she said her mind was made up."

Dash wrote on his notepad. "In your affidavit you state that you deleted that e-mail you just mentioned and also deleted the article. Why did you download the article?"

"I thought it would make it easier to look at it later. I was curious about what she was working on."

"Why did you delete the article and the e-mail?"

"When she said she wanted us to stop seeing each other, I probably overreacted but I was angry and frustrated and so I deleted the article and all the e-mails she had sent me."

"Isn't it true that you knew you had a backup to your laptop called Safe@HomePlate?"

"I'm not into computers. I really didn't know what Safe@HomePlate did and I didn't think about it at the time. I would get a bill from them once a year and I just paid it."

"Did you look at the bills to understand what you were paying for?"

"Not really."

"Are you in the habit of paying bills that you have no idea what you're being billed for?" Dash asked sarcastically.

"When it comes to my computer, yes. As long as my laptop is working, I keep things as they are and don't ask questions."

"Do you really expect this court to believe that?"

"Objection," Meredith said.

"I'll hear the witness' answer," Judge Neal said.

"I do expect the court to believe it," James said, "because it's the truth."

"Do you still have feelings for Ms. Clark?"

James shifted in his chair before glancing Noreen's way. "I do. I hope she'll give me another chance."

"Isn't your testimony today slanted in Ms. Clark's favor so that she might return your feelings?"

"If I did that, I don't think Noreen would have anything to do with me."

"Nothing further," Dash said.

"Ms. Sweeney. Do you have questions for Mr. James?"

"No, Your Honor."

"Then I suppose it's Mr. Nestor's turn," the judge said.

After being sworn in, Flash regarded Dash with his amused grin in place.

"Tell me, Mr. Nestor, how long have you been in business providing services involving computers?"

"You can call me Flash."

"That's not going to happen," Dash said. "Please answer my question."

"About five years."

"Let's see if we can cut to the chase. Are you one hundred percent certain that the article you retrieved from Mr. James' computer was created before Ms. Clark was accused of plagiarism?"

"No," Flash said, and Meredith heard a gasp from Noreen. "I'm ninety-nine percent certain. Would you like me to explain?"

"No," Dash said.

"I'd like you to explain, Mr. Nestor," Judge Neal said.

"You can also call me Flash."

"That's not going to happen. Please give your explanation."

"Whatever," Flash said. "First off, I know it's hard to believe, but there might be something out there that I'm not aware of. Also, it's possible to mess with dates. For example, something produced today could be backdated to an earlier date. In this case, I'm confident the recovered article was in existence in early

April. Both Ms. Clark and Mr. James have sworn that was the case. Mr. James' backup system, Safe@HomePlate, runs each night in the middle of the night and it's possible to tell when it first found a copy of the article and backed up the article. This happened on April sixth. When he downloaded the article attached to Ms. Clark's e-mail, his laptop made a new file for it and that occurred on April fourth. Also, when I recovered the article, I asked Mr. James a question to try to make sure he had received the article in early April when he said he did. Attorney Sweeney and Ms. Clark were present. Before Mr. James could look at the article, I asked him if he remembered the title of the article. He did remember the title, but he wasn't sure he had it exactly right. Then, without prompting from me, he said he also remembered the subtitle but again he wasn't sure he had it exactly right. I wrote down what Mr. James remembered. He was right. He didn't recall the title and subtitle exactly, but he was pretty close." Flash extracted a piece of paper from the pocket of his black shirt. "I made a chart comparing the actual title and subtitle of the article with Mr. James' recollection of those titles. Would you like to see it?"

"No," Dash responded.

"The court would like to see the chart," Judge Neal intervened. "Do you have copies?"

"Indeed I do." Flash reached down and extracted several papers from a large black duffle bag he had brought with him to the witness chair. "Here's five copies," he said to the court clerk.

The clerk presented Meredith and Dash with a copy of the chart and passed the remaining copies to Judge Neal.

Judge Neal studied Flash after reviewing the chart. "What made you ask Mr. James about the article's title and subtitle?"

Flash smiled. "Because I think ahead and wanted to make sure Mr. James was on the up and up." Meredith smiled as Flash pointed at Dash. "This joker claims there was backdating going on. I wanted to nip that bullshit in the bud."

Carpenter couldn't be sure, but he thought he glimpsed the judge's teeth when the jurist's beard parted. Was the judge smiling? Maybe beards weren't impenetrable.

"Continue, Mr. Dash," Judge Neal instructed.

"So you can't absolutely rule out backdating, correct?"

"I thought I just did. To accept a backdating conclusion, you'd have to ignore everything I just pointed to and that would be simply dumb and wrong."

Dash huddled briefly with his colleagues. "Nothing further," he said. "I do have questions for Ms. Clark."

Noreen regarded Dash evenly after having been sworn in. Meredith was uncertain whether her client's emotions were under control.

"Why did you provide Ms. Wheelwright with a copy of an article you knew wasn't ready for publication?" Dash asked.

"Because I didn't want her to think I had ignored writing the article. I explained my computer problems to her and never thought she would deny what I told her."

"Why didn't you show her the draft and then reclaim it?"

"That never occurred to me. I had my own copy of that early draft."

"Isn't it true that you never mentioned any computer problems to Ms. Wheelwright?"

"No, that's not true."

"Isn't it correct that you never wrote on the article you handed Ms. Wheelwright the word 'draft' or the words 'not for publication' or any similar caution?"

"That's right. All you had to do was look at the article to know it was a draft. Caryn had it in for me and has lied to you all."

"Objection," Dash said. "Move to strike the witness' answer. After 'That's right.'"

"Sustained," the judge ruled.

"Isn't it true that you've lied to this court by claiming you presented Ms. Wheelwright with a draft article?"

"Objection!" Meredith said.

"Overruled."

"No," Noreen said, glaring at Dash.

"Nothing further."

Once Noreen took her seat, Judge Neal leaned back in his bench chair and surveyed his courtroom, his expression unreadable. Carpenter expected the judge to take the case under advisement and delay making a ruling, but the judge taking his time might mean he was prepared to rule.

"Sometimes it's the little things that tip the balance in a case," Judge Neal said, leaning forward. "Those closed parentheses are little things but they speak loudly. I find it astonishing that neither Ms. Wheelwright nor Assistant Dean Warren were troubled by the closed parentheses and claim they never inquired as to what they represented. Both drafts of the article were attached to affidavits before me. I've compared the drafts. The recovered article that the law school regards as a fabrication, adds language in the precise places where the closed parentheses appeared in the document given by Ms. Clark to Ms. Wheelwright. There are three instances where closed parentheses appear in the recovered article and the locations of those three closed parentheses also appeared in the document given to Ms. Wheelwright. These circumstances weigh in the plaintiff's favor. Frankly, I find Ms. Wheelwright's version of events suspect."

Carpenter fought his natural instincts and began to entertain hope. Judge Neal appeared to be applying common sense.

"Of course the law school disputes the timing of the recovered article, claiming that the more complete article was an after-the-fact creation. However, that claim is defeated by Mr. Nestor's testimony and by the testimony of Mr. James. Mr. James received an e-mail from Ms. Clark in early April that contained an attachment. He downloaded the attachment and later deleted it. It was this attachment that was backed up by... Safe@HomePlate... and was easily recovered by Mr. Nestor who focused his search of the backed-up documents in April. Also, Mr. James' testimony as to when he received the article is backed up by his recollection of the article's title and subtitle which was largely correct. Fl... Mr. Nestor did think ahead when he asked Mr. James about the article's title and subtitle."

Meredith thought she heard Noreen softly crying behind her and forced herself to focus on the judge.

"I'm going to allow the plaintiff's motion for a preliminary injunction. The preliminary injunction will not go into effect for one week. That will give the law school an opportunity to seek judicial review of my order in the Appeals Court. My clerk will fax a copy of my order to counsel before the close of business today. I'm also going to set this case down for a trial on the merits in forty-five days. Both parties have had discovery through testimony. If there's any other discovery a party thinks is necessary, I want that discovery served on opposing counsel in ten days and I want the response to discovery served in ten days. If either party wishes to introduce a new witness, it must notify the other party of what the new witness will say and permit the other party to take the witness' deposition. Thank you, counsel. Court is adjourned."

Noreen Clark was pulling off the not inconsiderable feat of being giddy and weepy at the same time. Carpenter figured she was entitled to the mixed emotions. She had kissed Flash on the lips. "Nice," he had said. "You can have me any time."

Meredith beckoned Carpenter to join her. She had moved to a seat in the vacant jury box.

"What do you think the law school's going to do?" Meredith asked.

"Damage control."

"Clark has a claim against Wheelwright," Meredith said.

"I believe she does," Carpenter concurred.

"Do you think the law school will appeal Neal's order?" Meredith asked. She gestured toward Dash and his colleagues who were engaged in discussion while packing their briefcases.

"I'm not sure," Carpenter answered. "That assistant dean and Wheelwright were lousy witnesses. Wheelwright wouldn't look you or the judge in the eye. The assistant dean came across as incompetent. If I'm Dash, I'd be thinking of a way to make the case disappear. Even if Dash gets Neal's order reversed or put on hold, he's not going to want to go to trial with the witnesses he's stuck with."

"I guess we'll know in a week." Meredith motioned toward the counsel tables. "Incoming," she said as Dash approached.

"Do you have time for a brief chat?" Dash asked.

Meredith nodded and then introduced Carpenter.

"Does it make sense to try to quickly resolve this case?" Dash asked.

"What did you have in mind?" Meredith replied.

"A settlement agreement that is kept confidential but essentially obligates the law school to comply with your injunction requests. The case would be dismissed with prejudice."

"What about damages and attorney fees?" Meredith asked.

"I think damages would be a hard sell. We could talk about a reasonable figure for attorney fees."

Meredith turned to Carpenter. He was regarding Dash with his jaw muscles working, the sign he was considering settlement options. Meredith thought of taking a break to consult with Carpenter in private, but rejected that option. This was her case and she needed to take charge.

"Without damages," Meredith said, "I don't see this case settling. Your client conducted a half-assed investigation and set out to ruin Ms. Clark's career. She's already out ninety thousand. I think once a jury gets an eyeful and earful of your assistant dean and Wheelwright, the jury will come in with a multiple six figure verdict or even a seven figure verdict."

"Do you have a demand figure?" Dash asked.

"No," Meredith said. "I'd be prepared to consider presenting a demand figure if you tell me damages will be considered in any settlement."

"I'll get back to you," Dash said before turning to rejoin his colleagues.

"I suppose you would have played that differently," Meredith said to Carpenter.

"Not really. You're doing fine."

Meredith emitted a heartfelt sigh.

"Forget about this case for the rest of the day," Carpenter advised. "Tomorrow, when your head is clear, come up with a list of demands you want to make to the law school. I'd be glad to go over them with you."

"Why are you being so nice and helpful?"

"That's just my nature," Carpenter said deadpan.

"Yeah, right!" Meredith replied.

"Speaking of being nice, you might want to be nice to Nestor. That space shot came through for you."

"Don't worry. I'll be nice to him. If he'll let me."

86

Rachel sat beside Carpenter in the office suite's conference room reviewing the edits Philly had made to the complaint Rachel had drafted to be filed on behalf of Nathan Cohen. She found Philly's suggestions helpful. The final work product would be polished. First Carpenter had picked apart her draft, and now Philly was weighing in with constructive changes.

"I think we're done," Carpenter said. "Put it in final form."

"Who's going to argue the injunction motion?" Rachel asked. It had been a while since she'd appeared in court. The abrupt settlement of the Clyde Atkins case had eliminated a trial she would have shared with Carpenter.

"I'm thinking you should do the argument," Carpenter responded. "I know you have that class action motion coming up in the Spenser case. But my instincts tell me it should be you."

"That's fine," Rachel said, thinking that Carpenter's instincts were usually on the money. "Do you mind if I ask you something?"

"Why would I mind?" Carpenter said.

"I don't know," Rachel admitted. "Sometimes it's hard to tell what kind of reaction you're going to have to something. But I wanted to ask you why you spent so much time helping Meredith out."

Carpenter shrugged. "I had the time," he said. "Plus, her case interested me. And last but not least, I like her. There's something about her. I figured she could use having somebody around since it was her first case involving witnesses."

Rachel considered Carpenter's catalogue of reasons. "I know what you mean. There is something about her. I wish we could hire her."

"We all know that's not going to happen. We don't have the workload to take her on. But you never know what the future holds."

Rachel decided to further open up to Carpenter. "I was also wondering whether you were concerned that financially, this year isn't going to be as successful as last year."

"You're full of questions," Carpenter said, and Rachel was relieved there was no sign of irritability in his response. "Last year was probably extraordinary, so it would have taken a lot of luck to match last year. Yes, I'm concerned that we don't have a large inventory of cases. I'm sure you, Simon, and Philly share that concern. But this year is fine. We're making money, although not as much as last year. And most important of all, I think we're all happy. I can tell you I am."

Rachel found Carpenter's short speech heartfelt with no sign of the crabbiness he sometimes displayed. He seemed to have no regrets about the decision to form a firm.

"I'm happy, too," Rachel said. "Happiness can't be overrated."

Paul looked up from the report he was reading to find Evelyn looking at him. Evelyn's paperwork was stacked in the middle of her desk and Paul doubted it had received any attention. "What?" he asked.

"How did you know that Philly was the one for you?" Evelyn asked.

"What kind of a…" Paul stopped himself. Evelyn looked genuinely bereft. Her question probably had to do with Horace Benson and she had to be desperate if she asked it of him. Since they'd been working together, she hadn't revealed a personal, soft side but they had gotten along. He had become used to her and had learned to rely on her.

"There was just something about her that got to me," Paul said. "Her fiancé was in the hospital with no brain activity. He had been hit by a car while riding a bike. I had been the detective at the accident scene. I went to the hospital and there she was. She was trying to put up a brave front and my heart just went out to her. It's hard to explain."

Evelyn shook her head. "You've explained it very well. When I woke up in the hospital in Omaha, Horace was the first person I saw. He was looking at me with such concern and he didn't even know me. Nobody had ever looked at me that way before."

"Have you two talked about what you're going to do?" Paul asked.

"I'm afraid to bring it up. I'm scared about what he's going to say."

Paul's cell phone sounded. "Give me a sec. It's Philly."

"Come get me, now. My water broke and the contractions have started," Philly said.

"I'm on my way."

"Everything all right?" Evelyn asked.

"Philly's gone into labor. I've got to go."

"We've got to stop meeting like this," Dr. Amy Shumaker joked.

Philly wasn't laughing and Paul wondered whether she'd even heard Shumaker's quip. Philly was panting heavily, squeezing Paul's hand hard.

"You're doing fine," Shumaker reassured, and Paul decided to believe Philly's OB-GYN. Shumaker had delivered Daisy, and her sparkling green eyes above her surgical mask showed no sign of alarm or concern.

Philly's contraction stopped and she inhaled deeply, letting the air out slowly. Her black curls were plastered to her head with sweat.

"If you think I'm going to tell you the sex of this baby after you've waited this long to find out, you've got another think coming," Shumaker continued joking, and this time Paul found himself smiling.

"What are you grinning about?" Philly screeched. "You think this is funny?"

"Sorry," Paul said.

"Oh shit!" Philly shrieked. "Here comes another one!"

Paul had to remind himself that Philly was going through this without any anesthetic. She'd been fully dilated when wheeled into the delivery room so it had been too late for anesthesia.

"It's okay to push," Shumaker said.

"I am fucking pushing! What the hell did you think I was doing?"

"The baby has crowned," Shumaker said.

Philly paused and caught her breath.

"You're very close," Shumaker said.

With the next contraction Philly clenched her teeth and bore down.

"Excellent," Shumaker said.

Paul remembered when his daughter Jennie was born. He had been unable to focus what with all the noise and activity. But he was focused now and held his breath.

"Halfway there," Shumaker said. "Come on, just a little more. Okay!"

Shumaker held up a baby boy. Paul began counting fingers and toes and when he reached twenty, he bent over to kiss Philly's forehead. "Way to go, champ," he said.

Shumaker gave instructions on cutting the umbilical cord. Paul's hand shook as he made the cut.

"Let me see," Philly said, and Shumaker deposited the baby in Philly's arms. Paul watched as she checked the sex. "Daniel," she said as her breathing calmed.

"Daniel," Paul echoed, silently thanking the God he hadn't much believed in until this moment. Their son had thick black hair—nothing like Daisy's filmy, flyaway hair—and dark eyes. Paul couldn't tell which of them Daniel looked like and he didn't much care.

Philly settled Daniel on her stomach and Paul couldn't hear what she was whispering to him.

"Happy?" Paul asked.

"Happy," Philly said, closing her eyes.

Carpenter tried to keep a straight face as he herded Simon, Rachel, and Meredith into the conference room for a meeting he had described as an immediate emergency. He must have succeeded in maintaining a grim expression because Rachel was looking at him worriedly, poised to take notes, and Simon and Meredith sported serious expressions.

"Rachel, I want you to take notes. The rest of you just listen. This is serious. We have a crisis on our hands." Carpenter paused a few beats. "Philly gave birth to a boy."

Carpenter found the reactions of his two young partners predictable. Rachel's transformation into giddiness was instantaneous. Simon's broad grin was slower in coming but it did arrive. Meredith smiled politely as if she didn't quite know what to make of his announcement, and it occurred to Carpenter that Meredith's contacts with Philly had been largely through Skype.

When Rachel said, "We need to get her something," Carpenter realized Philly hadn't had a baby shower. Maxine would know whether it was proper to hold a baby shower after a baby was born. "I'll talk to Maxine and have her get in touch with Isabella. We'll work it out."

"I am so happy for her," Rachel gushed. "This is great. Is she okay?"

"Paul said mother and son are doing well," Carpenter replied, recalling that Paul had sounded on his cell phone so worn and tired that if it weren't biologically impossible, you might have thought he had been the one to give birth.

"So how do you guys handle one of you being out for a while?" Meredith asked.

"We handle it by not handling it," Carpenter said. "We'll try not to bother her, and chances are she'll be the one to bother us first."

"At Pinkerton there were all these rules on maternity leave," Meredith said.

"Rules are not our strong suit," Carpenter responded. "As you may have noticed." It occurred to him that Philly's absence might not be missed since work was down and she had dealt with the Glass case before giving birth.

"I feel like we should open a bottle of champagne," Rachel said.

Carpenter reached inside his briefcase and removed a bottle of champagne, which he placed on the conference room table. "What's stopping you?"

Meredith had wanted to meet and Carpenter had insisted on coffee first to wipe away the taste of champagne. When he was ready, he grabbed a notepad and joined Meredith in the conference room.

"Dash called me and said the law school would consider damages in any settlement," Meredith said. "I need to come up with a demand figure for Clark. I'm not sure how to go about it."

"Don't give me that," Carpenter said. "You evaluated your own case against Pinkerton. Of course you can figure out what to demand. It's all about the money, as you know from settling your lawsuit against Pinkerton. It's fine to request Sloan-Webster pay Clark's legal fees, but what about putting a dollar value on the emotional distress she's experienced? What about the fact that her reputation was tarnished? What about the fact that a ninety-thousand dollar starting salary was withdrawn by a law firm? And while we're at it, what about a pound of fucking flesh?"

Carpenter was obviously joking on that last point, but you couldn't tell it from the fierce look he was leveling. Meredith decided to ignore Carpenter's sharp tone and be grateful that he was taking the time to help her. She studied her settlement list: pay Clark's legal fees, clean up Clark's law school record, and mail retractions to anyone told that Clark had plagiarized. Her list also included the word 'damages' but didn't contain any sum.

"Maybe the place to start is the ninety-thousand dollar offer that was retracted," Meredith said.

"Go on," Carpenter said.

"Maybe the demand is for a multiple of that figure."

"I'm listening."

"A multiple of five?" Meredith hadn't intended to frame her response as a question but that's how it came out.

"How would you justify a multiple of five?" Carpenter challenged.

"By stressing that the worst thing you can do to a lawyer is falsely claim that the lawyer is a cheat," Meredith responded, finding that she was beginning to enjoy this back and forth.

"You know what Dash is going to say, don't you?" Carpenter said. "He's going to say the law school made a good-faith determination based on the evidence before it. He's going to harp on the fact that there was nothing to corroborate Clark's story. He's going to say that following the hearing when there was testimony on new facts that had recently come to light, the law school is acting promptly and in good faith to resolve the matter."

"To which I will say," Meredith replied, "that the law school's investigation was non-existent, thereby undermining any claim of good faith. At no time did the law school bring Clark and Wheelwright together to get a sense of which of them was credible, or take any steps to determine the plausibility of Clark's explanation"

Carpenter nodded slowly and Meredith wondered if he'd run out of things to say.

"Run what you're going to do by Clark and get her approval."

Meredith nodded. Dash was more experienced than she was, but she was beginning to think, 'So what?'

87

The preliminaries were over. Evan Morales, local counsel, had introduced Christopher Blaisedell to Judge Miriam Aronson and now the federal judge was consulting her trial notebook.

"You want me to certify this case as a class action," Aronson addressed Blaisedell. "But the defendant makes a number of telling points in opposition to your request, not the least of which is the fact that each graduate's situation is unique, so that no graduate may represent the interests of any other graduate. What do you say to that point?"

The judge was young with curly dark hair and a round, open face. She'd been a prosecutor during the ten years before her recent appointment to the bench with a focus on cases involving juveniles. Rachel suspected that for a judge who had been immersed in criminal law for a decade, making the transition to complicated civil motions wasn't easy.

"Of course, there are going to be differences among graduates of the law school," Blaisedell responded to Aronson. "But the core similarities between the named plaintiffs and the class they seek to represent predominate. The plaintiffs and the class they seek to represent are all graduates of Spenser New England School of Law. They are all without legal work. They were all promised a proactive placement office, which for years was moribund. They were all told more than fifty percent of the law school's graduates found legal work, but that inaccurate statement remained on the law school's website long after the statement wasn't true. These common, overriding elements warrant certification of this case as a class action."

"What do you say to Mr. Blaisedell's contention?" the judge asked.

"Let's consider Mr. Blaisedell's points one by one," Rachel replied. "There are a lot of reasons why a law school graduate may not have landed a legal job. Poor grades, no participation in extracurricular activities, poor interpersonal communication skills, and personal appearance are just some of the factors that come to mind. Therefore, Mr. Blaisedell's point that the plaintiffs and purported class members don't have legal jobs is off the mark because the reasons why each graduate doesn't have a job are unique to the graduate."

Rachel consulted her notes. "When it comes to the placement department, the named plaintiffs for the most part declined to make use of that office and, when they did, they received help. For example, we know that Felix Hennessey made the personal choice not to contact the placement department until he passed the bar exam, something that required three attempts on his part. We also know that once they got around to actually contacting the placement department, Marlon Gold and Tina Farrell have been given frequent updates from the placement office on jobs that are available. And the deposition testimony establishes that the placement office has helped with resume drafting in the case of Ms. Farrell."

Rachel paused. Carpenter was pleased that the judge was writing.

"There was nothing false or misleading about the law school's website. The website cited a survey of graduates conducted in 2008 as the source of slightly more than fifty percent of graduates finding a legal job. The school was under no duty to constantly change or update that information. Any of the plaintiffs was free to ask the placement office if the office had more recent data, but none of them did. And for 2008, the statement on the website was true."

Rachel consulted her one-page outline.

"Passages from the plaintiffs' depositions and other depositions that are before you focus on some harsh realities. First there is the fact that a poor academic performance at a law school that is not a top-tier law school may result in a graduate never finding a law-related job. Second, some graduates are not cut out to be lawyers. Third, a graduate who lands a law-related job may discover in short order that law is not for him or her. Fourth, the evidence is clear from all three named plaintiffs that the law school never guaranteed or promised any of them that any of them would find a law-related job. The plaintiffs for obvious reasons don't focus on these specifics since the specifics underscore the point that no graduate may stand in the shoes of another."

Rachel promptly sat and cast a sideways glance at Blaisedell. He too was writing and when he finished, he rose. "May I respond, Your Honor?"

Judge Aronson gestured for him to proceed.

"The 2008 website posting is misleading and the law school did have a responsibility to disclose more current, less favorable information on placing graduates in legal jobs. Secondly, if class rank and extracurricular activities are as important as Ms. Boyle claims they are, why did the law school remain silent as opposed to specifically informing law school applicants that their chances of obtaining a legal job fell between slim and none if they were in the bottom half of their class or if they declined to participate in extracurricular activities? And to the extent Ms. Boyle was suggesting that Spenser was not a top tier law school, why didn't the law school advertise that fact? Clearly the law school wanted to entice applicants so it could make money off them."

Blaisedell took his seat and Rachel was dismayed to see the judge writing. She rose and waited until the judge looked up from her note taking. "If I may, Your Honor, a brief rebuttal to what was just said. As our submission to the court shows, Spenser School of Law's ranking is determined by an outside rating agency that uses the term 'top tier.' Spenser did not rank in the rating agency's top tier, and the law school was not obligated to advertise the rating agency's determination. As a matter of fact, the law school did inform students that extracurricular activities were an important factor in obtaining legal employment. In our legal memorandum, we quote the law school's written materials on that point. Lastly, common sense comes into play here. If after completing high school and college, a law student wasn't aware that grades and extracurricular activities were factors in obtaining entry to the next level, in this case a law-related job, then the student probably doesn't have the common sense to be a lawyer."

Judge Aronson made a few notes but her expression gave nothing away. Rachel asked herself the question Carpenter liked to ask—which side would she rather be arguing? Her answer wasn't as clear cut as before the court hearing, but she still preferred the law school's position. "I'll take the matter under advisement," the judge declared.

88

Paul thought everyone in the house was being a good sport. Daniel hadn't slept more than two hours at a stretch. When he woke, he cried and there was nothing held back when he wailed; everyone in the house—and on their street for that matter—probably got an earful. But there had been no complaints from Raul and Isabella or from Sarah. The cries mostly had to do with hunger, which meant Philly was on duty. When she nursed Daniel anytime between two and four in the morning, Paul had made it a point to sit beside her in the living room. He'd taken the week off and wanted to help even if helping was nothing more than sitting next to Philly to give her company and reaching out to connect with Daniel's feet and toes when they were faced his way. During the early-morning nursing sessions in the living room, it seemed to Paul that time had stopped. He could hear Daniel sucking away and was conscious of Philly repositioning the baby and herself, but in the otherwise silent darkened room, it was if he had stepped out of his life into a still place where crime could not be imagined.

Philly took mid-afternoon feedings in their bedroom and sacked out with Daniel when they were done. Paul spent their sack time with Daisy and Rosalind and Jennie, who was staying over during the week he was off. Typically, they went to a park where the girls would run around. Jennie seemed to be storing up questions to ask about her half-brother, and Paul decided to let her choose the time to ask them.

Paul checked his watch. Three forty-nine in the morning. Philly and Daniel were asleep, still connected. Paul closed his eyes and matched his respirations to Philly's.

Meredith phoned Dash from the conference room so Carpenter wouldn't overhear her end of the conversation. She couldn't stand the thought of his silently second-guessing every word leaving her lips. Dash had listened without comment as she presented Noreen Clark's demand, and she was surprised by his first comment.

"What's your relationship with Carpenter?" Dash asked.

"What does that have to do with anything?" Meredith responded.

"Did he put you up to this?"

"What are you talking about?"

"If you think the law school is going to shell out four hundred and fifty thousand dollars plus attorney's fees, you're seriously mistaken."

Meredith regarded Dash's reaction as posturing. Dash was ethically bound to present her demand to the Sloan-Webster School of Law regardless of whether he thought the demand was reasonable. Posturing she could put up with, but Dash's remarks about Carpenter rankled. Dash was suggesting that Carpenter was pulling the strings on this negotiation and she was the puppet. True, Carpenter had given her advice, but she was the one making this call. 'The hell with Dash,' she thought; there was no reason to be nice to the man.

"Here's something to think about," Meredith said, striving to give her voice a hard edge. "Your client fucked up big time. I'm thinking of a jury being asked to imagine what it must feel like to have an incompetent assistant dean sign off on falsely accusing someone of fraud. I'm thinking Clark's demand figure will be chump change once a jury gets through with your client."

Dash didn't reply immediately, and Meredith wondered whether she had overreached. Dash had to know that she had never tried a case let alone a jury case. Was it possible Dash believed that Carpenter would handle the jury trial if the case wasn't settled?

"You've made an unreasonable demand and you know it," was Dash's comeback.

"I've done what I said I would do," Meredith replied curtly. "I've gotten back to you. I believe we're done."

"You've got that last part right," Dash said before hanging up.

Meredith replayed the conversation. She felt that she had held her own. Dash was now in a time crunch. He had appealed Judge Neal's order to the Appeals Court, but had scheduled the hearing in a week to permit settlement discussions to sort the case out. Dash also had to prepare for the trial Judge Neal had ordered. The law school had to be concerned about Dash's fees. Meredith knew what she would do in Dash's position: come back with a lowball offer.

October

From Meredith's Playlist

"The Logical Song"

Supertramp

89

Rachel couldn't recall a time when she felt more composed before a court hearing. Carpenter, sitting beside her at the plaintiffs' counsel table, also appeared calm. Behind them, in the first row of spectator seating, sat the Cohens, father and son, looking unperturbed but alert.

There were no surprises in the court papers submitted on behalf of the Edward Gibbon High School. The law firm representing the school had submitted an affidavit from the high school's principal, Bryson March, and a legal memorandum arguing that Nathan Cohen's T-shirt message crossed the line separating church and state and presented a potential risk to maintaining school discipline and order. Stanley Tyson would be representing the high school. Of medium height and a tad overweight, Tyson had presented Rachel with a genuine broad smile when they had exchanged legal papers.

"All rise," announced the court clerk. "The court is now in session."

Judge Agnes Doyle ascended the bench and favored the lawyers before her with a smile. Rachel thought there must be something in the water—everyone appeared to be in a good mood. Judge Doyle was in her third decade on the bench but, looking at her, you wouldn't have guessed she was pushing the mandatory retirement age of seventy. She reminded Rachel of Maxine: salt and pepper short hair, laugh lines quoting her eyes, a resolute mien.

"What is it about T-shirts?" the judge said. "One would think T-shirts are innocent enough, but here we are immersed in a court case because of one. How come this matter required litigation? Why wasn't it sorted out?"

Rachel felt a nudge. "You should take this," Carpenter whispered.

Rachel promptly rose and out of the corner of her eye saw Tyson easing back onto his chair. Either she had beaten him to the punch, or he had concluded that discretion was the better part of valor.

"Fair questions," Rachel said. "T-shirts are innocent enough, even though a case can be made that today they represent a poor man's billboard. And where the message on the T-shirt before the court is one of understanding, brotherhood, and tolerance, it is almost inexplicable that Nathan Cohen has had to resort to litigation in order to attend school wearing the T-shirt with its message of peace. But the sad truth is that the defendants have refused to let Mr. Cohen attend high school if he wears the T-shirt in question. So, reluctantly, Mr. Cohen was forced to seek legal redress to be able to exercise his first amendment rights."

"That's laying it on a bit thick, isn't it, Ms. Boyle?"

"Thank you, Your Honor. That was my intent."

"I see," Doyle said, and Rachel was relieved to see a judicial smile in acknowledgement of her attempt at humor. "The defendants raise their own first amendment argument. They point to separation of church and state which, in this case, they claim means keeping religion outside the classroom. How do you respond?"

Rachel and Carpenter had spent some time working on a response to this contention and, last night, Rachel had debated the issue with Josh, who ended the back and forth by tickling her silly.

"The defendants' first amendment argument is misconceived," Rachel said. She liked that word. Lawyers were constantly using words like "misplaced" or "misconceived" when politely debunking an argument, and there was something to be said for invoking such mannered words to suggest an opponent was full of shit.

"Let's suppose for a minute that my client, Nathan Cohen, had showed up at school wearing a T-shirt with the message, 'On the seventh day God rested.' Would this innocuous quote from the Bible have caused Mr. Cohen to be sent home for the day? I doubt that."

"Do you agree, Mr. Tyson?" the judge asked, and Rachel immediately took her seat, curious as to how her adversary would handle the judge's question.

"It is entirely possible Mr. Cohen would have been denied permission to wear a T-shirt sporting a Biblical reference that might be seen as offensive by atheists or non-Christians. One can easily imagine the havoc that would occur if nonbelievers had to contemplate a resting deity."

Rachel gave Tyson credit. Had he conceded that an innocuous Biblical reference wouldn't have resulted in a student being sent home, he would have undercut his legal position.

"Well, at least you're consistent," the judge said. "What's that quote? 'A foolish consistency is the hobgoblin of little minds?' Was it Emerson who said that?"

Rachel had no idea who was responsible for the quote and Tyson also appeared clueless about its source.

"It *was* Emerson," Carpenter said rising. "Many people misquote Emerson by leaving out the word 'foolish.'"

"Mr. Carpenter, I presume," Doyle said.

"The one and only," Carpenter replied before taking his seat.

"Where were we?" the judge asked, not evidencing any embarrassment over having lost her train of thought.

"Foolish consistency," Rachel offered. "I would also point out that the defendants' first amendment argument is undercut by the fact that no one associated with the school was wearing a T-shirt. The message on Mr. Cohen's T-shirt is a personal expression on his part, which does not implicate state action relating to church and state."

"No doubt Mr. Tyson would argue that by permitting Mr. Cohen to wear the T-shirt, the high school is taking a position that implicates church-state matters."

"I would indeed so argue," Tyson confirmed.

"But that argument would be unavailing," Rachel said, resorting to another of those words used by lawyers to politely deliver a zinger. "Jesus was a historical figure. What he said, what he did, should be part of a high school student's learning experience."

"Are you suggesting that more than two thousand years ago Jesus weighed in on homosexuality and transgender issues?" the judge inquired.

"No, I'm not," Rachel replied. "But today, people are now asking, in a host of modern-day situations, 'What would Jesus do?' Mr. Cohen is providing one answer on an issue that is publicly debated. I suppose if Mr. Cohen's message changed the word Jesus to Ghandi or Martin Luther King, the school would not object. Or would it?"

"Would it?" the judge asked Tyson.

"To avoid taking an inconsistent position, I suspect it would," Tyson said, his smile conveying his enjoyment of the back and forth of argument.

"What is the basis of the high school's position that Mr. Cohen's wearing the T-shirt in question would cause a breakdown in school discipline?" Doyle asked Tyson. "The evidence is that discipline was maintained during the few days Mr. Cohen donned his T-shirt before the school took action."

"The fact that discipline was maintained for several days is beside the point. The high school wasn't required to wait for a breakdown in discipline before taking action. The high school administration viewed Mr. Cohen's attire as a threat to order given the nature and subject matter of his message."

"Doesn't Mr. Tyson have a point?" Doyle asked Rachel.

"Not a valid point. As Mr. Cohen's affidavit points out, students in solidarity with his position protested the school's decision that he not be allowed to wear his T-shirt and there was a counter-protest in response to that protest. Thus, it was the school's decision to ban Mr. Cohen from wearing the T-shirt that threatened order and discipline. Mr. Cohen's actual wearing of the T-shirt posed no such threat."

"Ms. Boyle makes a fair point, doesn't she?" the judge asked Tyson.

"No she doesn't," Tyson responded. "If the T-shirt hadn't put in an appearance to begin with, there would have been no protests. If anything, the protests confirm the judgment of educators that Mr. Cohen's message was volatile and divisive. This court should show deference to the judgment of the high school's administration."

"I suppose Ms. Boyle would claim that the high school's real gripe was with the message on the T-shirt, and that maintaining discipline was not the real reason Mr. Cohen was barred from school if he wore his T-shirt," Doyle mused.

"Yes, that is exactly what I would claim," Rachel affirmed.

The judge became lost in thought. Rachel doubted she would rule from the bench, but stranger things had happened.

"I'm going to take this matter under advisement," Doyle suddenly declared. "I encourage the parties to try to find a solution to the problem before the court but, if I don't hear from counsel in a week, I will assume that no solution was reached. Anything further? No? Then the court shall be in recess."

"The judge seemed to think this was funny," Arthur Cohen complained outside the courtroom. "There's nothing funny about it."

Rachel privately disagreed. Judge Doyle hadn't regarded the case as funny; worse, the judge may have considered it trivial. Rachel tried to be diplomatic. "When there's no jury involved, some judges adopt a lighter tone when questioning lawyers."

"It didn't strike me as very professional," Arthur Cohen said.

"Is there any compromise that would be acceptable to you?" Rachel asked Nathan.

Nathan shrugged. "I don't know."

"It's okay to be creative on this," Rachel counseled.

"I'll think about it. But I don't think you have to worry. The high school will never agree to anything."

Nathan might be correct. Rachel had gotten a look at the high school principle, Bryson March, who had taken a seat in the rear of the courtroom. He was a large, unsmiling man who had the look of a disciplinarian. But his lawyer, Stanley Tyson, had displayed a sense of humor. Rachel had an off-the-wall idea. She decided to run it by Carpenter. If Carpenter didn't shoot it down, she'd present it to Tyson. Opposing counsel might turn out to be more reasonable than her own client.

90

"I have a counteroffer," Richard Dash said when Meredith picked up her phone. For a man presenting a counter proposal, Dash didn't sound like he was in a conciliatory mood. Meredith debated moving to the conference room. She was seated at the workstation in Carpenter's office, and he would hear every word she said. 'What the hell,' she thought. "I'm listening."

"My client's counteroffer on money is one hundred thousand dollars."

"One hundred thousand dollars," she repeated, raising her voice, and that caused Carpenter to look up from whatever he was working on. "That means we're three hundred and fifty thousand dollars apart. That's not a good sign when it comes to settling this case."

Carpenter was giving her his flinty stare and Meredith met his gaze. She was now in Dash's position. She would have to present his offer to Noreen Clark whether she liked it or not.

"Then maybe the case won't settle," Dash said tersely.

Carpenter slowly drew a forefinger across his throat.

"I'll present your proposal and get back to you."

Carpenter nodded approvingly.

"Is your client prepared to back down from the figure you previously presented to me?" Dash asked.

"As I said, I'll get back to you. Thank you for getting back to me." Meredith hung up her phone. If Carpenter hadn't been present signaling her to shut up, she realized that she might have explored reaching a middle ground with Dash.

"Now what?" Meredith asked Carpenter.

"You know what," Carpenter replied. "You have to tell Clark what was put on the table."

"I know that. But she'll ask me for my recommendation."

"So give it to her."

"I'm going to recommend that she reject the offer. I think she'd be making a mistake accepting the law school's proposal."

What passed for a smile played across Carpenter's lips. "You see? You do know what to do."

"But if Clark goes along with rejecting the offer, do I simply reject the offer? Or, do I make a counteroffer on Clark's behalf?"

Carpenter grew serious. "Those are the basic ways to play this. I'd be inclined to simply reject the offer and not make a counteroffer. I can't give you a rational reason for choosing that option. It's just my instinct. I could be wrong."

Meredith appreciated Carpenter's candor, but what he'd just said wasn't that helpful.

"What would you recommend to Clark as a monetary settlement?" Carpenter asked. "I think it's time to focus on that question."

"Two hundred and fifty thousand is what I've come up with."

Carpenter glared at her for a moment and then his gaze wandered and his jaw muscles started working.

Carpenter seemed to come out of a trance. "That feels about right," he said. "How did you come up with that figure?"

"I couldn't tell you really. It just seemed the way to go."

"Okay," Carpenter said. "This is the other discussion you need to have with Clark." He paused. "You look different. I was trying to figure it out. You're dressed up, right?"

"I'm going out. I've got a date tonight."

"I figured you were going to a funeral," Carpenter said. "You remind me of that guy Flash."

"That's who I'm going out with." Meredith couldn't believe how much time she had spent figuring out what to wear. She wondered what Flash's reaction would be when he saw her in ankle high black boots, black slacks, a black blouse and a half inch wide, solid black, silk choker necklace.

Carpenter frowned. "The Clark case isn't over. You might want to think twice about getting involved with a witness."

"You're probably right," Meredith said. "The advice you've given me has been great and I'm deeply appreciative. But I'm not taking your advice on this. The guy is hot!"

"Is this part of my witness compensation?" Flash asked.

"Shut up and fuck me!" Meredith said, panting. She was straddling him, grinding away and, yes, he was meeting her thrust for thrust, but she didn't want to be distracted by his grin or the amused look in his eyes. It was disconcerting enough that although they were both working, she was the one sweating, breathing hard. Flash looked and felt cool. His breathing appeared normal, which made her wonder whether he was one of those guys with the standing heart rate of a hibernating animal.

"Oh!"

Meredith couldn't believe how quick and strong Flash was. He had flipped her without warning and now her legs were hooked over his shoulders.

"How's my driving?" Flash said, his amused look still in place.

'Pretty damn good,' Meredith thought. Somehow, during the maneuver, they had stayed connected. The compliment Flash was due lodged in her throat. "Enough with the jokes already, okay?"

"No, not okay. Lighten up. We're having fun, remember?"

Flash's comeback took Meredith aback, broke her rhythm. Had she smiled once since they'd stripped down? When the hell had she become humorless? "You're driving is pretty good," she said, hoping her smile didn't come across as weak.

"Thanks. There's more where that came from."

Meredith reached up and worked loose the rubber band securing Flash's ponytail. His hair fanned out over his shoulders and, in the dim light, it could have been a woman looming over her if it weren't for a prominent male part inside her.

Flash's amused look remained, but she saw to that by closing her eyes. Concentrate, she told herself. She thought of Flash's body, long and lean, without an ounce of fat. If this guy didn't make her come, she was going to demand a refund.

"Oh!"

Now they were going at it doggie-style. How the hell did he keep them connected? "How about using turn signals next time?"

"You know what Tony V says about Mass drivers not using turn signals, don't you?"

"What the hell are you talking about? Who's Tony V?"

"Don't you ever go to the comedy show in Boston on First Night on New Year's Eve?"

"No."

"That's why you don't know who Tony V is. How can you not start off the new year with some laughs?"

"I don't give a shit who Tony V is!" She couldn't believe they were having this conversation while humping away.

"You should. The reason Massachusetts drivers don't use turn signals is because it's giving information to the enemy."

Flash began to laugh, and Meredith had to admit it was a pretty funny line. In fact it was a very funny line and she began to laugh as well. But mostly she wanted to stop chatting and let herself sink into the orgasm that was rising inside her.

"Are we having fun yet?" Flash asked.

"Stop it. I can't do this and laugh at the same time."

"Does that mean you don't know how to multitask?"

"Enough! Stop it!"

"You know, on New Year's Eve Tony V always gives advice for the upcoming year."

Meredith couldn't believe she was curious. "Like what?"

"Like never shoot a fat man who's above you on a flight of stairs."

Meredith tried not to laugh, lost the battle. "That's ridiculous."

"That's what Tony V says is what he usually gets as a reaction, but, as he points out, if the situation should arise, you're going to thank him."

Meredith started to laugh again. She couldn't remember the last time she had laughed out loud.

"Ready," Flash said.

"What?"

"Set."

"Wait a minute. What are you…"

"Go."

"Oh!"

Meredith startled awake. She remembered closing her eyes, trying to preserve and settle into the feeling of release. Christ! How long had she been out?

She rolled onto her side, facing toward the center of her bed, and found Flash staring at her, his ponytail again secured. "Sorry about dropping off."

"No need to apologize. Isn't it supposed to be the guy who conks out?"

Meredith couldn't read Flash's expression. He had just tried for humor, but his amused look had vanished and in its place was… God only knew—she couldn't get a read on him.

"I thought we were going out for dinner," Flash said.

Meredith realized that she was starving, but as hungry as she was, she couldn't move. "We are," she said. "You don't mind having started with dessert, do you?"

"Not in the least."

Flash had come to pick her up for dinner over an hour ago. She invited him into her apartment and then jumped him. What the hell had she been thinking? Nothing, obviously. "Do you think I've been a little too forward?" she asked, taking her own stab at humor.

"I just assumed this is how you treat all the witnesses in your cases."

"Very funny." She was relieved to see Flash's mischievous look return.

"So what was this all about?" Flash asked.

Meredith opted for the truth. "I was attracted to you the moment you walked into our conference room a while back. When I opened my door, I just decided to act on it."

"I'm not complaining."

"Neither am I." Meredith recalled only once before acting on a sexual impulse so directly. The woman she had come onto that time had been shocked, and she'd never figured out why she had so badly misread that situation.

Moving closer, Meredith reached out and stroked his face. "So what's the story with you?" she asked. "What do you do when you're not playing around with computers?"

Flash laughed. "So *now* you want to get to know me."

"I'm serious."

"Okay," Flash said. "I'm into yoga and meditation. I fool around with martial arts. I read books about computers. I surreptitiously audit advanced college courses on computers. I see to my consulting business." He paused. "Those are the highlights."

"Were you serious about wanting to be paid in cash?"

"*You* thought I was," Flash said.

"Yeah, I did."

"I guess you could say I was semi-serious. I usually throw that out just to see what someone will say. If I'm told that cash is okay and I can forget about receiving a 1099, then I become suspicious. Most of my clients are strangers, so I try to throw them a curve to get a read on them."

Meredith's stomach growled so loudly that Flash must have heard. Still she put off getting out of bed. "Are you seeing anybody?" she asked.

This time Flash was the one to reach out. He touched her face with the back of his fingers and Meredith found his touch cool, his expression again unreadable.

"I find myself looking at you," he said.

91

Philly eased out the back door into the chilly, predawn morning. Her sleep rhythms were out of whack. How else to explain her wandering around the backyard at five in the morning? She patted her spinning bike. Paul had gotten her an expensive, well-padded bicycle seat, but she was still too sore to use it.

She was wrapped in a robe but barefoot, and the damp grass chilled her feet. There wasn't much to the backyard—no trees, no shrubs, no flower beds—just grass and weeds. Philly was relieved that neither she nor her housemates were into gardening. The idea of nurturing one other living thing made her cringe.

Philly wished Paul could have extended his paternity leave, but she hadn't pressed him to do so. With Paul around, she'd glimpsed the possibility of successfully juggling all the things in her life. Now that he'd returned to work, she'd need help. Sarah Ferguson would never admit to not being able to fill Paul's gap, but was simply not up to the task. Some sort of daycare arrangement for Daisy was going to prove necessary.

After finishing a second circuit of the backyard, Philly sat down on the back steps. The cold of the concrete went through her robe but wasn't unpleasant. She breathed deeply in the cool morning air and stood up. She had less than an hour of alone time and resolved to use fifteen minutes to log onto her office computer, something she'd rarely done since returning from the hospital.

Once online, she saw that her partners were managing. Meredith's court case was turning out well. Nathan Cohen's lawsuit had been filed and the judge could be expected to issue a ruling shortly on Cohen's request for an injunction. Checking her e-mail messages, Philly felt that her law practice was at a remove. That mindset had to change. Keeping the balls she was juggling in the air required money and the only way money was going to come in was if she worked.

Simon had circulated Judge Miriam Aronson's ruling on the class action motion in the Spenser case to his partners and Meredith. He requested advice on how to present the judge's ruling to Dean Stockman and Professor Jamison. The judge, relying on many of Rachel's arguments, had denied the motion, but the denial had been without prejudice to the plaintiffs' renewing their motion after any additional discovery had concluded in the case or following trial. Among other things, the judge concluded that a plaintiff who never consulted the placement department timely, was not in a position to raise claims against the law school relating to that department. She noted that following trial, she would be in a better position to judge whether each plaintiff was suitable to represent a class.

Simon regarded the judge's ruling as a win for the law school. A denial was after all a denial. No class had been recognized by the judge; the three plaintiffs were on their own. But the judge had been clear that the plaintiffs could again try to represent a class once the discovery phase of the case was concluded or following the trial of the case. Which meant that the plaintiffs' class action options weren't permanently foreclosed. "Shit!" Simon exclaimed.

He swiveled his chair to face Philly's vacant office chair. Where the hell was Rachel? He wanted her feedback on the judge's ruling *now.* Which was not entirely true. What he really wanted was for Rachel to reassure him that the judge's ruling was a victory.

While waiting for Judge Aronson's ruling, Simon had put his recent free time to good use. He had made substantial progress on a first draft of a motion to dismiss the plaintiffs' case against the Spenser School of Law. That motion and the legal memorandum supporting it were nearly ready to be sent out for his partners' comments. True, the court wouldn't consider a motion to dismiss until the plaintiffs had concluded their discovery. But discovery was coming to an end. To date, Spenser School of Law had responded to all of the plaintiffs' discovery requests for information. Christopher Blaisedell had yet to depose Molly Grant and Dean Stockman, but those depositions were now scheduled.

For the first time, Simon could envision the Spenser case moving to a conclusion.

Meredith placed a call to Richard Dash. She now had Noreen Clark's approval to settle the pending lawsuit for $250,000. For the parties to get to that figure, Meredith was certain that more unpleasantness would precede the compromise.

"I hope you have good news," Dash said when he got on the line.

"I don't," Meredith said. "The law school's one hundred thousand dollar offer is rejected."

"Do you have a counteroffer?"

"No." Meredith said knowing that her response would drive Dash further up a wall.

"Is your client prepared to come down from her four hundred and fifty thousand demand?"

"Not at this time," Meredith responded, throwing Dash the small bone that Carpenter thought was appropriate at this juncture.

"Then when?" Dash demanded.

Meredith took her time before responding from the prepared script Carpenter suggested she follow. "I can't promise you anything, but if the law school puts an offer on the table that my client regards as serious, she might decide to move off her previous demand."

"I have to tell you that you're not being particularly helpful in trying to resolve this case. There's been no flexibility from you or your client on anything."

"I don't appreciate that at all," Meredith said, trying to sound more indignant than she felt. "The law school hasn't presented anything to be flexible about. Sorry, but I've got to run. There's another court matter I need to attend to."

Meredith set down her phone. Her last statement to Dash wasn't a total lie. She did have to get back to Simon on the class action ruling in the Spenser case. But outside of Noreen Clark's contingency case, she had nothing else going on.

Rachel was in the Spenser School of Law library reviewing the cases that Stanley Tyson had cited in the legal memorandum he had previously filed on behalf of Edward Gibbon High School. It was always worth checking. Some lawyers cited cases for legal propositions that the cases didn't support. Other lawyers' legal citations were always on the mark. Tyson's citations were in the latter camp. In a way, she was pleased that his research was well done. She had enjoyed arguing against him and had found his attempts at humor during the court hearing welcome. She decided to phone him while feeling charitable toward him.

"Ms. Boyle," Tyson said when he picked up his line. "Are you actually taking the judge up on her suggestion that the parties work things out? That would be a radical idea."

"Yes," Rachel said.

"I don't want to waste your time," Tyson replied. "I'm not optimistic that my client is prepared to be flexible."

"That's what my client said the high school's reaction would be. But hear me out. I have this wild and crazy idea that I want to run by you." As she explained what she had in mind, her idea sounded more off the wall than it did when she outlined it to Carpenter. Carpenter's reaction was that there was nothing to lose. But maybe there was something to lose. Her opposing counsel might think she was an idiot.

"Just so I'm clear, you haven't raised this with your client, correct?" Tyson asked.

"Correct."

"What you're suggesting is a little far out. But it's original and creative. Which probably means that my client won't have anything to do with it."

"I'm prepared to try to sell the idea to my client if you're willing to do the same with yours," Rachel said. "And since we're being direct with each other, you need to know that Nathan Cohen may tell me no."

Tyson didn't respond for a long moment. "You realize that if we do what you're suggesting, we run the risk of shooting ourselves in the foot."

"What do you mean?"

"I mean that this case would be a hoot to try. If we settle it, there's no trial."

Did Tyson actually say 'hoot?' "Does that mean you're in?"

"It does," Tyson said. "I'm in."

Carpenter entered the conference room to find Rachel, Simon, and Meredith huddled in front of a computer screen oohing and aahing over blurry Skype images of Philly's kids. When Rachel asked Daisy how she liked being a big sister, the little girl didn't answer, appeared self-conscious. Daniel, on the other hand, greeted Rachel's question with a full body wriggle followed by total repose.

"Daisy, why don't you see what Rosalind is up to?" Philly's voice sounded, and in a moment, Daisy's face vanished and Philly's face and shoulders filled the screen. Carpenter made out the top of Daniel's head, so Philly was holding the baby in her lap. Philly looked good if you ignored signs of exhaustion: dark circles under the eyes, droopy eyelids, a wan complexion even for Philly.

"I read the class action ruling," Philly said. "Congratulations."

"Thanks," Rachel said.

"But the ruling was without prejudice to the plaintiffs filing another class action motion," Simon said.

"So what?" Philly responded. "Let's say the judge denied the motion and left out the without prejudice part. Later on, the plaintiffs could still petition the court to change its mind."

"Do you think the law school will regard this as a victory?" Simon asked.

"It should," Philly said. "The plaintiffs didn't get what they wanted. If they come back later trying to get the court to change its mind, they're going to have to point to something new and different. That's easier said than done."

Simon looked unconvinced by Philly's reasoning. "I agree with Philly," Carpenter said. "Do you think the plaintiffs consider the judge's ruling a victory? I doubt it. They were flat-out turned down when it came to what they wanted."

"Let's both make the call to Dean Stockman and Professor Jamison," Rachel suggested to Simon. "If they complain about the result, I want to be around to argue that they should be happy with the decision."

Simon nodded at Rachel. "Tomorrow, I'll be sending you a draft of the pleadings seeking to dismiss the Spenser suit. Once the depositions of Molly Grant and Dean Stockman are taken, I want to be able to jump on the motion."

"Meredith," Philly said. "How's it going with your case against Sloan-Webster School of Law?"

"Forget that," Carpenter interjected. "Inquiring minds want to know how it's going with Flash."

"My lips are sealed," Meredith said.

"I'll bet they weren't," Carpenter replied, causing Meredith to redden.

Carpenter was working in the conference room, so Meredith didn't have to worry about privacy for this telephone discussion with Richard Dash. "Good morning," she said in as businesslike tone as she could muster.

Dash got right to the point. "My client is willing to increase its previous offer by fifty thousand dollars," Dash said without fanfare. "I've agreed to put back the hearing in the Appeals Court as you know. But if we have to argue the appeal of Judge Neal's order in the Appeals Court, my client will not settle and all offers are withdrawn."

Carpenter hadn't briefed her on this possible scenario; he had envisioned a low dollar figure from Dash and had recommended listening to the lawyer, waiting a few days, and then both rejecting his offer and coming back with a counteroffer of $400,000. Maybe the time to stop the cat and mouse game was now. She had authority from Noreen Clark to accept $250,000 so long as that sum didn't include attorney fees. The question was how to get Dash to throw another $100,000 into the pot.

"Have I reduced you to silence?" Dash inquired.

"Give me a fucking minute! I'm thinking!"

Meredith tried to regroup. She had just snapped at Dash because, on some instinctive level, she knew that was the way to deal with him.

"On behalf of my client, I appreciate your client's new offer. Unfortunately, we're still too far apart. Your offer is rejected. And if that turns out to mean we're in the Appeals Court, then so be it."

"Frankly, Ms. Sweeney, I'm sick and tired of you jerking me around. I'm not going to waste any more time negotiating with you. If you're not in a position to tell me what it will take to get the case settled then, fine, I'll see you in court."

On one level, Meredith had to applaud Dash for taking a hard line. On another level, she wondered whether her own hard line and gamesmanship had ruined the possibility of the case settling. "Three hundred and seventy-five thousand dollars," she said, not knowing whether she had made a fatal mistake by putting any figure on the table.

"You're right," Dash said. "We're still too far apart."

"I've already told you that," Meredith responded. "Again, thanks for making another proposal."

"Is there some middle ground that you'd be willing to recommend to your client?" Dash offered.

"What did you have in mind?"

"Two hundred fifty thousand is somewhere near the middle of the numbers we've been talking about."

Meredith felt her heart pounding. Surely Dash wouldn't have mentioned that figure if the figure was out of the question. She could tell him the number he had proposed sounded reasonable. Or she could jeopardize whatever progress they might now be making by being greedy. But wasn't greed good? "Here's what I'm prepared to do," she said. "I'm prepared to recommend to my client a settlement figure of two hundred and seventy-five thousand, if that's a number you are prepared to recommend to your client."

"What about the two hundred and fifty-thousand-dollar number I suggested? Again, I just threw the number out there. I haven't discussed it with my client."

"I told you what I'm prepared to recommend," Meredith replied. "I have no idea whether Ms. Clark will follow my recommendation. But it is a number I will try to sell to her if the number is something you will take back to your client with a favorable recommendation."

Dash remained silent. Meredith marveled at the ease with which she was able to seek a recovery above the $250,000 she was authorized to accept.

"Okay," Dash said. "I'll recommend the two hundred and seventy-five thousand."

"Excellent," Meredith said, trying to keep her tone neutral. "I should have an answer for you by noon tomorrow."

"It may take me longer to get my client to respond," Dash said. "Let's leave it that I'll call you when I have an answer."

"Okay," Meredith said. "Thank you for your time."

When she hung up, Meredith wondered whether she had played the negotiation correctly. She let her breath out and stood up to stretch. Carpenter, no doubt, would have criticisms as to her approach. And it was a little disconcerting to think that Noreen Clark's future was dependent on how she handled her learning curve when it came to settlement negotiations. Still, on balance, Meredith felt she had held her own.

92

"I think it's nuts," Nathan Cohen said dismissively. "It's also lame."

Rachel had phoned Nathan and explained her plan for settling his lawsuit. While the teenager's reaction wasn't unexpected, Rachel was surprised at how much his flat-out rejection stung.

"So what if it's nuts," Rachel replied. "You'd be getting your message across and might end up getting to wear your T-shirt whenever you wanted. Plus, your lawsuit would be resolved, and you and your parents would avoid further legal expense."

"I don't like the idea of anyone getting to say what I can put on a T-shirt."

"Of course you don't," Rachel said in what she hoped was a suitably supportive tone. "But you could end up losing your lawsuit, in which case, you'd have no chance to wear the T-shirt."

"What happens if Mr. March doesn't agree with any of this?" Nathan asked.

"Then we're back to letting the court decide."

"This sucks."

"Please think about my idea," Rachel said. "I want you to go over what I've said with your father and I'd like both of you to get back to me."

"Whatever," Nathan said, and Rachel wanted to strangle her client.

The law offices of Shapiro & Morales were more rinky-dink than their own, which made Simon realize that, to date, when it came to litigation, their opponents uniformly had had good-sized, decently-appointed offices. Shapiro & Morales didn't have a conference room. They were crammed into Evan Morales' office.

Christopher Blaisedell motioned for the stenographer to swear in Molly Grant. As Grant took the oath, she appeared composed. Playing the role of Blaisedell, Simon had subjected her to a long grilling. For the most part, she had responded well. It had taken some intense instruction, but Grant seemed to get comfortable with the idea that it was okay to admit that when she became the department head, the placement department had room for improvement.

"What changes did you make when you became the department head?" Blaisedell inquired after preliminary, background questions.

"One of the first things I did was create a more comprehensive electronic filing system. This included posting job openings on the school's website."

"Was that it?"

"No. I reached out to Massachusetts law firms and contacted hiring partners or their secretaries to arrange for job openings to be sent to my attention. I offered to meet with hiring partners, but I don't recall any of them accepting that offer."

"Have you finished your answer?"

Grant stared at Blaisedell. "No. I sent revised questionnaires to graduates seeking information about their current employment, and I catalogued the responses electronically."

"Anything else that you can think of?"

Grant paused and Simon was pleased that she was taking her time. "Those are the main things I recall. I know my office sent you a lot of documents. There may be something in those documents that would remind me of other changes."

"Was the placement office you took over less effective without the changes you implemented?"

"Probably."

"Did you ever meet with your predecessor?" Blaisedell asked.

"Yes. She provided me with a two-week orientation before she left."

Blaisedell had a copy of a page from the Spenser website marked as a deposition exhibit.

"Do you see the reference to more than fifty percent of graduates being placed in a law-related job?"

Grant nodded. "I see that."

"Do you see the 2008 reference to the more than fifty percent figure?"

"Yes."

"Does that percentage hold today?"

"The last information I looked at was based on 2011 questionnaires. About forty-nine percent of the graduates returning the questionnaire were in law-related jobs."

"Why wasn't the website changed to reflect that most recent information?"

"I don't know. When I send out questionnaires, I tabulate the responses and send a summary of the information to the dean's administrative assistant."

"Do you know why the dean failed to update the website with the 2011 information you just mentioned?"

"No."

Blaisedell listed the names of the plaintiffs in the lawsuit he had brought. "Do you have any views as to why the plaintiffs in this case have failed to obtain law-related jobs?"

"Objection," Simon said forcefully. "This witness can't possibly answer that question."

"I asked for her views," Blaisedell countered. "As the person at the law school in charge of placing graduates in legal positions, she may very well have views as to why the plaintiffs lack legal jobs."

"If you can, answer the question," Simon instructed.

"I don't know why they don't have legal jobs. I can't put myself in the shoes of employers that they have applied to for jobs. With the exception of Ms. Farrell, the plaintiffs didn't fare well academically. As I remember, none of the plaintiffs made a commitment to extra-curricular activities. These may be factors that have hindered them from obtaining a job. But again, I have no way of knowing for sure. It may be that prospective employers found other job applicants superior."

Simon was pleased with Grant's answer. She was keeping her cool and coming across as forthright.

"To your knowledge, does the law school ever inform applicants for admission that their chances of finding a legal job after graduation are approximately fifty percent?"

"I'm not involved in the admission process. I don't have knowledge about that one way or the other."

"Have you ever told a student or graduate what his or her chances were of landing a law-related job?"

"I don't recall ever telling that to a student or graduate."

"If the law school were to inform applicants for admission that their chances of finding a legal job after graduation were approximately fifty percent, would that be a true statement?"

"Objection," Simon said. "You're asking the witness to engage in pure speculation in an area she's not involved in." He turned to Grant. "If you can answer the question, please do so."

Grant asked for the question to be repeated. "Based on the questionnaire responses I mentioned before, the fifty percent figure is approximately accurate. It's close to the fifty-one percent figure on the website that you asked me about before. But I would qualify what I just said by adding that graduates who responded to questionnaires saying they didn't have a legal job may not have looked for a legal job or wanted one. On the other hand, some of those who didn't respond may have been working steadily as lawyers. It wasn't a random sample, just those who replied to the questionnaire."

Blaisedell made a note on his notepad. "Do you get involved with student loans?"

"No."

"Do you interact with law school personnel involved with student loans?"

"Sometimes. At staff meetings."

"What is the average debt for law school loans that a graduate of Spenser undertakes?"

"I don't know. I've heard a seventy-five-thousand-dollar figure mentioned."

"Do graduates consult you about paying back loan school loans?"

"Consult me? Not really. Some of them mention that they need to pay student loans back."

"What resources does the law school have to help graduates pay back law school loans when they don't have a job as a legal professional?"

"I really couldn't say one way or the other. It's not something I get involved in, as I already told you."

Simon couldn't understand why Blaisedell was asking these questions of Grant. Maybe he was tipping his hand as to the questions he would ask Dean Stockman.

Blaisedell consulted his notepad. "Let's start with Tina Farrell. What have you done to help her find a law-related job?"

Grant settled back in her chair looking more relaxed than at the start of the deposition. Simon was confident that she could answer in her sleep how she had helped each of the plaintiffs. Perhaps Blaisedell had run out of hard questions.

93

Meredith took a call from Richard Dash at her workstation in Carpenter's office. Carpenter was working at his desk, but Meredith didn't think it mattered what Carpenter heard.

"Good afternoon, Mr. Dash."

Dash got to the point. "If your client is on board, we have a deal at two hundred and seventy-five thousand."

"My client is on board," Meredith said, and she smiled when Carpenter gave her a thumbs up.

"How do you want to handle the paperwork to wrap this up?" Dash asked.

Meredith consulted her list. The money had been a sticking point, but the non-monetary issues were numerous and tricky. "I propose that you draft up the court filing that gets rid of the case and the parties' settlement agreement. I'd like to take a shot at drafting the notices to third parties and a document that would be included in Ms. Clark's law school record. I'll send you a current itemization of my legal fees."

"So you're giving me the easier of the tasks," Dash commented.

Meredith couldn't tell whether Dash was joking. "I hadn't thought of it that way, but you may be right."

"Okay," Dash said. "Let's try to exchange documents in a week. I'd like to keep the momentum going. I'll let the Appeals Court and Judge Neal's clerk know that we've reached a settlement in principle and need time to complete the documents."

"Works for me."

When Meredith set down her phone, she found Carpenter staring at her. "So how does it feel?" he said.

Meredith didn't really have to think about it. "Great."

"If you want me to look at any of the closing paperwork, I'd be glad to."

"Thanks." Meredith needed to do something nice for Carpenter. He really had come to her rescue.

"You know," Meredith said, "from a purely selfish point of view, I would have been better off being paid a third of the recovery than for my time."

"Are you complaining?"

"No."

"Good. That sometimes happens. It's happened to me. Sometimes the time you put in doesn't come close to matching a third of what your client takes home. But I've always felt that if I were paid for my time, I had no cause to bitch and moan. The client is the one who was damaged and if the client walks away with more money because a defendant is willing to pay for my time, good for the client."

Carpenter wasn't being paid for his time on this case, Meredith reflected. Maybe she needed to take a further hit to make sure that he put something in his pocket.

Paul and Evelyn had left the courthouse where they had been on call to testify in an armed robbery case that had resolved itself with a guilty plea, and almost as soon as their car was in gear, the dispatcher's voice sounded. "Domestic disturbance at 9 Elm Street near the intersection with Sea Crest Avenue. The man may be armed."

"Sullivan and Rodriguez," Paul responded into the police radio. "We're about three minutes away. We'll take it."

Evelyn set the car's lights flashing as she wove through traffic. Cars slowed down or pulled over, giving her room to maneuver.

"We haven't had one of these in a while," Evelyn said.

"We've been lucky," Paul replied. No cop welcomed a domestic disturbance call. You never knew what you were going to run into, but the luck of the draw was against you; escalated domestic situations were so prevalent that it was just a matter of time before one found you.

"The problem is on the second floor," the dispatcher reported. "There's a Marcus and Juanita Perez living there."

"Where are you getting this information?" Paul asked.

"A neighbor called."

The two-family house was rundown: peeling white paint, cracks in the walkway, a missing shutter on a second-floor window, more bare spots than grass on the small front lawn.

Evelyn killed the flasher. Paul was the first out of the car and as he started up the front walk, he caught sight of movement to his right. An elderly woman wearing a down parka over a housedress was making frantic arm movements. 'The neighbor,' he thought. "Stay by the front door," he told Evelyn. "Don't go inside."

"Did you call the police?" Paul asked.

The woman nodded, seemed out of breath. "He dragged her inside by the hair," she said, wheezing. "They're always fighting, but this was scary. She was screaming."

"Did you say that the man was armed?"

"I said he might be. There was something wedged into his belt in the back. You see on TV that's where they put their guns."

"Thanks for your help," Paul said. "Please go back inside your house."

The woman needed no urging; she appeared to be limping as she made her retreat.

"The neighbor thinks the guy may have had a gun wedged into his belt in the back," Paul said when he rejoined Evelyn. "We're going to assume that's the case. I'll lead."

The front door was open. Inside, a door to the left led to the first-floor unit, with stairs directly in front of them to the upstairs unit. Paul had just started up when a scream sounded above them. He picked up his pace. The second-floor landing was small and cramped. Paul thought of having Evelyn retreat to the first floor so that they weren't both exposed. But when another scream sounded, he realized there was no time. He tried the door at the head of the stairs and it opened. He leaned inside, Evelyn behind him. Another scream came from behind a closed door at the end of a hallway to his right.

Later, Paul tried to recall what made him turn around. He had been focused on the closed door and the screams from behind it, but something made him turn his head around. Behind them a man wearing a wife beater and sporting a red bandana had a pistol aimed at Evelyn's back. Paul lunged backward and tackled Evelyn; the explosion of sound was deafening as he landed on top of her. The shooter was still standing and he lowered his pistol toward them for a second shot. Paul rolled off Evelyn and got off his own shot, which tore into the man's shoulder and drove him backward.

"Jesus!" Evelyn's voice was breathless.

Paul stayed prone and steadied his revolver.

"Fuck," the wounded man snarled. He was holding his shoulder with his opposite hand, which still held his weapon.

Paul whispered to Evelyn to stay down. He was maybe twenty feet from the man. "I'm a police officer. Drop your weapon or I'm going to take you down."

"Fuck you," the man swore and when the man's gun hand moved off his shoulder, Paul fired.

For an instant everything was still. Paul couldn't move. He was conscious of Evelyn getting to her feet, stepping over him, and moving toward the shooter. He saw her kick the man's weapon behind her and feel for a carotid pulse.

"He's not going anywhere," Evelyn said. "I'm going to check out the other room."

Paul rolled to a sitting position trying to focus.

"You need to see this," Evelyn called out from down the hall.

Paul got to his feet and joined Evelyn in the room they'd been approaching. A woman was handcuffed to a narrow bed, each arm extended, secured to a side bar of the bed. Somehow, she had worked a gag loose. While Evelyn tried to soothe the terrified woman, Paul extracted his cell phone.

"We've got a situation at the Elm Street disturbance," Paul said when the station dispatcher picked up. "There's a shooter who's dead and a woman who may need medical attention. We need backup, big time."

Evelyn was bone-weary. The series of debriefings had taken hours. Their captain had given her the message that Paul would be finished shortly. She decided to wait for him at their joined desks knowing he'd return to check his messages before heading home.

Evelyn played back some of the events she had just finished describing in detail. The backup team had used a hacksaw to free the woman from the bed. The woman had been hysterical, which probably explained why she had failed to point out that the keys to the handcuffs were on her dresser. But Evelyn knew that what would stay with her the longest was the woman's reaction when she first saw her husband's body: the long pause, the angry glower, the glob of spit that had landed on the man's bloody shoulder.

Paul had saved her life. The shot fired by the dead man would have struck her between the shoulder blades. Once they'd freed the woman and she'd been led away, Evelyn had studied the part of the bedroom door shattered by the bullet and had walked back to the dead man, measuring the bullet path with her eyes. The dead husband had to have been in the kitchen when they entered the second story unit.

"Hey," Paul said, and Evelyn watched him collapse onto his chair.

"Thanks," Evelyn said. "You saved my life."

"That makes us even, or did you forget?"

"Are you okay?"

Paul shrugged. "Yes and no. I've never killed anyone before."

Evelyn had wounded a man before joining the force in Cambridge. She'd been shot at and had returned the fire.

"Did they tell you what's next?"

"Yeah," Paul said, nodding. "The shooting will be reviewed independently. The captain thinks I don't have anything to worry about."

"I agree," Evelyn said. She couldn't imagine a more justified use of deadly force.

Paul thumbed through his message slips and tossed the wad of paper on his desk. Then he checked his voice-mail messages.

"I'm out of here," Paul announced.

"Do you want to get a drink of something?"

"No. I want to go home. You look like you could use some rest yourself."

After Paul left, Evelyn stayed rooted to her chair. She picked up her cell phone and stared at it. Horace's cell phone number was the first one on her speed dial and with a jab of her forefinger, she made the connection.

Philly held Paul close, her head on his chest, the sound of his beating heart steady, loud. "Jesus," she whispered. "That's the last time I ask you how your day was."

"Very funny."

"I can't bear to think about what you went through."

"And I wish I could stop thinking about it."

Philly had already lost the father of her first child and now she tried not to think about almost losing the father of her second. She didn't want to consider the possibility that she was cursed and anyone who got too close to her was doomed.

"I had the guy in my sights," Paul whispered. "He was already down before I told him to drop his weapon. I could have gone for his other shoulder. I had the time. I'm a good shot."

Philly was surprised to hear Paul second-guessing himself. This wasn't the movies where sheriffs wearing white hats could shoot a gun out of a villain's hand.

"From everything you've said, he would have killed you if he'd had the chance," Philly responded. "You were aiming at his chest, just like you're supposed to do. Why should you have taken *any* chance? You're a hero. You saved Evelyn's life."

"I don't feel like a hero," Paul said as he rolled to his side of the bed.

Philly reached out and rubbed the back of Paul's neck. "Well, you're my hero and I'll bet you anything you're Evelyn's. And maybe you're a hero to that woman you rescued."

"I just want to sleep," Paul said in a flat, dispirited tone that made Philly wonder whether now was the time to worry.

November

From Meredith's Playlist

"Somebody Told Me"

The Killers

94

Evan Morales' office seemed cramped with Dean Stockman in it. Stockman was a large man. 'Two Molly Grants wouldn't equal the dean,' Simon thought. The dean's busy schedule hadn't allowed them much deposition preparation time; the dean had carved out two uninterrupted hours for Simon to pepper him with questions, and he had assured Simon that he'd read Molly Grant's deposition.

Blaisedell's introductory questions established that Dean Stockman had earned an MBA. He assumed his current position five years ago after serving for ten years as an assistant dean at a law school in the Midwest.

"Who was the placement department head before Molly Grant?" Blaisedell asked.

"That would have been Marion Cook."

"What were her qualifications for that position?"

"As I remember, she had been an administrative assistant in the school's business office and then applied for the job when the position fell vacant. She had excellent performance reviews in her previous position."

"Is it correct that she had no prior placement training or experience?"

"Yes, that's correct."

Blaisedell consulted his deposition outline. "Did anyone apply for the placement position who had prior placement training or experience?"

"I believe there was an applicant who had worked for a headhunter firm. That's my memory, but I could be mistaken."

"Why was Ms. Cook given the position?"

"She had demonstrated competence in her then current job, and we felt she could do the job as head of placement."

"What type of placement training did Ms. Cook receive before she actually took over the placement position?"

Stockman paused, looked thoughtful. "This happened a while back, so my memory isn't the best. But what I remember is that she shadowed the departing placement head for a couple of weeks."

"What were her performance reviews like as placement head?"

"Good, as far as I remember."

"Was 'placement department head' Ms. Cook's full-time position?"

"Yes."

"As placement department head, what did Ms. Cook do to help graduates find law-related positions?"

"I have to generalize here since I didn't work with her on a day-to-day basis," Stockman said. "She met with students and graduates, posted job openings, assisted students and graduates with their resumes if they requested help, and started a placement department website."

"Where were job openings posted?"

"I believe Ms. Cook utilized a placement bulletin board."

"So Ms. Cook didn't post job openings on the website she started, correct?"

"I believe that's correct. As I remember it, Ms. Grant began posting job openings on the website."

"Did graduates or students complain about the effectiveness of the placement department during Ms. Cook's tenure as department head?"

"Not to me."

"To anyone besides you?"

Stockman nodded. "Yes. Ms. Cook received e-mails complaining that her office wasn't effective. I believe you were given copies of those e-mails."

"Did Ms. Cook give you copies of those e-mails complaining about the effectiveness of the placement department at the time the e-mails were sent?"

"No."

"Were the complaining e-mails even known about when Ms. Cook received the performance evaluations you told us about before?"

"They weren't known to me."

"As you sit here today, what is your assessment of the placement department under Ms. Cook's tenure as department head?"

Stockman didn't answer immediately. So far he had responded to questions confidently. "There's nothing like twenty-twenty hindsight," he finally said. "Looking back now, I guess I would give the placement department a mixed review. On the positive side, Ms. Cook made herself available to students and graduates, and students and graduates met with her to seek help. On the negative side, I believe that the website could have been used more effectively. For example, posting those job opportunities you asked me about on the website might have improved the department."

"Under Ms. Cook, was the placement office knowledgeable and experienced, as noted in the law school's promotional materials?"

The dean paused again. "I would say yes. But there was room for improvement, as I just mentioned."

"How would you rank Spenser School of Law against other New England law schools?"

Stockman smiled. "That's a subject I've been known to talk about at length. But rather than risk boring you, I'll try to summarize my views. Spenser has been on the rise since I became dean. I'm not suggesting I deserve credit for its rise, but I'm proud of comments attributing the school's growing success in part to my efforts. We have a superior faculty in my opinion, and that's a key to a law school being successful *vis-a-vis* other schools. I've heard people say that Spenser is now on a par with Boston University School of Law, Boston College School of Law, Suffolk University School of Law, and Northeastern University School of Law. I don't completely share that view yet. But I'm confident that if I'm asked that question in five years, I'll be able to answer that we're on a par with those schools."

Blaisedell turned to his deposition outline.

"I'd like to add one more thing," Stockman said. "Spenser graduates are distinguishing themselves in the legal profession, and that is one of the reasons I believe par status with those other, better known schools will be obtained in the near future. Mr. Jeffries might find this embarrassing, but it's graduates such as Mr. Jeffries and Ms. Boyle, who are counsel to Spenser in this case, who are going to ensure that parity is achieved."

Generally, Simon didn't like a witness to give a speech when asked a question. But try as he might, he didn't see how the dean's self-serving words hurt the law school's case.

"Are law school applicants informed that upon graduation from Spenser they have a fifty-percent chance of landing a law-related job?"

"I believe a percentage figure around fifty percent is on the law school's website."

"Are you referring to the percent figure based on 2008 questionnaire responses?"

"I believe that is correct."

"Why wasn't that figure updated to include questionnaire responses for more recent years?"

"It simply wasn't. I believe subsequent years' responses were also close to the fifty percent figure."

"Today, how much is law school tuition?"

"Forty thousand per year."

"Is the law school profitable?"

"Yes. The law school's assets exceed its liabilities."

"Do you recall the law school's net income in 2011?"

"I do. I believe you have been supplied with that information. I recall a net income figure slightly in excess of one million dollars."

"Is it true that the more students the law school admits, the better its chances to have a positive net income figure for a given year?"

"Yes."

"This might be a good time for a ten-minute break," Blaisedell said.

Dean Stockman surprised Simon, saying he wanted to walk, and Simon figured the exercise would help the dean unwind. The dean had held his own during the deposition. If Blaisedell had intended to deliver a knockout blow, Simon believed that his opposing counsel had failed.

"From their point of view, what's the best thing they got out of me?" the dean asked without breaking stride.

"I'd say Blaisedell established something we already were aware of. Before Molly Grant, the placement department wasn't exactly proactive. After the break, he tried to beat you up about student loans, but I thought you handled that well."

The dean nodded, continued walking at a brisk pace. "We probably did hype the placement department's capabilities. As to student loans, it's not optimal that many of our graduates can't find a legal job to pay them back."

"Also something we knew about," Simon observed.

"Are you now going to move to dismiss the case?" the dean inquired.

"Yes. The motion has been drafted and the supporting legal memorandum is pretty much done. I need to decide whether I need an affidavit from you or Ms. Grant. It may be that your depositions will be enough."

They walked for a time in silence. Simon found that the cool air was dissipating the claustrophobic feel of Evan Morales' law office. He took a deep breath and let the air out slowly.

"I suppose this case can't be settled," the dean said. "Jamison believes that's not a possibility."

Simon hadn't seriously considered settlement. Strategically, he thought it was a mistake for Spenser to raise the subject. Maybe faced with a motion to dismiss, Blaisedell might broach settlement. "I don't think the law school should bring up settlement. If the other side raises the subject, we'll address it. Until then, I think we need to keep on doing what we're doing."

The dean slowed his pace. "I meant what I said back there. I think you and Rachel are doing a terrific job for us. Graduates like the two of you *are* going to help the law school."

"That's very kind," Simon replied. He had no doubt that if the case were lost, the dean would be singing a different tune.

Meredith stared at the two checks that Richard Dash had delivered to her by messenger, one for $275,000 made out to Noreen Clark, and one made out to her for $28,300, covering her legal time and the costs she had advanced in Clark's case. The case against the law school was over. Clark would be stopping by to pick up her check at noon and insisted on springing for lunch. Meredith couldn't recall a moment more gratifying or satisfying during her stint at Pinkerton.

With this payment, Meredith had held her own financially during the year without taking into account the settlement check she had received from Pinkerton. Periodic payments for her work on the Spenser and O'Day cases had kept her afloat. The Clark case payoff was gravy. She needed to think through how to repay Carpenter. But now it was time to think about tonight. Flash didn't know it yet, but they were going out.

95

Samantha Gray's smile was warm. The psychologist was genuinely glad to see him. They sat in their accustomed chairs. "I don't know where to begin," Paul admitted.

"Our schedules, the birth of your child, and the recent shooting delayed the session when we were going to discuss your original reason for coming to see me. I believe you now have the answer to the question that prompted you to see me."

"You've lost me," Paul said.

"Why did you come to see me initially?"

"I was concerned that I wouldn't act responsibly on the job because of all I had to lose."

"Exactly. I've read the reports of the shooting you were involved in. You saved your partner's life. You were courageous. I don't think you have to worry about responding appropriately in job situations. You passed that test."

Paul wanted to believe Gray. During the domestic disturbance, there had been no time to think of what he had to lose. "Instinct took over. I didn't stop to think. Is that passing a test?"

"In my opinion, yes," Gray said. "Don't over-think this. I believe you should feel proud about the way you responded. It's a good thing that your instincts kicked in."

"Okay."

"You don't sound convinced."

"It's just a lot to take in."

"Then take it all in and process it without over-thinking. If you still have concerns, I'm here to help you address them. But as far as I'm concerned, your original reason to come see me has been addressed. There's something to be said for the saying, 'Actions speak louder than words.'"

Paul nodded. Logically, what Gray had just said made sense. But when it came to the mind, logic didn't necessarily carry the day.

"Do you want to talk about the shooting?" Gray asked.

Paul had known this meeting with Gray would get into the shooting, but the shifted focus to that event nevertheless gave him a jolt of worry. "It was frightening," he said.

"I'm sure it was. Is there anything you want to say to me about it?"

Paul only hesitated a moment. He'd be a fool not to take advantage of Gray's counseling. So he told her everything.

"Why would you think in retrospect that somehow wounding this gunman was appropriate instead of shooting to ensure he was brought down? Wounding him might have placed you and your partner at risk."

"I'm a good shot and he was literally a sitting target. I can still picture him sitting with his back against the wall and his gun hand pressed against his wounded shoulder."

"You just told me that the man said 'fuck you' and was bringing his gun around to you and your partner. Why would you now even think that somehow trying to wound him was a viable option? You're losing me here."

Paul forced a smile. "Well, when you say it like that..."

"Is there any other way to say it?" Gray asked.

"I can't help feeling the way I do," Paul said, sensing that his response was somewhat weak. "I didn't have to shoot to kill but I did."

"Psychologists are not supposed to question the legitimacy of a client's feelings and I'm not questioning the legitimacy of yours. You feel what you feel. But one reason I'm here is to help officers consider whether feelings may be misplaced, given the facts. In this case, I believe it's important for you take a step back, look at the dangerous situation you were confronted with, and think about whether what you are feeling is appropriate given what you were facing."

"Okay."

"Again, you don't sound convinced," Gray said.

"I'll do what you just suggested," Paul replied.

"Excellent," Gray said. "How's your partner?"

"It was scary for her."

"Have the two of you talked about what happened?"

"Yeah. She's with you. She thinks I saved her life."

"Do you generally respect your partner's judgments?" Gray asked.

"I guess I do. Yes. She's a good cop."

"Then make her opinion one of the facts you take into account when you're reviewing this." And with that, Gray smiled and stood up to see Paul out of her office.

Evelyn headed for the front door of her apartment building and stopped short. Horace Benson was standing in the cone of the entryway light, an overnight bag in his hand. As soon as he saw her, he set the bag down and reached both arms out to her.

Horace was hugging her like he wasn't about to let go anytime soon. Evelyn pressed against him, felt the tension leave her body. "What are you doing here?" she whispered, trying not to cry. She'd never been happier to see anyone in her life.

"Oh, you know me. Impulsive to a fault. I had all of these unused personal days saved up and I was trying to think of someone I could drop in on unexpectedly."

"And you thought of me."

"I thought of you. I needed to see you and hold you. I wanted to make sure you were really all right." Gently, he moved her to arm's length, but without letting go.

"I am now. What are we going to do?"

"I've been thinking about that. Let's get inside. It's freezing out here."

"Wimp!"

Philly hadn't been able to sleep. As she stared at her computer in her second-floor office watching the election returns trickle in on a news channel, she remembered listening to Obama's inaugural address in 2009 and the hopes she held for his presidency. She had voted for him again this time around, too, and was glad that he'd been projected the winner. Although his programs had been derailed by conservative Republicans' kneejerk opposition so that his accomplishments were few, she trusted him. He had known hard times and seemed to remember them. Better Obama than the born-into-money shapeshifter he was running against. For some reason, more so than in 2008, she felt her vote this morning mattered.

Philly yawned. She needed to get downstairs and get some rest before Daniel next demanded to be fed. As she shut down her computer, the pollsters were sticking by their predictions that the president would carry Ohio.

Moving downstairs she couldn't get out of her head Obama supporters chanting "Four more years!" Four years seemed a lifetime. One year seemed a lifetime. For that matter, each day at a time sometimes seemed a series of barely manageable lifetimes.

96

As he approached his desk, Paul was surprised to see Horace Benson sitting adjacent to Evelyn in an extra chair he had pulled up to their joined desks.

"I didn't know you were in town," Paul said as he sat down.

"I was worried about your partner," Benson said. "I decided to check her out for myself. And by the way—thanks. You saved Evelyn's life. If there's anything I can ever do for you, just ask. I mean that."

Paul thought of downplaying his role and decided against that approach; Evelyn would challenge him if he played a modesty card. "That's very kind," he said.

An awkward silence followed. Paul couldn't read his partner's expression.

"There's something I need to ask you," Evelyn said, breaking the silence. "Horace and I have been talking. We want to give our relationship a shot. But that's not going to happen with me working here and Horace in Omaha."

Paul saw where this conversation would end up. He was going to lose his partner.

"Horace has talked to his captain," Evelyn continued. "His captain is okay with Horace doing a six-month tour of duty here. I know money's tight and it's probably not in our department's budget, but is that something we can do?"

Paul doubted their captain would go along with that plan. Money *was* a problem. An even swap of personnel for six months might work; but who in Cambridge would want to hang out in Omaha for half a year? "I don't know," Paul said. "I'm not sure what the captain would do."

"There's another option," Evelyn said. "Horace's captain is willing to take me on for six months. The Omaha PD would pay me while I was there."

Paul couldn't picture Evelyn working in the Midwest. "Is that something you really want to do?"

Evelyn looked at Benson before returning her attention to Paul. "When Horace said he'd be willing to work here, I knew what a big deal that was for him. He'd be doing it for me, and he'd be giving up a lot, including family. I figured that the least I could do was do the same for him."

"So you guys are serious," Paul said. It wasn't a question but both Evelyn and Benson nodded.

"What was I thinking when I sent you to Omaha?"

"I don't know," Evelyn said. "But it worked. And speaking of Omaha, I want to tell Grant Masterson at Sanborn Assisted Living Center that the real name of his tenant is Daryl Finch and that we've located his daughter. I'd like to give Masterson Heather's name. Then we tell Heather to call about the money her father never got to use."

"What about the sons?" Paul asked.

"What sons?"

Paul smiled. "Go for it," he said.

97

"You're looking down," Paul said to Evelyn across their joined desks. "I'm guessing Benson went back to Omaha."

Evelyn nodded. "Early this morning. I drove straight here from the airport."

Paul disliked having to contribute further to Evelyn's low mood. "I've spoken to the captain. He claims there's no money in the budget to bring Benson on for six months. But he's okay with you going to Omaha for six months."

"Shit!" Evelyn muttered.

Paul had figured that Evelyn's first choice was for Benson to come east. It was the first option she'd presented when the three of them had talked. "What are you going to do?"

"Shit on a fucking stick! I'm going to Omaha."

"I'm sorry," Paul said. "I wish the captain's decision had been different. When do you think you'll go?"

"I know you understand that I have to go," Evelyn said, ignoring Paul's question. "I remember telling you he took me to dinner after I got well enough to be discharged from the hospital. He was so transparent. He was mooning over me. He thinks I'm exotic. Whatever you do, don't tell him what a bitch I can be."

"Your secret's safe with me."

"So you agree I've been a bitch," Evelyn replied, and Paul was pleased to see her humor and sharp edges return.

"Your word, not mine."

"Yeah, right. I'm going to miss you."

They hadn't been friends exactly, but they'd worked well together and Paul had gotten used to her. She still hadn't answered his question about when she intended to leave, but maybe now was not the time to press the issue. "I'm going to miss you too," he said. "Wherever you go, you're going to be a success. The only advice I have for you is to take a deep breath every once in a while."

Evelyn gave him a hard stare and then her gaze softened. "I'm working on that," she said.

Paul took his usual seat in Samantha Gray's office and met the psychologist's earnest gaze.

"Where would you like to begin?" Gray asked.

"I thought about what you said about my instincts taking over," Paul answered. "I agree with what you said. After I had that gun pointed at me, I was afraid that I'd be paralyzed in some way and wouldn't be able to do my job out of fear of what I had to lose, or what my wife would lose, if something happened to me. Obviously, that didn't happen. I think I'll be okay in the future."

Gray nodded. "Good," she said. "What about the second incident, when you did the shooting?"

"I still wish it hadn't come down to having to use my weapon. But I think you were also right about that incident. I probably was over-thinking what happened. My instincts took over that time, too. When someone is about to use deadly force, we're taught to aim our weapon where a shot is likely to bring the person down. That's what I did. I think instinct took over and I fired in a manner that would most likely strike the guy. Am I sorry I didn't wound the guy? Probably. Am I going to beat myself up over it? No. Not anymore."

Gray didn't respond. She seemed to be examining his answer from different perspectives, as if he had presented her with puzzle pieces that she needed to turn this way and that to gauge where the pieces fit. Then she nodded.

"I don't believe in holding sessions for the sake of holding sessions," Gray said. "Unless you have something further to discuss, I believe that our work is done. If anything new arises or if anything further gives you concern about what we've discussed, all you have to do is make an appointment."

Paul felt a moment of unease. The sessions with Gray had helped. Now that she was cutting him loose, he realized he had nagging doubts about whether he had been cured—assuming cured was the right word. "Okay," he said.

"May I ask you something?" Gray said. "I'm curious by nature and I often try to get feedback from officers who see me."

"Sure."

"What was it that helped you come to terms with the issues you presented to me?"

"I don't think it was any one thing," Paul replied, after a moment of thought. "My wife said the same thing you said about the more recent shooting and, the more I thought about it, the more I realized what you both were saying was valid. It was the first time I had fatally shot someone and maybe I was having trouble processing what had happened."

Paul paused. He didn't expect to ever be free of the image of Marcus Perez leaning against the wall of the apartment with blood spreading over his wife beater, but he knew he could face the image.

"You suggested it was more than one thing," Gray prompted.

"The other thing has to do with my partner," Paul said. "Soon to be my ex-partner, which is a long story. She's fallen in love with a cop in Omaha, Nebraska of all places, and she's going to be on assignment there for six months. Anyway, I was talking to the two of them at the station and the way they were looking at each other reminded me of the first time I saw my wife. That's my present wife I'm talking about. And I realized that taking down the guy I shot was going to give them a chance together. I don't know. It just helped me come to terms with the shooting."

Gray nodded, didn't say anything.

"I'm sure that last part doesn't make any sense."

"There you go again—over-thinking," Gray said smiling. "It doesn't have to make sense. It just has to get you moving forward."

98

Father and son were both on this call and neither sounded happy.

"I'm telling you," Nathan Cohen reiterated. "Marsh will never agree to anything like this. And why would I agree to it?"

"Where did you come up with this?" Arthur Cohen demanded.

Rachel let the questions hang. "I want you to do two things for me," she said, adopting what she hoped was a calm, neutral tone. "First, forget about what Marsh and the high school will do. Put that out of your minds. Second, I want you to focus on whether the proposal I've explained to you is acceptable to you as a compromise that will resolve the case. I'm not asking you whether the proposal is what you want; we all know that it's something less than you want. What I need to know is whether the proposal is an acceptable compromise."

Rachel braced herself for further angry responses and was pleased when none were directed her way. Maybe the Cohens were evaluating the compromise proposal dispassionately.

"I like the idea of legal fees stopping if the case is settled," Arthur Cohen said.

"I don't know," Nathan said weakly. "There's a part of me that's sick to death of this whole thing. I guess I'd go along if the school went along."

"Okay," Rachel said, deciding to take the Cohens' comments as a direction to move forward on settlement. "Here's what's going to happen next. I will talk to the high school's lawyer and find out if the high school and March are on board with this approach. If they are, we may have to ask the judge to delay her decision until the details are worked out. If they reject the proposal, the judge will rule on Nathan's request for an injunction. Any questions? No? I'll get back to you."

"So, who wants to go first?" Stanley Tyson said when he picked up his phone.

"I called *you*," Rachel replied, "so I'll start. "Nathan Cohen will agree to the compromise if your clients are amenable."

"You may be surprised to hear that my clients *are* amenable," Tyson said.

"I'm not surprised," Rachel said. "Shocked is a better word." She debated whether to be further forthcoming with Tyson. In Carpenter's eyes, information volunteered, and unnecessary small talk were sins to be avoided. But she wasn't Carpenter and, while the man had admirable qualities, she didn't want to become him. "Does this mean we have clients who grudgingly have come to a middle ground?"

Tyson laughed. "I wouldn't use the word grudgingly with respect to my clients. Kicking and screaming are the words that come to mind."

Rachel laughed in response. She couldn't help liking her opponent and if that was a sign of weakness or mental impairment, so be it. "So how do we get this done?" she asked.

"I've had the misfortune to think about that. I would like to ask the judge to hold off her decision for another week to give the parties time to follow up on her suggestion to try to resolve the case informally."

"Agreed," Rachel said.

"My clients would prefer to have the case dismissed with prejudice and a side agreement executed that would be kept confidential and would not be filed in court unless a party sued for breach of the agreement."

Rachel realized that she was experienced enough to expect Tyson's approach. But there was the Nathan Cohen factor to consider; the teen would likely want some public recognition that he had won something in the suit he brought.

"I'm not sure Nathan Cohen will agree to that," Rachel responded. "Would your clients disclose the settlement agreement if someone asked for it under the Massachusetts Freedom of Information Act?"

"I never thought about that," Tyson admitted. "Good question. But suppose we reference the case in connection with the show you wish to put on? Would that work?'

"Show?"

"What would you call it?"

"Okay, show. I think your suggestion might work. How do you want to divide this up?"

"I'd like to do the first draft of the settlement agreement," Tyson said. "I will do my best to make it evenhanded."

Rachel believed Tyson, probably violating another Carpenter credo. "Okay," she said. "We have a plan."

99

Paul reached out to Philly, and she moved into his embrace.

"It's weird," Paul said. "I'm glad it's over but I'm sort of sad it's over."

"I know what you mean," Philly replied. They had completed their Thanksgiving Day marathon, taking in celebrations at her parents' house in Fall River, at Paul's family gathering in Cambridge, and finally at Philip's parents' house in North Andover. She and Daisy and Daniel had napped at various times while Paul drove uncomplaining. Daisy hadn't minded that she was not the undivided center of attention, taking adults cooing over Daniel in stride.

"Talk about three different family dynamics," Paul said.

Philly thought about their visits. With grandchildren to ooh and aah over, her distance from her parents wasn't center-stage and was less of a damper on the get-together. Kids ran loose at Paul's parents' house and the young girls present each wanted a chance to hold Daniel. When they picked him up, they did so solemnly as if in awe of one so little. Philip's mother's eyes teared when she first embraced Daisy and held Daniel. Philip's father had put a conforting arm around his wife's shoulders.

Philly rolled over in bed to look at Paul. "I wish I was closer to my parents," she confessed.

"You know they're proud of you," Paul said. "They may not say so, but I can tell you they are."

"They still don't know what to make of me."

"You're complicated," Paul said. "Good complicated."

"How come you're so close to your parents?" Philly asked.

"I think it has to do with growing up in a large family. My parents didn't have the time or energy to drive any one of us crazy."

"Philip's parents make me sad," Philly said.

"They're trying," Paul responded. "Given what they've been through, I think they're doing okay."

"They've still never asked if Daisy could stay with them for a long weekend."

"I'm pretty sure they'll do that when Daisy's a little older."

Philly wondered whether the future contacts with her family and Philip's family would continue to focus on July Fourth and Thanksgiving. She needed to get out of that rut. But maybe that would become one of those things that should get done but never happens, sort of like finding kids her own age for Daisy to play with.

"You can't do everything," Paul said, reading her mind, but Philly knew that she would damn well continue to try.

December

From Meredith's Playlist

"Pumped Up Kicks"

Foster the People

100

The scene playing out before Meredith would never have unfolded at Pinkerton. Philly had arrived mid-morning with her son. The baby was in one of those infant seat recliners set in the middle of the conference room table. The seat had a hand-hold bar on top and Meredith pictured Philly grippping the handle as she walked, swinging her baby like a lunchbox. Philly's partners were giggling and making faces at the baby who, as far as Meredith could tell, was asleep. Even Carpenter was acting goofy, making unintelligible noises and grinning broadly. Simon seemed relaxed as he stroked the baby's cheek with the back of a forefinger. Rachel was hyper and finally couldn't stand it anymore; with Philly's help, she extracted Daniel from the infant seat so she could hold him.

"He's so tiny," Rachel said, staring at the baby nestled in the crook of her elbow.

Meredith moved in for a closer look. Daniel was dark-complexioned and had a thick mop of dark hair. His features were scrunched up and every so often he smacked his lips.

"You're looking pretty good for a mother with two little ones," Carpenter said.

"As long as I don't sleep, I've got things under control. This morning I got on my spinning bike for the first time in ages. I am so out of shape."

"Is he an easy baby?" Rachel asked, nodding toward Daniel.

"That's an oxymoron," Philly said. "He hasn't fallen into a sleep routine yet. Although last night he actually zonked out for three straight hours."

Watching Rachel mooning over Daniel, Meredith wondered whether her own maternal instincts were on permanent sabbatical.

"Did anything special bring you in today?" Rachel asked.

"Of course. Today is the big day. You guys are filing the motion to dismiss in the Spenser case. Did you think I would miss that?"

Simon looked amazed. "You really came in because of that?"

"Don't flatter yourself," Philly said. "I came in because Daisy is being taken care of and I wanted to show Daniel off."

"You had me going there," Simon said.

"As you know, I've read everything you're going to file," Philly said. "You even incorporated some of the changes I suggested. I think you have a shot at getting some of the case thrown out. I like what you've put together."

"Thanks," Simon said as Rachel nuzzled Daniel.

Meredith was struck by how much the partners liked each other. She remembered the stories that would circulate at Pinkerton, tales of how departments were independent fiefdoms that ferociously guarded their respective turfs. There was one rumor, probably apocryphal, that the heads of the real estate and corporate departments had refused to sit down together for over a year.

Daniel's eyes snapped open. He first regarded Rachel with interest and then with concern. When he let out a piercing shriek, Rachel knew what to do. "Here, Mom," she said, passing the baby back to Philly.

"Hungry, aren't you?" Philly said. "If these jokers would give me a little privacy, I'll feed you."

Daniel's wailing stopped as soon as Philly spoke. She settled into a chair at the head of the table, Daniel in her lap. "Out," she directed, and Carpenter led the procession to the door.

Carpenter knocked softly on the conference room door and eased it open. "Everybody decent in here?" he said without entering.

"We're good," Philly said.

Carpenter took a seat next to where Philly was sitting at the head of the table. Her baby was back in the seat contraption. Carpenter noticed a stuffed backpack on the floor beside Philly, which he figured contained diapers and wipes and all the other shit you had to haul around for a newborn.

"Do you have time for a short business meeting?" Carpenter asked.

"Of course. I was kind of hoping we'd have a moment to chat."

"The filing of the Spenser motion to dismiss got me thinking," Carpenter said. "Once that gets done, there's going to be a lull in the billable-hour work we've got. We're just not picking up new business. And I think you know that Rachel is working out a deal to settle the T-shirt lawsuit."

"I know," Philly said dejectedly. "I think that while I'm out dealing with kids, you guys should split things three ways."

Carpenter had expected such an overture from Philly and had his response ready. "I don't think we should go there. You're being very generous, but it feels wrong to me."

"I don't know what to do about the lack of business," Philly said. "I think I've gotten spoiled. I just assumed new cases would roll in the door."

"I've never assumed that. I've learned that you're not guaranteed a fucking thing."

"What's our plan?" Philly asked as Daniel began to stir.

"I don't know," Carpenter grudgingly admitted. "It's driving me nuts. I'm going to brainstorm with Maxine. I'll figure something out."

Daniel cried out and Philly freed him from his seat, placing him against a shoulder. The kid was looking around, taking in his surroundings.

"He's got that same interested look his sister has," Carpenter said.

"I know. He likes being held up so he can look around, just like Daisy did."

Carpenter realized that his recently found calm about the firm's lack of business was a mirage. He felt responsible for Philly and Simon and Rachel. The notion that having partners meant he didn't have to shoulder business concerns himself was off the mark.

"What are we going to do with Meredith?" Philly asked. "There's no longer any Spenser work for her to do. I know you helped her with the case she landed. But she doesn't really have a future with us at the moment."

"You're right," Carpenter said. "I have to say, I enjoyed helping her out. You know, all the while I was giving her advice on her case, she reminded me of you. She's got this fearlessness you've got. Rachel was saying that she wished there was a place for her with us and I feel the same way. But I told Rachel that wasn't in the cards."

"How long are you going to let her camp out in your office?" Philly asked.

"I don't know. I may stay in denial a little longer. I try to give a different impression, but I don't like confrontation."

"That's not so. You *like* confrontation. You just don't like confrontation with someone you care about."

"Great," Carpenter said. "It's now official. I've become a fucking wuss."

Daisy and Daniel were asleep and Philly looked dead on her feet, poised to collapse on their bed. It was one in the morning and the house was quiet. For some reason, Paul didn't want to talk in the bedroom or living room. He snatched up the baby monitor and got Philly's attention. "Let's go outside."

"You're kidding, right? It's one in the morning and cold out there."

"Ten minutes," Paul said.

He made a quick trip to the entryway closet and returned with Philly's ski parka. He grabbed a sweatshirt for himself.

"Jesus!" Philly complained, but he saw that she was interested and soon she had her parka zipped up.

Outside in the backyard Paul gave Philly a hug. "Update time," he said, continuing to hold her close. It was a clear, cold night, starlit. Their breaths were visible. It occurred to him that they'd never had an extended, uninterrupted time alone. Daisy had been with them from Day One. When it came to one-on-one time, the best they were going to do was the odd day or two together when babysitting was in place. And moments like this.

"I'm finished with the department psychologist," Paul said. "I think I've put everything behind me."

"Define everything."

"The time Evelyn saved my life. The time I shot the guy when he was raising his gun at me and Evelyn."

"I was worried about you," Philly said.

"*I* was worried about me. But I think I did the best I could, and I think I acted correctly. I owe Evelyn big time."

"We should have her over."

"Then we're going to have to move fast," Paul said, and he explained Evelyn heading off to Omaha.

"That's too bad," Philly said.

"She's in love with the guy, so from her point of view it's good. I'm going to miss her."

"So why couldn't you tell me all this inside where it's warm?"

"I don't know. It's silly. I guess I just wanted us to be really alone. But you're right. It's freezing. Let's head back in."

"Not so fast, officer! I need to fill you in on a talk I had with Carpenter."

Concentrating on what Philly was telling him, Paul willed his teeth not to chatter. He had never considered Philly's firm to be at any risk. He'd just assumed that she and her partners had work. She'd make time to log into her office and he took those occasions to mean she was busy. "What are you going to do?" he asked.

"Carpenter and I don't have a clue. That's what's frustrating. We've got a great group of lawyers but not enough work. It's driving us nuts."

Paul couldn't stop his teeth from chattering. "Let me think about his," he said.

"*Now* we can go inside," Philly said. "Last one under the covers is a dork."

101

Simon responded to a phone message left by Christopher Blaisedell. He assumed that Blaisedell wanted additional time to respond to the motion to dismiss the case, so he was caught off guard by Blaisedell's first question.

"Have you given any consideration to settling the case?" Blaisedell asked.

"No," Simon replied, pleased that he could answer truthfully.

"Is settlement something that you'd be willing to talk about?"

"That obviously depends upon what you have in mind."

Blaisedell fell silent. Simon knew that this was a put-up-or-shut-up moment.

"Here's an outline of what I've been thinking of," Blaisedell said. "The law school would agree to make certain changes to the way it runs its placement department, would post on its website updated statistics on its graduates with law jobs, would agree to certain language in the promotional materials sent to applicants for admission, and would pay the plaintiffs' legal fees."

Simon finished writing and reviewed Blaisedell's listed points. Blaisedell had not mentioned any specific relief to be given to any of the plaintiffs and had not mentioned damages. "Have you discussed this with your clients?" he asked.

"No."

"Isn't this something you needed to broach with your clients before presenting it to me?" Why would a plaintiff agree to a settlement that didn't help the plaintiff personally?

"Not in my view," Blaisedell replied with certainty. "I'm simply calling to determine whether a settlement discussion is even possible. That's a lawyer-to-lawyer discussion. I've outlined some of the concepts I've been considering."

"You listed a bunch of things that the law school would do but you didn't provide any specifics," Simon pointed out.

"I'd be prepared to do that if the notion of settlement is something that your client will entertain."

The timing of Blaisedell's overture suggested some concern on his part that Spenser's motion to dismiss his suit might be allowed at least in part. Simon decided to push back. If he had leverage, now was the time to use it.

"I will report to my client that you've broached the subject of settlement. If you're serious about trying to resolve the case short of trial, you'll need to make a specific proposal. As you know, I have a duty to present to the law school whatever you propose. That's the way I'd like to proceed. A theoretical discussion about whether settlement discussions are possible accomplishes nothing in my view in the absence of specifics."

"I respectfully disagree," Blaisedell said. "I've frequently had occasion to sound out opposing counsel on whether settlement discussions were in order."

"Then we simply have to agree to disagree," Simon replied promptly. "If your clients are serious about trying to resolve the case, put something specific on the table."

"I'll have to get back to you," Blaisedell said.

"You know where to find me."

Simon put down his phone and began drafting an e-mail memo to his partners recounting the call. He thought he had played his hand well, but Carpenter might have a dissenting opinion.

Philly had drifted off to sleep after giving Daniel his early afternoon nursing. On waking, she settled Daniel in his crib and ventured groggily into the living room where she pulled up short at the sight of a girl with blue stripes in her black hair and an array of small rings embedded in each earlobe. With Sarah standing over her, the girl was kneeling on the floor, doling out crayons and drawing paper to Daisy and Rosalind. Isabella was standing behind Sarah looking uncertainly at the scene.

"Good afternoon, sleepyhead," Sarah said. "June, this is Mrs. Sullivan, but it's okay to call her Philly. Philly, say hello to June."

June nodded in her direction and Philly wondered whether the girl had reached her teens. She was dressed in a black long-sleeve turtleneck and black jeans. "What's going on?"

"June is my first babysitting student," Sarah declared proudly. "When she completes the School of Sarah, she will get an official diploma listing everything she's covered. It's a one-month course. Tuition is free."

Philly glanced at Isabella who shrugged in return. It was clear that Sarah had started her impromptu school without consulting the mothers of the house.

"Okay, you've armed the kids with crayons," Sarah said to June. "What do you need to be concerned about?"

June watched the two little girls intently. "You don't want them coloring on good things or on the floor," she finally said.

"Very good," Sarah replied. "Spreading newspapers is one option. Another is to use light, clear plastic like this."

Sarah handed a roll of clear plastic to June, who began to unwind the roll. "Hey, Daisy, will you help me?" June asked.

Daisy popped to her feet and held the edge while June backed up several yards. "Thanks, Daisy. You can let it go now."

June used a scissors to cut the plastic and she worked the protection under the girls and their artwork.

"That was a nice touch asking Daisy to help you," Sarah said. "I think you're a natural."

"What if they don't have this kind of plastic where I'm babysitting?"

"We'll talk about that later. One of the things I'm going to teach you is not to take a job until you check out the home and the supplies in the home. That way, you can say that you'd be glad to babysit but you need a bunch of things. Then you give the parents a list of what you need. Some parents may not hire you if you ask them to buy things, but that's a risk I think you should take. And by the way, if you're turned off by anything in the house or uncomfortable about anything, turn the job down."

"Cool," June said, and Philly was pleasantly surprised by how mature the kid seemed.

"Mothers!" Sarah declared. "You two are off duty. June and I are on duty, so you need to let us do our job."

Isabella headed for the kitchen and Philly followed. "So this is how Sarah's going to deal with an extra kid," Philly observed.

"This only works for the afternoons after school is out," Isabella said.

"Do you think she's got a plan for the mornings?"

"I wish I knew," Isabella said. "I suspect we'll find out shortly. I like this girl, June. God knows whether any of the others will have a clue."

"I think I'm okay with this," Philly said.

"Do we have a choice?"

102

As he thought about how his meetings with Rachel and Simon would play out, Carpenter considered that by the end of the day, he might have laid the groundwork for disposing of the few cases his new firm had left. What the hell was going on with people acting conciliatory and trying to settle litigation? What happened to the rallying cry of "Sue the bastards and never settle?"

"Christ!" Carpentered muttered. Then he did something he hadn't done in months; he rotated his chair to view the headshot photograph that years ago Philly had given him as a present. The black man's merciless, unforgiving stare seemed to bore into his soul. Carpenter wasn't looking for sympathy from the man in the photograph which he knew would never be forthcoming. Instead, he was looking for inspiration, for a jolt that would show him the way to get new business. The man's harsh glower told him what he already knew. He was on his own.

Meredith knocked on his door and entered his office, her dejected air palpable.

"You guys have been great," Meredith said, "but I was wondering how long you were going to let me camp out here."

Carpenter figured this was as good a time as any to get this conversation out of the way. "It's not a big deal," he said. "I'm thinking the end of the year give or take."

Meredith nodded, dispiritedly. If she made a move to give him a hug, he'd have to kill himself.

"I'm going to miss you guys," Meredith said.

"The feeling's mutual. We appreciate everything you did for us."

"This sucks," Meredith said with feeling, and Carpenter decided she'd correctly summed up the situation.

"This guy Tyson seems reasonable," Carpenter said to Rachel. They were in the conference room and had just completed reviewing Tyson's draft of the settlement agreement in the Nathan Cohen lawsuit.

"I like him," Rachel acknowledged. "And I agree with you that he's been reasonable. Although I have to confess that whenever he said something reasonable, I heard your voice telling me not to believe a thing he said."

Carpenter had communicated his distrust of opposing lawyers with one-liners that had apparently registered with his younger partners. "If you don't take on faith whatever your opposite number tells you, you won't be disappointed when what he tells you turns out to be a lot of crap," Carpenter replied, realizing that he had just delivered another cynical one-liner.

"I think I'm more trusting than you," Rachel said.

"You probably are. But you have good instincts and you're smart and you need to make your own judgments. Just remember, there's no downside to being cautious."

Carpenter realized what he had just done and laughed.

"What's so funny?"

"Me. I seem to have an unlimited supply of maxims."

"That's not so bad," Rachel said. "What's bad is that they stay with you. It's a little frightening to keep hearing your voice."

Carpenter refocused on the Cohen case settlement documents. "This is a pretty creative way to get rid of the case. What made you think of it?"

"I'm not sure," Rachel admitted, smiling. "It must have come to me at a time when I wasn't hearing your voice."

Carpenter studied his copy of the settlement outline Christopher Blaisedell had drafted in the Spenser School of Law case. Simon and Rachel each had a copy and they were waiting in the conference room for Philly to join them via Skype.

"Sorry I'm late," Philly said. She was without kids and looked all business.

"I wanted to talk before I sent this on to Dean Stockman and Professor Jamison," Simon said. "I previously told the dean that Blaisedell had raised settlement, and I had responded by telling him to come up with something specific. Now he has."

Carpenter consulted his notes. Blaisedell's proposal would require the placement department to hire a part-time assistant to Molly Grant for at least a year, would obligate the law school to include five years of data on its website relating to law-related job placements of graduates, and would require a statement in the law school's application materials informing potential students of the difficulties of obtaining a law-related job after graduation. In addition, Blaisedell's proposal would have the placement department conduct a job fair once a year for three years and block out two hours per working day in which students could meet one-on-one with Molly Grant or her new part-time assistant. Blaisedell noted that to date, his legal charges totaled $95,000.

"Carpenter's rubbed off on me," Simon continued. "I want to be prepared when the dean asks us for a recommendation."

"I'll start," Rachel said. "This proposal tells me that Blaisedell never came up with anything damaging during discovery. His proposal makes me think we could win our motion to dismiss."

"I agree with that," Philly said. "Blaisedell's suggesting ways to make the placement department better. But for the most part, the things he wants to correct are not things that showed the law school made any misrepresentation to law students or graduates."

"Blaisedell would disagree," Simon countered. "He'd claim that the law school misrepresented job placement possibilities both by including misleading information and by not including complete information. He'd argue that before Molly Grant, the placement department was useless rather than knowledgeable and experienced as advertised."

"But the depositions showed that no plaintiff relied on anything the law school said or didn't say," Rachel said.

Carpenter envisioned this back and forth going on indefinitely. "Let's go back to Simon's question," he suggested. "What are we going to recommend to the client?"

"But doesn't what we recommend depend on whether we think we can get the case thrown out?" Rachel asked.

"You're right," Carpenter replied. "And maybe we have the better of it when it comes to the motion to dismiss. We still need to think through what to advise the client."

"If the motion to dismiss is denied, do you think the plaintiffs would try to settle?" Philly asked.

"I don't know," Simon said. "They'd probably want more than what they're asking for now, but I can't think what more they could ask for. I don't see any plaintiff getting a refund of tuition payments. I'm thinking Blaisedell is worried about trying the case with the plaintiffs he's got. Felix Hennessey would be a disaster as a witness and Marlon Gold is not much better. Tina Farrell's appearance might give him a problem."

"Blaisedell has gotten other law schools to settle," Philly said. "Do we know what he got those schools to agree to?"

"No," Simon replied. "All his cases settled; none went to trial. The settlement agreements are confidential. The other cases were simply dismissed without the settlement terms filed in court. The court pleadings we looked at didn't reveal much, and the few law school lawyers we talked with were bound by confidentiality constraints."

"I'm leaning toward having the motion to dismiss go forward," Rachel said. "Although, what Blaisedell proposed doesn't seem too oppressive or unreasonable."

"That's kind of my thinking," Simon said.

When Philly stayed silent, Carpenter decided to add his two cents. "Here's the way I look at this. There's a tendency to regard a settlement offer from the other side as unreasonable simply because it's coming from the other side. None of us is falling into that trap. We agree that what Blaisedell put on the table is not unreasonable per se. He's not asking for money damages. Also, what he's proposing would make the placement department better. If that's true, that can only help the law school in the long run. To cut through this, I'm inclined to recommend to the law school that they try to hammer out a settlement. But I'd cap any legal fee payment at the ninety-five thousand Blaisedell mentioned."

Silence greeted his comments and Carpenter wondered if his recommendation was unexpected. After all, wasn't he supposed to be the no-holds-barred litigator?

"And there's one other small matter," Carpenter resumed, wondering whether he had saved the best for last. "What's to prevent Blaisedell from settling and then finding three other students to bring another suit against Spenser?"

Rachel and Simon turned pale.

"Shit!" Simon muttered. "Maybe we can't settle this case after all."

"What are we going to do?" Rachel said, and Carpenter picked up on the panicky tone to her question.

"If this case were certified as a class action," Carpenter said, "a judge would have to approve of any settlement and all members of the class would be bound by the settlement. Since a class has not been certified, we can settle without court approval. I think the best we're going to do here is prevent Blaisedell from either suing on behalf of students, or directly or indirectly getting anybody else to sue Spenser on behalf of students."

"Would Blaisedell ever agree to something like that?" Rachel asked.

"You're going to find out," Carpenter responded, "because that is going to be a dealbreaker if he says no."

"I'm trying to imagine the dean's and Professor Jamison's reactions if we recommend pursuing settlement given all these issues," Simon said.

"What we recommend shouldn't be predicated on what the client's reaction might be," Carpenter cautioned. "We recommend what we believe is in the best interests of the client. And if Blaisedell agrees not to bring or solicit additional litigation against Spenser and agrees to cap his attorney fees, I'm still in favor of settlement."

"I agree with Carpenter," Philly said. "This case came to you and Rachel and I'm inclined to let the two of you make the final decision on this. But I think you should make a recommendation on its merits without regard to the client's possible reaction. Which doesn't mean we shouldn't consider the law school's point of view."

Carpenter was relieved to see that Simon wasn't put off by Philly backing him up.

"And there are other things Stockman and Jamison should consider," Philly continued. "The law school wouldn't be admitting to liability. The case would go away, which would stop the school from incurring further legal fees. The school has certainly paid us a fair amount and, if the case goes to trial, our fees will be a lot more than we've already been paid. The changes Blaisedell is pushing for strike me as cosmetic. General language on the difficulties of finding a law-related job should simply state the obvious in my opinion. It's true that the law school would have to hire someone, which is money out of its pocket. But if the case went away on those terms and with Blaisedell's written agreement not to bring another suit, I think it's a win for the law school."

Carpenter hoped that Rachel and Simon were not viewing the more senior lawyers as ganging up on them.

"You're both convincing me," Rachel said.

"You're basically saying it makes sense to take a known proposal that isn't too onerous, over rolling the dice in litigation," Simon said.

"I think that's right," Carpenter said. "I was struck by you and Rachel not having any major difficulty with anything Blaisedell had proposed."

"Okay," Simon said. "I agree with the approach. I think the dean is going to have difficulty accepting anything other than an outright court victory, but that's his decision. God knows what Professor Jamison will make of all this. But when Rachel and I present this, I'm going to mention that we think we have the better side when it comes to the motion to dismiss the case."

"Go for it," Carpenter said.

"Are we concluded?" Simon asked.

"Yes, on the Spenser case," Philly said. "But I wanted to raise something with the three of you. When I'm not nursing Daniel, or changing diapers, or being run ragged, I've been thinking about how we're organized. A lot of big firms have managing partners and I'm wondering if we should have one too. I'm thinking of Carpenter. He's a sounding board to all of us and he's the most experienced of all of us. I'm thinking he should be in charge of managing the cases we have. I'm just throwing this out there."

Carpenter knew why Philly hadn't discussed this with him first. She probably had figured out that he'd have a negative reaction.

"I'm okay with that," Rachel said.

"So am I," Simon put in.

"Do I get a say in this?" Carpenter asked. "I appreciate the sentiment here. I really do. But I don't like the idea of titles. I have made more of an effort recently to stick my nose in the cases in the office, and I'm going to continue to do that if nobody has any objection. I think we have a system in place that's working and you all know what I have to say about that."

"If it's not broke, don't fix it," Rachel and Simon said in unison.

"Exactly. I've taught you well, young grasshoppers."

Rachel and Simon broke into laughter.

"Okay," Philly said. "It was just a thought."

103

"Were you surprised by this settlement initiative?" Professor Jamison asked.

The evidence professor and Dean Stockman were settled comfortably in adjacent lush chairs that surrounded a table set in the conference corner of the dean's spacious office. On this occasion, they struck Rachel as old, especially Jamison, who had been doing battle in the classroom for decades and sported the signs that went with longevity: a wrinkly wattle, longitudinal furrows in both cheeks, and age spots dotting his ample forehead. She had agreed that Simon would take the lead during this meeting and she now turned to her partner.

"Somewhat surprised," Simon said. "Previously, I gave you a heads up that Blaisedell had broached the subject in general terms. I asked him to present specifics and now he has."

"What do you recommend?" the dean asked.

"The short answer," Simon replied, "is that we recommend pursuing a settlement discussion."

Simon offered no further comment and Rachel silently applauded his approach. The dean and the professor plainly had not expected Simon's response. The dean, in particular, appeared taken aback.

"You're surprising me here," Jamison said. "The timing of this settlement initiative suggests the plaintiffs believe our motion to dismiss will be allowed. It seems to us"—and here Jamison inclined his head toward the dean—"that your motion has the plaintiffs on the run."

Simon regarded Jamison with a neutral expression. "Our recommendation to pursue settlement discussions reflects our weighing of all the factors that we believe need to be addressed," he said. "The motion to dismiss is only one factor and we are of the view that it is an extremely important factor. We think we have a better chance of prevailing on the motion, at least in part, than losing on the motion."

"I'm not a lawyer," the dean interrupted. "But haven't you just made the case that we should avoid talking with Blaisedell until the judge rules on the motion?"

"That's one way to look at it," Simon said. "It's a perfectly reasonable approach. However, it's not what we recommend. If the motion to dismiss is allowed, our recommendation would not be best for the law school. But we can't dismiss the prospect of the motion being denied entirely or in part. While we think we have the advantage on the motion, none of us can predict how the judge will ultimately rule."

"Since you think we have the advantage, I'm inclined to roll the dice and let the judge make a decision," the dean replied.

Simon nodded. "We took a hard look at what the plaintiffs are willing to settle for. With the exception of wanting legal fees paid and wanting you to hire a part-time employee for the placement department, we were struck by the fact that the changes the plaintiffs want to make are minor. Some of the changes they're looking for might even be beneficial."

"Why should we pay Blaisedell ninety-five thousand dollars?" the dean asked. "I'd rather pay you that money."

"As would we," Simon said, smiling for the first time, "but bear with us. We recommend that the law school put a ninety-five-thousand-dollar limit on plaintiffs' legal fees and make that clear up front. As for the part-time employee, we suggest sounding out Molly Grant on whether someone is needed. She might say yes because she would like some help. But we think she's a straight shooter and will give you an honest answer."

The dean frowned. Jamison was regarding Simon thoughtfully.

"We also considered the motion to dismiss being denied in whole or in part and the case going to trial. If that were to occur, the legal fees you would be paying us would greatly exceed the ninety-five thousand dollars that the plaintiffs have so far incurred. Lastly, the law school might not prevail at trial on all issues. In that event, the law school might end up having to pay some of Blaisedell's legal fees as well as ours."

The dean appeared to deflate. Rachel suspected he was searching for the high he was on when this meeting started.

"So, when we looked at all these factors, a settlement agreement along the lines that Blaisedell proposed seemed to us to be worth exploring. The law school would not admit to any liability. The settlement agreement would be kept confidential. The law school would put this matter behind it. A settlement might be the approach that proved least costly to the law school. And a settlement avoids dealing with the uncertainty of what a judge or jury might do." Simon paused. "There's one other matter," he added and then described the need to obtain Blaisedell's written agreement not to bring or solicit another suit against Spenser. "If Blaisedell agrees not to pursue another action against Spenser," Simon concluded, "there can be no guaranty that some other attorney won't come up with the idea independently of Blaisedell."

Stockman and Jamison went absolutely still. In Rachel's opinion, their silence defined the expression, "A pall fell over the room."

"This is not what I expected," the dean said. "It could go on and on."

Simon nodded. "That's a possibility. In settlement, we can't prevent another lawyer independently putting together a suit against the law school. But in this case we can insist that Blaisedell not sue Spenser and not solicit or encourage a suit against Spenser. We can also demand that Baisedell not discuss the law school with any other lawyer."

"Do you think Blaisedell will agree not to get involved with another suit?" Jamison asked.

"There's only one way to find out," Simon replied. "Blaisedell's agreement on that point is a dealbreaker in our opinion."

"Christ!" the dean muttered.

"You asked what we recommend," Simon said, "and we've told you. You're free to reject our advice. You need to decide whether agreeing to make the changes Blaisedell wants to make, capping legal fees at ninety-five thousand dollars, and backing Blaisedell off for the foreseeable future would be a win for the law school. We think it would be a win, and that's why we made the recommendation we did."

Rachel was struck by how Simon had commanded the dean's office. He had been calm and forceful. He had backed up every point he made. His tone had been respectful yet firm.

"You've given us a lot to think about," Jamison said. "We need some time to go over what you've said. I'm confident we'll be back to you shortly."

"Excellent," Simon said rising. "Any questions, you know where to find us."

104

Rachel had Stanley Tyson on speaker phone while she viewed on her computer the latest draft of the settlement agreement they had been working on. Tyson had been reasonable throughout, easy to work with. "This looks good to me," she said. "I'm going to have one of my partners take a final look and then deal with Nathan Cohen."

"Just don't give it to Carpenter," Tyson replied. "His reputation precedes him."

Rachel didn't bother with a comeback; Tyson was plainly joking. "Are you going to attend?" she asked.

"I wouldn't miss it for the world," Tyson said. "I always wanted to go back to high school although, to be frank, high school is not my fondest memory."

Carpenter and Maxine were walking along Mass Ave toward Cambridge. It was one of the companionable things Carpenter liked doing with her. Carpenter had his collar up against the evening cold but had held off wearing a hat in surrender to winter.

"I owe you a trip to Italy or Spain," Carpenter said.

"Yes, you do," Maxine replied. "Don't think I've forgotten."

"How about we do that when it gets warm?" Carpenter suggested.

"Delay, delay," Maxine said. "If we wait, you'll have a crisis at work that will prevent us from going."

"You're right," Carpenter conceded. "So how about right after the New Year we spend a week in the Caribbean? I've actually gone online and there are these hotel and airfare deals that seem pretty reasonable."

Maxine stopped abruptly. "*You* went online? *You* checked out deals?"

Carpenter shrugged. "I figured, what the hell? Right now I don't have to worry about work because there isn't any. We're settling everything in sight. If the Spenser case settles too, we're up shit's creek. So, to borrow a phrase from *Animal House,* 'road trip.'"

Maxine resumed walking. "Can I leave it up to you to book the trip?"

"Sure. I've printed out some of the deals. They're in my briefcase. Take a look and pick one. I'll set it up."

"Work really is dropping off for you," Maxine observed. "Now I'm really worried."

"You and me both."

105

The gymnasium of the Edward Gibbon High School was cavernous. The bleacher seats had been unfolded close to the long sides of the basketball court rectangle. Rachel was thrilled with the turnout. The place was packed. She spotted Stanley Tyson off to her right, caught his eye, and gave him a wave. The lawyer grinned broadly and made a thumbs up sign.

Seated at center court in three chairs arranged around a microphone were Nathan Cohen, Principal Bryson March, and Kathleen Stanton, Rachel's constitutional law professor at Spenser.

There was more than the undercurrent of idle conversation in the gymnasium. Rachel found the atmosphere electric. She might end up looking like a jerk when the evening was over, but if looking like a fool was the result of her off-the-wall idea, she could live with that outcome.

Rachel was pleased that the firm's contingent shared the excitement. Simon was looking about without his usual reserve. Meredith had exclaimed, "Wow!" when they had entered the gymnasium, and she still retained a slightly awed expression. Even their companions were caught up in the moment. Josh had served as a sounding board for her idea and had given her shoulder a squeeze when they had entered the gym and seen the turnout. "Cool," he had whispered. Frank Stevens was panning the crowd intently as if reliving his own high school moments, which were not so long ago. Flash had given her an approving wink. The Spenser School of Law contingent had one thing in common—each of them had latched onto a gorgeous guy.

Principal March advanced to the microphone and removed it from its stand. He tapped the mike several times before asking for everyone's attention. It took several moments for the crowd to become silent.

"We are very pleased to see such a large turnout for T-Shirt Appreciation Night," March began. "I'm going to offer up some preliminary remarks about how this night came to be. Nathan Cohen is here with me at center court. Nathan is now a junior and came to school toward the end of the last school year wearing a T-shirt with a message that I felt crossed a line."

March was interrupted by boos and he waited until the heckling stopped.

"I told Nathan that he couldn't come to school wearing that T-shirt and his response was to sue me and the high school for the right to wear the T-shirt. I'm pleased to report that the lawsuit has been settled. Nathan hired a creative lawyer, as did the school, and the lawyers came up with a settlement that provided for this T-Shirt Appreciation Night. Nathan is largely responsible for this event, and I believe he deserves a round of applause."

March's clapping could be heard on the mike and soon many in the audience joined him. Nathan offered an embarrassed wave.

"We've done a lot of intense publicity for this night, so I believe most of you know how we're going to proceed. But just so the ground rules for this evening are clear, I'm going to spell them out. Anyone wearing a T-shirt with a message he or she wants to share is welcome to come to center court and deliver the T-shirt's message and explain why he or she wants the message known. Anyone objecting to the message or simply wanting to comment on the message will then be given a chance to speak, again from center court. Offensive or hateful remarks will not be tolerated, and anyone making such remarks will be escorted out. We will conclude the discussion on each T-shirt message with a voice vote on whether it is appropriate to wear the T-shirt to school. A voice vote approving a T-shirt message doesn't mean that the T-shirt will be permitted at school, but the approval vote will be considered in making any final decision. When it comes time to talk about T-shirt messages we're going to start with Nathan and the T-shirt that led to his lawsuit. But before we start with Nathan, we are fortunate to have with us Kathleen Stanton, who teaches constitutional law at Spenser New England School of Law. Professor Stanton is going to say a few words about T-shirt messages and first amendment rights and a school's responsibility to maintain discipline and order. Professor Stanton will get us started, and she has graciously agreed to stay with us after her remarks, in case anyone has questions for her as the evening progresses. Nathan and I hope that this evening proves both enjoyable and educational for all of you. And now, Professor Stanton."

Rachel wondered how much Stanley Tyson had to do with Marsh's conciliatory, welcoming remarks.

Professor Stanton accepted the handheld microphone from March and said, "Good evening." The professor had been one of Rachel's favorite instructors at the law school and had agreed to join in the evening's program with genuine interest. Stanton was tall and thin and wore her wavy blond hair long. In the classroom, she had been the kind of professor to encourage debate and discussion. One of Rachel's regrets was that during law school, she had missed out on this back and forth because of her fear of public speaking. "I don't remember you from class," Stanton had said when they had met in the professor's office. "But

I looked you up and reread your final exam, which earned one of the highest grades I've ever given out."

"I'm thrilled to have been asked to be a part of this evening," Stanton began. "I believe everyone here has heard about the First Amendment to our constitution. The terms freedom of speech, freedom of the press, and freedom of religion are familiar to us. I firmly believe that freedom of speech is what makes our country both great and unique. Some of you students will have occasion to visit and even live in other countries and you may be struck by how those countries do not value and protect freedom of speech the way we do in this country.

"Mr. Cohen believed that he had the right to attend school wearing a T-shirt with a message that he will tell us about, and the school believed that it had the right to prohibit the wearing of a T-shirt that might disrupt the educational process. Many of you have probably asked yourselves who was right? Was Mr. Cohen correct that he could wear to school a T-shirt with any message he chose to put on it? Or was the high school right that it could prohibit any T-shirt message it found to be disruptive?

"There is no right or wrong answer to these questions. Questions of this type require a balancing of interests in connection with the facts of a specific situation. Mr. Cohen does have the right to express himself. The high school does have the right to ensure no disruption to the educational process. Courts are often asked to decide how those rights are to be balanced in a specific case."

Stanton paused and did a slow turn, making eye contact with each section of the bleachers.

"There's a famous quote from one of the former chief justices of our Supreme Court. The chief justice said that no one has the right to falsely cry fire in a crowded theater. What the chief justice meant was that not all speech is protected by the First Amendment. Speech that could lead to a public panic causing injury was not protected in the chief justice's view.

"Our Supreme Court has recognized a school's obligation to maintain discipline. Speech that might be protected by the First Amendment might not be protected when uttered in a school. For example, I believe that courts would take a dim view of T-shirt messages brought into a school that were filled with obscenities.

"How many students present this evening have lockers at the high school?"

Hands shot up in the bleachers.

"Some of you students may not be aware that school officials have more leeway to search a student's locker than police may have to search someone's house.

Information that a student has a weapon in his or her locker would likely justify school officials' search of that locker without the student's consent."

Stanton's pronouncement was greeted by boos and hisses.

"That reaction proves that we're going to have a lively evening. And now, without further ado, I'm going to turn the microphone over to Mr. Cohen."

Rachel spied Arthur Cohen sitting on a bleacher seat at floor level on the opposite side of the gymnasium. She had never been able to get a read on Nathan's father, and the absence of Nathan's mother had remained a mystery.

Nathan nodded slightly to Stanton as she handed off the microphone. The teen seemed composed, but he had struck Rachel as someone who would be uncomfortable in the spotlight.

"I'm wearing the T-shirt that started all this," Nathan said as he pulled aside a flannel shirt revealing a white T-shirt with writing that Rachel would have needed binoculars to make out. "It says, 'Jesus Loves Gays, Lesbians and the Transgendered.'"

There was a smattering of applause and scattered boos and Nathan accepted this mixed reaction with aplomb. He smiled sheepishly and Rachel was struck by her client's courage: it couldn't have been easy facing the large gathering.

"I'm interested in religion," Nathan explained. "I'm Jewish but I've studied other religions including Catholicism. Most people in this country are Christians, but I believe there is widespread intolerance especially from the religious right. There's intolerance at the high school when it comes to gays and lesbians and we all know it. I wanted to send a message that all people deserve God's blessing and I chose Jesus to convey that message because as an historical figure he comes across as someone who loves everyone."

Nathan looked toward March and held the microphone out to the principal. March rose and accepted the mike. "Does anyone want to come forward and respond to Nathan's message?"

There was silence. Then coming from behind Rachel and to her left, a booming voice bellowed, "Faggot!"

Rachel turned in the direction of the shout. She didn't have to guess who had yelled because a big burly teen with a blond buzz cut and wearing a school sweatshirt cupped his hands over his mouth and repeated the word: "Faggot!" He was accompanied by a several guys similarly dressed who clapped in his support.

"Shit!" Rachel muttered. Later she was to marvel at how quickly events proceeded. Frank Stevens left his seat and was moving down their row in the direction of the kid who had called out. Josh and Flash exchanged a look and they fell in behind Frank, working down the row of seats after him. Bryson March had fallen silent. He was staring in the direction of the shout but had not renewed his request for a response to Nathan's message. The shouter was sitting on an aisle seat across from seats occupied by the firm. When Frank reached him, he grabbed him by the throat, forced him up and out of his seat, applied an arm lock, and began marching him toward the gym floor. The kid struggled but couldn't dislodge Frank's hold. The kid's friends rose to action at once. Rachel watched in horror as two of them went after Frank. Flash let the first one pass him and delivered a short, quick, openhanded strike to the second one's chest that dropped him on the vacated aisle seat gasping for breath. His buddy was reaching for Frank but then was on the ground in the aisle. Josh had bent the kid's wrist back and slowly shook his head at the kid. Flash held up a hand and the rest of the shouter's entourage stopped advancing. Flash waved them backwards and to Rachel's amazement the group returned to their seats.

Frank now had the shouter at center court and took the mike from March. "This young man has something to say but he didn't seem to want to say it in front of everyone." Frank released his grip and stuck the mike in the kid's face. "Now's his chance."

The kid rubbed at his arm and stared at the mike but made no move to take it.

"Cat got your tongue?" Frank prodded.

Just as Rachel wondered why the beefed-up security for this evening hadn't sprung into action, three security guards moved from under one of the baskets toward center court. March got their attention and motioned them to stop.

Frank pointed at the kid. "This young man shouted out the word 'faggot.' Not once but twice. I think we all heard him. I took offense to that word. And I had reason to. I'm gay. It's just my opinion, but I don't think that word should be given first amendment protection."

Frank returned the mike to March and headed back to his seat. The kid who had yelled moved toward the exit door which was behind the security guards March had signaled to stand down. The guards parted and the shouter left the gymnasium without looking back.

A young girl wearing a school sweatshirt was now at center court and held out a hand for the mike. March passed it to her and took his seat. Rachel pegged the girl for a jock. She was tall and muscular. Her long blonde hair was done up in a single braid that hung down to just above her waist.

"I think most of the kids at school know me. I'm Pricilla Wazewski. I'm on the swimming team and I play goalie on the soccer team. I don't know Nathan, but I support his message. He's right. There is intolerance at this school. He's brought it out in the open and it's about time we recognized the problem. I also think he's right about what Jesus would say."

There was mild applause as Wazewski headed to her seat.

A boy with shoulder length black hair next took the mike. "Hi," he virtually snarled. "I'm George Lane and I'm the treasurer of the senior class. I don't think high school is the place for us to be told what Jesus would do, especially by a Jewish kid. I'm an atheist. As far as I'm concerned, Jesus and Moses and Buddha should be kept out of school. If people want to talk about them on their own time, fine. But not in school. The pledge of allegiance bullshit about this being one nation under God, is just that, bullshit." Lane returned the mike to March and left center court to a smattering of applause and a fair number of catcalls.

There was a line of students queuing up and Rachel felt her apprehension ease. She glanced at Stanley Tyson. The high school's lawyer had crossed his fingers and held them up for Rachel to see.

"I'm Billy Cooper. I'm president of the chess club. Jesus and Moses and Buddha lived. I think it's okay to say what they would do. I don't know Nathan Cohen, but his message wasn't hurting anyone. I don't see what the big deal is about this." Cooper turned to Professor Stanton. "Couldn't Nathan have put his message on a placard and stood with the placard across the street from the school?"

Stanton accepted the mike. "That's an excellent question. I would answer 'yes' so long as Mr. Cohen wasn't disrupting people coming to and going from school. This goes to a point I was making before. First amendment rights oftentimes depend on context. For first amendment purposes, a message delivered off school grounds may be treated differently than a message presented on school grounds."

Stanton passed the mike to the next student in line.

"I'm Gail Clancy," a short stout girl announced. "This all reminds me that Rodney King died this year. He was the guy who got viciously beat up by police during a riot. He's the guy who said, 'Why can't we all just get along?' I think that's a valid question. There are a lot of kids in our school who are gay or lesbians and we all know that they get weird looks that are not exactly friendly. I think that's wrong. We each have our own shit to deal with. I think we should be more tolerant of people who are different than we are. I support Nathan Cohen's message. I'm glad he said it."

Clancy retreated to her seat to the most substantial applause Rachel had heard this evening. For the first time, she could picture the evening ending well.

"This is the kind of dialog we hoped to have this evening," March said. "You should all be proud of yourselves. Who's next?"

"How are you doing?" Josh whispered to Rachel.

"A lot better than twenty minutes ago," Rachel whispered back.

For the moment, seated alone at the bar and starting on her second beer, Rachel couldn't wind down. Her mind was racing. T-Shirt Appreciation Night had come to an end a little before midnight. Bryson March had promised a second T-Shirt Appreciation Night within a month and that was probably the only reason people were willing to leave. There were so many highlights that Rachel found them blurring together: the voice vote endorsement of Nathan's message bringing a huge grin to her client's face that drove home the point that what he had just received was better than a legal victory; a voice vote that seemed equally divided on a T-shirt message that read, "If You're Here Illegally, Go Home!"; another equally divided voice vote on a message that said, "If You Think Evolution Isn't the Answer, You Haven't Evolved"; a voice vote disapproving a message that announced, "If You Were Born This Way It's Still Your F______ Problem." She had shaken Bryson March's hand at the end of the evening and congratulated him on his professionalism. Then there had been the shared, quiet moment with Stanley Tyson who had jokingly asked, "What are you going to do for an encore?" And Professor Stanton had taken her aside and requested that she keep in touch.

Rachel checked her watch. Close to two in the morning. The bar they had repaired to was a dive, but her friends didn't seem to mind. Josh and Flash seemed to have hit it off, their laid-back attitude simpatico. The way they had instinctively protected Frank's back probably meant that they were kindred spirits tuned into a wavelength only they received. Simon and Meredith stood on either side of Frank and were talking his ear off. All of a sudden Frank's mouth opened wide and he stared at the two of them. "*You're* the one," she heard Frank say, which got Simon and Meredith laughing uncontrollably. Rachel made a mental note to find out what was so funny, but she had the feeling that when she woke up tomorrow, she wouldn't remember a blessed thing.

Rachel took a slug of beer. 'The hell with it,' she thought. She wasn't driving.

106

Simon didn't think he'd ever worked this hard with a hangover, and it was hardly by choice. Professor Jamison had called Simon at ten in the morning on his cell phone, waking him and Frank. The dean worked better when he had something in writing to study, Jamison reported. So if it wasn't too much trouble, would Simon please draft a settlement agreement that he would be prepared to recommend to the law school and forward it before five? Hence the need to work, hangover or not. Coffee, which never failed to revive him in any situation, hadn't worked to relieve his hangover. Cold water and aspirin finally enabled him to focus. And for the first time since he had started working with her, Rachel was useless. She had arrived at the office, put her head down on Philly's desk and snored softly.

Two hours later, Rachel was awake and looking more like her usual self. It was four twenty and Simon had scheduled a partner conference call in ten minutes. Rachel was now reviewing his draft of a Spenser School of Law settlement agreement that he needed to e-mail to Professor Jamison.

"It seems to me you're giving Blaisedell everything he asked for," Philly said, participating in the conference by Skype.

"You're right. I reconsidered each of Blaisedell's requests, and I didn't find any of them unreasonable."

"I think you need to hold back on some concessions," Philly advised. "Otherwise, you won't have anything to trade."

Simon suspected that the grilling by his partners would be tougher than the grilling he would get from Dean Stockman and Professor Jamison. If nothing else, he'd be prepared for the client's feedback.

"That wasn't how I was looking at the negotiation with Blaisedell," Simon replied. "I'm not really envisioning a negotiation. Depending on what the dean and Jamison say, I was planning on telling Blaisedell that this was pretty much take it or leave it. And I was going to add that the attorney fee amount wasn't going to go up and that his personal agreement that neither he nor his firm would get involved in another suit was a dealbreaker for the law school. Either of those points may kill any deal."

"Then you're trying to sell this," Philly said.

Simon took his time considering Philly's point. "I suppose I am in a way," he finally acknowledged. "I think that if the case settled along the lines of what I've drafted, Spenser would make out okay. The way I approached this was to not fight about points that seemed reasonable and would make the deal attractive to Blaisedell in terms of what he proposed."

"What about holding back on hiring a part-time employee for the placement department?" Philly asked.

"Molly Grant said a part-time person would be useful to her. I think it helps the law school to add a part-timer."

"I think the dean and Jamison are going to want us to take a harder line at the outset," Rachel said.

"You're probably right," Simon said. "And that's fine; they can request that we take any hard line they want. If they insist and won't back down, then we'll take whatever hard line they come up with. But I don't think that's the way to go here if the objective is to settle the case. If settlement is the objective, then I think we should try to settle."

"Carpenter," Philly said. "You've been surprisingly silent."

"That's because I agree with Simon's approach. If settlement is the objective, let the other side have innocuous concessions if that's what it takes to get the deal done."

"I can't shake the feeling that we're going to have a serious problem with the client on Simon's approach." Rachel said.

"Of course you will," Carpenter replied. "Clients were put on earth to make lawyers' lives a living hell. What else is new? There's no harm in getting into it with a client. If the law school's interest in settlement is halfhearted, then settlement is probably never going to happen no matter what approach you take."

"I've got some wording changes I want to go over," Philly said.

"So do I," Rachel added.

"There's no time like the present," Simon answered.

107

"I don't get it." Dean Stockman frowned and shook his head. "My impression was that you were winning the case. Why are you willing to give the plaintiffs everything their attorney has requested?"

Simon glanced at Rachel who was regarding the dean neutrally. She had to be thinking "I told you so." They were back in the conference area of the dean's spacious office with Professor Jamison in attendance. Simon couldn't read the professor's expression. Previously, Jamison had taken a no-holds-barred position when it came to the litigation, so he probably had more of a negative reaction to settling than the dean.

Simon paused several beats to let the dean cool down. "For the reasons I mentioned when we last met, I think the law school should consider settlement. A settlement that doesn't require the law school to do much is in the law school's interest because it eliminates any unhappy outcome at trial. There are two main reasons why we included the other side's proposals in the settlement proposal you asked us to prepare. First, we didn't believe that the proposals were unreasonable. Second, we believed that their inclusion would make settlement more likely."

If honesty was the best policy, Simon wasn't sure that approach was working on the dean. Stockman's irritation was visible. Jamison remained a cipher.

"Adam, what's your view?" the dean asked Jamison.

"It really comes down to whether the law school should settle or roll the dice and press forward on the litigation. I have to say that at the outset, I was all in favor of waging a vigorous defense and taking the case to trial no matter what. I've spent a lot of time going over the specifics of what the plaintiffs have requested in any settlement agreement, and Simon's draft includes most of those requests. I don't really have a problem with providing five years of legal placement information or with cautioning applicants that graduation is no guarantee of finding a legal job. Also, I don't see any compelling reason to resist keeping the placement office open during certain hours for student conferences. However, I'm leery of agreeing to hire a part-time person for the placement department."

Simon felt vindicated.

"We can afford the part-time person," the dean said sourly. "And I suppose if we're promising to keep the placement office open for student conferences, an extra person would come in handy. I just hate giving in to these bastards."

Simon decided to let the dean and professor work their way through coming to terms with settlement without him selling it further.

"If we stopped legal bills in short order, those savings would probably pay for the part-time person," Jamison said.

"As some of our students are fond of saying," the dean responded, "this totally sucks."

Simon glanced at Rachel. She was smiling.

"Oh, what the hell," the dean said. "See what the other side says."

Simon rose and gathered his papers. Carpenter was always saying that when you got what you wanted it was time to get out of Dodge.

"Don't sound so enthusiastic," Simon said. "Besides, the attorney fee issue will probably kill any deal."

Simon had sent Blaisedell a copy of his draft settlement agreement attached to an e-mail. The draft document and e-mail had bold print disclaimers on every page: **FOR SETTLEMENT PURPOSES ONLY—NOT ADMISSIBLE IN ANY ADMINISTRATIVE OR JUDICIAL PROCEEDING.** In his e-mail, Simon said he'd be available to discuss the draft agreement.

Rachel checked her watch. Four o'clock. She was seated at Philly's desk. Simon had turned his chair so it faced away from his workstation and he was looking at her with a bored expression that she suspected matched her own. They had agreed to remain in the office until six because each believed they would hear from Blaisedell by the end of the day. Rachel envisioned the next hours passing with the two of them staring at each other not saying a word. Then she remembered something that, at the time, she was certain she would forget.

"What was so funny at the bar we went to after T-Shirt Appreciation Night? Frank said something to you and Meredith that cracked you both up." She couldn't remember Frank's exact words. They were tantalizingly out of reach.

Simon colored. The times when Simon appeared nonplussed were few and far between.

"I can't tell you," Simon said. "I promised not to tell."

"Who did you promise?"

"I can't tell you that either. Sorry."

"I'm trying to remember what exactly Frank said to get you both going."

Simon said nothing. Clearly he wasn't going to offer any help. "We're not supposed to have secrets from each other," Rachel complained.

Simon shrugged, stayed silent.

"This is driving me mad!" Rachel exclaimed.

"Josh and Flash seemed to get along," Simon said.

"You're trying to change the subject!"

"Am I succeeding?"

The phone rang causing both of them to start.

"We both know who that is," Simon said. "Why don't you pick up?" he added as he scooted his chair toward Rachel's desk.

"Rachel Boyle."

She nodded when Blaisedell identified himself. "Simon is with me. I'm going to put you on speaker phone."

"Good afternoon," Simon said.

"Thank you for forwarding the draft settlement agreement," Blaisedell said. "I thought it was evenhanded. To cut to the chase, I think we're close to a deal except for the attorney fees and my agreement not to bring another suit."

Rachel sat back in Philly's chair. They had agreed that Simon would do the talking.

"Then we may not be close to a deal," Simon replied. "Our client will not budge on the attorney fee figure and your agreement not to bring another suit. Ninety-five thousand is all our client will agree to pay for attorney fees in a settlement. Since this case isn't a class action, our client needs to preclude you and your firm from bringing or soliciting another action against the law school. Essentially, our client has agreed to make all of the changes you requested be made. But when it comes to attorney fees and your involvement in another suit, our client has drawn a line in the sand. What you're hearing from me is that this settlement negotiation is going to be brief. I know it sounds harsh, but what I sent over to you is pretty much take it or leave it."

"That is harsh," Blaisedell said. "I think if we sat down and discussed this, we might be able to work things out."

"No," Simon said. "I'm not authorized to bargain with you when it comes to attorney fees or your involvement in another action."

"Well, then you may be right. Maybe we aren't close to a deal. Do you have authority to agree to the settlement you sent over to me?"

"No," Simon repeated. "I received permission to send you the draft document I sent you. I'm to receive your reaction and report back to our client. If you were to tell me that the proposal I sent to you is acceptable, I believe I will get authority to settle the case on the terms I sent over."

Blaisedell didn't say anything for a while. "I'll have to get back to you," he finally said.

"That's fine," Simon said. "You know where to find us."

Rachel disconnected and regarded Simon. He had clearly enjoyed his back and forth with Blaisedell.

Simon opened his wallet and took out a ten-dollar bill. "Here's ten dollars that says Blaisedell will take the deal."

Rachel rooted around in her wallet. "Here's fifteen dollars to your ten that says Blaisedell will take the deal. I'm giving you odds."

"Thanks, but no thanks. Odds make no difference when it's a sure thing."

108

Carpenter had flipped his calendar over to January, saw the blank page, and then turned back to December. The settlement in the Spenser School of Law case left them with no billable work. Carpenter remembered lean times when he practiced on his own, but nothing like this. His brainstorming sessions with Maxine had come up with nothing. Philly's brainstorming efforts with Paul had also produced squat. When he turned the page on the calendar, 2013 promised to be beyond grim.

Carpenter looked up when there was a knock on his door. Simon and Rachel entered looking none too happy, and Carpenter guessed they, too, had figured out what the settlement in the Spenser case meant. Rachel took a seat in his visitor's chair and Simon perched on a corner of his desk.

"We can't tell whether Dean Stockman is happy," Rachel said. "He signed off on everything but didn't look too pleased about it. He never even said thank you."

Carpenter had carefully reviewed every document involved in the settlement. He thought Simon and Rachel and Meredith had done a good job on the case and that the settlement was a good result. "You know me," he said to his two young partners. "I've got a one-liner for everything. The one for the Spenser case is that a grateful client is an oxymoron."

"It makes me angry not to receive any kind of acknowledgment," Rachel went on. "So much for getting more business out of the law school."

"Any feedback from the professor?" Carpenter asked.

"Nothing," Simon said. "I still think we did a good job."

"So do I," Carpenter said.

"So where do we go from here?" Simon confronted the elephant in the room.

"I don't know," Carpenter admitted.

"When's Meredith leaving?" Rachel asked.

"The first of the year," Carpenter said. His follow-up discussion with Meredith had been short and to the point. She had thanked him profusely but there was little joy in his giving her a moving out date or in her accepting his message. He suspected that Simon and Rachel were even more upset with her leaving than he was.

"This sucks," Rachel said. "Maybe we should cancel the end-of-the-year dinner we've got planned."

"Yeah, it does suck," Carpenter acknowledged, "but we're not cancelling the dinner. Why should we? We've had a decent year. We've won a bunch of cases and settled a bunch of others to our clients' advantage. We've made money—not as much as last year, but last year was exceptional. So what if next year looks like a challenge?"

"It's next year that we're worried about," Rachel said, casting a quick glance Simon's way.

"I'm worried too," Carpenter replied. "But here's a suggestion. Take this down time as a time to have fun. Nothing says that you have to come to the office and spend a day staring at the walls. As a matter of fact, I'm about to leave. My suggestion is you both do the same. Isn't Frank around this week?" he asked Simon.

Simon nodded.

"Then what are you waiting for? Go have some fun."

His talk hadn't raised either Simon's or Rachel's spirits. Christ, his own mood hadn't elevated. But Carpenter decided to keep his word and leave. When in doubt, go to the gym.

Carpenter's late morning spinning class was nearing its end. He was soaked in sweat, his quads ached, and yet he was happy. It wasn't just the exercise that had mellowed him out. It was the way his mind wandered during a spinning workout that contributed to the drop in tension.

His mind had first drifted to the fact that, lately, the only time he thought about his CLL was when he went for his scheduled blood test. There was that brief period of concern until the test results came back, but once he received confirmation from Dr. Specter that the results were stable, he put the subject out of his mind. Was that some kind of hubris? Probably. Was he not giving sufficient thanks for having dodged another bullet? Probably. Was he becoming complacent that every test would produce a stable result? Probably. He knew he should be bracing himself for bad news on the cancer front, but his mindset wouldn't permit it. Another victory for mind over matter.

Thinking about Maxine was more enjoyable. He was looking forward to spending this afternoon with her. He had surprised himself as well as Maxine when he had called her with the suggestion. Since when had he become spontaneous? And they'd be heading to sun and sea after the first of the year.

Carpenter heard a buzzing; he looked down beside the front wheel of his bike to see his cell phone was announcing a call. The spinning class was almost over. Whoever was calling could wait.

Carpenter started his car and waited for the heat to kick in. He remembered his cell phone and saw that he had a message from Clyde Atkins. Hearing from a former client typically brought bad news, but in this case Carpenter didn't think it would.

"Hi. This is Clyde Atkins. I left a message on your machine at work. You made the mistake of giving me your cell phone number so I thought I'd try you. I gave your number to a guy named Henry Frazier. He seems to be in the midst of a dust up involving a family business. Sound familiar? Let me know if he contacts you. Being out of the family business has been great. No regrets even though the business does have a contract with PowerArm and there's a prediction for lots of snow this winter. Give me a call and I can fill you in."

Carpenter debated whether to retrieve messages from his office phone to see if Frazier had contacted him. He decided to wait. Maxine was on his mind and he wanted her to stay there.

109

Carpenter had held firm to his position that the lawyers meet first at the office and then link up with their significant others at the restaurant to celebrate

New Year's Eve. He didn't really like champagne, but because champagne was a big deal to some people, he had sprung for two bottles, a bottle of expensive sparkling water for Philly, and some plastic glasses and a bucket of ice. He had arrived at the office suite early to set out his purchases on the conference room table. He surveyed the room and couldn't hazard a guess as to how many hours he had spent inside it. The room had a tired look to it, but an upgrade was low priority and was probably one of those tasks that would never get done. Especially given their prospects for 2013.

Philly was the first to arrive, followed immediately by Simon, Rachel, and Meredith. His partners seemed restrained—there was nothing resembling the exuberant high of last year, which had ended with two million-dollar jury verdicts. For Meredith, this had to be a bittersweet occasion. She would get to enjoy a final moment with the firm, but she had to be thinking that she would be stopping by his office to retrieve her belongings after the New Year.

Winter coats were shed and Carpenter started to work on one of the bottles of champagne. He twisted off the securing wire and started easing the cork out of the bottle. He was conscious of the somber tone of the room and felt all eyes on him. The phone started ringing as the hollow pop of the cork being released sounded.

"Let's let it ring," Simon said.

"It could be a personal call for one of us," Rachel pointed out. "Maybe someone forgot where the restaurant was."

"Or a call from a babysitter," Philly said as she strode to the conference room phone. "Carpenter, Sullivan, Jeffries, and Boyle."

"It's for you," Philly said, handing the phone to Simon.

"This is Simon."

Carpenter joined the others in the room watching Simon listen to the caller. As the call progressed, Simon's serious, determined look began to lighten.

"I understand the urgency," Simon said, "and yes, we can help. We're taking the second of January off so it will have to be the third. Ten AM is fine. We'll see you then."

Simon set down the phone and claimed a glass of champagne. "I propose a toast," he said, and then waited until everyone had a glass in hand.

"To Christopher Blaisedell," Simon lifted his glass. "It seems he's just brought suit against the Sloan-Webster School of Law. That was the dean of the law school, Janet Martin. Dean Stockman suggested that she give us a call."

Carpenter broke the silence. "To Christopher Blaisedell," he seconded. "It appears you were wrong," he then said to Rachel.

"What do you mean?"

"You said you couldn't tell whether Dean Stockman was pleased with your work. You just got your answer."

Rachel reddened. "I see what you mean."

"I have a few toasts of my own," Carpenter announced as he made the rounds topping off glasses. "First, to Clyde Atkins, who referred Henry Frazier our way. Henry claims that he remained in the family business in reliance on the promise that his father, the business' founder, would step down as president of the company and put Henry in charge. According to Henry, his father has reneged on that promise. So, while Simon and Rachel will be meeting with yet another law school dean on the third, I will be meeting with Henry Frazier and Philly will be joining me either in person or by Skype."

"To Clyde Atkins," Philly said, raising her water glass.

"Now for my second toast," Carpenter said. "Here's to all of you. For me this was a challenging but fun year. I think it was a good year for all of us. We won some cases and settled others. We made some money. And we had some laughs. To my partners, I'm grateful beyond measure. I couldn't think of a better group to go into battle with. As for you, Meredith, I'm pleased you could join us tonight. You were a tremendous help during the year and we're grateful. Before you clear out of my office, let's hear from Simon and Rachel on what the dean of Sloan-Webster has to say."

"But I sued them," Meredith pointed out. "They're not going to want to have anything to do with me."

Carpenter shook his head. "Simon and Rachel will tell this dean that we used you on the Spenser case and might well use you on this one. They will ask the dean if that presents a problem for her. She will think about it for a second and say it's not a problem."

"But I sued her law school," Meredith repeated.

"And you won. Which is why the dean won't have a problem with you helping in this case should we be hired. Rest assured that this dean knows all about you and that's the strongest thing you have going for you."

"Works for me," Meredith said. "And before I forget, Noreen Clark has authorized me to bring suit against Caryn Wheelwright, the editor of the law school journal who lied about Noreen presenting a draft article. I might need some help with the case."

"Good for you," Rachel said.

"Enough about new business," Carpenter snapped. "Drink up, damn it," he ordered. "Then let's get the hell out of here."

The dessert dishes had been cleared and Carpenter was ready for the evening to end. Philly sat down next to him and for a moment they looked at the gathering in the private dining room and didn't say anything. Maxine and Paul were in earnest conversation in a corner of the room. The three young couples had congregated in a small group and Rachel was entreating Frank about something, but Frank kept shaking his head as Simon and Meredith stood off to the side sporting broad grins and Flash and Josh regarded the four of them with bemused expressions.

"Look at them," Carpenter said. "What a crew."

"That was nice what you said back in the office."

"Yeah, and I meant it. Did you ever think the two of us would end up with a cast of characters?"

"No," Philly admitted. "But I'm glad it happened."

"Me too."

"By the way," Philly said. "That meeting you have on the third? The guy Atkins referred? I'll be there in person."

"Good," Carpenter said. "It'll be like old times. Does that mean your kids are squared away?"

"Don't jump to conclusions. It just means that for that one morning, it's going to be under control. Do you want to hear about how much milk I have to express in the next two days to make it to the meeting?"

"I'll pass. Too much information."

"Wise choice."

"By the way. You may be on point for a short time on that case Clyde Atkins sent our way. Maxine and I are going to the Caribbean after the New Year."

"I thought you didn't like to travel."

"I don't like a lot of things, but on getting out of town, I'm becoming more flexible."

"Good for you."

"How come you and Paul aren't joining the gang for later tonight?" Carpenter asked.

"I can't speak for Paul, but for me, it's because I'm becoming an old fart like you. Besides, I've caught Tony V's act on First Night."

Carpenter caught their waiter's eye and signaled for the check.

The waiter approached sheepishly. "It's been taken care of," he said.

"What are you talking about?"

"That tall, young lady took care of it," the waiter said, pointing in Meredith's direction.

"That's ridiculous!" Carpenter erupted.

"She said that you would object and that if you were to object, I was to tell you politely to fuck off. I apologize, but she insisted I use the f-word or I wouldn't get a tip."

"Christ!" Carpenter grumbled as Philly broke into laughter and the waiter beat a quick retreat. "I should have seen this coming. Herb McCauley gave me a call. Meredith bought McCauley and Freedman thousand-dollar gift cards."

"No shit!" Philly exclaimed.

"You know what her picking up the tab means, don't you?" Carpenter went on. "It means we're never going to get out of here. It means I have to make another goddamn toast!"

Author's Note

I am indebted to Molly Rookwood for her edits, comments, suggestions and cautions.

I am also indebted to Meredith Larson, who asked to read a nearly finished version of *Lines in the Sand,* and then proceeded to produce helpful edits and comments on the draft sent to her.

Bob Vient and Andy Brody graciously answered my questions concerning one of the plot lines in the novel. Thank you both.

Paul DeLuca and Bob Sproull each went beyond the call of duty. Like Carpenter I am a technophobe when it comes to computers, e-mails, and the Internet. Paul and Bob each answered my questions in these areas, spent time researching several issues, and outlined alternative plot lines for my consideration. I am beyond grateful for the expertise, kindness, graciousness, and patience Paul and Bob afforded me.

I want to thank Jon Behar for proofreading the novel and finding nits that I failed to pick.

Any and all errors are mine.

Made in the USA
Monee, IL
04 November 2026

67385369R00280